D1030827

CHAUCER AND THE
FICTIONS OF GENDER

CHAUCER AND THE FICTIONS OF GENDER

ELAINE TUTTLE HANSEN

University of California Press
Berkeley · Los Angeles · Oxford

University of California Press
Berkeley and Los Angeles, California

University of California Press, Ltd.
Oxford, England

© 1992 by
The Regents of the University of California

Library of Congress Cataloging-in-Publication Data
Hansen, Elaine Tuttle, 1947–
    Chaucer and the fictions of gender / Elaine
    Tuttle Hansen.
    p. cm.
    Includes bibliographical references and index.
    1. Chaucer, Geoffrey, d. 1400—Characters—
Women. 2 Chaucer, Geoffrey, d. 1400—Political and
social views. 3. Feminism and literature,
England. 4. Sex role in literature. 5. Women in
literature. I. Title.
    PR1928.w64H36   1991   91–13025
    823'.1—dc20   CIP

Printed in the United States of America
9 8 7 6 5 4 3 2 1

Quod tho Criseyde, "Is this a mannes game?
What, Troilus, wol ye do thus for shame?"

Troilus and Criseyde, III.1126–27

Contents

Acknowledgments

A number of people have read parts of this book, have patiently engaged in conversations about its ideas, or have been an inspiration in both direct and indirect ways. Many of these people, including some I have never met, are acknowledged in the footnotes to this study; among and in addition to these colleagues, I am especially grateful on various fronts to Abbe Blum, Julia Epstein, Thelma Fenster, Sheila Fisher, Janet Halley, Stan Hansen, Marsh Leicester, Mary Poovey, Libby Potter, Ellen Rose, and Eve Sedgwick. For careful and generous readings of the entire manuscript, I thank Arlyn Diamond and Carolyn Dinshaw. For her enthusiasm and expertise in matters pertaining to the publication of the book, I thank Doris Kretschmer. For their help in cheerfully producing a finished manuscript, I thank Carol Wilkinson and Mary Ann Carr.

The completion of this study was made possible by the sabbatical leave granted to me by Haverford College, and support for indexing was provided by the Faculty Development Fund given to the College by John Whitehead. I am also grateful to the College for a regular supply of undergraduates willing to read and talk about Chaucer with me. Various presses and journals have kindly granted me permission to include previously published materials here. Part of the introduction is taken from "The Feminization of False Men in Chaucer's *Legend of Good Women*," in Janet Halley and Sheila Fisher, eds., *Seeking the Woman in Late Medieval and Renaissance Writing* (University of Tennessee Press). Chapter 8 is a revised version of "The Powers of Silence: The Case of the Clerk's Griselda," published in Mary Erler and Maryanne Kowaleski, eds., *Women and Power in the Middle Ages* (University of Georgia Press). The first part of Chapter 2 originally appeared in *Women's Studies*, and the second part in *Exemplaria*. Finally, a shorter version of Chapter 3 appeared as "The Death of Blanche and the Life of the Moral Order" in *Thought*.

1

Introduction

FALSE MEN IN THE *LEGEND OF GOOD WOMEN*

A decade or so ago, my emerging interest in what it might mean to approach Chaucer from a feminist perspective took me to a poem that seemed to focus most exclusively on images of the female: the *Legend of Good Women.* If I could argue from the evidence of this recalcitrant work, one that other feminist scholars had already despaired of understanding, I thought I might pin down the elusive author and determine whether he was or was not a friend of women. I have recanted some of the conclusions I drew when first looking into Chaucer's Legends, and the questions about women, feminism, and male authors that I am asking now are somewhat different. The story of how and why my reading of Chaucer's last dream-vision changed may serve to introduce the project this book comprises.

My first reading of the *Legend of Good Women* emphasized an overall design in the narrator's curious treatment of his ten heroines.[1] If her traditional reputation is passionate and aggressive, even wicked in some way (like Cleopatra's, say, or Medea's), he domesticates the heroine's forcefulness and covers up her iniquity; where she is known for innocence and goodness (like Thisbe, Lucrece, or Hypsipyle), he hints at other flaws in her character, devalues her virtues, and punishes her model behavior. At the same time, the narrator reveals from the outset his own interest in the manly world of politics and war. In the opening *Legend of Cleopatra,* Antony's failed career is foregrounded, and the sea battle at Actium is lovingly detailed; as other readers have noted, the narrator's boredom with the stories of loving women he has been coerced into telling becomes ever more patent as the poem proceeds. Al-

---

1. "Irony and the Antifeminist Narrator in Chaucer's *Legend of Good Women,*" *Journal of English and Germanic Philology* 82 (1983), pp. 11–31.

though for the most part he obeys Alceste's orders to tell stories about "false men" (G.476) and debunks his heroes as well as his heroines, this narrator does not finally hide his identification with "us men" (920), and he even joins in their efforts to fool "ye women" (see, for example, 2559–61).

So overt are the biases of the narrator, I decided, that readers are prevented from trusting him and obliged instead to see how his selection and treatment of good women ironically define the double bind in which the female in his culture is caught: victimized if she follows the rules of love and lives up to medieval ideals of the feminine; unworthy, unloved, and unsung if she does not. The line between unreliable narrator and trustworthy author in this characteristically ironic Chaucerian fiction is less overt. I ventured to conclude that probably both the narrator and Cupid were to be regarded as unaware of the antifeminism inherent in their idealization of women, although I also suggested that there might be a further irony. The narrator might well be awake to the implications of his storytelling and thereby poking fun at Cupid by giving him a poem whose effect is just the opposite of what the tyrannical male god demanded. The narrator might be much closer to the author, then, but the object of the irony, I argued, is still the antifeminist tradition; the narrator merely dons the mask of the antifeminist to make his satiric point. Other critics had already argued that many of the revisions in the *Prologue* reveal Chaucer's concern with freeing himself from the limitations of courtly convention. I added that in his attempt to move toward "a poetry more of the world and less of the garden," the poet becomes more aware of and ironically exposes the imprisonment of women in that garden.[2] I drew the line at imputing antifeminist sentiment to Chaucer as implied author because of the way I then read his treatment of women in other works; because I thought the blatant antifeminism of the Legends was unworthy of the subtle intelligence that is obviously Chaucer's; and because I failed to understand why an antifeminist work would impugn men, too, in the insistent way that this poem does.

Not long after completing this reading of the Legends, I was asked to participate in a debate about the poem at a meeting of the New

2. R. W. Frank, *Chaucer and the Legend of Good Women* (Cambridge: Harvard University Press, 1972), p. 36.

Chaucer Society, and for that purpose I decided to explore more fully the question of how and why the narrator did, as I had observed, impugn men too.[3] As I noted, he deflates his heroes as well as his heroines and, following Alceste's instructions, attacks the male characters with increasing harshness; I saw this treatment originally as both mask and symptom of his overriding interest in his own sex. The more I looked, the more it seemed that the *Legend of Good Women* was best thought of as a poem about men, not women, and specifically about two kinds of oddly related men: those who can't seem to help loving women, for one reason or another, and those who can't stop trafficking in stories about women. Part of what makes both types "false men," I began to see, was their feminization. Since this is an issue I return to throughout this study, let me pause here to spell out in some detail how the Legends articulate the problem of feminized men: those who sometimes act as women are said to act and who are treated as women are often treated.

For the literary heroes of the Legends, heterosexual union is clearly presented not as a good or even attainable end, but as a serious, perhaps insuperable problem, a necessary yet perilous part of the quest for stable masculine identity and social bonds between men. What is most dangerous about heterosexual desire, according to the Legends, is the feminine position, itself a divided one—vulnerable, submissive, subservient and self-sacrificing on one hand, crafty and duplicitous on the other—that men in love or lust for a woman seem forced to assume. By this reading, the heroes of the first two legends, Antony and Pyramus, appear not as exceptions to the rule Cupid laid down, as "trewe" male lovers set apart from all the other tricksters, rapists, and cowards in the poem, but as early object lessons in the fate of men who give themselves wholeheartedly to a heterosexual passion or to the idea of one. In different ways, both are utterly unmanned by their submission to the service of Love. For the love of Cleopatra, Antony loses his reason, his freedom, and his interest in the public realm: "love hadde brought

---

3. Fifth International Congress, Philadelphia, March 1986; the session on the *Legend of Good Women* included papers given by Sheila Delany, Arlyn Diamond, and myself. My second reading of the Legends was subsequently published as "The Feminization of Men in Chaucer's *Legend of Good Women*," in *Seeking the Woman in Late Medieval and Renaissance Writings*, ed. Janet Halley and Sheila Fisher (Knoxville: University of Tennessee Press, 1989); the rest of the first section of this chapter is taken directly from that article.

this man in swich a rage, / And hym so narwe bounden in his las
. . . That al the world he sette at no value."*[4] The narrator similarly
implies that Antony's motive in killing himself, after the defeat at
Actium, is not so much the loss of Cleopatra as the loss of manly
honor and prowess that he has suffered on account of love: " 'My
worshipe in this day thus have I lorn,' " he says, in the line just
preceding the report of his suicide (660–61). The adolescent Pyramus
is presented as a less tragic figure in that he has little manly "worshipe" to lose in the first place. From his unexplained tardiness in
arriving at Ninus's tomb, we can infer that he is not as bold or
appetitive or eager as Thisbe, nor as able and willing to leave the
domestic sphere; as the narrator notes in his translation of the Ovidian story, "al to longe, allas! at hom was he" (824). Revealing his
own fear of women and heterosexuality, Pyramus misreads Thisbe's
bloody veil as a sign of her death; it more accurately represents, in
this version of the tale, her confrontation with the feminine aggression and appetite figured in the lioness, forces that the nubile maiden
also hides from but is not undone by. In his only speech in the
legend, Pyramus is less concerned with the loss of Thisbe than with
his own failure as a man to protect her (833–41), and his immediate
response to this blow to manly pride is, like Antony's, suicide.

For both Antony and Pyramus, unbearable flaws in their masculine identity—as warrior/ruler in Antony's case, as sexually mature and independent adult male and defender of helpless women
in Pyramus's—appear to have been caused or at least exposed by
their faithful efforts to establish and maintain a heterosexual relationship. It seems plausible to conclude from their stories that these
heroes consequently choose suicide not because they cannot live
without the women they love, but because they cannot live with
themselves in the emasculated state to which they have been reduced. But, ironically, their suicides confirm how they have been
feminized by love, for suicide is defined by the poem, and the long-
lived traditions from which it draws, as the last recourse for a woman
who is raped, abandoned, or otherwise troubled by the vagaries of
her inevitable heterosexual relations, or who, like Alceste, sacrifices

---

*All Chaucer quotations are from *The Works of Geoffrey Chaucer*, 2d ed. Edited by F. N.
Robinson (Boston: Houghton Mifflin, 1957).
    4. *LGW* 599–602.

herself for her husband.[5] Antony and Pyramus, the only two "good men" the narrator can find, serve then to introduce the real agenda of the Legends by representing the danger to men in love at either end of the masculine life cycle. Antony is the mature hero lamentably feminized and finally doomed by ungoverned heterosexual desire, Pyramus the boy who does not reach manhood because he rushes (admittedly not quite fast enough) into the dangerous path of love before he is equipped to negotiate the perils along the way (notably without his father's guidance, let alone approval).

If the first two Legends suggest that manhood is difficult both to attain and to maintain, the remaining stories extend the problem of feminization from those men who try to serve love to a number who are not so naively loyal to women or to the God of Love's ostensively woman-centered code. Most of the other heroes, older than Pyramus and wiser than Antony, seem to know that heterosexual union is sometimes a pleasant or necessary diversion—it confirms one element of their manhood and often saves their lives—but a dangerous state in which to settle down, a place in which the manhood they are supposedly proving is in fact deeply threatened. These others survive the mortal dangers of love by betraying and abandoning women, but the problems of feminization are not so easily solved.

All of the remaining heroes are presented as characters caught up—like women—in the plots of other men (weak fathers, jealous uncles, and warring rulers), constrained by forces beyond their control and unable to rule their own destinies. Those few males who are circumstantially freer, apparently more in control of their lives, are presented as even more inescapably in bondage to an internal force, the irrational effect of what is characterized as innate, gratuitous male lust. Tereus rapes Philomela because of an unexplained, unmotivated, perhaps involuntary, and clearly brutalizing desire;

---

5. Saint Augustine, for example, links the discussion of whether a man's lust can pollute a Christian woman (i.e., if she is raped) with the discussion of suicide, with much consideration of Lucrece, whom he pronounces guilty. In carefully explaining, in his version of the story, that Lucrece fainted before she was raped, Chaucer seems to be vindicating her of the suspicion that Augustine raises, one often held against victims of rape: what if she enjoyed it? "Quid si enim (quod ipsa tantummodo nosse poterat), quamvis juveni violenter irruenti, etiam sua libidine; illecta consensit, idque in se puniens ita doluit, ut morte putaret expiandum?" (*De Civitate Dei*, I. xix, *Patrologia Latina* 41, p. 33).

Tarquinius rapes Lucrece on account of a somewhat more explicable passion, as male competition routed through women (who has the most faithful wife?) fuels the fires of his lust and violence. The male characters' status as victims and pawns—like women, again—of external and internal forces beyond their rational control is also emphasized and aggravated by the frequent reversal of roles, anticipated in the story of Pyramus and Thisbe, where Thisbe is more aggressive, more eager, and even more manly than her lover, or at least as capable of taking care of herself in the woods. While the narrator downplays the unfeminine characteristics of his heroines to make them fit his model of "good women," most of them (including Dido, Ariadne, Phaedra, Medea, Phyllis, and Hypermnestra) are or could be in positions of material power over their lovers. The sexual anxiety that this circumstance generates in men is brought into the open in the plot of the last story, the legend of Hypermnestra, when Hypermnestra's father gives her a knife on her wedding night and commands her to kill her husband (who is also his nephew) in their nuptial bed. But Chaucer's women are themselves already mutilated creatures, not castrating agents. Hypermnestra is said to be congenitally unable to wield a blade, and she and all the women of the narrator's subversive tradition are uninterested in using their past and present powers except to rescue men from life-threatening situations, usually in the hope of marrying them afterwards.

The hero, then, is initially feminized by circumstances, fate, or innate weakness; and he finds that the strategies he can subsequently employ to escape this status in fact only confirm it. To secure a more powerful woman's assistance, for instance, a hero is often forced, like any victim, to play up his weakness. Aeneas weeps and threatens suicide; Theseus begs and bribes and makes false promises; and Jason is as "coy as is a mayde" (1548), while his friend Hercules serves as his pander. Tarquinius and Lucrece's husband Colatyne leave their post in the Roman camp to steal into the "estris" (1715), the inner spaces, of Lucrece's chamber (recalling Troilus's hideout in Book III); in that domestic enclosure, Tarquinius's proper masculine reason and honor is defenseless against "his blynde lust" (1756). Tereus, inflamed by the vulnerable beauty of Philomela, uses his "wiles" (2294) to take her from her father's protection; and again the feminizing quality of his lust is illustrated by the underscored interiority of the space where the rape occurs, in a "derke cave" within a forest (2310–12). After prostituting himself to win (with little effort) the lady's undying affection, or removing himself to a feminine place where he can indulge in his lust, the hero must then attempt to recover his masculine position—his independence, nobility, and devotion to more important issues—by eschewing the heterosexual union in which he is dependent on a woman. And yet, for the heroes of the Legends, abandoning a woman, like the earlier process of seducing one, is emasculating in one way or another: men's infidelities and betrayal of women in this poem always involve them again in lies and storytelling, wiliness and other duplicities, ignoble escapes out of windows, and the complete failure of the chivalric obligation to protect the lady herself.

By the end of the poem we might well conclude that feminization is hard to avoid in this world because the rules of patriarchy are incompatible with the rules of love, and that men are caught in the consequent contradiction as they try to establish stable gender identity. Whereas patriarchy devalues the culturally feminine and insists on the difference between men and women as well as the power of men over women, the heterosexual love idealized by the laws of Cupid values traits associated with femininity such as irrationality, self-sacrifice, submission, and service, and thus diminishes in theory both the difference and the power differential between male and female. The problematic lack of difference that such a conception of love entails is clarified and developed in various ways: note, for example, that the women in the poem who give themselves utterly to men are in fact attracted not by otherness and virility, but by the male's temporary or apparent *sameness*, his passivity, coyness, vulnerability, and dependence (and even, in the case of Jason, his looks)—those very characteristics that also signal the heroes' feminization. When women are raped, there is no suggestion of their sexual arousal or complicity—Lucrece is not even conscious. What might be construed as the women's unconscious desire, like the men's, to remain connected to one of their own sex cannot be gratified for long by the hero, who for his part must necessarily be unfaithful if he is to demonstrate his manhood, his dominance and difference. Moreover, the actual, fatal loss of gender differentiation that a successful heterosexual union would bring about, if two actually became one, is perhaps hinted at in the essential similarity of the most innocent and true lovers in the poem, Pyramus and Thisbe, who speak in one voice, both "wex pale" and are separated only by the cold wall their fathers have built, in vain, to keep them apart.

If the poem suggests that there is something wrong with the laws of love, it also reveals a serious problem in the rule of the fathers. Fathers are, in theory at least, men who have negotiated that treacherous path of heterosexual desire. The institution of patriarchal rule should facilitate the next generation's passage to adulthood: hence a father must at once protect his daughters and pass proper standards of manliness on to his sons. But the contradiction in this charge is brought out in the Legends by the fact that all the men of the fathers' generation fail in one way or another to see their offspring to sexual maturity, whether through absence, incapacity, or malevolence. Cleopatra's story, as told by this narrator, opens pointedly "After the deth of Tholome the kyng" (580), and so too we are reminded early in the linked stories of Medea and Hypsipyle that Aeson, the father of their common seducer, Jason, is dead. Living fathers, like Anchises and Pandeon, are sometimes too weak to protect their sons and daughters; or, as is more often the case, they cause active harm, intentionally or not, to the next generation. Thisbe's and Pyramus's fathers inexplicably prohibit love and so indirectly cause their childrens' deaths. Aeetes unwittingly seals his daughter Medea's doom when he bids her to sit at the table with Jason. Theseus passes on his good looks and his false ways with women to his son, Demophon, while Jason and Lyno are both objects of schemes by jealous uncles. In the latter story, we also see a strong suggestion of incest in Egiste's bizarre speech to his daughter, Hypermnestra. In the same breath the father vows his love and threatens to kill the girl if she refuses to murder her bridegroom-cousin, Lyno, and it is difficult to avoid the conclusion that this is the story of a Lear-like father who cannot let his daughter grow up and sleep with another man. The public, institutional consequences of such unresolved Oedipal situations—of the patriarchal failure to help sons become men—reach epic proportions in the legend of Lucrece, where the narrator frames his story with reminders that Tarquinius's irrational lust brings an end to the whole line of Roman kings (1680–84, 1862–64).

Turning briefly to the figure of the dreamer/narrator himself as he is characterized in the *Prologue*, in retrospect we find arguably sufficient explanation for his only partially concealed antipathy toward women and his complex anxieties about the infectious feminization of men as lovers and fathers alike. The narrator of the *Legend of Good Women* presents himself in the well-known opening lines (F.1–209, G.1–103), before the dream-vision, as a bookworm who is drawn from his fanatic devotion to reading by only one "game" (F/G.33), the cult of the marguerite. His situation emphasizes both the literary man's prior lack of interest in actual heterosexual love and his professional obligation to take part in an elaborate courtly word game, here one in which the explicit substitution of the daisy for the lady at once covers over and underscores the unimportance or irrelevance of real women.[6] The dream that follows suggests the multiple anxieties of the figure of the court poet in such circumstances, including his fear of a tyrannical male ruler who (perhaps anxious to demonstrate his own superior status and potency) blames his servant for writing antifeminist poetry and also calls attention to that servant's inability to perform as a lover: "Thow . . . art therto nothyng able," the God of Love says (F.320, G.246). The figure of the poet is further feminized by the intervention of a powerful, aristocratic woman who speaks the kind of rational words that he for some unexplained, but psychologically and historically plausible, reason cannot.[7] His indifference to real women can perhaps turn to active antipathy when he is, in effect, treated like a woman himself, not recognized as a man by the male ruler and blocked from proving his manhood either by loving an actual female or by ignoring the subject of women altogether. As in the case of the heroes of the Legends, the only strategy the narrator can use to escape the censure and embarrassment revealed in the dream actually requires one type of stereotypically feminine (and uncourtly) behavior: wiliness and

6. On the displacement of the actual lady as object of medieval love poetry, see R. F. Green, *Poets and Princepleasers* (Toronto: University of Toronto Press, 1980), pp. 99–134.

7. Omitted from my argument here but worthy of fuller consideration as part of the historical context of the poem is the notion thoroughly explored, but not analyzed, in early twentieth-century scholarship that the *Legend of Good Women* was an occasional poem commissioned by (or presented to) a royal female patron: either Queen Anne or, possibly, Joan of Kent, wife of the Black Prince and mother of Richard II. For an overview and bibliography of the historical argument, see John H. Fisher's review in *Companion to Chaucer Studies*, rev. ed., ed. Beryl Rowland (New York and Oxford: Oxford University Press, 1979), pp. 464–76.

duplicity, as he apparently submits to and then subtly betrays Cupid's purposes and instead writes to his own ends.[8]

FEMINIST CHAUCER?

And trusteth, as in love, no man but me.
Legend of Good Women, 2561

To the extent that feminist discourse defines its problematic as "woman," it, too, ironically privileges the man as unproblematic or exempt from determination from gender relations.[9]
Jane Flax, "Postmodernism and Gender Relations in Feminist Theory"

This analysis of feminization in the Legends brought me to conclusions different from my earlier ones. I did not find myself retracting the observation that this poem is not performing traditional antifeminist satire, or that it criticizes the less subtle forms and traps of misogyny inherent in certain already tired discursive conventions. However, it became clear to me that I needed to think harder about my naive assumption that a literary critique of the socio-gender system and its constraining effects on masculine identity and the male writer has anything to do with a pro-woman position. This book records the results of that effort. The *Legend of Good Women* is usually thought to represent Chaucer's return to a genre he has outgrown, but focusing on the problematic of "false men" marks the late dream-vision as central, not marginal, and affords a point of entry into the particularities of this poet's apparently lifelong engagement with the woman question. By turning in the next chapter

8. We need go no further than Chaucer's *Troilus and Criseyde* for a restatement of the widespread misogynistic assumption that women are craftier than men. In Book IV, when Pandarus wants Criseyde to stop crying and start plotting, he observes: " 'Women ben wise in short avysement; / And lat sen how youre wit shal now availle' " (IV.936–37). Later, in conversation with Troilus, Criseyde tries to claim for herself the potential power of feminine wiles that Pandarus invokes (" 'I am a womman, as ful wel ye woot' " [IV.1261–67]), but Troilus knows better, and tells her she won't be able to fool her father: " 'Ye shal nat blende hym for youre wommanhede, / Ne feyne aright' " (IV.1462–3). The pattern here is repeated throughout Chaucerian fictions: in the hands of women, stereotypical feminine powers turn out to be unavailing in a world that men control. Men actually use feminine strategies more successfully, in the short run, than women do, but they cannot be admired for doing so.

9. The quotation from "Postmodernism and Gender Relations" is taken from *Signs* 12 (1987), p. 629.

to questions about his most infamous female character, in the *Wife of Bath's Prologue* and *Tale*, I aim to establish the priority of two issues: first, my prevailing concern with (the representation of) women, although my explicit topic is as often as not men, the masculine imagination, and the male author; and second, my equal regard for Chaucer's fictions and for the fictions of Chaucer formulated by the modern critical reception of the texts, which is nowhere more interesting than in response to the Wife of Bath. The rest of the book moves from the early dream visions through *Troilus and Criseyde* and then concludes with five more of the *Canterbury Tales* that seem most pertinent to my inquiries. Attending to the representation of gender difference and gender relations throughout these works, with an ongoing regard for the feminization of both male characters and male figures for the poet, I have found myself no longer interested in defending Gavin Douglas's well-known dictum that Chaucer was "euer, God wait, wemenis frend."[10] What then, I have inquired, is the nature and function of a late twentieth-century feminist analysis of these canonical, male-authored late medieval texts?

As I have pursued this question, I have become convinced that in Chaucer studies, the uncertain footing of any feminist approach to premodern works has been made even more slippery, ironically, by the unusual ease with which a prima facie case for the importance of women as characters and Woman (and gender, where the feminine is the marked position) as topic can be made. Under the influence of recent mediations in the practice of literary criticism, a growing number of scholars—including, as I have said, myself at an earlier point—have concluded in one way or another that the representation of women in Chaucerian fiction testifies to the poet's open-mindedness and even intentional subversion of traditional antifeminist positions. This view is sometimes part of a move to make Chaucer studies more theoretically au courant and to draw analogies between various contemporary approaches and Chaucer's insights and methods. There has been no systematic and thorough attempt to posit the evolution of the protofeminism that many have identified in Chaucer and his poetry. However, if the implications of separate studies were brought together and extended, it would be possible to see that they sketch a developmental poetics in which the female

10. From Douglas's *Eneados* (1513), cited in Caroline F. E. Spurgeon, *Five Hundred Years of Chaucer Criticism and Allusion, 1357–1900* (Cambridge: Cambridge University Press, 1925), vol. I, p. 72.

voice itself, as speaker instead of spoken about, gradually enters Chaucerian fiction, while, as one recent critic sees it, Chaucer "abandoned his career as a poet of women."[11]

I claim, however, that the attempt to recuperate a feminist Chaucer who does not threaten the humanist Chaucer, based on the assumption that Chaucer is sympathetic to women's problems and that we hear in his poetry either a female voice or an *écriture féminine* (in the vernacular of the fourteenth-century East Midlands), is misguided. Such efforts, moreover, have so far prevented feminist critics from making much difference in the way we read and theorize about Chaucer and have contributed to the difficulty of finding or creating the larger audience that our work might address. While I have moved beyond my early efforts to determine Chaucer's sexual politics, it has remained important to me to interrogate readings that recover Chaucer as a protofeminist or continue to adulate him as a humanist because such readings may stand in the way of the necessary activity of making new models for feminist interpretations of Chaucer and other male authors.

I have stressed, then, that in the very real continuity of concern throughout Chaucerian fiction with the representation of women, I hear not a swelling chorus of female voices entering the text and speaking for and about themselves, but something of a monotone making known both feminine absence and masculine anxiety. As I listen, what often sounds like a woman's voice, what is spoken in the name of women inflected by different and highly realistic, sometimes subversive dialects, always enters and leaves Chaucerian story not as the enunciation of an autonomous speaker, but as an urgent problem for the gendered identity of male characters, male narrators, and (?male) readers. The problem is always represented in large part as a problem of the feminization of men. The repetitive return to the fraught depiction of women and of male speakers, characters and narrators alike, who in various ways resemble those women in turn documents the dubious nature of gender difference: the fact that men and women are similar and dissimilar, depending on how, why, and when we are looking at them, or that all human beings have both feminine and masculine characteristics.

---

11. This is Lee Patterson's claim in " 'For the Wyves Love of Bath' ": Feminine Rhetoric and Poetic Resolution in the *Roman de la Rose* and the *Canterbury Tales,*" *Speculum* 58 (1983), pp. 656–95. References to other scholars who find a "feminist" Chaucer will be found throughout this study, and especially in Chapter 2.

This understanding of a fundamental similarity between male and female is consistent with orthodox medical and scientific views that prevailed until the late eighteenth century. As Thomas Laqueur has observed:

> For several thousand years it had been a commonplace that women have the same genitals as men, except that, as Nemesius, bishop of Emesa in the sixth century, put it: "Theirs are inside the body and not outside it." Galen, who in the second century A.D. developed the most powerful and resilient model of the homologous nature of male and female reproductive organs, could already cite the anatomist Herophilus (third century B.C.) in support of his claim that a woman has testes with accompanying seminal ducts very much like the man's, one on each side of the uterus, the only difference being that the male's are contained in the scrotum and the female's are not.[12]

Belief in the genital homology of male and female did not translate into assumptions of their social, political, or moral equality; the female's insufficient heat accounted medically for the internalization of her organs of reproduction and her natural inferiority. Moreover, the paradigm of homology equated the male with the human, and female difference was not inquired into. For example, Laqueur points out that until 1797 no one thought to reproduce illustrations of female skeletons: "Up to this time there had been one basic structure for the human body, the type of the male."[13] While it is usually assumed that the perceived similarity and mutability of biological gender were tightly controlled in premodern thinking by a firm sense of natural and proper hierarchy, Chaucerian fiction seems to call this assumption into question. Chaucer seems to insist, as some of us might put it today, that gender is socially constructed and historically experienced as protean, provisional, intermittent, and discontinuous, and his poetry explores the consequent difficulty that men face in securing masculine identity and dominance.

This concern with the instability and incompleteness of gender difference undermines the uncomplicated assumption that we can hear

---

12. "Orgasm, Generation, and the Politics of Reproductive Biology," in *The Making of the Modern Body*, ed. Catherine Gallagher and Thomas Laqueur (Berkeley: University of California Press, 1987), p. 2 (originally published as *Representations* 14 [*Spring* 1986]). For an overview of the scientific discussion of whether and how women differed from men, see also Vern L. Bullough, "Medieval Medical and Scientific Views of Women," *Viator* 4 (1973), pp. 485–501.

13. Laqueur, "Orgasm, Generation, and the Politics of Reproductive Biology," p. 4.

women speaking when the author describes or impersonates a woman. Chaucer, it could be argued, is the last to imagine and give voice to something we can categorize with useful certainty as a female speaker, for the poems attributed to him are among the first to problematize the notion of singly gendered subjectivity, even as they may in various ways imply that in all the orthodox prescriptions of gender roles by which experience is given social meaning, women's voices are precisely those that have been silenced. In Chaucer, moreover, the foregrounded problem of representing the silenced woman characteristically intersects the problem of poetic authority in general and the self-authorization of the individual poet's voice in particular. According to certain authoritative discourses of the Middle Ages (not unlike some postmodern discourses in this regard), writing itself occupies a feminine position in a culture that insists on the inherent and necessary inferiority and absence, both materially and symbolically, of women. As we see in the *Legend of Good Women*, the figure of the male poet in Chaucer dreams of impotence, of being treated like a woman—marginalized, for instance, in the court, or misread by future audiences—and yet he is obliged to write about women in order to compete with other men and enter into a privileged discourse. In response to this position, he employs a striking and, in certain obvious ways, effective strategy: he underscores and imitates the charge, exploits the negative, subversive powers of nonrepresentability assigned to the female, the feminine, and the poetic—and then shows, or works to show, that there is still a masculine position to be taken within writing.

Representations of the vicissitudes of masculine identity in a patriarchal culture, then, do not necessarily entail abandoning its potential privilege. In Chaucer, moves to reclaim the boldly destabilized notion of integral maleness, to occupy the space that has been opened up by the inversions and subversions of courtly love in particular and thus to manage the woman question, characteristically implicate an equally insistent re-essentializing of gender and a re-marking of gender difference—for women especially. If the difference of the female is not fully clear and plausible, it has to be repeatedly reconstructed. To this end the female character is always redefined as other than the male characters and speakers in the texts in a variety of predictable ways: she is generically fixed and fully engendered; in every instance she is dead, or mutilated, victimized, violated, anesthetized, abandoned, mystified; or she lacks art, or she lacks desire.[14] The figure of the male poet, by contrast, is drawn

14. Compare Naomi Schor's argument in "Dreaming Dissymmetry: Barthes, Foucault, and Sexual Difference," in *Men in Feminism*, ed. Alice Jardine and Paul Smith

beyond gender; he is represented as variously asexual (or postsexual), alive, creative, playful, uncertain, neutral, or empty to the point of vanishing, and yet full of desire. In other words, the poet exploits his insight into the indeterminacy of gender difference and the social construction of gender relations as part of his efforts to produce himself as multiply, resistantly, and evasively as possible. Moreover, he repeatedly represents other men and other male poets as having foundered over the problems of feminization and gender instability entailed in loving or desiring a woman and/or telling her story. At this early stage in the history of English poetry, the figure of the poet constitutes his own authority by entering into classical and earlier medieval traditions of discourse about women and sexuality and negotiating the problems of doing so more successfully than others have done. If Chaucer abandons his career as a poet of women, then, it is not once but repeatedly, always as a gesture of one-upmanship in a world where writing about women is what literary men do, and always to take up the problem of "false men" and "true women" again in the next text.[15] The figure of the poet in Chaucer tells us that no one can write woman even as he does so. In this way, Chaucerian fiction is representative of the Western literary canon at perhaps its most interesting and certainly its most subtly problematic for late twentieth-century women readers and feminist scholars.

"FEMINIZATION" AND "CHAUCER"

Tunc effeminati passim in orbe dominabantur indisciplinate debachabantur sodomiticisque spurciciis foedi catamitae flammis urendi turpiter abutebantur. Ritus heroum abiciebant, horta-

---

(New York and London: Methuen, 1987), pp. 98–110, on re-essentializing and denying women's specificity. And from a forthcoming essay by Jane Gallop, Schor quotes: " 'The wish to escape sexual difference might be but another mode of denying women' " (100). See also Leslie Wahl Rabine's discussion of the Derridean move: in his works such as "The Double Session," *Glas*, and *Spurs: Nietzsche's Styles*, she observes, "the feminine or woman comes into play but serves to make the male hero . . . bisexual or multi-sexual, in a move that continues to exclude and marginalize women" ("A Feminist Politics of Non-identity," *Feminist Studies* 14 [1988], 16).

15. Again, compare Rabine's formulation: "The repression of the feminine that founds his masculinity is not an isolated event but an ongoing and continuous process. In other words, his apparently stable, self-identical ego rests not on a solid foundation but on this unstable process" ("A Feminist Politics of Non-identity," 20).

menta sacerdotum deridebant, barbaricumque morem in habitu et uita tenebant. Nam capillos a uertice in frontem discriminabant, longos crines ueluti mulieres nutriebant, et summopere comebant, prolixisque niniumque stictis camisiis indui tunicisque gaudebant.

Orderic Vitalis, *Historia Ecclesiastica*

(At that time effeminates set the fashion in many parts of the world: foul catamites, doomed to eternal fire, unrestrainedly pursued their revels and shamelessly gave themselves up to the filth of sodomy. They rejected the traditions of honest men, ridiculed the counsel of priests, and persisted in their barbarous way of life and style of dress. They parted their hair from the crown of the head to the forehead, grew long and luxurious locks like women, and loved to deck themselves in long, overtight shirts and tunics.)[16]

"No, I don't want to destroy you, any more than I want to save you. There has been far too much talk about you, and I want to leave you alone altogether. My interest is in my own sex; yours evidently can look after itself. That's what I want to save."

Verena saw that he was more serious now than he had been before, that he was not piling it up satirically, but saying really and a trifle wearily, as if suddenly he were tired of much talk, what he meant. "To save it from what?" she asked. "From the most damnable feminization!"[17]

Henry James, *The Bostonians*

In looking at Chaucer's career as a poet of women from the standpoint of my reading of the *Legend of Good Women,* I rely on a couple of terms that merit some discussion at the outset. First, I have retained the word "feminization" to describe circumstances that are represented in various forms in all the texts I have included here. It refers throughout to a dramatized state of social, psychological, and discursive crisis wherein men occupy positions and/or perform functions already occupied and performed, within a given text and its contexts, by women or normatively assigned by orthodox discourses to Woman. There are various reasons for speaking of feminization as opposed to either "emasculation"

16. Both the Latin and the translation are taken from Marjorie Chibnall, ed. and trans., *The Ecclesiastical History of Orderic Vitalis,* IV, Books VI and VII (Oxford: Clarendon Press, 1973), pp. 188–89. Two recent discussions brought this passage to my attention: Sharon Farmer, "Persuasive Voices: Clerical Images of Medieval Wives," *Speculum* 61 (1986), 517–43; and Brian Stock, *The Implications of Literacy* (Princeton: Princeton University Press, 1983), pp. 481–82.

17. Henry James, *The Bostonians* (New York: Modern Library, 1956), pp. 342–3.

or, to use a more symmetrical and common term, "role reversal." The emasculation of men is indeed often explicitly the problem for male characters and types: hence all the drooping courtly lovers, from the Black Knight, Troilus, Palamon, Arcite, and Aurelius to the most clearly comic and parodic version of all, Absolon; hence, in a different way, the coy and maidenly Clerk of Oxenford and his prototype, the impotent Geffrey himself in the *House of Fame*, and the heroes of his own tales, the henpecked Melibeus and sweet young Sir Thopas. In some senses and at some moments, feminization and emasculation are interchangeable effects, and I do not intend to set up or adhere to a rigorous distinction between the two. But in calling the problem one of feminization rather than one of emasculation, I want to emphasize my assumption that various fictional failures of manliness can be read as signs or results of another issue, one that always puts men whose stake is in their own gendered identity and their relations with other men into a situation involving women and Woman. To speak of emasculation is to privilege the exclusively positive valence of the masculine, to see maleness as the ideal state from which something is sometimes, and always problematically, missing or taken away. To speak of feminization is on the contrary to suggest that the feminine, in this cultural context a pejorative mark and a set of subordinated or marginalized positions historically occupied most often by female human beings, may have a certain potency and priority, although this possibility is just what it is repeatedly necessary to disprove.

Role reversal is a somewhat broader term, often used by anthropologists, that would cover much of the symbolic and practical terrain I want to explore here, but it implies a symmetry not found in the material I have examined, in which women are rarely "masculinized." Sometimes the feminization of men is indeed an effect in part of their apparent relation to women on top, so to speak; thus the narrator in the *Prologue* to the *Legend of Good Women* is silenced by the rational, authoritative voice of Alceste, and in the *Book of the Duchess* the Black Knight looks more womanly when he talks about his submission to the dominance of White. But White and Alceste are represented as archetypally feminine figures, in ways I shall explore. Chaucerian fiction as a whole suggests that role reversal really only goes one way; both the risks and the benefits of gender instability are for men only. For women, the crossing of gender lines is often fatal (White and Alceste are dead), and in many poems, the implication that a woman might be masculinized is explicitly foreclosed, as in the *Legend of Good Women* and in figures like Dido in the *House of Fame* and Criseyde.

Caroline Walker Bynum's recent work on what she often speaks of as role reversal in medieval religious experience and theological writing reveals a similar pattern. Men were more likely to "become" women— not in practical terms, where cross-dressing would have been of little benefit to them, but in the stories they told about their psychic experiences and the theories they devised to account for them—than women were to become men. Bynum sees this phenomenon as both a site for social rebellion and a safety valve for maintaining normative social order; "descriptions of God as female and the startling reversal at the heart of the mass provided an alternative to and critique of the asymmetry between the sexes in the ordinary world."[18] While I do not focus here on Chaucer's relations to this religious context or to theological writings about gender (a study that would require a different background and would attend more carefully to another group of Chaucerian fictions as well), it seems clear that Chaucer, like the medieval men whom Bynum studies, found symbolic cross-dressing fascinating, useful, inevitable, and frightening.

My use of the term "feminization" is connected to but markedly different from its usage in studies of later periods, such as Ann Douglas's *Feminization of American Culture* or Nancy Armstrong's *Desire and Domestic Fiction.*[19] To put the principal difference, as I see it, most simply, Douglas and Armstrong are both talking about the influence of historical women and of frequently positive female roles on culture, which it is possible to do in the nineteenth-century America and England they study. I am talking about the influence of a negative cultural position or function, as reconstructed from authoritative and prescriptive discourse in the medieval period—and related to the activity of actual women in ways that it is difficult, if not impossible, to assess in this period, even as we keep the problem in mind—on the men who produce the cultural

18. *Holy Feast and Holy Fast: The Religious Significance of Food to Medieval Women* (Berkeley: University of California Press, 1987), especially Chapter 10, "Women's Symbols," pp. 277–96.

19. Ann Douglas, *The Feminization of American Culture* (New York: Knopf, 1977); Nancy Armstrong, *Desire and Domestic Fiction: A Political History of the Novel* (New York: Oxford University Press, 1987). Perhaps I should add that I do not use the term "feminization" in the way that has been used by some modern feminist writers, either, to suggest that the feminine is a subversive position in culture, a positively transgressive site from which phallocentrism can be attacked and deconstructed.

artifacts by which we have traditionally known the Middle Ages and by which our own culture has thus been shaped.[20] But as the work of Armstrong, Douglas, and others indicates, the concept of feminization has a history, and that history begins well before and continues long after the Middle Ages.[21] It is not my project in this study to trace either the full course of this history or the long stretch and complicated shape of its medieval chapters. Within a field circumscribed by my interests and training, I attempt to examine with care and specificity one momentous and consequential engagement with the problem.

Before I proceed, however, it may be useful to point out that other modern scholars of medieval culture, like Bynum, have also begun the task of identifying and analyzing from various perspectives what I am calling the feminization of men and male writers; although they may not use exactly this term, their work intersects my findings in interesting ways and suggests the outlines of historical contexts that I do not explore further here. Toril Moi, for instance, building on Marc Bloch's earlier observations on the influence of noblewomen on aristocratic males of the *courtoisie*, explains what she terms the "effeminisation" of the knightly classes from the twelfth century on as strategic to the naturalization of class differences: "Signalling their cultural superiority, the 'ef-

20. I assume throughout this study an understanding of medieval misogyny and notions about women and Woman based on several recent works, including Hoffman Reynolds Hays, *The Dangerous Sex: The Myth of Feminine Evil* (New York: Putnam, 1964); Katharine M. Rogers, *The Troublesome Helpmate: A History of Misogyny in Literature* (Seattle: University of Washington Press, 1966); Shulamith Shahar, *The Fourth Estate: A History of Women in the Middle Ages*, trans. Chaya Galai (London: Methuen, 1983); Bynum, *Holy Feast and Holy Fast; Sisters and Workers in the Middle Ages*, ed. Judith M. Bennett, Elizabeth A. Clark, Jean F. O'Barr, B. Anne Vilen, and Sarah Westphal-Wihl (Chicago: University of Chicago Press, 1989), and many others specifically and gratefully acknowledged in subsequent notes.

21. For a study of Greek drama that would permit interesting analogies to be drawn between the blurring and refixing of gender difference in Chaucerian fiction and classical tragedy, see Nicole Loraux, *Tragic Ways of Killing a Woman*, trans. Anthony Forster (Cambridge: Harvard University Press, 1987). Recent works suggesting that the history of the relations between male writers and women/Woman extends through the Enlightenment into the modern period include Ruth Salvaggio's discussion of Swift in *Enlightened Absence: Neoclassical Configurations of the Feminine* (Urbana: University of Illinois Press, 1988); Margaret Waller, "*Cherchez la Femme*: Male Malady and Narrative Politics in the French Novel," *PMLA* 104 (1989), pp. 141–51; Barbara Johnson, "Mallarmé as Mother," in *A World of Difference* (Baltimore: Johns Hopkins University Press, 1987), pp. 137–43. Relevant to this history, too, would be studies considering the different position in relation to writing occupied by a female subject; for a discussion of "feminization in the writing subject" that focuses on a female writer in another premodern field, see for instance Catherine Gallagher, "Embracing the Absolute: The Female Subject in Seventeenth-Century England," *Genders* 1 (1988), pp. 24–39.

feminisation' of the aristocracy paradoxically enough comes to signify their 'natural' right to power. It is precisely in its insistence on the 'natural' differences between rulers and ruled that courtly ideology achieved its legitimising function, a function which operates long after the feudal artistocracy has lost its central position in society."[22] By such a reading it appears that for certain political and socioeconomic purposes, one important difference, class, tends to override or alter the orthodox configuration of another prominent difference, gender. But this exigency creates enormous pressures, as Chaucerian fictions often suggest, and the ensuing strains, so marked in the literature of courtly love, remind us that gender difference has never historically remained a "weak difference" for long.[23]

While the courtly model of aristocratic behavior feminizes the male lover—rendering him subservient, weakened, infantilized, privatized, and emotional—Georges Duby has pointed out that in the twelfth century a countermodel also elevated the ideal of the "fruitful couple," the married man and woman "temporarily entrusted with the husbanding of a patrimony." This model, in contrast to the courtly model, required and reinforced strong gender difference: "The same attitude which at that time led to greater differentiation between male and female attire also established different models of behavior for the two sexes: it was fitting for boys to be aggressive, but girls should be prudent and guarded."[24] The feminization that functioned to reinforce class difference, according to Moi, coexisted then with an ideology that implied the kind

22. "Desire in Language: Andreas Capellanus and the Controversy of Courtly Love," in David Aers, ed., *Medieval Literature: Criticism, Ideology, and History* (New York: St. Martin's Press, 1986), p. 19. For useful comments on the complex relation of the figure of the male poet and the female to whom his poetry is addressed in an earlier medieval period, see E. Jane Burns, "The Man Behind the Lady in Troubadour Lyric," *Romance Notes* 25 (1985), especially pp. 263ff. Where I am interested in the male's feminization, Burns stresses that the lady is masculinized and suggests that the purpose of this kind of writing is "to attenuate the menace of female sexuality by codifying desire and seduction, enclosing them within a safely idealized framework" (p. 267).

23. In speaking of a "weak difference," I am borrowing from D. A. Miller's work on *Middlemarch* in *Narrative and Its Discontents* (Princeton: Princeton University Press, 1983), pp. 110ff. Miller argues that in any narrative a number of "weak differences" are suppressed so that "strong differences" may be foregrounded and used to counter threats to the "social arrangements" that they maintain.

24. *Medieval Marriage: Two Models from Twelfth-Century France,* trans. Elborg Forster (Baltimore: Johns Hopkins University Press, 1978), p. 15.

of distrust and hostility towards fashionably effeminate men recorded elsewhere.[25]

Duby maintains that these two apparently opposing "shifts in ideology," courtly love and the ideal of the "fruitful couple," were "actually profoundly compatible and indeed complementary," together managing the division between "youths" and "elders" within the aristocracy. "Their combined impact," Duby affirms, "constituted a welcome aid in safeguarding what had now become, more clearly than ever, the keystone of the dominant society—the married state."[26] The *Franklin's Tale*, as I read it, narrates precisely how "the married state" accommodates incompatible ideals of gender identity and gender relations, although elsewhere in the poetry of Chaucer contradictions and concussions within and between models that regulate gender may seem more visible than strategic complementarity. As a longstanding focus of Chaucer criticism makes clear, by the late fourteenth century, at least, the keystone is showing signs of the stresses it holds in balance, and marriage is represented as a prominent site of discussion and anxiety for dominant elements of society.

The difference between Duby's analysis of twelfth-century France and my observation about the writings of a fourteenth-century English poet may reflect in part the fact that the perception of inadequate or instable gender differentiation is increasingly acute for the secular poet in the late medieval period, given the poet's material and intellectual position. In the centuries before Chaucer wrote, one important strain of medieval thinking linked poetry and rhetoric with social and sexual deviance. Some recent scholarship has focused on the influential text of Alan of Lille's *De planctu naturae*, and, as R. Howard Bloch puts it in his discussion of *De planctu*, "It is, ultimately, the mobility of poetic language and of sexual identity that represents for Nature the most potent threat to the *straightness* ... of grammar and to the continuity of lineage."[27] In another study, Bloch pushes the argument to the conclusion that the medieval poet from the early patristic period to the late Middle Ages is,

25. See, for example, the passage from Orderic Vitalis used as an epigraph for this section.

26. Ibid., pp. 13–15.

27. "Silence and Holes: The *Roman du Silence* and the Art of the Trouvère," *Yale French Studies* 70 (1986), pp. 81–99; see also Jan Ziolkowski, *Alan of Lille's Grammar of Sex* (Cambridge, MA: The Medieval Academy of America, 1985).

by definition, a woman.[28] Eugence Vance has also recently offered a reading of the twelfth-century romance as serving the interests of a new class and ideology. Most interesting for the purposes of my study of Chaucer, Vance considers the identification of a court poet writing two centuries before Chaucer, Chrétien de Troyes, with his fictional female characters, the silk workers in the Pesme Avanture episode of *Yvain*, and suggests that it reveals the author's anxiety that the male worker of texts, like the female weaver of textiles, will be exploited by the new ideology.[29]

In his study of the court poet in the specific period during which Chaucer flourished, R. F. Green, like Duby, Bloch, and Vance, does not use the term "feminization," nor does his analysis include the category of gender. But Green's work may indicate certain analogies between the position of the male poet and the (aristocratic) woman in later medieval society. The writer is a marginalized figure at the fourteenth-century English court, one who must be careful not to offend those of higher rank and authority. He seeks to please and entertain those who have real and theoretical power over him as both interpreters of texts and patrons of art. Moreover, Green observes that some familiar features of the poetic texts we know from the period may be explained as a function of the social situation; the poet's "self-effacement" and "obliqueness," in particular, reflect the caution necessary in claiming authority in the court. At the same time, the poet could bond with aristocratic men (and perhaps women) by displaying his expertise in the literary game, the game of love-talking. Green believes, however, that the poet in this period could not acquire much social importance through poetry, and he points out that we have no evidence that Chaucer's reputation as a poet furthered his career as a court official.[30] It may be possible, and it would certainly be interesting, to uncover more historical evidence of this sort to flesh out what we see in Chaucer about the poet's concern with the perceived instability of gender identity in an age when a hierarchical ordering of the sexes was said to be both natural and divinely ordained. Socially, the poet is put in a position more like that of women and yet forced to compete with men; to write poetry is to violate the

28. "Medieval Misogyny," *Representations* 20 (1987), pp. 1–24. For critiques of the latter by several feminist medievalists, including myself, see *Medieval Feminist Newsletter* 6 (Fall 1988), pp. 2–15.

29. "Chretien's *Yvain* and the Ideologies of Change and Exchange," *Yale French Studies* 70 (1986), pp. 42–62.

30. Green, *Poets and Princepleasers*, pp. 99–134.

proprieties of grammar and gender, to submit to the judgment and authority of the audience, and yet it is also to play a man's game—and in Chaucer to constitute the rules of the game, I shall suggest, so that only men can or will play.[31]

A second term I want to comment on before I proceed with this project is of a rather different order; it is not a concept I have chosen to use in preference to other possibilities, it is not susceptible to brief remark, and its meaning is in one sense the subject of all that follows: it is the term "Chaucer." Today more than ever the name of the author is thrown into quotation marks by the conjunction of the longstanding textual and historical difficulties of reconstructing the fourteenth-century author and postmodern efforts to deconstruct notions of the writing subject's identity and intentionality altogether. Like dramatic readings of the *Canterbury Tales*, claims about Chaucer's intentions and authority can always be challenged by sobering reminders of how little we know, how conjectural our assumptions must be about this author's biography, the dating of individual texts, and even the authority (or authorship) of (parts of) the texts we now have. To tell a story about Chaucer's agency, to try to seek out and reveal his real intentions, moreover, is to presuppose what postmodern thought no longer lets us rely on: the unity or knowability of any authorial position or any subjective stance. Daring to speak about Chaucer at the close of the twentieth century, we might only want to say that he mirrors and compounds both the historical and theoretical problems by self-consciously erasing himself from his fiction, most notably through the varying forms of his infamous irony. Chaucer seems thus to represent, even exaggerate the dilemma par excellence for the literary critic, as succinctly articulated by Peggy Kamuf: "The undecidable trait of the signature must fall into the crack of the historicist/formalist opposition organizing most discourse about literature."[32] At the

31. Relevant here in ways that I can only allude to are discussions of the changing status of poetic authority in late medieval theorizing about language and meaning; see, for example, Holly Wallace Boucher, "Nominalism: The Difference for Chaucer and Boccaccio," *Chaucer Review* 20 (1986), pp. 213–20, and, more generally, Jesse Gellrich, *The Idea of the Book in the Middle Ages* (Ithaca: Cornell University Press, 1985). For discussion of the relation of poets and their authority over their texts to historical changes in reading practices, see Susan Schibanoff, "The New Reader and Female Textuality in Two Early Commentaries on Chaucer," *Studies in the Age of Chaucer* 10 (1988), pp. 71–108.

32. *Signature Pieces: On the Institution of Authorship* (Ithaca: Cornell University Press, 1988), p. 13. See also Michel Foucault's discussion in "What Is an Author?" in *Language, Counter-Memory, Practice*, ed. D. Bouchard (Ithaca: Cornell University Press, 1977), pp. 113–38; in Foucault's words, "The author's name is not a function of a man's civil status, nor is it fictional; it is situated in the breach, among the discontinuities, which gives rise to new groups of discourse and their singular modes of existence" (p. 123).

same time, those moments throughout the Chaucer canon when so much is given to suggest the presence of a historical author with intentions (that is, after all, one implication of both irony and evasiveness), and even with worries that we will misinterpret them, may make some readers understandably reluctant to deconstruct Chaucer too far. More importantly, perhaps, the emergence of forces that would politicize postmodern theory militates against surrendering all sense of authorial (and critical) presence and agency.

It is both from and about the crack, as Kamuf describes it, that I speak, then, when I use the word "Chaucer." One thing I am implicitly asking throughout this study is whether and how we can demystify and politicize rather than reify the undecidability and unknowability of the author, the problem of the signature, seemingly so perfectly embodied in Chaucer, and whether in particular we can do so from the perspective of gender asymmetries. Does the history of gender, as written in part by literary traditions, have anything to do with the fact that most modern and postmodern discourse about literature *is* organized, one way or another, around the principle of authorial undecidability? Is the shifting, provisional nature of the author function that Chaucer so often seems to epitomize in tension or in collaboration with the humanist fiction of the unimplicated, all-seeing artist whom Chaucer also represents to so many readers? With such questions at the fore, I suggest, we can discover in Chaucerian fictions—the poems that have come down to us under his signature and the fiction of Chaucer they have made possible—something about the formation of liberal views of the (male) author as both an individual "unencumbered" personality and a transcendent self with authoritative insights into universal human nature, at a liminal moment in its history.[33] While "Chaucer," then, comprises our historical and the-

---

33. For an early instance of a discussion that tackles these questions and draws helpfully on postmodern theorizing, see H. Marshall Leicester, "The Art of Impersonation: A General Prologue to the *Canterbury Tales*," *PMLA* 95 (1980), pp. 213–24. Leicester's most recent writing about Chaucer in *The Disenchanted Self: Representing the Subject in the Canterbury Tales* (Berkeley and Los Angeles: University of California Press, 1990) was unfortunately published after my work on this book was completed. Recent discussions of the history of reading and authorship that examine this liminal moment include Gellrich, *Idea of the Book*, and, without explicit consideration of Chaucer but in terms that usefully flesh out crucial background, Susan Noakes, *Timely Reading: Between Exegesis and Interpretation* (Ithaca: Cornell University Press, 1988). For a clear description of the feminist critique of the "unencumbered" self, see Seyla Benhabib and Drucilla Cornell's "Introduction: Beyond the Politics of Gender," in *Feminism as Critique*, ed. Benhabib and Cornell (Minneapolis: University of Minnesota Press, 1987), pp. 10–13.

oretical lack of knowledge about the author and in that way identifies the author with neutrality, absence, and obliqueness, so too, I suggest, "Chaucer" comprises strategic obfuscations that are part of a sexual politics and that cannot be divorced from a sense of gendered agency in the production and reception of literary texts. This agency can be conceived of as dispersed and fragmentary, sometimes authorial, sometimes scribal, sometimes critical, sometimes textual and discursive. I henceforth retain the term "Chaucer" (and the adjective "Chaucerian") without quotation marks to refer to this potent, evasive, multipartite, and internally divided agency not to avoid the problems it raises, and not for want of better words, but because one of my main aims is to intervene in the ongoing critical enterprise of constructing in the name of Chaucer a literary father figure, like many fathers powerful and attractive by virtue of his distance and absence, a magisterial authorial self "we" can know and trust.

2

The Wife of Bath and
the Mark of Adam

The wyf of Bathe take I for auctrice
þat womman han no ioie ne deyntee
þat men sholde vp-on hem putte any vice.
Hoccleve, *Dialogus cum
Amico*, ca. 1422

From the early fifteenth century to the late twentieth, one fact about the elusive Wife of Bath has never been disputed: where they agree on nothing else, her numerous commentators, like Hoccleve, take the Wife "for auctrice," as "a woman whose opinion is accepted as authoritative."[1] Controversy over the precise meaning and value of the Wife's opinion effectively ensures her authoritative status, and now, perhaps more than ever before, she has become a figure to be reckoned with by anyone interested in the history, both factual and literary, of women before 1500. Faced with the problem of women's absence and silence in the past, feminist historians and literary critics turn with enthusiasm to the Wife as a rare instance of woman as agent, speaker, and, most recently, reader.[2] More than any other well-known literary character, she is frequently compared with historically real personages, from Christine de

---

1. The epigraph is taken from Caroline F. E. Spurgeon, *Five Hundred Years of Chaucer Criticism and Allusion, 1357–1900* (London: Cambridge University Press, 1925), Vol. I, p. 33; "autrice" is defined thus in the *Middle English Dictionary*, ed. Hans Kurath and Sherman Kuhn (Ann Arbor: University of Michigan Press), B.1, p. 515.

2. For discussion of the Wife as an "aural reader," see Susan Schibanoff, "Taking the Gold out of Egypt: The Art of Reading as a Woman," in *Gender and Reading*, ed. Elizabeth A. Flynn and Patrocinio P. Schweickart (Baltimore and London: Johns Hopkins University Press, 1986), pp. 83–106.

Pisan to Simone de Beauvoir.[3] Where treated as a fictive character, she is often read in a sociological and historical context, as a sign of Chaucer's empathy with real women and/or understanding of feminine power; a realistic, historically plausible foil to the idealized views of femininity found in prescriptive texts of the period; possibly even "a truly practicing feminist"; and indubitably a survivor and a spokeswoman.[4]

Here I interrogate this majority view, first by offering a relatively conventional close reading of the poem, treating the Wife and other characters as if they were psychologically verisimilar human beings from whose reported speech and actions the audience of the text identifies and interprets a living self in a social context. I read this self differently, however, from many recent critics, in a way that emphasizes its powerlessness, self-destructiveness, and silencing, and I argue that the Wife's discourse in the *Prologue* and *Tale* belies her apparent garrulity, autonomy, and dominance. At this level of interpretation she paradoxically represents not the full and remarkable presence with which modern readings have tended to invest her, or even some feminine strategy of negativity and subversion that might be glimpsed through the text, but a dramatic and important instance of woman's silence and suppression

---

3. Schibanoff actually compares the Wife with the quasi-autobiographical narrator "Christine" of the *Book of the City of Women*. Lawrence Lipking, "Aristotle's Sister: A Poetics of Abandonment," *Critical Inquiry*, 19 (1983), pp. 61–81, puts the Wife in the company of women writers ranging from Sappho and Lady Murasaki to Virginia Woolf and Simone de Beauvoir. See also Chapter 1 of this study.

4. I oversimplify by grouping all of the following critics together, but the kind of recent scholarship I have in mind is exemplified in works such as W.F. Bolton, "The Wife of Bath: Narrator as Victim," *Women and Literature*, 1 (1980), pp. 54–65; Mary Carruthers, "The Wife of Bath and the Painting of Lions," *PMLA*, 94 (1979), pp. 209–22; Arlyn Diamond, "Chaucer's Women and Women's Chaucer," in *The Authority of Experience*, ed. Diamond and Lee Edwards (Amherst: University of Massachusetts Press, 1977), pp. 60–83; Robert W. Hanning, "From Eva and Ave to Eglentyne and Alisoun: Chaucer's Insight into the Roles Women Play," *Signs* 2 (1977), pp. 580–99; Kenneth Oberempt, "Chaucer's Antimisogynist Wife of Bath," *Chaucer Review* 10 (1976), pp. 287–302; and Hope Phyllis Weissman, "Antifeminism and Chaucer's Characterization of Women," in *Geoffrey Chaucer: A Collection of Original Articles*, ed. George D. Economou (New York: McGraw-Hill, 1975), pp. 93–110. Maureen Fries refers to the Wife as "a truly practicing feminist" in " 'Slydynge of Corage': Chaucer's Criseyde as Feminist and Victim," in *Authority of Experience*, p. 59. A few protests have been lodged against the tendency to overly lifelike readings of the Wife; see for example David S. Reid, "Crocodilian Humor: A Discussion of Chaucer's Wife of Bath," *Chaucer Review* 4 (1970), pp. 73–89; Ellen Schauber and Ellen Spolsky, "The Consolation of Alison: The Speech Acts of the Wife of Bath," *Centrum* 5 (1977), pp. 20–34; Wayne Shumaker, "Alisoun in Wanderland: A Study in Chaucer's Mind and Literary Method," *ELH* 18 (1961), pp. 77–89.

in history and in language. In the subsequent phases of my argument, I consider the ramifications of my insistence on the Wife's negation for our understanding of the literary inscription of prominent cultural myths about male authors and about women, in fiction and in fact.

But she was somdel deef, and that was scathe.
I.446

It is hardly necessary to rehearse the reasons why the Wife of Bath might well be read as a woman who defies the stereotype of the properly chaste, submissive, and fundamentally silent female, that orthodox ideal celebrated in the antifeminist heroines who, in one authoritative ordering of the Tales, bracket her own performance: the Man of Law's long-suffering Constance and the Clerk's patient Griselda. Against the background that they figure, the Wife stands out even more prominently as the chatterbox, the gossip, the obsessive prattler, a type prominent in medieval literature and given mythical stature in the *Merchant's Tale*, when Proserpina debates the woman question with her husband Pluto and is made to proclaim: " 'I am a womman, nedes moot I speke, / Or elles swelle til myn herte breke' " (IV.2305–6). The Wife may also figure the female storyteller, overtly challenging and at the same time emulating both male authority and the male author, and presenting us with one of our earliest literary images of the female as verbal artist. Sandra Gilbert and Susan Gubar's description of the wicked queen in Snow White might serve equally well to characterize the Wife: "a plotter, a plot-maker, a schemer, a witch, an artist, an impersonator, a woman of almost infinite creative energy, witty, wily, and self-absorbed as all artists traditionally are."[5] In her *Prologue*, moreover, which is twice as long as her *Tale*, the Wife lays claim to the power of language to control the behavior of others. Through verbal attack, as she alleges and demonstrates, she gained and kept the upper hand in her first three marriages. She views words as strategic weapons, like sex and money, in the war between the sexes, and she describes her verbal tactics as repayment in kind against the men in her life: "I quitte hem word for word. . . . I ne owe hem nat a word that it nys quit" (422–25). One might well argue

---

5. *The Madwoman in the Attic* (New Haven: Yale University Press, 1979), p. 30.

that she successfully frees herself and requites the whole antifeminist tradition by turning the tables on male authority, parodying its rhetorical strategies and thus revealing its prejudice and absurdity by impersonating the male voice.[6]

But views of the Wife as triumphant and powerful, often accompanied by the assumption that Chaucer intends to criticize or at least poke fun at antifeminist arguments, may be qualified, as other readers have suggested, by a recognition of the Wife's limitations, which the *Prologue* and *Tale* make equally clear. Despite her putative ability and eagerness to speak, I suggest, the Wife of Bath is not essentially more free, self-determined, or self-expressive than the good, silent woman, like Griselda or Constance, and her own words oblige us to understand the constraints upon her.

Throughout her *Prologue*, the Wife's language reflects precisely the power differential overtly dramatized in other of the Tales, especially the Clerk's. The first 170 lines of the *Prologue* consist mostly of direct and indirect quotation from both biblical and patristic texts, and so they are punctuated with tags that taken together underscore the gender of official speakers and critics: "quod he," "thus seyde he," "he speketh," "th'apostel seith," "Mark telle kan," and so on. Although she begins to speak of her own "experience"—she has "had" five husbands—only nine lines into her speech she cites her first authority, and the terms in which she does so are particularly salient. "But me was toold, certeyn, nat longe agoon is, . . ." she says, that biblical injunction forbids multiple marriage (9). The sudden appearance of the adversative at the beginning of line 9 immediately signals the oppugnant stance she is assigned to take throughout the rest of the *Prologue*. The use of the passive transformation, "me was told," puts the Wife first in the surface structure of the sentence; she is indeed self-absorbed, the phrasing suggests, and attempts to use her words, like her church offering, to affirm her preeminence. But in the deep structure of the sentence, "someone told me," the Wife is the object of the verb, or, in case-grammar terms, the "patient." Magically transformed, like the old hag in her tale, the Wife

---

6. For this view see Marjorie M. Malvern, " 'Who peyntede the leon, tel me who?' Rhetorical and Didactic Roles Played by an Aesopic Fable in the *Wife of Bath's Prologue*," *Studies in Philology* 80 (1983), pp. 238–52; Barry Sanders, "Chaucer's Dependence on Sermon Structure in the *Wife of Bath's Prologue and Tale*," *Studies in Medieval Culture* 4 (1974), pp. 437–45; and James Spisak, "Antifeminism Bridled: Two Rhetorical Contexts," *Neuphilologische Mitteilungen* 81 (1980), pp. 150–60.

occupies a place in the surface structure of her utterance that disguises her fundamental status, seen only in the base sentence, as a person acted upon rather than acting, a human being whose behavior is subject to the criticism and correction of some higher authority. Furthermore, although later in the *Prologue* the Wife repeatedly identifies the "auctoritees" against whom she argues, the subject in the deep structure of this sentence remains unexpressed. As the audience would presumably know, the antifeminist argument to which she alludes comes from St. Jerome; but it is not clear whether the Wife has it directly from his writings or, as is more likely, from some male reader of Jerome like her fifth husband. All we learn from the *Prologue* is that someone, at some unspecified time in the relatively recent past ("nat longe agoon is"), told the Wife that her behavior was immoral, and she does not say who. Perhaps she has forgotten or does not wish to identify a living critic, or perhaps she does not know exactly who, just as she cannot say quite when: no one told her, and everyone told her. The authority against which she rebels is not that of any single person; there is no tyrannical lord in her life as there is in Griselda's. The Wife is defending herself against a much vaguer and more obscured force of social disapproval, powerfully unnamed and unnameable, and her later attempts to meet specific arguments are self-defeating efforts to pin down and triumph over that generalized, mystifying, and hence invincible hostility that she meets from all sides.

This crucial vagueness and uncertainty, this Orwellian mystification of the power behind language, is further reflected in the opening lines as the Wife claims that she does not fully understand the meaning, although she understands the hostility and disapproval, of the arguments against her. She goes on to cite the highest authority of "Jhesus, God and man," and tellingly, the story of Jesus she relates is one that reveals not his loving-kindness, but his apparently gratuitous reproof of the Samaritan woman. The Wife's professed inability to interpret the meaning of his rebuke serves both to challenge its authority and to reveal her own nebulous insecurity:

> What that he mente therby, I kan nat seyn;
> But that I axe, why that the fifthe man
> Was noon housbonde to the Samaritan?
> How manye myghte she have in mariage?
> (20–23)

She asks her bold questions of no one in particular, and of everyone. We see again the generalized feeling that someone out there knows more than she does. Immediately afterwards, instead of rejecting an authority that she does not understand or that conflicts with her own experience (whatever that may be), she proceeds to choose another "gentil" text to support her argument: "God bad us for to wexe and multiplye" (28). This is all strategic on her part and no doubt meant to be very funny. It also underlines a serious truth about the nature of power in her world. God's characteristic speech act is a command; created in His image, all men, even Christ, speak sharp words to women, for reasons that are purposefully obscure and obscured; and the Wife, along with all women, is "told" by received opinion that her behavior is wrong. She struggles to understand why, she seems to want both to subvert and to be right and "good,"[7] and so she asks questions and tries to find or make authorities that speak on her side. Despite the admonitions of many exegetical critics, those of us who are not horrified by her blasphemy will admire her resilience and persistence and courage. We also see, however, that as long as she accepts (or, what amounts to the same thing, attempts to invert) the basic power differential and the obfuscation of power reflected and supported by the language she uses, her struggles are in vain. As will become clearer after my discussion of the *Clerk's Tale*, this protofeminist, this "archewyf" and "auctrice" is not even as critical of her true masters, as awake to her less obvious but equally fundamental subjection, as patient Griselda.

The rest of the *Prologue* provides evidence that supports this reading. In telling us about her first three old husbands, the Wife quotes herself, demonstrating how she verbally attacked them and always won; but ironically, since her method was to accuse her husbands of standard antifeminist attitudes, for yet another 150 lines we are subjected (as she was) to a deafening stream of misogynist platitudes, here from folk rather than learned tradition. The repeated "thou seist" tag, again necessitated by the quotation within quotation, emphasizes the fact that she is fighting against the power of male voices to control her behavior and that at some level she knows it. Again, ironically, all is false; her first three husbands, she implies, were not bright enough to talk this much, but she is trying to pin down that invisible and omnipresent power that she knows will control her if she gives it a chance. And with her fifth husband, the Wife herself is aptly repaid for all her earlier deceits. She

7. Gloria K. Shapiro makes this point in "Dame Alice as Deceptive Narrator," *Chaucer Review* 6 (1971), pp. 130–41.

undergoes a perverse version of wish fulfillment—an experience she uses and revises when she tells her tale—when the story she invented to control her first three husbands comes true. Janekyn really does attack her, that is, with antifeminist doctrine, this time of a learned and hence even more authoritative variety. In the final section of her *Prologue*, as she describes the contents of his antifeminist miscellany by quoting from it at great length, the Wife yet again gives the stronger voice in the text, as in reality, to the opposition.

One might argue that all this quotation merely shows us what a woman is up against and therefore highlights the Wife's victory over it, but it is also essential to remember that throughout her performance the Wife both consciously and unconsciously endorses the antifeminist stereotypes she cites, illustrating again that, as Fredric Jameson puts it, "transgressions, presupposing the laws or norms or taboos against which they function, thereby end up precisely reconfirming those laws."[8] She boasts, for instance, of her traditionally feminine powers to lie and deceive and manipulate men, and this unwitting self-deprecation is not so very different from the idealized statements of victimization that "good" women, like Constance or Griselda, are willing and even eager to utter. Both the dumb woman and the wily, witty, creative woman live in a world where their protest against received opinion is normally silenced and dialogue precluded; and so the patient and the impatient woman— the norm and the transgression—are presented as two sides of the same coin, able to see themselves and speak for themselves only in terms provided by the dominant language and mythology of their culture. The Wife's loss of hearing is caused, as we are told at the end of her *Prologue*, by one act that is not a speech act, her violent nonverbal attempt to destroy Jankyn's book, the written word that has made her what she is. This cryptic, unsettling, and foreshortened drama of role reversal, mock murder, and humiliation discloses the mutual degradation that marital relations entail in her world, and the Wife's mutilation serves as a climactic symbol of the simultaneously muting and deafening effect of the dominant discourse and the gender hierarchy it enforces.

The *Wife of Bath's Tale* has sometimes been seen as an antidote to the use of male authority and endless quotation in her *Prologue*, but on closer examination things are not really very different. For a while, the tables

8. *The Political Unconscious* (Ithaca: Cornell University Press, 1981), p. 68.

do seem genuinely turned: the tale begins with a casual rape, but the rapist is sentenced to death, and the queen (thanks to the "grace" of the king) is granted power over his life. She gives him a twelvemonth and a day to find out what women want most, and now the story sounds as though the pronouns have been reversed. The Knight can save his neck if he finds out what the opposite sex really desires; the price he is asked to pay for the correct answer is one more often exacted from women, as he is required to satisfy the lawful sexual appetites of someone old and physically repulsive to his suddenly refined sensibilities. The heroine of the tale, an elf queen disguised as an old hag, is a powerful artist, able to transform herself and gain mastery over her husband through her wise and "gentil" (and thoroughly orthodox) speech. But the ending of the tale, like the ending of so much Chaucerian fiction in this regard, safely returns us to a more familiar plot and a more suitable alignment of the sexes. The rapist not only saves his life but is also rewarded by the promise of that impossible being, an unfailingly beautiful, faithful, and obedient wife; the hag who gave him the answer, who had all the power, gives it up, and transforms herself into a Constance or Griselda. Thus the denouement implies that the Wife herself lacks confidence in the female's powers of speech. Although the hag/elf queen, like the queen in Snow White, has the creative drive of an artist, it is thwarted and used self-destructively to reveal that her true identity is what every man is said to want most, a woman "bothe fair and good" (1241) who "obeyed hym in every thyng / That myghte doon hym plesance or likyng" (1255–56). The hag chooses that silent beauty which only in a fairy tale is anything but fleeting and dangerous. With the happy ending the heroine relinquishes her power and dissolves into literal silence and alleged submission, the archetypal feminine transformation.

The Wife, of course, does not; she has the last word, and I think we can begin to see why that word must be a curse on men:

> And eek I praye Jhesu shorte hir lyves
> That wol nat be governed by hir wyves;
> And olde and angry nygardes of dispence,
> God sende hem soone verray pestilence!
> (1261–64)

The speaker who utters a curse assumes, as the Wife always does, that language has power in more than a metaphorical sense. She wishes to injure the addressee, or the person or persons cursed, and reduces the object of her imprecation to linguistic powerlessness: there is no effective response to a curse, no way to ward it off, and it can work without the addressee's knowledge of it. Its efficaciousness depends not, however, on the speaker's power, but on the power of some external, presumably divine or supernatural, force whose aid is invoked for the purposes of destroying the opposition and closing off communication. The curse, at once vague and all-encompassing, is only a response in kind, then, to the hostility that the Wife meets on all sides and an application of the repressive training in the power of language that a patriarchal culture has given her. It is by the same token not a response, but an involuntary, extraverbal cry of anger that implicitly denies the autonomy of both speaker and addressee and undercuts the Wife's putative attempt to speak of and for herself.[9]

Who peyntede the leon, tel me who?
By God! if wommen hadde writen stories,
As clerkes han withinne hire oratories,
They wolde han writen of men moore wikkednesse
Than al the mark of Adam may redresse.

III.692–96

In any discussion of the Wife of Bath as a speaking subject, the Wife's intriguing question—who painted the lion? from whose point of view is this story being told?—requires close attention. In the lines quoted above, the character is made to allude self-reflexively to the problem that I have been arguing is most central to feminist interpretations of this text, to the actual silence and absence of the Wife and/as Woman. If women had ever authored stories, she points out, they would be very different ones; although actually, as she imagines it here, they would also be much the same—equally determined, that is, by the anxieties of gender difference and the resultant, allegedly inevitable competition between men and women. A female character thus indirectly but unequivocally reminds

9. See Margaret Homans, " 'Her Very Own Howl: The Ambiguities of Representation in Recent Women's Fiction," *Signs* 9 (1983), 186–205, for an analogous discussion, in a very different historical period, of the question of women's relation to language and the specific issue of what happens (in literary texts, at least) when women fail or destroy themselves in their attempts to appropriate the dominant discourse and are left to utter a "referentless" cry of rage that takes them outside discourse.

us at the very center of her fictional narrative not only that an author's gender, as constructed by a set of binary oppositions between female and male, always colors the written (and spoken) word, but also that this text affords no exception to the rule that women have *not* written the story. A male author created the Wife, and "her" teasing, playful, characteristically hostile, and arguably unconscious reference to this fact mirrors and confirms what we have seen in both the *Prologue* and the *Tale*: a feminine monstrosity who is the product of the masculine imagination against which she ineffectively and only superficially rebels. It is an apparently paradoxical but finally explicable and revealing fact that the one woman in the *Canterbury Tales* who is so often viewed, for good or bad, as an autonomous being is the one from whose mouth comes the reminder that "she," like every female character in the male-authored text, never existed at all. In an important sense the Wife is not only as powerless and silent, but also as unreal, as unrepresentable, as saintly Constance, patient Griselda, or the transformed hag at the end of her tale, and the fact that she herself voices this understanding is consistent with the variously self-deprecating pronouncements we hear from many Chaucerian heroines.

The passage on the painting of lions signifies, in other words, that the Wife's actual failure of self-expression and empowerment through language, analyzed at the mimetic level in the first part of this chapter, is a symptom of the alleged impossibility of her speaking, by virtue of her gendered exclusion from the role of storyteller. This claim ensures at every level the Wife's and Woman's negation, as even the most wordy and verisimilar of female characters is (de)constructed by her own words as that which is not actually speaking and not actually being represented, that which stands outside the bounds of language and literary convention altogether. The way she is characterized thus manages to conflate real women and the absent Woman as firmly as possible. And it is precisely this negation of the Wife that makes her an important figure for feminist analysis. As H. Marshall Leicester has put it, in a reading of the Wife that I return to in later parts of this chapter, "there is no Wife of Bath."[10] Understood as a construction of the text, this fact can help us to read this complicated, convoluted poem for the insights it affords us into the ways and means by which the literary tradition has maneuvered

10. "Of a Fire in the Dark: Public and Private Feminism in the *Wife of Bath's Tale*," *Women's Studies* 11 (1984), pp. 157–78.

within, accounted for, and profited from the socio-gender system as we know it, in all its complexity, fragility, and historical variability. My reading of the Wife, like all subsequent readings in this study, thus intends to challenge in particular the bipartite myth of Chaucer's special sympathy or empathy with women and his aesthetic or moral transcendence.

To interrogate this myth, I first want to consider two arguments that seem to support the remarkable notion that Chaucer sympathizes not merely with female characters like the Wife, but even with the particular insights of late twentieth-century feminist criticism into the social construction of Woman. First, one argument might go, the position of the feminine exemplified by the Wife—a position finally outside the bounds, as we have seen, of the representable—may be viewed, like all marginal positions, as a potentially subversive one. Above all, the mandated silence of women and the concomitant impossibility of representing a real female speaker threatens both the author's control and the audience's ability to understand the character and the poem: the evanescence of the Wife and Woman's position marks the limits, in other words, of both representation and interpretation.[11] To argue that we can never know "who she is" because she is "not anyone" seems to state the obvious and beg the question, but it also calls into question the effectiveness of precisely the kind of reading—or its opposite—that I have offered in the first part of this essay. Viewing the Wife as a psychologically verisimilar, speaking self and concluding that either she is or is not empowered, such readings allow us to assume a momentary, illusory power over the character and the world, to situate ourselves, as Leicester again puts it, in "a position superior to her from which she can be fixed and placed, understood and dismissed." And so it could be argued that by inscribing the silence and enigma of the Wife as/and Woman in the many ways I have suggested, Chaucer refuses to let us rest securely and comfortably in that dominant position, and hence at least tacitly advocates a tolerant, antiauthoritarian stance that the modern feminist reader must value.[12] But

11. Compare Shoshana Felman's discussion of Balzac's "The Girl with the Golden Eyes," in "Rereading Femininity," *Yale French Studies* 62 (1981), pp. 19–44: "It is thus not only the conventional authority of sovereign masculinity that Paquita's femininity threatens but the authority of any representative code as such, the smooth functioning of the very institution of representation" (p. 32).

12. This is H. Marshall Leicester's reading of Chaucer's sexual politics in "Of a Fire in the Dark"; the quotation is from pp. 161–62.

I shall argue here and later that defining Woman as mystery, that is, defining the feminine as resistance to closure, reifies both her status as Other, that which can never be fully known or present, and the unrelenting dynamics of binary gender opposition as surely as do totalizing, patriarchal readings. In the latter part of this chapter I comment in more detail on the theoretical and practical problematics of such a position.

Second, a case might be made for Chaucer's allegedly feminist leanings on the basis of a closely related issue: the similarities between the position of women and the apparent position of the poet. The *Canterbury Tales* as a whole seems structured to highlight and even exaggerate a situation common to all (literary) texts. Stories both reveal and create tellers; no tale can be interpreted except as the product of a human speaker, and yet the human speaker behind each tale is also firmly identified as the fictional creation of yet another speaker. This situation creates a possibility of infinite regression, a dramatization and literalization of the *mise en abîme* of language, and hence a fundamental and threatening absence of identifiable authority that leads to a well-known interpretive problem: how do we locate "Chaucer the poet" (not to speak of "Chaucer the man") at any moment? Or who, at any point, is speaking? The voice of the poet creates, at best, a slippery, ironic persona who, like the Wife of Bath, offers us someone who is not really there, who is only, in Leicester's words again, "the traces of a presence that asserts its simultaneous absence."[13]

Like the Wife: what interests me here and throughout this study is the repeated perception that the figure of the poet and the woman are represented as similar in many ways. At the level of historical realism, Chaucer and the Wife may seem particularly homologous in their (in)-subordinate position. Recent scholars have suggested that the medieval poet may well be understood in terms of the ambivalent, insecure, and inferior position that he held in the fourteenth-century court;[14] as marginalized and subordinated figures, poets and women alike may be si-

---

13. Leicester, "The Art of Impersonation: A General Prologue to the *Canterbury Tales*," *PMLA* 95 (1980), p. 220.

14. See R. F. Green, *Poets and Princepleasers* (Toronto: University of Toronto Press, 1980); Richard Waswo, "The Narrator of *Troilus and Criseyde*," *ELH* 50 (1983), pp. 1–25; and for a comparable argument based on a later continental situation, Paul Zumthor, "From (Hi)Story to Poem, or the Paths of Pun: The Grands Rhetoriqueurs of Fifteenth-Century France," *New Literary History*, 10 (1979), pp. 231–62. See also my discussion of this issue in Chapter 1.

multaneously complicitous with and suspicious of both the ideology that tries but fails to define them and of the audience to and for whom they speak. Both the Wife and Chaucer tell lies that subvert the power of words to speak any truth at all, stories that threaten any correspondence between utterance and meaning and that undermine orthodox assumptions about the nature of intention and identity. In their silence and absence, both poet and woman stand together, by this reading, in the position of the limit of that which can be represented. Disclosing the other side of all this potential subversiveness, as verisimilar selves they seem to share an ideologically sanctioned fantasy of silent submission and wordless transformation that their excessive fluency covers and belies. The happy ending of the Wife's *Tale*, although qualified by both her *Prologue* and her curse, seems oddly analogous to the poet's famous *Retraction*, problematized by its uncomfortable relation to all of the work that precedes it.

But it is at just this point that the provocative analogy between Chaucer and Wife, great Poet and quintessential Woman, breaks down in a way I find particularly interesting, and the case for Chaucer's tolerance, sympathy, or identification with women again becomes at best moot. The Wife's curse once more is telling: it functions as a commentary on her own fantasy, for which we find no counterpart following the *Retraction*. Chaucer's strategy in the *Canterbury Tales*, as we shall see again in the last part of this book, displaces the commitment that speaking entails onto other voices in an attempt to remain as free of the constraints of fallen language, as powerfully apolitical, muted, unaccountable, unnamed, and unspoken as possible. The poet does exercise (to this day, one might argue) the power of silence, and the *Retraction* in a sense simply reinforces that silence without deconstructing the work it ostensively retracts. The figure of the male author constructed by the *Canterbury Tales* as a whole can only caution us against thinking we can know anything at all about him—including his sexual politics.

The Wife's curse, on the other hand, reveals that the female character created by Chaucer retains a paradoxical and fatal faith in language that is self-destructive: invoking the power of words to destroy rather than create, she at once discovers and betrays her own commitment to speaking, validates the patriarchal authority she seeks to resist, and renounces the power of silence that the poet seems more able to exploit. From this perspective, the Wife's performance demonstrates that Chaucer's Woman suffers from a delusion that the implied author does not reproduce. Her curse, in particular, serves to distinguish her dramatically from the figure of the male poet, and, more important, to disarm the very threat of women's silence and unrepresentability that the poet acknowledges, appropriates, and strategically counters. The lesson of the Wife's *Prologue* and *Tale* seems to be that a naive faith in language does not serve women well because language is, according to the *Canterbury Tales*, an instrument for reproducing the conventions that constrain and deny both the experience of women and the representation of that experience. But this is just the lesson that the Wife, unlike the poet, is not allowed to learn or profit from—because she is the lesson. As learned in "scolematere" (1272) as any clerk, she cannot escape the convention of the happy ending that legitimates the knight's originally illicit and violent desire by subordinating and silencing the hag/elf queen any more than she can escape the need to transgress and thus reinforce the laws of language and the myths of culture that at once silence her and condemn her to speak.

———————

It is odd that many have found the Wife of Bath lifelike. If she is, it is not in a way that those who see her as a marvel of naturalistic invention would accept. In common sense human terms she is absurd and grotesque, a figment of that anti-feminist gallimaufry, the Prologue to her Tale. That many take her as a triumph of Chaucer's mellow and humane art tells us more about the place of women in our tradition than about the words before us. True, Chaucer was civilized; he shared the enjoyment of his courtly, humanist civilization in baiting women and the middle classes. But we are middle class, even if we think the middle classes ought not to be baited; and women are not to be baited really, for their place has changed. In short our idea of civilization is different from Chaucer's. So it can hardly be that those who talk of the mellowness and humanity that went into the Wife really mean they whole-heartedly enjoy Chaucer's curmudgeonly and old-fashioned humor; or if they do, they are less than frank about it. It seems much more likely that they have found a way of misunderstanding Chaucer. And we have other ways as well, for our different ethos has not given us a detached view of the real nature of the Wife's comedy. It has made her an embarrassment, so that, fearing for Chaucer's good name, we misunderstand her elaborately.[15]

David S. Reid, "Crocodilian Humor"

———————

15. "Crocodilian Humor," p. 73.

I am not the first to stand outside the general consensus that the Wife of Bath is an authentic female speaker who testifies to both real female power (or lack thereof) and Chaucer's own extraordinary virtues and virtuosities. The paragraph cited above opens David S. Reid's discussion of Chaucer's Wife of Bath in an essay published almost two decades ago, and while there are many things to be said about Reid's iconoclastic position, the questions I address here are these: Why has the critical community since 1970 been unmoved by his exposé of the misreadings of the Wife that have, he alleges, been generated by the modern canonization and adulation of Chaucer? Why do we still find the latest and often most theoretically sophisticated Chaucerians still apparently fearing for Chaucer's good name, and what is it that they fear, exactly? Putting aside for the moment the equally important and deeply implicated problem of class politics that Reid alludes to, and that I will touch on in later chapters, I propose that the politics of literary adulation so clearly practiced in those elaborate misunderstandings of the Wife and other Chaucerian women are prominently and preeminently sexual politics.[16] A late twentieth-century feminist critique that persists in scrutinizing the male-authored canon can call into question the continuing practice of such politics in literary studies in general, as well as in Chaucer studies.

To this end, I want to explore more fully the history of the reception of the *Wife's Prologue* and *Tale* as a pro- or antifeminist document, and the implications of that history for current feminist readings. For the purposes of my argument, I begin by cavalierly and hypothetically dividing the history of Chaucer criticism into three political ages: the prefeminist, the feminist, and the postfeminist. I want to say very little about the first age, somewhat more about the second, and more yet about the third. In the long prefeminist era, dating from somewhere near the end of the fourteenth century to the second half of the twentieth, what we may now want to read as blatantly "sexist" responses to Chaucer's female characters are abundant and various. It would be easy but no longer very newsworthy to document the ways in which the two broad traditions of critical response to the Wife of Bath in particular cover the fears that the talking woman inspires in a predominantly male audience: she

16. I take the phrase "the politics of literary adulation" from the conference of that name held at West Chester University in April 1985, where I delivered a very early version of this chapter.

is the butt of Chaucer's broad, jolly, ironic humor, or the target of his righteous, Christian, ironic scorn. Whether the Wife is seen as "amazing" and "vividly feminine" or as a "blight and scourge,"[17] neither the female character nor the woman question is of serious interest to the critics; the author, Chaucer, is the literary hero, a great, wise, godlike creator of characters whose human foibles he captures and exposes, be it lovingly or sternly.

The second, comparatively brief era in the history I am constructing here was occasionally prefigured in earlier studies of Chaucer's alleged empathy with women but began to flourish only in the 1970s.[18] I will call this the feminist era, although I do not want to suggest that whatever feminism means, it refers to a monolithic project or in any sense a completed one. I use the term "feminist" at this point to describe a kind of critical activity in the academy that developed in response to sociopolitical events of the last two decades. I also use it elsewhere in this study to refer to current critical practice and theory, including my own recent work, that sees itself working within late twentieth-century feminism and yet builds on and differs from the feminist criticism of ten years ago (including, again, my own) in significant ways, even to the point of questioning how the feminist position, as construed in certain ways, can actually achieve the goals its occupants desire.[19]

It is in the 1970s, at any rate, that the question of sexual politics becomes an explicit one addressed by scholars who ask us to view Chaucer

17. The views I cite belong, respectively, to George Lyman Kittredge ("The Wife of Bath is one of the most amazing characters that the brain of man has ever yet conceived"), *Chaucer and His Poetry* (Cambridge: Harvard University Press, 1915), p. 189; Walter C. Curry, *Chaucer and the Medieval Sciences*, 2d. ed. (New York: Barnes and Noble, 1960), p. 91; and William Blake, "Sir Jeffry Chaucer and the nine and twenty Pilgrims on their Journey to Canterbury," cited in Spurgeon, *Five Hundred Years of Chaucer Criticism*, vol. II, p. 45.

18. One early "feminist" reading that prefigures the work of the 1970s is Constance Saintonge, "In Defense of Criseyde," *Modern Language Quarterly* 15 (1954), pp. 310–20.

19. For an example of my more recent critique of my own earlier "feminist" writing about Chaucer, see "The Feminization of Men in Chaucer's *Legend of Good Women*," in Janet Halley and Sheila Fisher, eds., *Seeking the Woman in Late Medieval and Renaissance Writings* (Knoxville: University of Tennessee Press, 1989), which revises "Irony and the Antifeminist Narrator in Chaucer's *Legend of Good Women*," *Journal of English and Germanic Philology* 82 (1983), pp. 11–31, and my discussion in the preceding chapter. I see the enterprise of using and "revising" earlier feminist work in a different, more positive light than some critics do; contrast, for example, Nina Baym's warnings (meant as part of her case against "theory") against feminist criticism that "succeeds . . . only when it ignores or dismisses the earlier paths of feminist literary study as 'naive' and grounds its own theories in those currently in vogue with men who make theory" (*Tulsa Studies in Women's Literature* 2 [1983], p. 45).

as a social critic analyzing individuals as products of conventions and ideology. By this view, the poet specifically and self-consciously offers understanding or even radical criticism of the antifeminist tradition as he knew, used, and, some would say, intentionally subverted it. Among Chaucerians explicitly concerned with modern questions of feminism and antifeminism, however, there appears again a difference or double-ness of opinion on Chaucer's infamous Wife of Bath. As I noted before, some emphasize the degree to which she is a strong, autonomous, rel-atively free woman, a realistic, historically plausible foil to the idealized views of femininity found in prescriptive texts of the medieval period, and even, as Maureen Fries claims, "a truly practicing feminist."[20] Others, on the contrary, contend that she is presented as a victim, speaking not from a position of even relative strength but in the "manipulative, hostile voice" of a woman suffering from "the wounds of gender."[21]

This debate refracts through a new lens the old division among pre-feminists: to the feminist critic of this era, the Wife as blasphemous female monster is a heroine; as "vividly feminine" or comic female gro-tesque, she is a victim. This period certainly brings a new focus on institutions and the way they construct selves or individuals; and we see unaccustomed investment in, perhaps even identification with, the fe-male character. But the literary adulation of Chaucer persists; most critics read through the character and their interpretation of her circumstances and significance to the presence, authority, and (good) intentions of the author. Whether the Wife is seen as victim of misogyny or avatar of liberation, then, Chaucer is often credited with "insight into the roles women play," and the ostensive empathy with his female characters that traditional criticism had often noted more or less in passing is reaffirmed and made central to his poetic vision in ways that accord with the de-mands of a twentieth-century liberal consciousness and the academic institutions within which these texts are read.[22] Arlyn Diamond, who stands virtually alone in this period in suggesting that Chaucer's sym-pathy is "limited by his fundamental conservatism," concludes her per-suasive feminist critique by rehabilitating Chaucer, to an extent, on very interesting grounds—on the basis of his "discomfort with categories": "he means to be women's friend, insofar as he can be, and it is this

20. " 'Slydynge of Corage,' " p. 693; see also note 5 above.
21. Bolton, "The Wife of Bath: Narrator as Victim," p. 63.
22. As Hanning argues in his essay "From Eva and Ave to Eglentyne and Alisoun."

painfully honest effort, this unwillingness to be satisfied with the formulas of his age, which we as feminists can honor in him."[23]

It is my contention, and my purpose in this study as a whole to demonstrate, that the feminist era in Chaucer studies is not over in any sense: important feminist scholarship is still being written, and feminism has yet to make the difference that it might make in the way that male authors like Chaucer are read. But in the work of recent Chaucerians, as in the wider worlds of literary criticism and the culture in which it is practiced, I discern at least the potential for an emergent third era that I shall call, with reservations, postfeminist. I qualify my use of this term because I do not wish to imply that something like the postfeminism announced by the American media since the early 1980s is irrevocably upon us, or that it is somehow necessary or inevitable that on the fast track in academe we now move on beyond feminist criticism and theory.[24] Nor do I mean to invoke another use of this term, in the intellectual discourse of *Le Postféminisme* in France in the 1970s.[25] But the term "postfeminist" serves to describe some of the specific implications, although not necessarily the intended or actual argument, of two recent essays on the Wife of Bath. I use the term postfeminist, then, in reference to these works in certain specific ways: they are post-*feminist* in the sense that they seem, at one level, to take up the contemporary feminist project by focusing powerful critical attention on the literary representation of women and the rhetorical construction of gender; implicitly or explicitly, they find Chaucer himself something of a feminist—or at least not an antifeminist—in his sexual politics. Each essay may be termed *post*-feminist, however, in that each may imply, as I see it with an admittedly pessimistic eye, some of the ways in which a "merely" feminist reading of Chaucer is both out of date and beside the point. Chaucer is constructed in both essays as a male poet writing for and about men; in both, moreover, the specifically gendered woman reader may be excluded or limited by the critic's interpretive assumptions. (In neither piece are the categories "men" and "women" either historicized or decon-

23. Arlyn Diamond, "Chaucer's Women and Women's Chaucer," p. 83.

24. For an early announcement of what is now more or less taken for granted in the media, see Susan Bolotin, "Voices from the Post-feminist Generation," *New York Times Magazine*, 17 October 1982, pp. 28ff.

25. For an insightful discussion of this topic, see Mary Russo, "Notes on 'Post-feminism,'" in *The Politics of Theory*, ed. Francis Barker et al. (Colchester: University of Sussex, 1983), pp. 27–37.

structed.) At the same time, the benefits and demands of a certain kind of political feminism seem to have been accepted by both critics: given their determination of the author's irreproachable attitude toward women, Chaucer can still be read and valued for his humanist insight into and sympathy for the female other as well as his dispassionate artistic greatness. Taking up only one aspect of each critic's interpretation of Chaucer's Wife, in looking at the arguably postfeminist implications of these essays I intend not to distort or diminish their efforts and achievements, nor to exaggerate or reify their role in opening a new age, or the uniqueness of their positions, but rather to view them as part of a very long history of criticism. My concern as a feminist in the late twentieth century is that history can and does repeat itself.

The first of these essays is Lee Patterson's " 'For the Wyves Love of Bath': Feminine Rhetoric and Poetic Resolution in the *Roman de la Rose* and the *Canterbury Tales.*" Patterson does not situate his work openly in relation to current feminist thought, but his essay affirms what might seem a useful premise for any feminist reading of Chaucer: questions of gender are "of central importance in Chaucer's efforts at poetic self-definition." The poet has and shares insights into the ways women (and poets) are victimized by literary tradition, and moreover "acknowledges his own complicity" in the process. The Wife of Bath is, as Patterson so fundamentally understands, "a creature of the male imagination." It is when Chaucer "uses" the Wife's voice, however, "to counter the authoritative tones of the Man of Law," Patterson concludes, that "he is in effect abandoning his claims to the 'maistrye' of an 'art poetical' that is based on the submission of women."[26]

Such a claim raises more questions about identity and intentionality in discourse than Patterson even begins to answer in his essay, but I am less interested here in his predictable assessment of the blamelessness of Chaucer's sexual politics than in his pervasive assumptions about the way gender intersects and connects the position of the writer and the reader. Repeatedly, he presupposes that both "the medieval poetic consciousness" and the modern critical consciousness are male or masculine, that a transhistorical notion of male heterosexuality is essential to the task of reading (women), and that reading women is a constitutive ac-

26. Lee Patterson, " 'For the Wyves Love of Bath': Feminine Rhetoric and Poetic Resolution in the *Roman de la Rose* and the *Canterbury Tales,*" *Speculum* 58 (1983), pp. 656–95; quotations in this paragraph are found on pp. 688–87 and 693.

tivity (and again a transhistorical one) for authors and audiences alike. For example, Patterson speaks of the Wife's rhetorical come-on in her Prologue and notes that *"for the male audience* feminine speaking *is never* wholly divested of the titillating ambivalence of eroticism" (my emphasis); again, "the self images of the first two parts [of the Prologue] are ways of testing the patience and persistence of *the masculine audience"* (my emphasis). Patterson also acknowledges, indirectly at least, that he, like the historical and ostensively ideal or implied reader of Chaucer, is a member of a timeless, heterosexual male readership: he notes, for instance, that there are "appealing moments" in the otherwise "appalling" *Prologue,* moments when "the very intimacy of her revelations assures us that *we* are not old and foolish, that we might even be one of those with whom she has shared 'many a myrthe' " (Patterson's emphasis).[27]

Patterson's use of "we" in such formulations may obviously confound some late twentieth-century female readers and feminist critics, who cannot in good faith include themselves in that rhetorical first-person plural because they simply cannot be turned on (or off) by the Wife as Patterson implies that their male colleagues are, if indeed reading this text is inevitably charged with gendered sexual interaction.[28] This model of interpretation, based on one falsely universal paradigm of heterosexual male response—the reader is he who wants to be assured by a come-hither look from a lusty woman that he is not old and foolish—is by no means new or unusual in literary studies. As some recent critical studies have demonstrated, for instance, the notion that writing and reading can be described as sexual, gendered practices is common in medieval theorizing about the moral and epistemological function of literature.[29] In modern criticism, assumptions like Patterson's govern much authoritative prefeminist scholarly discourse (in spirit, if not in date of publication) on Chaucer's female characters; if we turn back just a few years to the commentary of a more venerable Chaucerian like E. Talbot Donaldson,

27. Ibid., pp. 662, 678.
28. In Patterson's words, the Wife of Bath's text "solicits both body and mind, and it requires for its explication both an erotics and a hermeneutics. Who is equal to its demands? 'Yblessed be God that I have wedded fyve! / Welcome the sixte, whan that evere he shal' (44–45)." (" 'For the Wyves Love of Bath,' " p. 658).
29. See, for instance, recent work by R. Howard Bloch, including "Silence and Holes: the *Roman de Silence* and the Art of the Trouvère," *Yale French Studies* 70 (1986), pp. 81–99; "Medieval Misogyny," *Representations* 20 (Fall 1987), pp. 1–24; and Carolyn Dinshaw, *Chaucer's Sexual Poetics* (Madison: University of Wisconsin Press, 1989).

for example, or to an essay on Chaucer published not so long ago in the pages of the most widely circulated professional journal in the literary field, we find precisely the same sort of presuppositions about the gender and sexualized response of "the" reader.

In the last sentence of a well-known essay on *Troilus and Criseyde*, Donaldson indirectly addresses alleged contradictions in his own and the male characters' sexual feelings about that other infamous Chaucerian woman, Criseyde, by invoking an all too familiar homosocial couple: the "sensitive" but "sensible" male reader, and his mentor across the centuries, that great male artist who simultaneously represents (and masters) the female character and sustains the myth of woman's mystery. "Every sensitive reader," Donaldson concludes, "will feel that he really knows Criseide—and no sensible reader will ever claim that he really understands her."[30] Again, as in the case of the Wife and so many Chaucerian women, we see the easy conflation of real women (women we really know) with Woman as mystery, absence, Other (that which we will never really understand). Evan Carton's discussion of *Troilus and Criseyde*, appearing in *PMLA* in 1979, makes this gendered and sexualized model of the allegedly universal reader's response more explicit, and it does so with somewhat more theoretical sophistication and self-consciousness. Carton views Pandarus's activity, verbal and sexual, as "paradigmatic for all participants in the narrative," including narrator and reader. Pandarus desires "to take Criseyde" and so too *"We* must reach out to seize our prize" (emphasis added)—where the prize is meaning itself as well as the now openly incestuous seduction of the woman.[31]

Countless examples could be adduced, but let me return to my main point: my fear of what I see as a postfeminist position in Patterson's work is thus in large part the fear that the scholarly community, along with much of the real world, will return easily and quietly to the prefeminist status quo, where there is no place for the woman reader and critic of Chaucer (or for the male who does not respond as many critics imagine he does).[32] In what sense can a self-consciously female human being

30. E. Talbot Donaldson, *Speaking of Chaucer* (London: Athlone Press, 1970), p. 83.

31. Evan Carton, "Complicity and Responsibility in Pandarus' Bed and Chaucer's Art," *PMLA* 94 (1979), pp. 47–61.

32. I am reminded here of Nancy K. Miller's comment on the historical continuity between what I am calling prefeminist and postfeminist ways of thinking, in "The Text's Heroine: A Feminist Critic and Her Fictions," *Diacritics* 12 (Summer 1982): "Indeed, society did not wait for the invention of man to repress 'woman' or oppress women, and the 'end of man' in no way precludes the reinscription of woman as Other" (p. 49).

in the late twentieth century belong to a community in which member-
ship requires "taking" Criseyde? Unless she is, as Carton indeed imagines Criseyde (and perhaps all women) to be, thoroughly immasculated,
identifying with alleged male sexual pleasure and vicariously gratified
by it, she cannot, by this model of language and interpretation, join in
the primal, communal act of "constituting meaning." If critics like Carton
and Patterson are right—and even some feminists would certainly seem
to agree that they are[33] —the kind of meaning criticism wants is a male
possession; and women can only read poems like *Troilus and Criseyde*
or the *Canterbury Tales* (or by the most extreme view enter into discourse
at all) if we are complicitous in the sexual exploitation and silencing of
the female character and in strategies for constituting the culturally feminine (and masculine) that reify hierarchy and exclusion.

It seems almost too easy to point out, with a degree of self-righteous-
ness I would like to avoid but probably cannot entirely disown, the
exclusion of the woman reader from the prominent strain of critical
interpretation that such readings represent. Using a critic like Donaldson
is perhaps a cheap shot, and yet his views have been highly influential
on a generation of prominent Chaucer critics and hence on subsequent
generations of students, and his sympathy with and interest in both
women characters and his own masculinity make him a virtual replica
of the modern Chaucer that many scholars admire and work hard to
preserve. But the more difficult project of proposing alternative models
has only begun. If some of "us" are not titillated by the Wife and do not
desire Criseyde, and yet "we" do not want to jettison the hard-won
recognition that readers and writers (and maybe reading and writing)
are, have been, or can be gendered, in some sense—so that, among other
things, women can read and speak about texts and their histories—then
we need to continue to develop new practice and theory that accounts
for, among other things, the relations between women as one group of
(formerly excluded) readers and canonical, male-authored works. We
need models and methodologies that allow us to constitute ourselves as
readers, and hence to constitute meaning itself, in a way that does not
involve either "taking," in various senses, the female characters or the
feminine position as culturally constructed, *or* letting them go, to be

33. For just one discussion of the complicated question of whether the dominant discourse is available to the female speaker (and reader), which includes an excellent bibliography of the debate, see Homans, " 'Her Very Own Howl.' "

constructed and interpreted, as always, by prefeminist or postfeminist positions.[34]

The second article I want to speak about is Leicester's "Of a Fire in the Dark: Public and Private Feminism in the *Wife of Bath's Tale*." This piece seems at first, like Patterson's work, to belong more properly to the feminist era, for indeed the overt, central, and compelling argument of the piece is that troubling contradictions in the Wife's self-presentation, reflected in the unresolved critical debate I have already described, testify to two types of feminism that she practices: first, a "polemical, reactive, necessarily 'illiberal' " public feminism (again, what was known in pre-feminist days as her monstrous, unpalatable appropriation of male power), and, second, a "deeper," subtextual, private feminism, which is "more humanist (in the sense of being interested in what individuals can make, positively, of the culture and institutions that precede and sur-round them) and more humane—or at any rate 'nicer.' " Both private and public feminisms, Leicester concludes, bear witness to Chaucer's own nice, humane, feminist-humanist personality, for, after all, the char-acter's feminisms can finally be nothing more or less than the author's: "This lack of closure in the Wife's life and personality is, finally, an aspect of Chaucer's feminism, since of course there is no Wife of Bath." In the inconclusiveness and ambivalence of his portrait of the Wife, moreover, Leicester finds evidence, as I noted earlier, for his view that the author can be commended for attempting to bring a woman to life "by trying to sustain her mystery, her possibility, and her independence."[35]

Near the end of his essay, however, Leicester offers a very interesting qualification of his own authority to judge these issues: "While I think from the evidence that Chaucer knew a lot about women, I am not in a position to speak with authority on this topic, *since, like the poet, I lack*

34. A recent collection of essays that speaks to this concern and provides several such models is Fisher and Halley, *Seeking the Woman*. Another example of recent work that offers a possible model and methodology of the sort I speak of here is Marguerite Waller's "Usurpation, Seduction, and the Problematics of the Proper: A 'Deconstructive,' 'Feminist' Rereading of the Seductions of Richard and Anne in Shakespeare's *Richard III*," in *Re-writing the Renaissance: The Discourses of Sexual Difference in Early Modern Europe*, eds. Margaret W. Ferguson, Maureen Quilligan, and Nancy J. Vickers (Chicago and London: University of Chicago Press, 1986), pp. 159–74. Waller proposes a reading that she calls an "anti-seduction," "one that performs an act modifying rather than reinforcing the reality suggested by either approach [deconstructive or feminist] in the absence of the other" (p. 161).

35. "Of a Fire in the Dark," pp. 162, 175, and 176, respectively.

certain essential experience" (my emphasis).[36] My response to this comment is mixed, and I am troubled not so much by Leicester's argument
or conclusions (although, as readers of this study will recognize, they
greatly differ from my own in terms of the emphasis I lay on the Wife's
textuality) as by the full implications for women readers and for feminist
theory of his frank, personal statement. On the one hand, Leicester reminds us again that authors and readers alike are gendered people, a
point that feminist criticism has to date often insisted on in its efforts to
point out that the idea of the universal or neutral human perspective
serves to mask the interests of a particular class, race, and gender. He
also seems to validate rather than exclude the voice of the putative female
reader in a way that reverses traditional notions of who has what when
he speaks of his own lack, the absence in the male of some "essential
experience" that empowers the female to "speak with authority" on the
topic of Chaucer's insight into women.

But at the same time, taken another way, Leicester's observation exposes a more problematic aspect of the situation of women readers who
would read male authors with any attention to the problems of gendered
subjectivity: the poet was male. So, in theory and more often than not
in fact, at least in the history of the poem's reception to date, is the
reader/critic by whom the poem is interpreted.[37] The familiar presupposition, made usefully explicit here, is that Chaucer and the male reader
thus share their (again transhistorical) maleness, whatever that means;
and identification with the author is still possible, if not required, as in
earlier models. And if my different gender position does give me the
"essential experience" that Chaucer and Leicester lack, and hence special
knowledge about women as a topic, then men too (like Chaucer and
most of his historical audience) must have their own gendered experiences and topics about which I am in turn unable to speak with authority.
In fact I seem to be specially licensed by my gender only to determine

36. Ibid., pp. 175–76.
37. An interesting and complicated point that goes beyond the scope of this study
involves the possibility that some at least of Chaucer's poems, like other medieval works,
were written for female patrons. But most modern critics seem to assume that the reader
and critic is always male; again, Donaldson enunciates this assumption quite explicitly for
us. Here, for instance, is the last sentence of his essay "Four Women of Style": "I am
happy to think that even after five and a half centuries the Prioress is continuing her
journey to Canterbury in the company of her three priests, probably making a fool of
herself, but surely capable, like other attractive women, of making even bigger fools of *us
male critics*" (*Speaking of Chaucer*, p. 64; my emphasis).

whether Chaucer got it right, whether he and the male critic do or do not know "a lot about women." Such a position is coherent with certain poststructuralist claims about feminism; Julia Kristeva, for instance, has said, "A woman cannot be; it is something which does not even belong to the order of being. It follows that a feminist practice can only be negative, at odds with what already exists so that we may say 'that's not it' and 'that's still not it.' "[38] To me, however attractive theoretically and however visible in practice (especially, it sometimes seems, my own practice, with its insistent critique of other readings), this assumption does not, finally, foster a fully satisfying way of engaging texts or developing a rich feminist framework for analysis, nor does it suggest a good enough reason for continuing to read Chaucer, or for urging my readings upon communities of feminists not professionally committed to medieval studies.[39]

Leicester's comment, then, obliges me to think harder about what feminist criticism intends and achieves by its insistence that the gender of author and reader/critic matters, for in the way I have suggested here this insistence, unqualified and unhistoricized, may lead a woman reader of canonical male-authored texts (like the Wife herself) to something of a critical dead end: not excluded from response, perhaps, but highly limited, helplessly constructed by the very discourse she seeks to demystify. It also obliges me to urge, therefore, that as we pursue the elusive history of the female reading subject, we keep in mind a point made recently by feminist theorists. As Mary Jacobus puts it, the male reading subject is not an unconstructed, "natural," or neutral position (nor, I would add, an ahistorical one). "If reading as a woman is a paradoxical act, reading as a man," Jacobus argues, "must involve a similarly double or divided demand."[40] Chaucerian fictions confront pre-

38. "Woman Can Never Be Defined," in *New French Feminisms*, ed. Elaine Marks and Isabelle de Courtivron (New York: Schocken Books, 1981), p. 137. Linda Alcoff also cites and comments on this passage; see "Cultural Feminism versus Post-structuralism: The Identity Crisis in Feminist Theory," *Signs* 13 (1988), p. 418.

39. For a discussion of the theoretical dangers of equating Woman and negativity, see Drucilla Cornell and Adam Thurschwell, "Feminism, Negativity, Intersubjectivity," in *Feminism as Critique*, Seyla Benhabib and Drucilla Cornell (Minneapolis: University of Minnesota Press, 1987), pp. 142–62.

40. Mary Jacobus, *Reading Woman: Essays in Feminist Criticism* (New York: Columbia University Press, 1986), p. 11. I am indebted to Jacobus's arguments at other points in this chapter as well. On this particular issue, see also Nancy K. Miller, "Changing the Subject: Authorship, Writing, and the Reader," in *Feminist Studies/Critical Studies*, ed. Teresa de Lauretis (Bloomington: Indiana University Press, 1986), p. 115.

cisely this fact that reading (and writing) as a man is a paradoxical act. The dream-visions, *Troilus and Criseyde,* and several other *Canterbury Tales* all explore that masculine doubleness and division, as experienced particularly by men who love women and/or tell stories about them. Women in Chaucerian fictions are in fact not excluded from powers, especially powers of language, to which (most) men have access. As a donnée of the *Canterbury Tales* in particular, pilgrims of either sex are both "speaker" and "spoken"; all human beings in this textual world are, as a precondition of their existence, the "kind of fiction" usually associated in Western culture with women "in that they are defined by others as components of the language and thought of others."[41] If the garrulous woman and the silent woman are, as I argue, two sides of the same coin, it is the common medium of exchange in this fictional economy.

But through the construction of notorious female characters such as the Wife, the division within men is occluded and these human problems and anxieties are displaced onto Woman and women; the feminine gender becomes what we may usefully think of as "marked," in various senses of the word. In the language of linguistics, "markedness" refers to the fact that one of a minimal pair may be more specifically characterized or delimited in its usage than the other; in the minimal pair constituted by masculine and feminine in our culture, the latter, in the text as in the world, bears an identifying mark, a visible sign and even a predestined character, it seems, of sexual difference. This markedness by virtue of gender is inscribed in modern English in the prominent fact of the generic masculine, and linguists educe from their study of this and other features of the language precisely what I find in the Wife's characterization and its subsequent interpretations: "a tendency, on the one hand, to equate humanity with the male sex and, on the other hand, to assume that femaleness defines women, whose individuality becomes submerged in categorizing principles that treat all women as identical."[42]

41. Myra Jehlen, "Archimedes and the Paradox of Feminist Criticism," *Signs* 6 (1981), pp. 575–601.

42. Sally McConnell-Ginet, "Linguistics and the Feminist Challenge," in *Women and Language in Literature and Society,* ed. McConnell-Ginet, Ruth Borker, and Nelly Furman (New York: Praeger, 1980), p. 9. See also Monique Wittig, "The Mark of Gender," in *The Poetics of Gender,* ed. Nancy K. Miller (New York: Columbia University Press, 1986), pp. 63–73. Subsequent to the original publication of this chapter, I also discovered a brief discussion of the female as the marked term in Nancy Armstrong, "The Gender Bind: Women and the Disciplines," *Genders* 3 (1988), p. 2.

"Femaleness defines women": so, too, females, marked by their gender in ways that males in Western culture consequently seem not to be, are kept within marks, limits and boundaries that define and contain their "individuality," and the Wife turns out to be a reflection of "categorizing principles" rather than a speaking subject. Wearing and reproducing the mark, the brand, the inscription, of the gender system as we know it, she, like any female, becomes the mark at which hostile forces aim, the object, the target of antifeminist attack in both the *Canterbury Tales* and many of their modern interpretations. When we focus on the centrality of the thematic of the feminine and interpret its textual manifestations as evidence of the female character's authoritative status or of the male poet's tolerant feminism, wise humanism, dispassion, or incandescence, we miss or dismiss too quickly what a feminist analysis of Chaucerian fictions discloses about the structures of antifeminism, about the displacement and usurpation of female silence, and about the hidden "mark of Adam," the fact that males are also constrained and constituted by gender.

> Could it be argued that the only way of avoiding these constant historical loops which depart or return from the conviction of women's natural dispositions . . . would be to make a grander gesture—to stand back and announce that there *aren't any* 'women'? And then, hard on that defiant and initially absurd-sounding assertion, to be scrupulously careful to elaborate it— to plead that it means that all definitions of gender must be looked at with an eagle eye, wherever they emanate from and whoever pronounces them, and that such a scrutiny is a thoroughly feminist undertaking. The will to support this is not blandly social-democratic, for in no way does it aim to vault over the stubborn harshness of lived gender while it queries sexual categorisation. Nor does it aim at a glorious indifference to politics by placing itself under the banner of some renewed claim to androgyny, or to a more modern aspiration to a 'post-gendered subjectivity'. But, while it refuses to break with feminism by naming itself as a neutral deconstruction, at the same time it refuses to identify feminism with the camp of the lovers of 'real women'.[43]
>
> Denise Riley, "Does Sex Have a History?"

43. *Am I That Name? Feminism and the Category of 'Women' in History* (Minneapolis: University of Minnesota Press, 1988), p. 3.

As I have indicated, "Chaucer's mellow and humane art" is indeed the apparently irrepressible, irresistible constant in the modern literary assessment of his work, the perceived center of timeless truth that endures ostensive historical revolutions in taste and critical practice and that actually serves, I submit, to hide in various ways the driving force of sexual politics. Arguments of the prefeminist school ignore the question of sexual politics (even when they recognize it as a question that engaged the fourteenth-century literary community)[44] and claim with no sense of embarrassment at all that "Chaucer's specialty was mankind," as the revered George Lyman Kittredge repeatedly put it. Arguments looking explicitly at Chaucer's attitude toward women with recent feminist questions in mind know that "mankind" is a suspect entity, and so they have to date tended to modify this claim by reminding us that Chaucer's specialty was really, and to an unusual degree, womankind. What I have termed postfeminist arguments at one level or another return the real focus to mankind, now in a gender-specific sense of the term. To the extent that they begin to explore the interaction of feminine textuality and masculine identity, their work offers exciting new interpretive possibilities. At the same time, while usefully attesting the maleness of Chaucer's imagination and intended audience, they may directly or indirectly reconfirm the irrelevance or marginality of real females and now feminists to his work. Moreover, their claims for his tolerant humanism and humaneness (or sometimes, recently, for his political subversiveness) often rest on findings that Chaucer knows a lot about women (but not everything), deplores their victimization, and even espouses the cause of their freedom and equality.

Many Chaucerians thus end up adulating this artist for reasons that ought to seem internally contradictory: at one and the same time he is compassionate and dispassionate, a friend of women and a neutral stage manager. One thing that is confirmed in the case of Chaucer studies is that "bias" and "greatness" are still generally and deeply believed to be

44. See, for example, Wolfgang Clemen's discussion of the Dido episode in the *House of Fame*, in *Chaucer's Early Poetry*, trans. C. A. M. Sym (London: Methuen, 1963). Toward the end of his comments on Chaucer's rivalry with Ovid and Virgil, Clemen notes that "For Chaucer's *audience*" (Clemen's emphasis), the Dido episode would be perceived as part of "a controversy which had become fashionable since the *Roman de la Rose*" and would also anticipate the later exploration of the same controversy in the *Legend of Good Women*. Without further ado, however, Clemen dismisses the relevance of the audience's understanding of this literary and political context and simply states: "It is obvious, however, that Chaucer himself did not take this controversy seriously" (p. 86).

mutually exclusive, for great poets and great criticism alike. And freedom from the bias of gender in particular (as Virginia Woolf tellingly and sometimes self-destructively argued) is especially crucial to that notion of negative capability that underpins romantic and postromantic definitions of literary excellence.[45] Chaucer is mellow and great, in other words, because he transcends the personal, the biased, the situated and above all the gendered position; and as a male poet, he proves this transcendence by his ability to imagine and represent the point of view of the Other, that is, the woman or other outcast. But the notion of transcendence depends on the notion of something to be transcended, something limited and bound up in ordinary experience, something immanent and, as Simone de Beauvoir first pointed out, in Western culture, often, something feminine. Universalizing myths of great humanist art may fundamentally depend, then, like the local, historical example of Chaucer's poetry that I examine in the rest of this study, on sympathetic and tolerant representations of Woman that in fact perpetuate her cultural status as victim and Other.

In examining the even more widespread and already often abandoned myth of Shakespeare as humanist author par excellence, Leah Marcus defines this myth in terms that correspond quite precisely to still current assumptions about Chaucer: "The author is in the heavens, from which nothing but benign influence can be imagined to flow. His plays offer 'light' to those capable of recognizing the good, 'cheere' to those needing inspiration, and chiding to those needing correction." But, according to Marcus, no one can really take this view seriously any more; "the demise of the transcendent bard" took place some time ago. "It can be argued," Marcus notes, "that by the 1960s and early 1970s, interpretation governed by humanist assumptions about the transcendence of Shakespeare was already playing itself out."[46] This seems to be far from true in Chaucer studies, however, and in wondering why, it has occurred to me that in part it is because the case for the humanist Chaucer has always in some ways been more difficult to make. To the extent that it requires some ingenuity, as Reid points out, to overlook the ways in which Chaucer is not quite as firmly invisible and godlike as Shakespeare, the critical

45. In *A Room of One's Own* (New York and London: Harcourt Brace Jovanovich, 1957), especially pp. 58–59.

46. *Puzzling Shakespeare: Local Reading and Its Discontents* (Berkeley: University of California Press, 1988); the quotations are found on pp. 30 and 31, respectively.

interest in making him so—responsive, I hasten to add, to the ways in which his poetry invites such treatment—lives on. Throughout the 1980s Chaucer is still praised for "a magisterial and dispassionate deployment of inherited literary forms"; "the myth will live," we are admonished, "because it symbolizes profound convictions and elevates the human mind."[47] But the magisterial and dispassionate Chaucer the poet coexists with Chaucer the pilgrim, the dreamer, the narrator of *Troilus and Criseyde*, all dramatized figures of anxious, passionately involved authorship. In fact, then, a highly postmodern version of the author—the fragmented, provisional, shifting, subversive *I* of so much medieval poetry—is in tension with humanist wholeness and transcendence in Chaucer, and this tension is often reflected in and managed by his representation, again, of women and Woman.

The representation of Woman as the absent Other, together with the exclusion of women from acts of representation and acts of criticism, also enforces and depends on a myth observed as often as not in the breach, as it were, by Chaucer: the myth of gender difference itself. Construed in one way, the feminist project sustains, even depends on, this myth, but feminist readings that foreground first the Wife's difference and absence and then the way this difference and absence are constructed, rather than essential, natural, invariable, can help to complicate the myth in useful ways. To this end I suggest we make something different of Leicester's accurate and yet all too easily dismissed observation that "of course there is no Wife of Bath" and of Patterson's perception that "she is so evidently a creature of the male imagination." The textuality or impossibility of Woman and the absence or silence of women are not the points I end with (or the penultimate points, just before I invoke the canonical author); they are the points I suggest we begin from, both theoretically and in the kind of practice this book follows. They do not lead me back (not immediately, at least, and never unproblematically) to the male author's presence, or to his alleged efforts either "to think himself inside a woman's head," on the one hand, or "to respect her privacy," on the other. The Wife's absence and textuality, taken into the context of Chaucer's obsessive concern with the double or divided demands of reading and writing as a man, is a fact first to be foregrounded

---

47. Patterson, " 'For the Wyves Love of Bath,' " p. 658; John H. Fisher, "Animadversions on the Text of Chaucer, 1988," *Speculum* 63 (1988), p. 793.

and parsed, "looked at with an eagle's eye," not read through and put aside, or acknowledged in theory and then overlooked in practice.

From such a vantage, it can become apparent that what we may speak of as the absence and silence of Woman and women in Chaucerian fiction is overdetermined. Chaucer's career as a poet of the masculine imagination begins, if the standard chronology is correct, with a poem about a dead woman, the Duchess of Lancaster; through the creation of female caricatures from the perfect "White" to the fallible Criseyde and beyond, Chaucerian fictions repeatedly reenact "her" death, bringing a woman to represented life in order that she may be killed off, lost, silenced, and erased. At the level of theme and character, the narratives concomitantly and strenuously argue for women's difference from men, and they define feminine desire—as did the fourteenth-century literary culture in general—as a point to be debated. The Knight in the *Wife of Bath's Tale* enters into this debate, and thus, like so many elements of Chaucerian fiction, stands as avatar of the modern Freudian quest in his compulsory search for "what thyng is it that wommen moost desiren" (905). He putatively finds the answer, but nevertheless the question persists. Female characters in Chaucerian fiction are always problems for other male characters and, at another level, for the (male) audience, and these problems are, as we shall see, consistently coterminous with the "larger" interpretive problems of language and authority. But reexamining these problems, I pose different questions, such as: Whose interests are served by the death, abandonment, or defeat of a woman, or by the prevailing position to which the female and the feminine are assigned? And why is "the woman question" so often the site of the Chaucerian investigation of "the language question" and of the insistent challenge to literary tradition and authority?

My efforts to answer such questions in the pages that follow will repeatedly lead me back, by various routes, to questions about male characters, masculine identity, and the issue of male authorial and critical presence—not construed now as a solution or a center of fixed, knowable truth (either Chaucer is woman's friend, or Chaucer is another in a long line of antifeminists) but as in itself a complicated problem for feminist, not postfeminist, study. "There is no Wife of Bath"; that is to say, she is a fiction, and she marks the limits of representation; she is a part of the poet, and she is an embarrassment to his good name and to the humanist claim that the canonical male author speaks for all humanity. The misunderstandings that attempt to conceal these facts, and that fail to interrogate the gendered construction of both authorial and critical subjectivity on the alleged absence of women aligned with the carefully orchestrated textuality of Woman, can only confirm a link between past and present that medievalists might understandably prefer to ignore: "our idea of civilization" is in some respects not so different from Chaucer's.

3

The Death of the Duchess

When Blanche died her body was transported to London for
burial by a thousand horsemen, with due pomp and decorum. When this cortege reached St. Albans, however, decorum was rudely shattered by an unseemly jurisdictional
dispute between the abbot of St. Albans and the leader of
the cortege, the bishop of Lincoln. The bishop wished to
celebrate high mass for the duchess, but the abbot suspected
this as a subtle manoeuvre by the bishop to insinuate himself
into the abbey in order to strengthen the jurisdiction which
bishops of Lincoln had long claimed to exercise over the
abbey, and which the abbey had long strenuously resisted.
For an entire day the wrangle continued, until eventually the
bishop was induced to put his seal to a document acknowl-
edging that he entered the abbey on suffrance and not as of
right. The episode was not one to be lightly forgotten at St.
Albans, where the abbot's defence of his "liberties" was recorded in circumstantial detail by the historian of the abbey.
For our purposes, the key feature of his account of this unsavoury episode is the very feature which made it memorable
to him: the presence of the bishop of Lincoln. For the bishop's
itinerary shows that he could easily have been in the vicinity
of St. Albans at the right time in 1368, but not in 1369.

> J. J. N. Palmer, "The Historical
> Context of the *Book of the Duchess*:
> A Revision"

The *Book of the Duchess* is generally considered to be an elegy for Blanche,
Duchess of Lancaster and wife of the author's patron, John of Gaunt.[1]
The precise date of Blanche's death, and hence the terminus a quo of
Chaucer's text, has been the subject of some scholarly dispute; in the
passage cited above, John Palmer tells the story of the altercation be-

---

1. The article from which the epigraph is taken is in *Chaucer Review* 8 (1974), p. 256.
Palmer takes this anecdote from *Gesta Abbatum Monasterii S. Albani*, ed. H. T. Riley, Rolls
Series, vol. III, pp. 274–77.

tween the abbot of St. Albans and the bishop of Lincoln in support of his claim that Blanche died in 1368 rather than 1369, as others allege. For my purposes, however, "the key feature . . . of this unsavoury episode" is not the date it establishes but the analogy it provides to my reading of what actually happens when the more famous ceremonial commemoration for the dead Duchess is attempted, in Chaucer's first dream-vision.

While her body lay in its coffin outside the monastery of St. Albans, the intended celebration of a mass for Blanche became the occasion for another chapter in a struggle for power between two men and the two institutions they represented, competing within the larger institution of the Church for jurisdictional rights. So too in the poem, the lady's dead body turns into a site of both conversation and contestation between two men, here not Christian priests but devotees of love, and two positions or roles within the institution of (court) poetry. What makes the episode memorable to its male participants is not Blanche herself, or her death, but their own interaction. In both the historical and the literary instance, as the men wrangle and bond, all that seems to remain of the Duchess is either the neglected corpse, uncelebrated and displaced from center to periphery by the territorial dispute, or the allegorical figure of White, through which the poem idealizes the historical Blanche out of existence in the battle for control over meaning and intention.

This is not the way previous scholars have usually understood the poem. The exact nature of the consolation offered by the *Book of the Duchess* has seemed problematic to several modern readers, but shining through the interpretive haze is the beautiful White, virtually always taken both as a clear allegorical representation of the historical personage Blanche, Duchess of Lancaster, and as the poem's center of spiritual value, the key to the moral and perhaps aesthetic order it presupposes and teaches.[2] While White may represent different specific ideals to dif-

2. For overviews of the "consolation" debate in modern scholarship, see Joerg I. Fichte, "The *Book of the Duchess*—A Consolation?" *Studia Neophilologica* 45 (1973), pp. 53–67, and Helen Phillips, "Structure and Consolation in the Book of the Duchess," *Chaucer Review* 16 (1981), pp. 107–18. Other recent attempts to complicate or revise our understanding of the nature of the consolation offered in the poem include Denis Walker, "Narrative Inconclusiveness and Consolatory Dialectic in the Book of the Duchess," *Chaucer Review* 18 (1983), pp. 1–17; and Rose A. Zimbardo, "The Book of the Duchess and the Dream of Folly," *Chaucer Review* 18 (1984), pp. 329–46. My own reading is indebted to the quite different approach to the poem taken by Maud Ellmann, "Blanche," in *Criticism and Critical Theory*, ed. Jeremy Hawthorn (London: Edward Arnold, 1984), pp. 99–110.

ferent readers, her perfection appears to be indisputable.³ As one recent critic puts it, "She has ascended to a nearly divine position out of time, much like the daughter in Pearl."⁴ But feminist inquiry into literary representations of women calls into question the grounds and implications of the assumption that White, like so many other female paragons in medieval works, functions as a core of human value in the poem, and it attends in a different way to the abundance and prominence of dead women in the literary tradition. What further does it signify when the emblem of moral perfection, in both secular and religious masterworks, is a woman, and a dead one? When her death is overdetermined at all levels of interpretation, as it is in the *Book of the Duchess*, what threat to proper order might we infer that this loss dispels? What strategies of dissipation and containment do we see at work, and how successful are they? The Chaucerian elegy suggests some interesting answers to such questions. In both the narrator's pre-dream reading and in his subsequent dream itself, I shall argue, the poem foregrounds and implicates through its treatment of White two intersecting problems: the mutability of gender, for men at least, and the instability of meaning.

THE FEMINIZATION OF THE BLACK KNIGHT
AND THE NARRATOR

> Provoking the spectator or reader to hover between denial and acknowledgement, these narrative representations of death (whether visual or textual) serve to enact that any "voyeur" is always also implicated in the field of vision and that the act of fragmenting and objectifying the body of another ricochets back by destabilizing the spectator's position as well.⁵
>
> Elisabeth Bronfen, "Violence of
> Representation—Representation
> of Violence"

---

3. Compare, for example, John Fyler's view that Blanche serves as "a modern exemplar of chaste fidelity" and other ancient, secular virtues who "keeps the Golden Age alive in the iron world" (*Chaucer and Ovid* [New Haven: Yale University Press, 1979], pp. 79–80) with James Wimsatt's argument that she represents the explicitly late-medieval Christian virtue of Marian holiness ("The Apotheosis of Blanche," *Journal of English and Germanic Philology* 66 [1967], pp. 26–44).

4. Diane Ross, "The Play of Genres in the *Book of the Duchess*," *Chaucer Review* 19 (1984), p. 10.

5. *Literature Interpretation Theory*, I, p. 314.

The mutability and indeterminacy of gender is prominently figured in the blurring of normative assumptions about gender difference in the two male protagonists of the *Book of the Duchess*, the narrator and the man about whom he dreams, the Black Knight. Each, in his own way, is feminized—shown or said to be like actual women, with womanly characteristics, or put in positions defined by the poem and by other discourses of the period as feminine positions, ones that women are said to occupy or told to occupy. The Black Knight's feminization is apparent from the moment when the dreamer finds him sitting under an oak tree, with his head hanging down. Although "Of the age of foure and twenty yer" (455), he appears to be just on the threshold of manhood, barely displaying secondary sex characteristics: "Upon hys berd," for instance, there is "but lytel her" (456).[6] Moreover, the man in black shows no knightly aggression toward the intrusive dreamer. Instead of challenging the man who intrudes on his private sorrow, he apologizes to the dreamer for his own aloofness and attempts to assuage the anger he seems to expect another man would exhibit: "I prey the, be not wroth" (519).

It is worth pausing over the initial materialization of the Black Knight in the dream to consider how the mysterious, liminally male stranger encountered by the questing dreamer may be said to occupy a position filled elsewhere in romance by fairy ladies. In the story of Sir Launfal, for example, an alienated young knight, cast out from Arthur's court, journeys into a forest, just as Chaucer's dreamer does. There he meets women from an otherworld who eventually help him solve (or avoid) his problems, just as the dreamer meets the Knight. The fuller ambiguity and complexity of gender alignments in the Chaucerian version, however, is suggested by the fact that the Black Knight actually plays a part similar to that of both the dejected, unloved, isolated knight and the lady who magically appears to him. For the dreamer, the Knight in many ways takes the place of the female apparition; at the same time, it may not be coincidental that the Knight's literal position is similar to that of Sir Launfal himself, in the Middle English version of the story, at the moment when the fairy damsels first appear to him. On the day he rides

---

6. The conventional youthfulness of the Black Knight reflects the pervasive topos of the infantilization of men in courtly love; for an early and insightful discussion of this topic, see Herbert Moller, "The Meaning of Courtly Love," *Journal of American Folklore* 73 (1960), pp. 39–52.

out from court, the weather is hot, so Sir Launfal sits down on his cloak, "In þe schadwe, vnþer a tre . . . yn sorow and sore" (lines 226–29).[7]

It is instructive to note, moreover, that both the Black Knight and Sir Launfal suffer from feminization but that the cause and effect of their suffering implicate sexual identity and gender relations in very different ways. Sir Launfal mourns the loss of his male companion's love and comradeship, but he eventually replaces these bonds with the love of the fairy mistress whose passion for him proves his manly ability to attract a lady more beautiful than Queen Gwenevere. Thus the romance hero escapes from the realities of his feminization (his poverty, marginalization, and abandonment) into a dream-world where historical relations of money and power among men are simply irrelevant, and the fantasy of heterosexual union with an enchanting woman offers a timeless and perfect escape from the problems of playing the part of an adult male. In the *Book of the Duchess*, the inverse occurs. The Black Knight mourns the absolute loss of his actual lady, whom he turns into a fantasy. To the extent that he may be restored by his companionship with the male dreamer, he may return, healed, to court and to an historical identity. Another version of the Sir Launfal story, Marie de France's *Lanval*, underlines the problematic of masculine identity embedded in this plot. In this telling, when the poor knight refuses the lustful queen's advances, she accuses him directly of homosexuality. He is so angry that he boasts of his affair with the fairy mistress; thus breaking his promise, he almost loses the lady, but at the last minute she forgives and transports him. Again in Marie's version the Sir Launfal story solves problems of uncertain masculinity with an escape into fantasy, whereas the *Book of the Duchess* seems to leave the lady alone in the dream-world while men recuperate reality and reaffirm male friendship.[8]

As the narrator's dream unfolds, the Black Knight's feminization is extended, and various developments suggest that he resembles not only Sir Launfal but also countless other courtly lovers who undergo role reversal. When he speaks of his past, for example, this gentle Knight predictably represents himself as rendered passive and imprisoned by love and the lady, "ykaught" (838) by his very first sight of the captor, White: "She had the herte, / And who hath that, may not asterte" (1153–54). He describes his fearfulness (1251), his infantilization (1095), and his

---

7. Thomas Chestre, *Sir Launfal*, ed. A. J. Bliss (London: Thomas Nelson and Sons, 1960).
8. Marie de France, *Lais*, ed. A. Ewert (Oxford: Blackwell, 1944, reprinted 1965).

retreat to his bed (1253–55). He is like other aristocratic male lovers in the literary culture he belongs to in that he is, ironically, womanlike: receptive, irrational, and secluded in the private world of dream and lyric.

Textual allusions comparing the Black Knight to well-known women who died for love confirm this highly conventional feminization at yet another level. In his early efforts to alleviate the mourner's excessive and self-destructive grief, the dreamer compares him not to male heroes but to a series of well-known ladies betrayed by men, who subsequently (and foolishly, the dreamer implies) killed themselves: Medea, Phyllis, Dido, and Echo (725ff.).[9] Interestingly, the list ends with one male example of such "foly," Samson, whose story also confirms what the Knight reveals: a man is made weak and womanly by too much love for a woman. When the Knight himself images traitors to love, he reminds us that in Western mythology it is usually men who betray and abandon, for he chooses the male exemplars of Achitofel, Antenor, and Ganelon (1116–23); near the end, he realigns himself with women by proclaiming his sorrow at the lady's refusal to be greater than Cassandra's (1246). Earlier, he also seems to suggest a similarity between himself and the beloved lady, or at least to imply that he shares qualities associated with her highly symbolic name and the feminine virtues of innocence, purity, and receptivity it signifies. In lines 779–81, he describes himself as naturally "thralle" to the idea of love long before he met any specific object of desire, and he speculates on the causes of his apparently innate aptitude for the role of lover: "Paraunter I was thereto most able, / As a whit wal or a table. . . "

From the beginning, moreover, the most important figure in the poem to whom the Knight is obviously analogous is Alcyone, the bereaved female partner in the narrator's pre-dream reading. Later I shall identify decisive differences, too, between Alcyone and the Black Knight, but my object at this point is to emphasize an obvious connection between the narrator's reading and his dream: the story of the faithful wife's loss of her spouse serves as a structural analogue for the Black Knight's affliction, and a central sign of the identification of men with women in this poem that both reveals and exaggerates the feminization of the courtly male inherent in the conventions and texts of love.

9. Coming at the end of this speech, the narrator's final rebuke invokes a gender-specific sense of the term "man" and thus may tactfully remind the Black Knight that he is acting in an unmanly way: "But ther is no *man* alyve her / Wolde for a fers make this woo" (740–41, my emphasis).

Turning now from the Black Knight to the narrator of the poem, we find evidence that confirms and extends such a claim. While the mournful Knight, taken by topical readings as a figure of the poet's actual, powerful aristocratic patron, is feminized only within the licensed and highlighted fictionality of the dream, the narrator of the poem claims to be already feminized in the waking world. The causes and effects of his predicament both resemble and differ somewhat from those of the Knight's. At the very beginning, the narrator intimates his own loss or failure in love when he speaks at some length of his sleeplessness (a stereotypical lover's malady) and when he refers to the one physician who could heal him. But in this poem, this hint is notably couched *as* a hint, whereas in the text's sources it is made explicit. The narrator's own (milder) case of lovesickness may serve partly to signal his bond with the Knight; it is perhaps nothing more or less than a badge he must initially display in order to enter into the aristocratic male game of talking about love. It also suggests the symbolic inseparability of the roles of poet and lover in courtly literature, the link between the act of writing and the act of desiring the unattainable woman that is also underscored in the Knight's own highly literary discourse and in the poem as a whole. But insofar as the roles, like the ranks, of lover and poet may be distinguished, too, the narrator's feminization specifically implicates the particular circumstances of the medieval court poet and explicitly draws into the problem of gender instability the problems of meaning and interpretation. For the narrator, even more than the Black Knight, is identified with Alcyone, and above all with the one aspect of Alcyone's situation that he himself has added and underlined in telling her story: her self-conscious epistemological uncertainty, centered on her inability to know for sure whether the absence of her beloved spouse is to be interpreted as a sign of his death.

These salient elements of the Chaucerian Alcyone are foregrounded if we compare the *Book of the Duchess* to its two main sources, as modern scholars have identified them, Ovid's *Metamorphoses* and Machaut's *La Fonteinne Amoreuse*.[10] In both, Alcyone is a figure of fear, devotion, jeal-

---

10. Guillaume de Machaut, "La Fonteinne Amoureuse," in *Oeuvres de Guillaume de Machaut*, ed. Ernest Hoepffner (Paris: Librairie Ancienne Edouard Champion, 1921), vol. III; and Ovid, *Metamorphoses*, ed. Frank R. Miller, 2d ed. (Cambridge: Harvard University Press, 1921), XI.410–750. James Wimsatt, in "The Sources of Chaucer's 'Seys and Alcyone,' " *Medium Aevum* 36 (1967), pp. 231–41, also considers Chaucer's use of Statius's *Thebaid*, the *Aeneid*, and *Ovide Moralise* in his version of the Ceyx and Alcyone story.

ousy, and grief. She has just one long speech in Ovid's tale, in which she begs her husband not to leave her, or at least not to go by boat. After a long description of the storm at sea in which readers learn that Ceyx is drowned (omitted in Chaucer's version), Ovid notes that Alcyone, still waiting for her husband's return, prays at Juno's shrine "that her husband may be kept safe from harm, that he may return once more, loving no other woman more than her."[11] It is Juno who, unable to endure the woman's ignorance of Ceyx's drowning and eager to "free her altar from the touch of the hands of mourning," arranges to send Alcyone a vision that will tell her the truth.[12] In Machaut's version, where the emphasis is on the male friends who share this story, we find the love of Ceyx and Alcyone all but deleted from the opening of the tale and an Alcyone who speaks only two lines in the entire episode, when she vaguely asks relief from suffering: "Je te pri, / Riche deese, oy mon dolent depri."[13]

The *Book of the Duchess* follows Machaut in emphasizing a relationship between two male interlocutors in the dream itself but contrasts sharply with both Machaut and Ovid in its treatment of Alcyone. In Chaucer, this woman is the central character of the story the narrator says he read, and as such she is a vocal being less grief-stricken than dying to know one thing: "And wher my lord, my love, be deed?" (91). In Ovid, despite her initial forebodings, Alcyone seems naively sure that her husband will return to her; she weaves the robes that the two of them will wear at his homecoming. In Chaucer, she takes the practical initiative and conducts a search for her husband, "bothe eest and west" (88). When it fails, she invents another plan to alleviate her ignorance. Instead of asking Juno to keep Ceyx faithful or to take pity on her grief, Chaucer's Alcyone herself proposes that the goddess send her a dream which will tell her the truth and thereby refix the crucial boundary, the line between living and dead, that the absence of Ceyx has obscured:

> "Send me grace to slepe, and mete
> In my slep som certeyn sweven
> Wherthourgh that I may knowen even
> Whether my lord be quyk or ded."
> (118–21)

---

11. The translation is Miller's, II.161; the Latin reads: "veniebat ad aras / utque foret sospes coniunx suus utque rediret, / optabat, nullamque sibi praeferret," XI.579–81.

12. "utque manus funestas arceat aris," XI.584.

13. "La Fonteinne Amoureuse," 559–60.

By a stratagem that I want to say more about later, Alcyone is granted the certain knowledge of Ceyx's death that she so urgently seeks, and in Chaucer's version she promptly dies. In Ovid, by contrast (and, with less emphasis, in Machaut), Alcyone's death is dramatically transmuted at the last minute: just as she is about to fling herself into the sea, where her husband's body floats, the gods take pity and transform wife and husband alike into birds.

The Chaucerian omission of this metamorphosis raises questions that I intend to elucidate, but first let me underscore the similarities between the narrator of the *Book of the Duchess* and the Alcyone he constructs. Before he retells her story, he explicitly signals the crossing of gender lines (as well as the lines between story and history, literary character and the merged figure of author/reader) when he identifies himself with Alcyone on account of her sorrow:

> Such sorowe this lady to her tok
> That trewly I, which made this book,
> Had such pittee and such rowthe
> To rede hir sorwe, that, by my trowthe,
> I ferde the worse al the morwe
> Aftir, to thenken on hir sorwe.
>
> (95–100)

Even before this, however, we may retrospectively identify the narrator's position and Alcyone's on critical grounds. In the opening lines of the poem, he tells us that he has lost the capacity to know the difference between crucial binary oppositions upon which the power to make morally informed choices depends:

> . . . I take no kep
> Of nothing, how hyt cometh or gooth,
> Ne me nys nothyng leef nor looth.
> Al is ylyche good to me—
> Joye or sorwe, wherso hyt be.
> . . . .
> Suche fantasies ben in myn hede,
> So I not what is best to doo.
>
> (6–10, 28–29)

Anticipating his Alcyone, who swoons after her prayer to Juno, the speaker describes himself before his dream as "a mased thyng, / Alway in poynt to falle a-doun" (12–13). He stresses that his condition is unnatural, "agaynes kynde" (16), and, like Alcyone, he bargains with a divine power for a dream that will restore his natural, necessary reason, his ability to differentiate—and then act—properly. The narrator light-heartedly bargains with a lesser deity (Morpheus, not Juno) and, in return for a good night's sleep, offers a richly ornamented feather bed rather than his own eternal devotion. Through this joke, he may trivialize the woman's more impassioned bargaining—and I shall suggest some reasons why it might serve his interests to do so—but he also imitates it.

Within the dream, the dreamer finds or puts himself in a state even more exactly like Alcyone's: he fails to understand, or acts as if he has not yet heard, the news sounded in the Knight's clear formulation, in the first lyric we hear the mourner speak: "My lady bryght . . . Is fro me ded and ys agoon" (477–79). Many modern readers have debated whether the dreamer has actually failed to understand the literal meaning of the Knight's lament or merely pretends not to for therapeutic purposes, but it is not possible or necessary to decide this question. What matters is that in either case he thereby takes up a position, like Alcyone's, of unknowingness. More specifically, even, he appears not to know precisely what Alcyone does not know, and what the audiences of both stories already know: a beloved spouse is dead. His subsequent move to certainty and the knowledge of death sustains the analogy, for at the end of a charade as elaborate as that in which Ceyx's dead body speaks to Alcyone, the dreamer, like the fictive woman, understands the truth, regains his ability to make distinctions, to interpret the absence of the loved one as the final and irreversible difference of death.

The climactic message from the dream world is the same, in other words, for the narrator and the bereaved woman: the certain truth is death, the final absence of the beloved. Compare Ceyx's "For, *certes, swete,* I nam but *ded*" (204, my emphasis, with the last exchange between dreamer and Knight: " 'She ys *ded!* ' 'Nay!' 'Yis, be my *trouthe!* ' " (1309, my emphasis). As in the case of Alcyone, the dreamer's vision suddenly dissolves when this message has been received. Alcyone dies; the narrator is released, moved by his certain knowledge to act, in his case to perform the poem we have just heard. He awakens in bed, with the book of "Alcione and Seys the kyng" in his hand (1327–29), and abruptly closes the poem with these lines:

> Thoghte I, "Thys ys so queynt a sweven
> That I wol, be processe of tyme,
> Fonde to put this sweven in ryme

As I kan best, and that anoon."
This was my sweven; now hit ys doon.
(1330–34)

Together, the parallels between Alcyone and both the dreamer and the man (or the part of his own manhood) he dreams about indicate, then, the crossing and blurring of gender lines and the feminization of the court poet as well as the courtly lover; they concomitantly foreground and thematize an issue I shall take up in the last section of this chapter, the problem of uncertainty and misunderstanding, of communicative as well as gender disorder. At the same time, as the dream closes, crucial differences between Alcyone and these male characters become apparent, and I want to turn now to a more extended reflection on these differences. First, I will suggest how the distinctions between the bereaved woman's response to the death of her husband and the men's response to the death of Blanche/White may enable the male characters to limit and resist the debilitating effects of feminization by restoring a sense of normative, stable gender division. If we wish to speak of this dream-vision as a poem of consolation, it may be more accurate to say that it works to console men not for the loss of the perfect woman but for the loss of their own solid sense of masculinity, the gender identity that is put at risk by both the pursuit and the attainment of heterosexual love. Second, turning my argument in another direction, I argue that such consolation and restoration are at best partial and temporary in this text, for the femininization that men seem to suffer as lovers of real women is in fact symptomatic of a problem both between and within men, one that cannot be resolved by the erasure of women or the retreat from romantic love, but inherent and inescapable in the kind of discourse that narrator and Black Knight undertake together in their efforts to face and displace the truth of death.

"She is ded!" "Nay!" "Yis, be my trouthe!"
(1309)

To clarify the substantial difference between Alcyone's experience and that of both the narrator and the Black Knight, I want first to return to the pre-dream matter and particularly to the putative origins and consequences of Alcyone's own dream. The elaborate mechanics that are entailed in the production of Alcyone's vision, based on details found in

Ovid and Machaut, literalize the way in which dreams effect the transgression of certain fundamental boundaries. Rather than merely appearing to Alcyone herself or sending a direct message, Juno sets a complicated performance in motion. First, she despatches a messenger to the god of sleep. In all versions of the story, this messenger then quite literally begins the process of staging Alcyone's dream by crossing the boundary between above and below; he descends from the world of the gods to the Cave of Sleep, a sphere of darkness and night that is elaborately described (especially in Ovid) in terms of its difference from the ordinary world of day, domesticity, and activity. The *Book of the Duchess* compresses a lengthy catalogue of negative comparisons in Ovid into three lines (157–59), but the violation of physical boundaries is emphasized in another, original way: Juno's instructions to Morpheus entail an apparently unique detail, as he is told to "crepe into the body" (144) of the dead Ceyx in order to appear before the sleeping Alcyone. Morpheus as shape-shifter thus crosses the lines between inside and outside, living and dead, speaking spirit and inanimate corpse. In a way particularly pertinent to my reading, with its emphasis on the underlying problem of how gender can be stabilized and grounded in any fundamental way, Morpheus violates the integrity of the body as a container of the living spirit and the intactness of the identity it putatively dictates and ensures. The news he thereby brings, however, as formulated in Chaucer's version, clearly restores meaning, identity, and a binary order of opposition, as it also echoes the closing lines of Alcyone's prior prayer: "For, certes, swete, I nam but *ded*; / Ye shul me never on *lyve* yse" (204–5, my emphasis; compare "Whether my lord be *quyk* or *ded*"[121]).

This paradoxical show—the dead body momentarily inspirited in order to speak of its own silence and absence, the apparition come to say that what it seems to be is no longer to be seen—establishes the dream world that Chaucer repeatedly visits in his poetic career as one in which borders and oppositions are unfixed and refixed, and the hard truth is told through the performance of elaborate fictions. At the same time, and somewhat ironically, Alcyone's immediate death, once she has heard the news, suggests both that such uncanny play with boundaries and limits within dreams seeps dangerously over into the waking world, and that there are fatal, self-destructive consequences of the certainty she sought. Assured of the difference between life and death for Ceyx, Alcyone looks no further: "With that hir eyen up she casteth / And saw noght" (212–13). The Chaucerian Alcyone, at the beginning of the story so vocal and active in seeking knowledge and pressing Juno to send her "som certeyn sweven" (119), now takes her seemingly proper and inevitable place as a bereaved wife (a woman without a man): " 'Allas!' quod she for sorwe, / And deyede within the thridde morwe" (213–14).

Two differences are obvious between Alcyone and the male characters with whom she is deeply identified. First, Alcyone dies, in Chaucer, without a murmur of regret or protest, and it is especially interesting that she is never allowed any expression of the love that she has known and lost. From the beginning, her passion for Ceyx, so central in the Ovidian tale, is hardly mentioned. Alcyone's longing for her husband is merely referred to as "a pitous thing / To telle," "For him she loved alderbest" (84–87). Morpheus, speaking from the corpse of Ceyx, could be referring to their married love when he didactically offers the Boethian lesson, " 'To lytel while oure blysse lasteth!' " (211), but, unlike the Black Knight, the bereaved woman herself never elegizes that specifically connubial "bliss" she has supposedly enjoyed. Characteristically, the narrator even points to his omission of the part of the story in which Alcyone just might have voiced the consoling memory of former love. After swiftly recording her demise in the lines quoted above (213–14), the narrative pauses for a moment to mark this crucial silence with *occupatio:*

> But what she sayede more in that swow
> I may not telle yow as now;
> Hyt were to longe for to dwelle.
> My first matere I wil yow telle.
>
> (215–18)

By contrast, in the poem's "first matere," the Black Knight, the bereaved husband, is forced by the dreamer to express his deep love for his dead spouse in incrementally precise utterances. In lines 1285–97, he is finally able to verbalize what one critic calls "the ecstatic mutuality" of their relationship; this expressive, verbalizing, and memorializing capacity, here reserved for men, is what many readers see as the central value that the dreamer helps the lover to realize.[14]

More important, perhaps, is the second difference between the bereaved woman and the bereaved men: the narrator's vision, as told, works to neutralize the dangerous effects of the unfixing of boundaries within the dream state for both the narrator and the Black Knight, in a

---

14. Robert B. Burlin, *Chaucerian Fiction* (Princeton: Princeton University Press, 1977), p. 62.

way that sharply differentiates their experience from Alcyone's. In the narrator's dream, as in Alcyone's, certain fundamental distinctions are initially blurred or problematized: gender differences are destabilized; the border between life and death is reopened as the dreamer fails or pretends not to understand White's actual demise; the ambiguous nature of his misunderstanding itself, like the Black Knight's circumlocutions, throws into relief the difficulty of deciding what is real and what is fantasy. The thrust of his dream is, however, toward a restatement of the same fatal certainty that Alcyone attained: the loved one is dead, and ideal love is lost. But to this experience and to this uniquely certain knowledge the male characters respond very differently. When he first appears, the Black Knight seems to be on the verge of death, and all too eager for it, but in fact he is not dead; both he and the dreamer are still alive when the dream begins, some time after White's death.[15] Even before the dreamer undertakes his talking cure, the narrative pauses to describe the internal forces, figured as the blood rushing to warm his heart, that keep the Knight from expiring despite his "harm" (486–99). And by the end of the dream and the poem, both the narrator and the Knight seem even more alive, able to see and do more. The Knight has been roused from his stupor, has recognized and conversed with another man, and may be able to rejoin the hunt; even more emphatically, the narrator wakes from a good night's sleep (after eight years of insomnia) into reality, and we are left to assume that Chaucer in effect enters into a poetic career.

Since the Knight and the narrator are like Alcyone in so many ways, why don't they too just expire when they know that the beloved, the ideal woman, is irrevocably lost? One prominent implication of the asymmetry thus constructed between the fates of male and female mourners is that proper gender difference has been restored by the poem. In the extreme and liminal case of lost love, the death of a spouse, the

15. The poem does not of course specify how long "White" or Blanche has been dead. Edward I. Condren, in "The Historical Context of the *Book of the Duchess*: A New Hypothesis," *Chaucer Review* 5 (1970–71), pp. 195–212, argues that the "eight year sickness" to which the narrator refers in the beginning of the poem means that eight years have passed since Blanche's death, and so dates the poem as late as 1377; for a refutation of this possibility, see Palmer, "The Historical Context: A Revision," p. 257. For the suggestion that the poem was written up to three or four years after the Duchess of Lancaster's death, see Howard Schless, "A Dating for the *Book of the Duchess*: Line 1314," *Chaucer Review* 19 (1985), pp. 273–76. Another strenuous denial of this possibility is made by Donald Howard, *Chaucer: His Life, His Works, His World* (New York: E. P. Dutton, 1987), pp. 148–50.

difference so threatened by heterosexual relations is reestablished: the bereaved woman simply dies, alone and in silence; the bereaved man lives on to enter into conversation with another man, and on the basis of their interaction in the dream world, he moves at least tentatively back into the world outside the poem. On the constantly slipping, now newly refixed oppositions between life and death, presence and absence, metaphor and reality, and male and female, the poet and the Knight have together reconstructed meaning and discourse. The Knight returns to history (or so the historical puns in 1318–19 suggest), the poet to his audience and his craft.

It is thus reasonable to conclude that in the *Book of the Duchess*, to the extent that the Knight and the poet are consoled, they are consoled not *for* the death of the lady but *by* it. Both Knight and poet were in danger of being permanently trapped in the negative, feminized state—apathetic, mournful, solitary, irrational, and unnatural—to which both love and its irrefutable loss reduced them. But the deaths of two loving and good women, insistently represented and confirmed within the discursive experience of the poem, appear to restore them, in some way that modern readings have never fully faced, to reason and action.

Whether we speak of the reality of women or the idea of Woman that both Alcyone and White may signify, we can now see contextual reasons why life might well go on for the Knight and the speaker precisely because "she ys ded." Alive, the Duchess of Lancaster, or any historical woman, is more than the object of male exchange or the topic of discourse she appears to be in so many male-authored texts, literary and otherwise. From any number of perspectives, the historical woman is threatening to what we know about masculinity and male entitlement in the fourteenth century: her sexual presence, for instance, is a danger to male self-containment, or, theologically speaking, to the chaste soul, or, both politically and psychodynamically speaking, to the absolute power of paternity and purity of lineage. The economic self of a noblewoman (even if she is empowered chiefly by her representative status) imperils the interests and male prerogatives of aristocratic men, as of court poets. And while the Duchess's class and socioeconomic power distinguish her from most women of her era, recent feminist historians assure us that there were other powerful women and other sociopolitical powers exercised by women in all classes.[16]

16. Several recent studies of the question of women's powers in the medieval period provide both discussion and bibliography crucial to this topic; see, for example,

The more immediate historical context of the poem also supports this reading by reminding us that after Blanche's death, John of Gaunt was freed to marry again, according to D. W. Robertson, "for the sole purposes of fulfilling his political ambitions."[17] Palmer opens his discussion of the date of the poem by considering the evidence of a letter in which negotiations for another wife for Gaunt were carried on within a few weeks of Blanche's death, according to his dating of events. He points out that this document "does highlight in the starkest manner the contrast between the conventions of aristocratic *amour courtois* on the one hand, and the political realities which shaped the marriages of the aristocracy on the other."[18] And, as I have said, the elegy for Blanche inaugurates Chaucer's career as we know it today.

If we think, too, of the idea of Woman represented by the two fictive ideals, Alcyone and White, we may draw similar conclusions. The story that ends in the death of Alcyone, the fabled woman to whom both men are so symptomatically analogous, at first clearly offers the narrator a way out of his paralyzing disorder; he both identifies with her grief and is imaginatively moved by it. By the end of the poem, however, at another interpretive level, her response to bereavement retrospectively enunciates a clear difference, as I have noted, between legendary female experience and that of both the male narrator and the male character. For the bereaved woman, the proper act is suicide; for the bereaved man, life must go on. The poem closes quite firmly when and only when this preeminent cultural distinction between male and female, a distinction threatened both by love and its absence, has been performed. Within the dream, Alcyone's status as the ideal woman—a dead one—is mirrored in White, the Blanche who is immortalized, fixed, pinned down, and frozen in a state of proper difference that confirms the manhood of those men who celebrate her. One side of the conflicted double image of the female that pervades medieval culture, White is a paradigmatic figure of the completely perfect and totally absent woman upon whom the moral

---

the essays collected in Mary Erler and Maryanne Kowaleski, eds., *Women and Power in the Middle Ages* (Athens: University of Georgia Press, 1988); in Renate Bridenthal, Claudia Koonz, and Susan Mosher Stuard, eds., *Becoming Visible: Women in European Society.* 2d ed. (Boston: Houghton Mifflin, 1987); and in the special issue of *Thought* (64 [1989]), ed. Thelma Fenster, in which a portion of this chapter first appeared.

17. *A Preface to Chaucer: Studies in Medieval Perspectives* (Princeton: Princeton University Press, 1963), p. 466.

18. Palmer, "The Historical Context," p. 260.

and social order depends, as this order is collectively conceived by the otherwise often competing institutions of courtly love, Christian theology, and poetic convention. She, Alcyone or White, is a crucial fiction, in other words, for the male lover, the male moralist, and the male poet; she is the figure of both difference and stable gender identity essential to the healing of the polymorphous, disordered condition of historically gendered subjectivity and discourse.

"Thou wost ful lytel what thou menest."
BD 743, 1137, 1305

As I have suggested, however, it is equally possible and necessary to observe that the healing process enacted in the *Book of the Duchess* is far from complete. The problems on which the poem turns remain only partially and imperfectly resolved, and in my view the claims made for aristocratic masculine identity, like those made for poetry and poets, are not made with the "easy confidence and exuberant enthusiasm" that some other readers have noted in the poem.[19] The unevenness and fragility of conclusions in the poem, so characteristic of Chaucerian poetics, are apparent in the considerations that I turn to now.

As so much of the critical commentary suggests, the resolution of the narrator's dream and the ending of the poem in particular are troublesome; if, as I have argued, a certain fundamental gender difference is clearly illustrated, little else is. Many readers have complained that the poem ends too abruptly. In less than twenty lines, the Black Knight disappears, reality subliminally intrudes (with the historical puns and the ringing bells), and the dreamer awakens. There seems to be no obvious, final message of consolation, as many readers have pointed out, no summarizing statement in the text of what the dreamer or the Black Knight has learned, and no definitive promise of specific future change in the state of either figure. Within the dream, moreover, what climax or sense of ending there is stems from two closural gestures that on closer inspection are especially problematic and interesting: first, the Knight's cathartic ode to mutuality, and second, and more formally, the near or exact repetition of two earlier utterances that bring the dream full circle.

---

19. Burlin, *Chaucerian Fiction*, p. 74.

Both closural devices may be read as symptomatic of the predicament of masculine identity explored in this dream-vision.

Let us look more carefully, first, at the Knight's "ecstatic" evocation of his perfect union with the dead woman, a few lines before the end of the dream and the poem:

> "In al my yowthe, in al chaunce,
> She took me in hir governaunce.
> Therwyth she was alway so trewe,
> Our joye was ever ylyche newe;
> Oure hertes wern so evene a payre,
> That never nas that oon contrayre
> To that other, for no woo.
> For sothe, ylyche they suffred thoo
> Oo blysse, and eke oo sorwe bothe;
> Ylyche they were bothe glad and wrothe;
> Al was us oon, withoute were.
> And thus we lyved ful many a yere
> So wel, I kan nat telle how."
>
> (1285–97)

In this passage, as a consequence of his conversation with the dreamer, the Knight celebrates the myth of mutuality and merged identity in romantic love. He voices precisely what Jacques Lacan, a modern analyst of questions about sexuality and language similar to those that Chaucer insistently poses, has identified as the starting point of the idea of romantic love: "We are as one"; "Al was us oon." But, as Lacan also observes, this ideal of mutuality and unity is to be seen as a myth that persists in the face of its unreality. Lacan writes: "*We are as one*. Of course everyone knows that it has never happened for two to make one, but still *we are as one*."[20] And in the Knight's speech it is the real *im*possibility of mutuality, of ideal oneness in love—"everyone knows that it has never happened"—that is brought to the fore by the implausibility of the kind of perfect happiness and mutual accord that he alleges. For within his highly conventional utterance, there is above all a radical and unresolved disjunction between the Knight's opening affirmation of the lady's superiority and his own feminine-like inferiority—"she took me in hir governaunce"—and his subsequent declaration of their equality and

20. Seminar XX, cited and translated in *Feminine Sexuality*, ed. Juliet Mitchell and Jacqueline Rose (New York: Norton, 1982), p. 46.

similarity—"Oure hertes wern so evene a payre. . . . Ylyche they were
. . . Al was us oon." The lady's supervisory skills must indeed be remarkable; in the space of a few lines she raises the childlike, erring,
subservient and feminized lover to her own ideal state, a state of perfection either quite masculine in its own right, or perhaps beyond the difference and limits of embodied gender and untroubled by the problems
of heterosexuality.

Other commentators have observed, but glossed over, this difficulty.
Michael Cherniss, for example, refers to the Knight's first service to love
in the abstract as "no more than the first sexual stirrings of the average
male adolescent," and even the Knight's initial adoration of White herself
suggests to Cherniss "the obsessive, puppy-like devotion of a teen-aged
boy." But, Cherniss adds with no discussion of the problem, " 'Another
yere,' however, he was apparently able to convince her of his maturity."
The poem does not (and cannot) show us, however, how the transition
between such puppy love and "mature" love is possible.[21] The transformation from feminine to masculine, from the inferior to the equal, the
passive to the active, the irrational to the rational that is required of the
feminized male lover who actually marries his lady is one of those consequential matters that can only be situated in what the story does not
tell. This metamorphosis is clearly too incredible to be believed or to be
located in time and hence in narrative: "I kan nat telle how." The role
of the courtly lover in which we see the Knight throughout the dream,
indeed that of the male adolescent (with a scanty beard), is the opposite
of the proper role of the husband in medieval society.

Recent social history might suggest that this apparent contradiction
in masculine ideals reflects and contains the real differences of entitlement among men of a single class, the aristocracy. In his study of aristocratic marriage in twelfth-century France, Georges Duby sees two shifts
in ideology, responding to "the major fault-line" dividing younger sons
(juvenes) who were forced to remain bachelors and elders (seniores) who
were able to marry and thereby acquire, according to Duby, wisdom and
power. The ideals of chivalric adventure and courtly love served to com-

21. Michael Cherniss, "The Boethian Dialogue in Chaucer's *Book of the Duchess*," *Journal of English and Germanic Philology* 68 (1969), pp. 660–61. Robertson takes another tack:
he reads the "uncomplimentary" aspect of the Black Knight's portrait in this regard as
evidence that the character should not be identified too closely, if at all, with John of
Gaunt (*Preface to Chaucer*, pp. 463–65).

pensate the former for their exclusion; at the same time, an alternative ideal, available only to the married man, was expressed in the celebration of "the fruitful couple."[22] In the passage from the fourteenth-century English poem that I have just discussed, precisely the same fault-line is represented as an internal division in the Knight's individual (and archetypal) experience, as we see in his retrospective description of his movement—or rather his implausible leap—from adolescence into wedded bliss.

Duby views the two conflicting ideals as actually compatible and complementary; they are both "safeguarding . . . the keystone of the dominant society—the married state." Courtly love expressed "profound hostility" to marriage but was in fact a strategy controlled by the *senior:* "By exhibiting his largesse to the point of letting his lady pretend that she was gradually giving herself, he was able to gain an ever stronger hold over the young men of his household, to domesticate them in the proper sense of the term."[23] But throughout Chaucerian fiction, the compatibility of the opposing ideals of courtly love and fruitful marriage is repeatedly put to the test, and the conflict between lovers and husbands, youths and elders, appears as a crucial site of both external hostility between men and psychological division within men. In the *Book of the Duchess,* the strategic complementarity of the courtly lover and the married husband is presupposed and celebrated in the poet's dream of the Black Knight in ways that seem to flesh out Duby's thesis. Feminist analysis, however, foregrounds the fact that whatever stability and wholeness this divided masculine ideal attains is based on the absence of Woman and women. Moreover, I am arguing, it is possible to read in and through the poem division within the ideal and to feel the effect of its strains. The actual impossibility of the "fruitful couple"—the impossibility that two can make one, that the problems of gender difference between the male and female, and more importantly within the male, can be resolved by notions of ideal love—is not explored extensively in the *Book of the Duchess;* further investigation of this problem comes later, and repeatedly, in Chaucer's writing. For now the impossibility of love, as we see in the deployment of the Knight's ode to mutuality and unity,

22. *Medieval Marriage: Two Models from Twelfth-Century France,* trans. Elborg Forster (Baltimore and London: Johns Hopkins University Press, 1978), especially pp. 12–15. See also my discussion of this issue in Chapter 1.

23. Ibid., p. 14.

at once figures and conceals the difficulty of a unified, integral masculine selfhood; it stands as the topic of male conversation, the bracketing ground of discourse. It is both the instigation to speech and writing and its terminal point, both the consolation that the Knight is allowed and an impasse beyond which his story cannot go. Taken any further, after all, the myth of union in love—"Al was us oon"—threatens the myth of proper gender difference; better that it has never happened.

Turning from the Knight's speech to the closural effect generated by key verbal repetitions framing the dream, we further see that conversation between men is occasioned here not by the loss of love alone, but by the two issues that the dream brings together: the lady's death and the dreamer's misunderstanding. The first repetition I want to consider is the one that encloses the dialogue between the two male characters with the simultaneously obvious and obscured fact of White's death, at once the given and the object of quest. In his opening words, spoken, he thinks, to himself and set off in a lyric format, the Knight unequivocally says that "my lady bryght . . . Is fro me ded" (477–79); several hundred lines later, at the climax and close of the dream vision, he merely reiterates what the readers of the poem have known all along: "She ys ded" (1309). This anticlimactic epiphany tells the audience what it has understood for at least a thousand lines, if not longer, but it apparently hits the dreamer with the force of sudden revelation. Adding no information, the rehearsal of old news serves not only to foreground what is most important about White, her deadness, but also to remind us that the dream is an event of both elegiac celebration and mistaken interpretation, of (intentionally or otherwise) mishearing and misreading, a dramatized instance of the infamous instability and indeterminacy of language and the gap between utterance and uptake, intention and effect, that the poet dreams of healing. Poetry in this fundamental case quite literally depends on, embodies, and contains a communicative misfire, and hence exposes the risk of lost meaning said by many medieval and modern thinkers alike to be inherent in all efforts at human speech; and here again this risk is linked to, even caused by, the risk of lost love, the inherently unattainable ideal of heterosexual union.

This metapoetic point is underscored and extended by analysis of a second closing repetition, this one an exact quotation of a punctuating couplet spoken twice before by the Knight in response to instances of the dreamer's misunderstanding: " 'Thou wost ful lytel what thou me-

nest; / I have lost more than thow wenest' " (743–44, 1137–38, 1305–06).[24]
In the third and final repetition of this couplet, only thirty lines before
the end of the poem, the Knight explicitly quotes himself and calls the
dreamer's attention to the repetition, prefacing his observation with an
imperative: "Bethenke how I seyde here-beforn" (1304). The self-citation
underscores the refrain-like quality of the lines, their status as cryptic
moral or message of the poem itself, an epigrammatic, rhyming summary
of its meaning that the audience is exhorted, like the dreamer, to ponder.
It again links the problem of (male) meaning, "what thou menest," with
the problem of (male) loss, "I have lost. . . ."

The first line of the couplet, "Thow wost ful lytel what thou menest,"
actually goes much further: it calls into serious question the dreamer's
understanding as well as the possibility of meaningful utterance and
interpretation in general. For what the Knight says here, after all, is not,
"You don't understand what *I* mean," but, "You don't understand what
you mean." This is an apparently illogical or impossible statement—how
can it be that, how can we talk if, the *speaker* doesn't know what he
intends to say? How would communication proceed if I knew more
about what you meant than you did? The *Middle English Dictionary*
glosses this sentence under *menen*, verb (1), sense 1.d, "to refer to (sb. or
sth.), speak of, mention" as an instance of a modern idiom of which it
is the only example listed: "you do not know what you are talking
about."[25] For the purposes of the dictionary, and of making idiomatic
sense of the lines, this is a pragmatic solution that cannot explain away
the fundamental problem. Glosses for all senses of the verb *menen* include, explicitly or implicitly, the notion of intention and fidelity to the
speaker's will—hence "to intend to convey (sth.) . . . to intend . . . plan
. . . aim"; "to desire (sth.), want, strive for . . . "; "to say (sth.), assert;
speak (the truth), express (one's thought) . . . "; "to remember . . . "; "to
believe."[26] The Knight is charging the dreamer, then, with lacking access

24. Actually, line 1137 is slightly different from lines 743 and 1305: it reads " 'Yee!' seyde
he, 'thow nost what thow menest.' " The second line of the couplet is exactly the same
in all three citations.
25. *Middle English Dictionary*, M.3, p. 306.
26. Even in all other cited instances of *menen* listed under sense 1.d, "to refer to," the
speaker's awareness of his own intention is never refuted or questioned, except in one
passage from Rolle's *Meditation on the Passion*: "I fynde no swetnes but speke as a lay,
and nou3t wrote what I mene." Here the speaker refers to his own self-alienation, the
loss of accord between utterance and intention, apparently as a sign of his despair and
disorder, and consequently his inhuman, meaningless speech: "I speke . . . as a lay."

to or control over his own meaning, his own will and intention. The dream thus seems to express as deep an anxiety about the possibility of certain knowledge and true interpretation as any twentieth-century deconstructive reading could wish to impute to it. In this poem, speaking is quite obviously risky business; misunderstanding is the norm, even speakers cannot fully know or control the meaning of their own utterances, and the author is not the arbiter of meaning.

In the second line of the couplet, the indirection of the Knight's statement of loss, "I have lost more than thow wenest," might be read as a mark of his emotion; so severe is the mourner's grief, it is often assumed, that he cannot speak of it openly. Such an assumption about the character's psychology might fit with and account for the Knight's elaborately distanced discourse throughout the poem, beginning with the obscuring metaphor of the chess game with Fortune, in which the lady is his "fers," and only gradually, in response to the literal-minded dreamer's (insistence on) misunderstanding, telling the real story. But the formulation also gestures in two other directions. First, it exemplifies the mystification of the woman's death that has been such a crucial goal of the entire dream-conversation; it emphasizes and insures once again the erasure of Blanche that is the inevitable underside of all this elegiac, figurative celebration of White. The lady even disappears from the surface structure of this line; she is referenced by the cryptic "more than thow wenest"— and as I have argued, what the Knight has lost is indeed more than anyone will understand who reads the poem only as an elegy for Blanche. Second, the statement reiterates what is clear in the first line: the Knight's contempt for the dreamer and the distance between the two men. What the lover has lost is "more than *thow* wenest": something more valuable, more perfect, than the unloved dreamer can hope to understand; something unnamed, ineffable, or identifiable only as that which exceeds the dreamer's limited interpretive grasp. Blanche refigured as White functions, then, as a sign of the male lover's superior comprehension, his higher experience, his finer appreciation; the idea of the perfect woman is a site not only of conversation but also of competition between the two men, where the lover articulates his authority over the writer.

In retrospect, this distance between the dreamer and the man he dreams about is implied in various ways throughout the dream. In discussing their analogous feminization and their resistance to it in the first two parts of this chapter, I spoke as if the dreamer and the Knight were separate individuals who share a common, even essential maleness, and I might be taken to mean that these men, suffering from a common disease, cooperate in their mutually beneficial cure, however partial it is. This assumption is, it seems to me, an effect that the poem seeks. The dreamer goes to some lengths to develop a (com)passionate relationship with the man in black, for reasons that are not made explicit. Perhaps they are obvious: John of Gaunt is a powerful patron; male friendship is a theoretical and practical virtue throughout the Middle Ages; the homosocial, as recent scholarship is making us see, is a long-lived, celebrated, and empowering tradition.[27] But at the same time, as the Knight's refrain stresses, there is a distinct and constant undercurrent of friction between the two men. A note of exasperation is heard in the Knight's corrections of the dreamer's condescending assumptions and in his insistent calls to better attention (e.g., 750–58). On one occasion, the narrator observes that the Knight's looks bespeak a less polite response than his words: "With that he loked on me asyde, / As who sayth, 'Nay, that wol not be' " (558–59; readers of Chaucer may be reminded that the Knight here acts just like another literary woman, Chaucer's Criseyde, in the opening scene in the temple: she too looks "a lite aside," and her sideways glance is then verbalized, by the narrator, as a reproof; see *Troilus and Criseyde*, I.290–92). Most overtly, the Knight's refrain, as I have analyzed it, seizes interpretive authority from the dreamer by insisting that in the paradigmatic instance at hand, if not in all cases, the hearer knows better, is a more successful interpreter and reader of intentions, than the speaker: you don't know what you mean (but I do).

As a complex and summative comment, the Knight's refrain thus implies what I see as the poem's pervasive concern with the difficulties

---

27. The passionate nature of the dreamer's relationship with the Black Knight has been observed by other commentators. Robert Hanning, for one, points out that in both Machaut and Chaucer, "the lover's complaint leads to the formation of an idealized intimacy between the lover (representing 'experience,' but also the lyric mode) and the narrator (representing the poet as recorder of experience and agent for transforming lyric conventions into the narrative mode)" (p. 132). Hanning suggests that consolation comes from the establishment of a "*human* community" (my emphasis) between the two men, leading to "personal acceptance and renewed creativity" ("Chaucer's First Ovid: Metamorphosis and Poetic Tradition in the *Book of the Duchess* and the *House of Fame*," in *Chaucer and the Craft of Fiction*, ed. Leigh A. Arrathoon [Rochester, MI: Solaris Press, 1986], pp. 121–63). However, in the light of work like Eve Sedgwick's *Between Men: English Literature and Male Homosocial Desire* (New York: Columbia University Press, 1985) on the male homosocial tradition in Western literature, and as I seek to confirm throughout this study, it is impossible to regard the bonding of dreamer and Knight as a model for fully "human" engagement.

either of a unified, unique male selfhood or of harmonious and enabling bonds between men conceived of as intact individuals in discrete but mutually respected social positions. The man in black's accusation that the dreamer doesn't know what he, the dreamer, means suggests that the instability and indeterminacy of language is an intrasubjective as well as an intersubjective problem, reflecting not merely a gap between knower and known but, even more disturbingly, a division or confusion within the allegedly singular (male) speaker. This problem is congruent and coterminous with what we actually see about the instability of gender: as I suggested in the first part of this chapter, for both dreamer and lover, the problem is not only the woman outside but also what we might call the woman inside. Other commentators have seen the Black Knight and the dreamer as two aspects of a single consciousness; what I am adding to such arguments is that this internally divided, double self is specifically perceived and described in the poem as a masculine consciousness, at once defined and recuperated by its difference and separation from the feminine and imperiled by both the woman outside and the woman inside.[28] Previous critical conclusions about the *human* consolation of the poem, I would insist, must therefore be viewed with serious reservations.

At the same time, the poem is interested in the fragility of bonds between men. The division within the male is not accidentally figured in the dream as a dialogue between two distinct and distant male characters, and the Knight's refrain repeatedly confirms that the internally fragmented male may also come into conflict with other males whose positions, experiences, and psychological strains are different from his own. And in conclusion I want to raise just one more possibility: the competition between this particular dreamer and the man he dreams of may speak not only to the conflict within and between men over the idea and the reality of women and normative gender identity but also to historical changes in (often gendered) assumptions about the authority of texts versus readers, authors versus audiences.

Jesse Gellrich has recently suggested that in Chaucer's poetry (as in Dante's, only even more radically) we see the beginning of such a change

---

28. One proponent of the view that the dreamer and the man he dreams about are "two aspects of one person" is Condren, "The Historical Context: A New Hypothesis." For dissenting arguments, see for example Robertson, *Preface to Chaucer*, pp. 465–66 (cited also in note 24 above) and Palmer, "The Historical Context: A Revision," p. 257.

that poetic (or "fictive") discourse initiates, a change from the idea of the Book, with "grounding in fixed meanings validated in a definite origin," to "discourse that recognizes its own impossibilities and proceeds by locating the authority for making sense no longer in the pages of the past, but in the hands of the reader."[29] Without disagreeing with Gellrich's general argument, I would suggest that the *Book of the Duchess*, a text Gellrich does not examine, actually says at least as much about the problems of such a change, the difficulties, for the writer (who is male, in fact and theory) of transferring authority from the Book to the reader (who is also male). It does so by thoroughly unfixing, in the dream world, another boundary, one that was, if historical reconstructions of the period are accurate, also being broken down in the real world: the boundary between speaker and hearer, poet and audience.

Just as the Knight has both masculine and feminine attributes and roles, so too he functions as both parties in the communicative exchange. While in the couplet I have just dwelt on he plays the part of the corrective reader of the dreamer's words and intentions, in the dream he figures chiefly as a speaker himself—and notably as a poet himself, one who begins by singing a lay and who uses highly metaphoric, conventional, literary language throughout. The narrator shifts even more dramatically back and forth between the theoretically distinct roles of speaker and listener, author and audience. He is constituted as the speaker/author of the whole poem but then characterized as a reader in the pre-dream sequence and as a listener and interpreter in the dream itself.

Both inside and outside the dream, as a reader or listener, it is the narrator who most dramatically embodies both the power and the limits of reader's claims to authority and validity in interpretation. The best we can say of him as a reader of Ovid, Machaut, and other possible sources is that he is selective and self-interested. Within the dream, he generates conversation and possibly therapy by deliberately or unwittingly misreading the Black Knight's words, and the ambiguity of his intention, as I noted before, is neither incidental nor resolvable; it is crucial. As reader of both books and people, he does display a creative, even controlling role. But as the Knight insinuates, it is never clear whether he knows what he's talking about. His misreadings are far from authoritative in

---

29. Jesse Gellrich, *The Idea of the Book in the Middle Ages* (Ithaca: Cornell University Press, 1985), p. 27.

the dream; one can never be sure that he knows when he's misreading, for the written text of the dream strategically offers no explicit interpretive gloss whatsoever, no final message of consolation, or despair, that we might agree or disagree with, or even simply locate as this reader's reading. The Knight's charge, "Thou wost ful lytel what thow menest," may be a case of the pot calling the kettle black, but it nevertheless accurately describes this figure of the poet as a speaker who doesn't know what he means, who is not in control of his own intention, and as a listener who doesn't quite know what anyone else means either.

If the author is threatened as well as empowered by the authority of readers, and aware that the binary oppositions of speaker and listener, writer and reader, like the difference between masculine and feminine, are less stable in fact than in theory, then perhaps this is the cleverest strategy of all: to resist the notion that the reader (in the historical context, most often a socially superior figure) has interpretive authority, but to do so by taking on himself the role of the reader, so that overt competition is neatly displaced. And the strategy mirrors his politic negotiation of the problem of gender. The (medieval) poet is inevitably a figure divided against himself, unsure of his gender and how to avail himself of the putative privileges of masculinity, uncertain of the grounds of his authority, engaged in an activity that promises no certainty and no actual escape from time and loss, from history and death, from ideology and theology. Writing fiction, indeed, cultivates the risk of being misread, subjected to the reader's power, exploited: again, of being feminized. By taking on some aspects of the role of the woman in culture, the male author at once disguises the competition between men across class and professional ranks and erases the real woman.

Previous generations of readers have not been concerned with this erasure or with the smudges it has left on the pages of so many canonical masterworks and the interpretations that have canonized them. In reading Chaucer in particular, they have marveled instead at the poet's alleged ability to bring Woman, in all her various and wondrous forms, to full literary life. But late twentieth-century feminist scholars may pore over the limited evidence of those smudges in order to marvel at something quite different. We find that Woman, in the form of the female character, is brought to represented life precisely in order to be killed off, silenced, displaced, ignored, again and again. The murder, however, is always only attempted. White is, the Black Knight says at one point, "to

myn yë, / The soleyn fenix of Arabye" (981–82). Many modern commentators have taken this to mean that she is an allegorical figure for
both Christ and Mary. It suggests at the same time another possibility:
it is White as a figure of the feminine, and above all the problematic idea
of Woman's difference and similarity, who cannot finally die. The culminating realization of the central male characters in this poem seems
to be the anticlimactic truth that readers have known all along: "she"—
White/Blanche, Alcyone—"ys ded." But as an elegy, however imperfect
an example of the genre, the poem still brings the dead woman to a kind
of imaginative life—"to myn yë." And other "she's"—Criseyde, the Wife
of Bath, Griselda, May, and so on—are in fact reborn in all of the most
interesting Chaucerian poems, as in the ongoing literary tradition of
which they are part.

In some sense, then, I am also suggesting that the figure of the poet
remains, throughout Chaucerian fiction, as cannily opaque or as unbe-
lieving as the dreamer of the *Book of the Duchess*, up to the very end of
his dream. In one sense he never quite understands or accepts the fact
that he sets out to confirm, that "she ys ded." He knows, that is, that
without the subject of Woman, there would be nothing for him to talk
about with men like the Black Knight. It is not accidental, and it is only
superficially paradoxical, that the statement of loss that initiates their
conversation, because the dreamer plays at misunderstanding, is precisely what brings his interchange with the Knight to an end. Descriptions of women metaphorized (as the Knight's "fers," for instance, in
lines 618ff.) or idealized as the perfect and unattainable object of love
keep the interchange, and the poem, going. Once the Knight is brought
to admit that White relinquished her static, perfect, inaccessible state to
become his flesh-and-blood wife, he too has almost nothing left to say;
and once the dreamer responds as if to the fact of an actual death, his
discursive partner, the bereaved lover, disappears.

The poet also knows that "she"—the idea of Woman—is a fiction, the
figure of a constructed difference and the function of a notion of stable
gender identity that is precarious and that fails to correspond to the
behavior of historical males and females. As a fiction, that which does
not exist, she is neither quick nor dead; as an undeniable part of both
the dreamer and the Knight, she can be neither silenced nor brought to
full life. The problems and possibilities that the idea of Woman and the

fact of women represent to poetry, as it is known, and to masculine identity and therefore to the social and moral order, as they are known, must be insistently confronted. Like the Book of the Duchess, Chaucer's subsequent fiction feeds on and cannot escape the specter of Woman's and women's presence, just as it inscribes but cannot guarantee her, and their, absence.

4

"We wrechched wymmen konne noon art":
Dido and Geffrey in the House of Fame

Playing with one's own name, putting it in play is, in effect,
what is always going on. . . . The very structure of the proper
name sets this process in motion. That's what the proper
name is for. At work, naturally, in the desire—the apparent
desire—to lose one's name by disarticulating it, disseminating
it, is the inverse movement. By disseminating or losing my
own name, I make it more and more intrusive; I occupy the
whole site, and as a result my name gains more ground. The
more I lose, the more I gain.

Jacques Derrida,
The Ear of the Other

DIDO AND THE CRITICS

In the *Parliament of Fowls*, in the narrator's rendition of the book he reads
before his dream, Africanus offers his grandson Scipio a celestial vision
that begins with a brief, dismissive glimpse of Carthage, the earthly city
whose destruction is essential to Scipio's career as a Roman militarist.[1]
In the next chapter, I shall argue that Scipio's dream represents, among
other things, a perspective rooted in the history of gender relations, and
that Carthage might also be remembered as the city ruled by the legendary queen Dido. Dido is the female figure who is not named, the
femininity that is repressed in Scipio's dream at the beginning of the
Parliament, but her story—the story of how her *name* was lost—is told
twice elsewhere in the Chaucerian canon, in the *Legend of Good Women*,
and, before that, with more apparent interest and sympathy, in Book I
of the *House of Fame*.

1. The epigraph appears in the English edition, ed. Christie V. McDonald (New York:
Schocken Books, 1985), p. 76.

In the *House of Fame*, as in the *Parliament of Fowls*, the poet's dream-vision begins in Venus's temple. After a brief description of his surroundings there (119–39), the narrator launches directly into a rendition of the one classical legend he seems to find most noteworthy among the temple's wall inscriptions, the story of the *Aeneid*. This story itself is told in highly compressed form until Dido appears on the scene, in line 241. The first Chaucerian version of her encounter with Aeneas characteristically conflates at least two sources, Virgil's epic and Ovid's *Heroides*. Two apparently original touches are also added: a long monologue spoken by Dido, the only character to whom reported speech is given in this episode, and the narrator's own sententious interjections: for example, he moralizes, "Allas! what harm doth apparence, / Whan hit is fals in existence!" (265–66).

The function of Book I of the *House of Fame* as it now stands has been the subject of much critical debate. Some modern readers have noted that it is a markedly unconventional beginning; Wolfgang Clemen, for instance, points out that unlike other medieval love visions, the *House of Fame* does not open with an allegorical representation of Love, and Chaucer's readers, Clemens thinks, "must have been surprised to find Venus depicted solely by means of the Dido-episode."[2] Robert O. Payne goes so far as to insist that Book I is irrelevant to subsequent material: "It does not suggest anything which follows, and critics have been able to correlate its 'sentence' with the rest of the poem only by abstracting to so great a degree as to vitiate comparison."[3] But many scholars have contended otherwise. The story of Dido, taken as a classic case of an already ambiguous legend whose ambiguities are only heightened in Chaucer's rendition, is said to bring to the fore questions about loyalty, about sympathy, and—central to arguments for the cohesiveness of the poem—about interpretation. Along these lines, critics have commonly addressed questions such as: Whose side is the narrator on, at any given point? Dido's or Aeneas's? Ovid's or Virgil's? Whose side was Virgil on, for that matter?[4]

---

2. *Chaucer's Early Poetry* (London: Methuen, 1963), p. 79.

3. *The Key of Remembrance* (New Haven: Yale University Press, 1963), p. 133. For a recent, somewhat more moderate restatement of this position, see Larry Sklute on the *House of Fame*, in *Virtue of Necessity: Inconclusiveness and Narrative Form in Chaucer's Poetry* (Columbus: Ohio State University Press, 1984), pp. 35–47, where Sklute notes that "each of its books concerns different conceptual problems, the logical contingencies of which are not fully apparent."

4. John Fyler takes up the latter question in *Chaucer and Ovid*, (New Haven: Yale University Press, 1979), p. 39.

Even critics who agree on the cohesiveness of Book 1 with the rest of the poem, however, differ sharply in their answers to such questions about the nature and course of the narrator's sympathies and tone throughout the episode. Opinion has ranged from those who see an essentially pro-Dido (and/or pro-Ovid) version here, and attribute it to Chaucer as well as to the narrator, to those who view Dido as a representative of carnality to whose evils the narrator is blind, while Chaucer (like Virgil, or at least like medieval commentators on Virgil) is not.[5] Some find the tone of the poem consistently "light-hearted," "entertaining," even "gay, buoyant," and "fun-filled," while others find it disturbing or at least "faintly unpleasant."[6] Insofar as such disagreements have created two camps, one (possibly like Ovid) reading Dido as more or less innocent victim and one (possibly like Virgil) more or less hostile to Dido and sensitive to the mitigating circumstances surrounding Aeneas's desertion of the queen of Carthage, modern commentary has replicated the very controversy that the poem inscribes in its display of conflicting evidence from the sources and in its own departures from them. And several of the most recent and interesting studies of the poem concur that this, at last, brings us to the real point of the Dido episode: it is not meant to evoke sympathy for or hostility toward Dido or the womanly attributes, good or bad, that she represents, but to introduce the epistemological, moral, and hermeneutical questions that the poem goes on to explore in Books II and III. For John Fyler, for instance, the episode proves the narrator's "disillusionment" with the literary tradition of love, whose enigmas "deny the possibility of understanding and discriminating judgment. All one has left in the face of the incomprehensible is a pious hope."[7]

---

5. The pro-Dido position is taken, for example, by J. A. W. Bennett in *Chaucer's Book of Fame* (Oxford: Clarendon Press, 1968), p. 38. For the opposing view that Dido is a symbol of "libidinous love" and that Chaucer's "extravagant sympathy" for her is another instance of ironic humor, see B. G. Koonce, *Chaucer and the Tradition of Fame: Symbolism in the House of Fame* (Princeton: Princeton University Press, 1966), pp. 112, 114.

6. See, respectively, Clemen, *Chaucer's Early Poetry*, pp. 67, 73; Larry D. Benson, "The 'Love-Tydynges' in Chaucer's *House of Fame*," in *Chaucer in the Eighties*, ed. Julian N. Wasserman and Robert J. Blanch (Syracuse: Syracuse University Press, 1986), p. 3; and Fyler, *Chaucer and Ovid*, pp. 35–39, 47.

7. *Chaucer and Ovid*, p. 40. Fyler follows the position taken by Sheila Delany, who puts it thus: "Chaucer grants the validity of conflicting truths and confronts the problem with no way of deciding between them," and "to transcend the given terms of the choice is the purpose of the narrator's prayer at the end of Book I" (*Chaucer's House of Fame: The Poetics of Skeptical Fideism* [Chicago: University of Chicago Press, 1970], p. 57).

More recently, Jesse Gellrich has questioned whether even "pious hope" really resolves the problem that the *House of Fame* as a whole confronts. Although Gellrich does not focus on Book I—which he describes, interestingly enough, as "the treatment of sources about *Aneas*" (my emphasis)—he suggests that the conflict between Virgil's story and Ovid's "is appropriate to the *larger* subject of Chaucer's poem" (my emphasis) because of its ambiguity. Chaucer is not unable to choose between Ovidian and Virgilian versions, but he refuses to do so in order to call into question the power of narrative itself to moralize. The poem as a whole, Gellrich argues, does not leave us with hope or skepticism, but positively rejects "the Book of the past," and its accompanying myth of language and moral closure, in favor of "his own text, the language of poetry and its capacity to explore old books." The subversive power of the fictive and the arbitrary in turn authorizes the poet as and only as a fiction, "a creation of the text."[8]

Like Gellrich, Jacqueline Miller also self-consciously uses contemporary theoretical concerns and methods in her investigation of authority and authorship at the heart of the *House of Fame*. Miller, however, is less confident that the poem wholeheartedly valorizes poetic language or the poet's voice. Arguing that the dream-vision is inherently a form that allows the writer to explore the conflict between "external" authority and "individual vision or voice," Miller contends that the narrator oscillates between the two alternatives, finding at times "confidence in the personal vision" that is "forceful but not total," but ending with a "not entirely hopeless" silence that serves "to salvage the image of an anonymous figure whose authority is merely suggested, and never tested."[9]

Like Gellrich, too, Miller focuses little attention on Dido, but what she does have to say about Book I is for my purposes highly suggestive: she sees it as a discussion of language, not love, and points out, as others have done, that Dido's problem, her betrayal by a man with "godlyhede / In speche" (330–31) but no "trouthe," is analogous to the nar-

---

8. *The Idea of the Book in the Middle Ages* (Ithaca: Cornell University Press, 1985); quotations are taken, respectively, from pp. 174–75 and 198.

9. *Poetic License: Authority and Authorship in Medieval and Renaissance Contexts* (New York and Oxford: Oxford University Press, 1986); the quoted sentences are found on pp. 47, 67, and 72, respectively.

rator's problem. The Virgilian and Ovidian versions represent not contradictory truths, but contradictory attitudes toward authority: is it absolute, or "something more local, relative, and individual"?[10] In his
invention of Dido's long lament, according to Miller, the narrator himself
asserts his growing "self-reliance." Yet just as Dido's speech does not
save her or her name from abandonment and disrepute, so too the
narrator is not empowered by his departure from tradition, for he returns
to a reliance on external authority (in Book I, in the catalogue of betrayed
women, "as the book us tellis" [388–426], and in the sudden lurch to
present the "Virgilian" view of Aeneas's motives, as "The book seyth
. . . "[427–32]). And he images the terror and loneliness of self-reliance in
the vision of emptiness and sterility that closes the Dido episode and
Book I.

I give somewhat extensive summaries of Gellrich's and Miller's readings because they seem to offer such persuasive and rich ways of placing
the House of Fame at the center of our current revaluation of the Middle
Ages as a period more formative of and analogous to our own than has
sometimes been thought, with a poetic tradition highly conscious of the
intersecting problems of language, authority, and subjectivity. Perhaps
only in the context of a study like mine, with its insistent and single-
minded focus on the histories and historicity of women, gender, and
sexual politics, do their considerations still leave something out. The
questions I want to pursue are already predictable and in formulation,
at least, simple. Why does a poem that turns out to be about the illusory
nature of fame, truth, and interpretive authority start as the story of a
woman's response to a man's sexual betrayal? What is the significance
of the poem's representation of Dido as a woman, and what can be said
about its depiction of a male narrator, addressed as Geffrey, who seems
both to sympathize with and resemble his female character? Given the
similarities between male narrator and female character, what signification may we assign to Geffrey's closing claim to self-sufficiency and self-
possession of a name ("Sufficeth me . . . That no wight have my name
in honde," 1876–77) as opposed to Dido's insistence that she has lost her
name (345ff.)? The assertion that Chaucer is interested not in the Dido
story per se but in the "larger" conflict between Ovid and Virgil begs
these questions and invites criticism—following the lead of the text and
the old story it retells—to abandon the woman once again.

10. Ibid., p. 54.

Clemen suggested several years ago that the Dido episode "could be taken as an anticipation and prelude leading up to the *Legend of Good Women*," and that although Chaucer does not make this point explicit, his audience would have recognized his attempt to tell a famous story about a woman's abandonment and a "man's untrouthe" as part of the contemporary controversy over *Le Roman de la Rose*, a crucial source of the long-lived *querelle des femmes*. Clemen pursues this line of reasoning no further, and in fact summarily dismisses the importance of the connection he has perceived: "It is obvious, however, that Chaucer himself did not take this controversy seriously."[11] If Chaucer did not enter the late medieval debate over Woman seriously, however, he certainly did so frequently, even obsessively. From my perspective it is obvious that Dido's story, taken in the context of this obsession, raises and helps to answer hitherto unasked questions about relations between the male author and his female characters. In this chapter I want to consider again, then, how "the woman question," as it emerges in the late fourteenth century—as a question about the nature and meaning of sexual difference, "men" versus "women," often particularized in the thematics of betrayal versus loyalty and domination versus submission—functions as the origin of the Chaucerian challenge to literary tradition, as the ground and instigation of the poet's subversive encounter with authority and authoritative discourse. Here, as in the *Book of the Duchess*, problems that the defense of Woman and the discourse of love bring to the fore are coterminous with problems of meaning and intention; and the text's complex representation of a female character and her putatively typical femininity to some extent strategically addresses those problems. And I suggest that the development of the poetic self, of subjectivity itself, of what Miller calls "the promotion of the speaker as the only authority principle," both constructs and depends on the gender system as we (still) know it and as it constrains and constitutes the authoritative (male) speaker and engenders authors and authority.[12] In the next section of this chapter, I focus on key aspects of the contrast, first, between the marginal, irrelevant Dido and the central female figure of Chaucer's first dream-vision, White; then I suggest that there is also some common ground between the two visions with regard to the narrator's characteristic representation of women and the concomitant problem of artistic

11. Clemen, *Chaucer's Early Poetry*, p. 86.
12. Miller, *Poetic License*, p. 51.

authority. In the concluding section, I turn to the figure of the poet, here, uniquely, named with the proper name of the author, Geffrey (729), to explore the strategic function of his feminization, which serves paradoxically to characterize a self-constructing difference between him and his female character, Dido.

DIDO AND WHITE

To some modern scholars, Dido clearly and straightforwardly embodies lust and worldly appetite, and thus she would seem to stand in clear opposition to Chaucer's first female character, the paragon White.[13] It is hard to find evidence in the *House of Fame*, however, for this view of Dido's character. Her passion and sexuality are downplayed by the narrator's trivializing, prudish circumlocutions. For example, he describes her sexual relations with Aeneas thus: "she . . . let him doo / Al that weddynge longeth too" (242–44). His worst accusation seems to be that she has done "amys" (269), and is guilty of "nyce lest, / That loved al to sone a gest" (287–88), while Aeneas is, by implication at least, charged with "many a shrewed vice" (275). The Chaucerian version of Dido's story does not accord her the implicit power and purpose suggested by the stereotypical view of Woman and female sexuality as evil incarnate. Dido in the *House of Fame* is indeed presented as a foil to White, but in ways that stress how weak, not evil, she is, and how constituted and constrained by certain allegedly typical attributes of her gender. If White and Dido together bespeak something of the radically split view of Woman that we can trace throughout the medieval period and into later centuries, they suggest that this split is less between spirit and flesh, virgin (or chaste wife) and whore, in fact, than between the strong exception and the weak rule; consequently, the rule, the norm, the reality of Woman is all the more firmly equated with the weak.

Following the dictates of courtly convention, as I suggested in the last chapter, White is depicted as a woman both exemplary and singular; among ladies she was "oon / That was lyk noon of the route" (*BD* 818–

13. See Koonce, *Chaucer and the Tradition of Fame*, pp. 89–136, for the fullest statement of this position. I should also note that reading the *House of Fame* as the second in the sequence of Chaucerian dream-visions is itself somewhat problematic, since the dating of the early poems is conjectural; for a standard discussion of the theories that suggest 1379–80 as a reasonable date for this poem, see Robinson, p. 779.

19); formed, moreover, so as to have "surmounted" the planets, moon, and stars (*BD* 826); "chef ensample" of all Nature's work (*BD* 911). When the dreamer in that poem implies that the Black Knight's superlatives may reflect his biased (not to mention conventional) perspective—"Yow thoghte that she was the beste" (*BD* 1049)—the Knight launches into a long, densely allusive defense of White's status as paragon and exception, concluding as he began, "She was as good, and nothyng lyk" (*BD* 1085). Although Dido too is portrayed in previous literary works as a queen of superlative beauty, wealth, and power who could offer a poet matter for another conventional depiction of the potent and peerless courtly lady, she is deflated in Chaucer's first rendition of her story to the most common female denominator. In marked contrast to incomparable White, this Dido is a mundane embodiment of any and every woman, especially in terms of her natural victimization at the hands (or, more precisely, at the words) of an equally typical, deceptive male stranger.

White also differs from Dido in that she properly resists the appeals of the Black Knight for some time. In contrast to the aloof paragon whose reluctance is the subject of so many flattering couplets in the *Book of the Duchess*, Dido falls in love with Aeneas two lines after she is introduced to the story. The narrator alleges the typicality of this behavior, telling us that she quickly and regrettably "dide hym al the reverence . . . That *any woman* myghte do" (259–61, my emphasis), and he goes on to moralize in the same terms: "Loo, how *a woman* doth amys / To love him that unknowen ys! . . . For this shal *every woman* fynde" (269–70, 279, my emphasis). Dido herself authorizes the narrator's intepretation of her meaning and status as typical, foolish, seductible Woman—a woman, any woman, every woman. She represents her own experience as the typical and universal experience of "wymmen" versus "men," "we" versus "ye," artless victim beguiled by smooth-talking victimizer:

> Allas, that ever hadde routhe
> Any woman on any man
> Now see I wel, and telle kan,
> We wrechched wymmen konne noon art,
> For certeyn, for the more part,
> Thus we be served everychone.
> How sore that ye men konne groone,
> Anoon as we have yow receyved,
> Certaynly we ben deceyvyd!
>
> (332–40)

Here, as well as later in this speech, a second and paramount preoccupation emerges, identified once more as a typically feminine one and one that constructs Dido, an everywoman, in opposition to White, the paragon. White's name, the Black Knight insists, was no metaphor: "She hadde not hir name wrong" (*BD* 951). Her love of the propriety and virtue of that perfectly faithful name was in itself the safeguard of her most important womanly quality, her sexual purity: "No wyght myghte do hir noo shame, / She loved so wel hir owne name" (*BD* 1017–18). Dido, on the other hand, has no name whose transparent fidelity to the idea it signifies guarantees her honor, nor does she live in a world where such accord between the word and the deed, referent and reference, is deemed possible. The power and propriety of language, the capacity of the word to invoke and control reality that White putatively embodies and makes coterminous with female sexual purity, is as lost as White is dead, and Dido's fall is in more ways than one a linguistic issue.

Dido is deceived by the prevailing gap in this poem as a whole between utterance and intention. She is taken in, specifically, by the words of Aeneas: as the narrator tells it in his brief summary of their wooing, Dido listened to Aeneas's story and then gave him her love, "Wenynge hyt had al be so / As he hir swor" (262–63). She herself similarly blames Aeneas's duplicitous and seductive words and indicts his godlike rhetorical skill as a typical male endowment: " 'O, have ye men such godlyhede / In speche, and never a del of trouthe?' " (330–31). A few lines later, in the long passage cited earlier, Dido contradicts one widespread assumption about women by alleging that she, like all women, differs from men in her lack of this rhetorical talent, the capacity to be artful, to deceive: " 'We wrechched wymmen konne noon art' " (335). But her own professed honesty and humility—virtuous enough qualities, in the abstract—do not empower her or safeguard her chastity; on the contrary, it is her rhetorical innocence that guarantees her sexual guilt. Lacking the necessary understanding that speech is not always true, or coming to this understanding just too late, she is the one who loses (the capacity to play with) her "name"—a concept that imbricates, as for White, control over sexuality and textuality, power over her own body and over the words that will represent that body to present and future speakers and listeners (and readers):

> "O, wel-away that I was born!
> For thorgh yow is my *name* lorn,
> And alle myn actes red and songe

> Over al thys lond, on every tonge.
> O wikke Fame! for ther nys
> Nothing so swift, lo, as she is!
> O soth ys, every thing ys wyst,
> Though hit be kevered with the myst.
> Eke, though I myghte duren ever,
> That I have don, rekever I never,
> That I ne shal be seyd, allas,
> *Yshamed* be thourgh Eneas,
> And that I shal thus juged be—
> 'Loo, ryght as she hath don, now she
> Wol doo eft-sones, hardely;'
> Thus seyth the peple prively."
> (345–60, my emphasis)

As my emphasis indicates, these lines embed the rhyme of "noo shame / hir owne name" that we heard in the *Book of the Duchess* (1017–18), but here the phonetic cohesion is so dissipated as to go unnoticed because of Dido's fall, alleged to be both inevitabe and storyworthy. In her world, words are unreliable; men rely on that unreliability to seduce and abandon women; and women are incapable of resisting, although with hindsight they can both lament their doom and avow its universality and predictability. The only truth and certainty, according to Dido, is that her shame will be "red and songe . . . on every tonge." Thus, as Dido's assertion might further suggest, *her* role in the affair is the one thing that is actually not in dispute; rather, it is *Aeneas*'s motives that are differently construed by Ovidians and Virgilians—and in this sense Gellrich's reference to Book I as "the treatment of the sources about Aneas," which I cited earlier, may not be as insensitive to the interests of the text as it seems at first glance. The very complexities and ambiguities in which the story is enmeshed, the "myst" in which it is all the more emphatically covered by the narrator's particular manner of telling, only make the certain "fact" of Dido's emblematic experience more solid and real, the single common denominator of an allegedly problematic "dual tradition."

At the same time that the poem establishes such a contrast between White and Dido, and between the ideas of Woman and the theories of language that they respectively embody, the Dido episode also permits us to see in the *House of Fame* precisely what we saw in the *Book of the Duchess:* a poem, a male poet's dream of enabling and storyworthy discourse, that is grounded in and takes off from its concern to fix the reputation of a (dead) woman. Dido, like White, is brought to imaginative life and made into a speaking subject in Book I of the poem, but then she is forgotten, left behind, and killed off. In suicide, she confirms her proper sense of shame and, like Alcyone in the *Book of the Duchess*, her seemly femininity. Alcyone's powerlessness to act or do, as I argued in the last chapter, is underscored by the narrator's subtle omission of even the minimal agency that suicide requires: he just notes that she "deyde," and then uses *occupatio* to get on with the story. Dido's suicide is mentioned as such, but undercut as an act of any real importance by the narrator's familiar matter-of-factness: "when this was seyd and doo, / She rof hirselve to the herte, / And deyde thorgh the wounde smerte" (372–74). As in the case of Alcyone, moreover, the narrator's putative disinterest in expanding the story in certain directions is signaled by a narrative rupture, *occupatio* (381–82), and an intertextual allusion that at once invokes and dismisses literary precursors: "whoso to knowe hit hath purpos, / Rede Virgile . . . Or the Epistle of Ovyde" (377–79).

If White, along with the power of women and Woman that she represents, is as threatening to men and to models of meaning, in both her presence and her absence, as I have argued in the preceding chapter, then the representation of Dido serves in another way to disarm that threat. Dido, the poem insists, is generic and typical; most women aren't like White; there's no need to worry quite so much about their power or their loss. After White's all but paralyzing death and its enunciation in poetry, we are left to imagine the poet of the *Book of the Duchess* going on to write about other topics with "renewed creativity."[14] The *House of Fame* seems to fulfill this promise. In the continuation of the dream, in Books II and III, having fixed Woman and women in a proper, typical, and inescapable position of weakness, difference, and linguistic vulnerability, the figure of the poet moves on to explore his so-called larger interest in some of the issues that implicitly arose in the interaction between the narrator and the Black Knight: his anxious verbal rivalry with male precursors and figures of authority and the struggle for power, within the institution of literature, between reader and writer.

14. Thus argues Robert W. Hanning, in "Chaucer's First Ovid: Metamorphosis and Poetic Tradition in the *Book of the Duchess* and the *House of Fame*," in *Chaucer and the Craft of Fiction*, ed. Leigh A. Arrathoon (Rochester, MI: Solaris Press, 1986), p. 125.

DIDO AND GEFFREY

To stop with this observation, however, is like stopping with the absence and textuality of the Wife of Bath or the marginality and erasure of Blanche/White. Such a partial reading, accurate as far as it goes, nevertheless occludes further dimensions of the problem that the topic of women, construed as a category, forces the author, construed as a man, to negotiate. It accedes, moreover, to the notion that Books II and III are the central portions of the poem in which Chaucer explores his more important concerns, concerns beyond the problems of gender difference and heterosexual love. The poem is to an extent strategically constructed to reinforce precisely this viewpoint. The narrator, having told Dido's story with a characteristic display of ambivalent sympathy, appears to abandon the topic of Woman and the representation of women as suddenly and completely as Aeneas sets sail for Italy. A more persistent reading of what follows can suggest, however, that it is actually impossible for the figure of the poet as represented here to leave Woman and women behind him completely, in part because femininity as Dido represents it is so obviously integral to his own nature and experience. Here too, as in the *Book of the Duchess*, the problem is not just what we might speak of as "the woman outside," either the perfectly unattainable and transcendent paragon, White, who resists, or the all-too-available and tempting victim, Dido, who yields. It is also "the woman inside": the fear and the demonstrated actuality, with all its attendant consequences, that gender differences may not be so clear and fixed as Dido's insistent "we wymmen" and "ye men," sealed off in Book I, would suggest. The female character's self-denigrating essentialism is demonstrably inadequate to account for the behavior and experience of the narrator of this poem, the instability or fluidity of whose gender is brought out from the beginning. Three indications of the feminization of this figure of the male poet are prominent: first, his self-characterization as a womanly type in the Proem to Book I; second, his sympathy and identification with Dido and his confirmation of the linguistic lesson she learned, too late; third, his relation to the manly (and preposterous) golden eagle of Book II. The narrator's self-representation before and during his dream undermines the simplistic, categorical and clichéd opposition of male and female enunciated and embodied by Dido. Paradoxically despite and because of this, the poem reintroduces a fundamentally self-constructing differ-ence between Geffrey and his female character at the close (as we now know it) of Book III.

In the Proem to Book I, the narrator presents himself as someone learned but remarkably confused about the possible causes of dreams. His hyperbolic confusion recalls the similarly foregrounded uncertainty of the narrator in the prologue to the *Book of the Duchess*, an uncertainty that he shared in that poem with Alcyone, and that accords with me-dieval assumptions about female irrationality in general. In the *House of Fame*, I suggest, his opening remarks quietly embed a detailed corre-spondence between the narrator and another legendary woman, the Wife of Bath. "For hyt is wonder, be the roode, / To my wyt, what causeth swevenes . . . " (2–3), the narrator announces, for example, at the beginning of the poem. He catalogues a wide range of possible explanations for dreams in the next fifty lines, and then simply ends this discussion by restating the initial claim and dismissing the subject:

> But why the cause is, noght wot I.
> Wel worthe, of this thyng, grete clerkys
> That trete of this and other werkes;
> For I of noon opinion
> Nyl as now make mensyon . . .
>
>   (52–56)

The terms of this disclaimer are much like those of that similarly disin-genuous strategist, the Wife of Bath, whose own opening claims for experience over authority are supported by her repeated protestations that she cannot fully understand clerkly disputation and will pit her own brand of common sense against it. Her comment on Jesus' reproof of the Samaritan who had five husbands, for instance, sounds much like the narrator's "But why the cause is, noght wot I" (*HF* 52): "What he mente therby, I kan nat seyn . . ." (*CT* III.20).

The analogy between the narrator of the *House of Fame* and Chaucer's most famous female character is even more clearly brought out by his next moves in the Proem. Following his disavowal, for the moment at least ("as now") of any sure "opinion" about dreams, the narrator says that he will offer instead only the story of his own personal experience, his dream of December 10—although what follows, like the Wife's alleg-edly personal experience, will turn out to be a compendium of citation, a discourse constructed fairly obviously of a patchwork of authoritative, traditional material. In concluding his proem, he prays for a blessing on all those in his audience who "take hit wel and skorne hyt noght" (91)— and a vicious curse on those who "mysdeme hyt" (97). He self-critically sums up the meanness of his sentiment: "I am no bet in charyte!" (108).

The Wife repeatedly calls attention in this same way to her mental and spiritual shortcomings. She argues, for instance, that Christ intended to recommend poverty "to hem that wolde lyve parfitly; / And lordynges, by youre leve, that am nat I" (*CT* III.111–12). One of her most notable moral imperfections, according to the *General Prologue*, again identifies her with the narrator of the dream-vision: when others precede her to give their offerings at church, "she was out of alle charitee" (*CT* I.452). She ends her tale, just as the narrator ends his Proem to Book I, with a curse on her enemies, a curse whose primitiveness and viciousness strikes me as highly similar to his: she asks that God shorten the lives of unruly husbands and "sende hem soone verray pestilence!" (*CT* III.1264), while the narrator of the *House of Fame* prays that his detractors may suffer "every harm that any man / Hath had, syth the world began" (99–100).

Assuming the chronology of composition that is usually accepted by modern scholars, the text of the *House of Fame* can only retrospectively bring to bear these marked parallels between male narrator and female character. But I am not arguing that the narrator is directly modeled on the Wife, or the Wife on the narrator. My point is that the Wife and Geffrey share many traits: their disingenuous claims about the limits of their own understanding; their sarcastic distinctions between their own powers of reasoning and those of clerks; their misleading citation of allegedly personal experience, although again and again they actually take on and subvert authoritative discourse; their strategic self-criticism; and their final recourse to the curse, which implies their sense that the power of language can be tapped into but is ultimately outside and above human control. In her *Prologue* and *Tale*, these traits identify the Wife, many readers seem to agree, as a stereotypically feminine being, a real woman, Chaucer's most convincing portrait of actual female experience. If so, then the same traits so prominently displayed by a male character must surely call his proper masculinity and the integrity and difference of maleness into some question.

The narrator's self-presentation in the Proem, moreover, lays a foundation for his alleged and oft-noted sympathy for Dido, which borders on a possible identification with her. For, like the narrator in the *Book of the Duchess* and his Alcyone, Geffrey and his Dido share two serious worries.[15] First, neither can trust words, nor the appearances they create, though both are eager to do so. The narrator, like Dido in her long speech, shows sound hindsight in his allegation that this woman's experience teaches an obvious lesson: "Hyt is not al gold that glareth" (272). Given this truism, he should also be forewarned that there is something glaringly wrong with his vision, at the end of Book I, of an eagle "of gold" (503; in case we miss the reference, the eagle is also compared to a sun made of gold in 506, and his feathers are "as of gold" in 530). The golden eagle's failure to provide a solid, transcendent, authoritative vision is made clear in the next episode of the dream, in Book II. The narrator will be similarly disillusioned by false appearances in Book III, from the opening moment when what looks like shining rock or glass in Fame's temple turns out to be ice. Second, even before the dreamer arrives at the House of Fame, he and Dido are both troubled by a related concern about words: both worry about what "wikke Fame" will say of them. Dido/any woman/every woman knows she will be subjected to both Fame and the wicked tongues of "peple pryvely." The narrator from the beginning is worried about his similar subjection to both the authorities of the past and the readers of the present and future, those who "mysdemen" his work, "Thorgh malicious entencion . . . thorgh presumpcion, / Or hate, or skorn, or thorgh envye, / Dispit, or jape, or vilanye" (93–96).

In Book II, the narrator's feminization is also brought out not only by his similarities to women inside or outside the poem but also by his womanish display of fear, passivity, and speechlessness and by his subordination to a manly figure who at once terrifies him and gives him great pleasure. The golden eagle speaks "In mannes vois" and with all the authority of those "grete clerkes" from whom the narrator dissociates himself in the Proem. Geffrey's position throughout Book II, by contrast, is almost completely passive and submissive to the authority of his guide. Literally he is seized "as I were a larke" (546) by the "grymme pawes stronge" (541) of the eagle; he is all but overcome with "drede, / That al my felynge gan to dede" (551–52); later he sweats with fear (1042). He is also all but silenced by the eagle's authoritative discourse and responds to his captor/mentor's long speeches mostly in monosyllables. But he is

15. As Miller also points out in *Poetic License*, p. 53.

impressed as well as petrified by the eagle's manly voice of authority. Near the end of his flight, just after he has been shown the Milky Way and given its mythological explanation, the dreamer expresses his delight in the new heights, literal and figurative, to which the eagle's discourse carries him: "He gan alway upper to sore, / And gladded me ay more and more, / So feythfully to me spak he" (961–63).

Is the golden eagle, then, the man that Aeneas wasn't—a faithful speaker who can bring true pleasure to the fearful narrator in the dream of a homosocial relationship wherein the narrator plays the part of the woman? Most modern readers have said no, for they see the eagle as "tiresome" and "windy," and some have suggested that the dreamer's silence during the flight is a sign less of fear than of disinterest, boredom, or growing disenchantment.[16] The narrator, however, never explicitly voices a critique of the eagle but leaves that to his audience. Within the dream, his self-proclaimed feelings of pleasure and his apparent suscep-tibility to a powerful authority that also terrifies and silences him resem-ble, again, the feelings of many of Chaucer's female characters—like Criseyde, another "sely larke" (TC III.1191), and her dream of silent sub-mission to an experience that ought to be painful but is actually thrilling, and that incidentally also involves a manly eagle.

The problem of his feminization is also implicated and illuminated in the dreamer's curious refusal, a few lines later, to learn more about the stars, a refusal of supposedly higher, truer knowledge, of things beyond the power of normal human vision—and a refusal, the allusions of the poem suggest, that markedly differentiates the dreamer from certain mythic male heroes. He explains his demurral by saying that he will believe what is written, and that to look at the stars "shulde shenden al my syghte" (1016). At this point, the dreamer seems to fear the heights to which other men, as the eagle already pointed out, have fatally as-pired; we are even higher, the eagle tells him (914 ff.), than Alexander, or Scipio, or Daedalus and Icarus. In other words, he fears the pride of men, particularly men in the mythical role of sons, who wish to surpass their fathers, to see for themselves what lies beyond the limits set for human understanding; he does not imagine himself to be like Scipio, able to have a transcendent vision.

16. Donald K. Fry, "The Ending of the House of Fame," in Chaucer at Albany, ed. Rossell Hope Robbins (New York: Burt Franklin, 1975), pp. 31, 33; John Leyerle, "Chaucer's Windy Eagle," University of Toronto Quarterly 40 (1971), pp. 247–65.

At this point, and especially in thus ostensively settling for faith in authority as opposed to his own confirming or transcendent vision, the dreamer's characterization brings out the paradoxical double bind of proper masculinity as it is often normatively defined in Western culture and the deep and complex feminization that is involved in the very reliance on authority that authoritative discourse recommends. Authoritarian arguments espouse the possibility of one truth, of fixed and absolute standards; moreover, they assume that enlightened individuals will see and agree on this truth and these standards. Practically, however, they tend to measure enlightenment in terms of orthodoxy, and they require submission, a passive acceptance of authorized doctrine, in lieu of an individual quest for truth. As the stories of Icarus and Phaeton suggest, the son who takes the power allegedly given into his own hands by the father is never strong enough or wise enough to control it; the individual ambition and personal aspiration of sons is, in these myths, quite literally suicidal. (The alternative tragedy for men is the Oedipal fate.) There is an inherent flaw or trap, then, in theories of patriarchy. And so in fact the man who respects authority, who is a good and faithful reader and learns his lesson well—a good Christian, and a man like the dreamer in Book II, at least—in one regard forfeits masculinity.[17] To choose experience, as women like the Wife are said to do, is to run great risks, and in Book II there seems to be little to gain by doing so.

By the end of Book II, in the ways I have suggested, Geffrey's complex feminization has become clear and is part and parcel of the problem that the dream seems designed to work out. The simple, generic, essentializing opposition between a/any/every man and woman that the story of Dido and Aeneas enforces and embodies is falsified both by the narrator's self-characterization and by his experience within the dream. No wonder that this unstably gendered narrator, whose own telling of the Dido story seems to bring out the innate and inevitable opposition of men and women, is confused, unable to take a stance or to make the sources or signification of his dream clear and single. Book I suggests that at some level he would like to endorse accepted views of gender difference, just as he would like to take pleasure in the golden authority that glitters in the form of the eagle. But both his self-presentation in the

17. For a fuller elaboration of the inherent feminization of the good medieval Christian, see Caroline Walker Bynum, *Holy Feast and Holy Fast* (Berkeley and Los Angeles: University of California Press, 1987).

Proem to Book I and his experience in the dream either belie the conventional wisdom about men and women or prove that he is an unnatural man. Thus it is in this man's likeness to women, in his femininity
or perhaps androgyny, that the narrator differs from, and is superior to,
Dido. The womanly Dido sees "we wymmen" and "ye men" as innately
different and inevitably antagonistic, and she firmly endorses her own
subjugation within the totalizing category of women. The unmanly,
sympathetic narrator, by contrast, articulates in his self-representation
the ambiguity and fluidity of gender, which become readable as the
possibility of transcending the problems of gender and heterosexual relations altogether. The woman loses her name, even as her reputation is
fixed; the poet puts into play his proper name even as he flaunts its
fictive status (that is, as he names himself a character within his fiction)
and proclaims his independence and individuality. In Book III, in particular, as the dreamer displays a more openly iconoclastic, less submissive
attitude toward authority, his difference from Dido becomes even more
overt and even more enabling, for the ambiguity that proves fatal for
Dido is comprehended by the narrator's claim to artful, creative evasion
and subjectivity.

At the end of Book III, the narrator specifically claims to escape the
submission to the feminine figure, the powerful, unreliable Fame, that
Dido abhors but accepts.[18] By disavowing any interest in or subjection
to Fame, he differentiates himself from women like Dido and resists that
feminine and feminizing power to which poets in particular are subjected. Dido's final words in Book I, quoted earlier, simply acknowledge

18. My focus here is not on the femininity of Fame, which Chaucer did not invent or
underscore and which would merit another kind of discussion. It may be worth noting
here, however, that his description of her shifting size, taken from Boethius, precisely
sums up at a prominent point in the poem what we see to be true of the paradoxical
representation of women in Chaucer—even in just the first two dream-visions—and more
generally in medieval culture. At first glance, this "femynyne creature," unlike anything
else formed by Nature, seems less than the length of a cubit; in a little while, however,
she stretches herself out so that her feet are on earth and her head touches the heavens
(1364–76). Similarly, as we look at the figure of Woman in the Middle Ages, at one moment
she seems to be a vanishingly small object (and subject), hardly visible in the record of
the culture, but from another perspective (look at the Virgin Mary, or the Wife of Bath)
she seems to us both a superhuman figure and a colossal problem, looming large on the
psychic horizon of male thinkers from the church fathers to the writers of secular romance,
overshadowing and some would say provoking the ideologies of theology, courtly love,
and even the feudal state. (Boethius makes a further claim that the *House of Fame* omits:
in her fullest extension, Fame not only touches heaven but also blocks men's sight of it.
In the Chaucerian translation: "Whan che hef hir heved heyer, che percede the selve
hevene so that the sighte of men lokyinge was in ydel," *Boece*, Bk. 1, pr.1, p. 817).

that she is now the helpless and hopeless victim of "wikke Fame" (349). The dreamer, by contrast, emerges from his absorbed vision of the pageant of the nine petitioning groups with a clear and firm declaration of his independence. Asked by the unnamed "frend" if he has come to Fame's court to get some for himself, he denies it vigorously:

> "Nay, for sothe, frend," quod y;
> "I cam noght hyder, graunt mercy,
> For no such cause, by my hed!
> Sufficeth me, as I were ded,
> That no wight have my name in honde.
> I wot myself best how y stonde;
> For what I drye, or what I thynke,
> I wil myselen al hyt drynke,
> Certeyn, for the more part,
> As fer forth as I kan myn art."
>
> (1873–82)

In this passage many commentators have heard Chaucer the poet proclaiming the authority of art and the individual author. In Gellrich's words (although not in specific reference to this passage), Chaucer is alleging that "the 'origin' for knowledge in the poem can only be the text itself." Fictional language—the "craft" that Chaucer practices—"is its own authority . . . and its author (notwithstanding his testimony to the 'soth' of what he 'sawgh') a creation of the text, a pure fiction, and even given a name—in order to sever finally the anonymous myth of the Book from the only authority the poem can have—'Geffrey.' "[19] Miller also cites this passage directly and reads it as "the final and firmest expression of faith in self as artist—as principle of conception, judgment, and interpretation—that the narrator delivers," although she goes on to emphasize, in contrast to Gellrich, that the "tone of confidence," strongest here, is still only fleeting, one swing of the pendulum that carries the poet back and forth between "forthright independence" and "self-effacing subservience."[20]

Miller also mentions the echo, in the narrator's reference to "myn art," of Dido's earlier admission of powerlessness, "We wrechched wymmen konne noon art . . . " (335). Pointing to the contrast between the dreamer's claims for authorial independence (temporary, in her view)

19. Gellrich, *Idea of the Book,* pp. 198–99.
20. Miller, *Poetic License,* pp. 64, 67.

and Dido's self-denial of her own authority, Miller sees both passages as part of "a unit where denial and assertion of autonomy become inextricably, almost reciprocally merged."[21] Insofar as the relation between Dido and Geffrey does form a "unit" bespeaking the fluidity of gender boundaries—for one of them, the man—by highlighting the narrator's own womanliness, and insofar as the narrator's resistance to his feminization is strategically incomplete, I agree with Miller's reading. It leaves out, however, the gendered distinction between Geffrey's assertion and Dido's denial, the one certainty that the poem affirms. Dido, here as always, emphasizes that her lack of control, her lack of art, is an inescapable condition of her gender: she speaks, again, only as one of an invariable class, "*We* wrechched *wymmen . . .* Thus *we* be served *everychone.*" The dreamer's claim, whether we see it with Miller as temporary or with Gellrich as final and complete, affirms his autonomy and subjectivity as an individual, whatever his gender or whatever the uncertainty thereof. Thus he differs from Dido and claims that, feminized as he is by circumstances and perhaps by predilection, he is finally *not* a woman, and not like women/any woman/every woman. He lays claim, in telling his own dream, to both a position of subjectivity, by contrast to the archetypal woman's subjugation, and again a proper *name:* precisely what Dido, of course, has lost, and what Gellrich understands to be so important to the authority of poetry and the fictiveness of poets: "even given a name."

In Book I, it is ironically the otherwise arbitrary and wicked Fame who allegedly inscribes what Dido herself avows as the only certain truth: the repeated, inevitable story of woman's seduction and abandonment, about which "everything is wyste." But the evasive narrator cannot and will not be seduced and abandoned or subjected to judgment; he alone remains covered in a truly enabling, self-created mist. Instead of being taken in by ambiguity, like Dido (and later others, most notably Criseyde), he takes it into his self-representation. In complicated gestures of submission and resistance to male authorities that play with and thereby play out his own femininity and his own name, he leaves Dido behind (for now) and distinguishes his career from hers. Thus he lays claim through the very act of sympathetically representing a woman to the authority of his own imagination and discourse. As he says in introducing the self-incriminating dialogue he invents for Dido:

21. Ibid., p. 66.

In suche wordes gan to pleyne
Dydo of hir grete peyne,
As me mette redely;
Non other auctour alegge I.

(311–14)

Better the open-ended silence at the (in)conclusion of the *House of Fame*,
better by far the resolution to hold on to and play with the name "Geffrey" (the more fictive, the better), than the capacity to speak, like the
kind of fiction of Woman that Dido represents here, only in the first
person plural.

5

Female Indecision and Indifference
in the *Parliament of Fowls*

> "I wol nat serve Venus ne Cupide,
> Forsothe as yit, by no manere weye."
>
> *Parliament of Fowls, 652–53*

> It seems more probable that men really fear, not that they
> will have women's sexual appetites forced on them, or that
> women want to smother and devour them, but that women
> could be indifferent to them altogether, that men could be
> allowed sexual and emotional—and therefore economic—ac-
> cess to women *only* on women's terms, otherwise being left
> on the periphery of the matrix.
>
> Adrienne Rich, "Compulsory
> Heterosexuality and Lesbian
> Existence"

In the *Book of the Duchess*, the Black Knight repeatedly details White's
"godnesse" (*BD* 985), the virtue that shines forth from her "benygne"
(*BD* 918) face to her perfectly proportioned limbs, as well as from her
words and deeds.[1] According to the Knight, moreover, "the goddesse,
dame Nature" (*BD* 871) herself took great pleasure in creating this "chef
patron of beaute / And chef ensample of al hir werk" (*BD* 910–11). In the
Parliament of Fowls, the dreamer imagines a very similar manifestation
of this ideal woman, again formed and here actually accompanied by
the goddess who delights in her own female creation:

> . . . Nature held on hire hond
> A formel egle, of shap the gentilleste
> That evere she among hire werkes fond,

---

1. The article from which the epigraph is taken is in *Powers of Desire: The Politics of
Sexuality*, ed. Ann Snitow, Christine Stansell, and Sharon Thompson (New York: Monthly
Review Press, 1983), p. 187.

> The moste benygne and the goodlieste.
> In hire was everi vertu at his reste. . . .
>
> (372–6)

The similarity of these conventional descriptions suggests that the courtly lady figured in White, like "the soleyn fenix of Arabye" (*BD* 982) to whom she is compared, is in some sense to be reincarnated in the formel eagle. Or perhaps the avian metamorphosis denied to Alcyone, that other version of virtuous woman in the *Book of the Duchess*, is realized in the *Parliament* in the dreamy resuscitation of the dead wife as a living, talking bird. In any event, the problems that White and Alcyone represent are still at large in what we take to be the later poem, although the exemplary female has come back to life in a rather different plot.

In the *Parliament* as in the elegy for Blanche, the frustration of the male lover(s) and the impossibility of oneness in heterosexual love are the issues on which the story of the dream turns. But now these conventional incentives to narrative are caused not by the death of a lady who has surrendered "al hooly / The noble yifte of hir mercy" (*BD* 1269–70) but by the female's refusal or at least deferral of any such wholehearted and merciful consent. While the lady's resistance is a cliché of much medieval love poetry, it may strike readers of Chaucer as unusual: it is rare enough that women in his secular stories are reluctant to yield to men's sexual importunities, and even in the few instances we do have of female resistance and unavailability, the plot that ensues comes to closure because the lady capitulates (or is forced to capitulate) and/or dies. Indifference is an attitude usually reserved for a few male characters—Troilus, for example, at the end of Book V of *Troilus and Criseyde*. In the *Parliament*, by contrast, certain kinds of narrative closure are prominently blocked by the formel eagle's unexpected but sanctioned unwillingness—as yet—to yield. She promises that her consent will come—but in a time outside the bounds of the narrative itself, in a future beyond the ending of the dream and the poem.

Either despite or because of the apparently unique place of the formel eagle in Chaucerian fiction, however, most modern commentators have not considered this female character or her naysaying in much detail, and what literary scholarship to date has said about the formel reveals that notable unevenness of opinion that Chaucerian women seem designed to evoke.[2] Whereas to one scholar she represents "instinctive

---

2. See Donald C. Baker's review essay and bibliography on the *Parliament* in *Companion to Chaucer Studies*, rev. ed., Beryl Rowland (London: Oxford University Press, 1979), pp. 428–45.

femininity" and Chaucer's laudable advocacy of "free choice" for
women, "even when the maiden is of such rank that her betrothal is the
whole commonwealth's concern," to several others she is indicative of
nothing more or less than the narrator's own troubled or amused inde-
cisiveness, his desire to keep an aloof or genial distance from the courtly
tradition he critiques or his exploration of "problems of consciousness."[3]
Despairing in the face of such critical disarray, at least two scholars have
recently argued that the real reason for the formel's indecision is as
impossible to determine as the motives for Chaucer's own "no doubt
... deliberate ambiguity."[4] Others have suggested that the formel's indecision, ambiguous as it and she may be, is simply not to be taken very
seriously. According to D. S. Brewer, the point of the poem "lies in the
humour and interest of various attitudes to or ideas about love, and not
in whom the formel will choose."[5] David Lawton hypothesizes that the
formel could be judged "in the wrong" for seeking "an escape from love,
an escape from experience," but then dismisses his own suggestion as
"too heavy an interpretation"; the Parliament is, as Nature puts it, merely

3. The formel's "instinctive femininity" is proposed by J. A. W. Bennett, *The Parlement
of Foules: An Interpretation* (Oxford: Clarendon University Press, 1957), p. 177. Several other
scholars have subsequently argued that the formel reveals more about the narrator than
about feminine nature, and in particular that her indecision is a figure of his own lack of
commitment to anything as definite as "free choice." See Wolfgang Clemen, *Chaucer's
Early Poetry,* trans. C. A. M. Sym (London: Methuen, 1963), p. 123; John Fyler, *Chaucer and
Ovid* (New Haven: Yale University Press, 1979), p. 85; James Dean, "Artistic Conclusiveness
in Chaucer's *Parliament of Fowls,*" *Chaucer Review* 21 (1986), p. 23. But critics who agree in
reading the formel's indecision as an analogue to the narrator's (or poet's) do not in turn
concur on the thematic valence of that analogy. R. W. Frank, for one, stresses that the
formel's indecision is "right" and analogous, again, to Chaucer's, because in the poem as
a whole he "is not taking sides," but remains merely "amused" by the overly serious
nature of competing points of view ("Structure and Meaning in the *Parliament of Fowls,*"
PMLA 71 [1956], 538–39). Clemen somewhat similarly argues that a genial and sympathetic
Chaucer "keeps his distance" from the courtly tradition (p. 169). Charles O. McDonald,
although committed to Chaucer's "genial irony, . . . sympathy and understanding," seems
to see a more positive identification of a "goal" in the poem: the celebration of "common
good achieved through natural married love" ("An Interpretation of Chaucer's *Parliament
of Fowls,*" *Speculum* 30 [1955], pp. 454–56). Unlike those who focus on the poem as social
satire, Fyler sees the inconclusiveness of the debate and the role of "Diana" as crucial to
"the unsatisfying, loose-ended quality of the dream" (p. 84) and hence to the ways in
which the poem articulates above all the "problems of consciousness" (p. 88).
4. Jack B. Oruch, "Nature's Limitations and the *Demande d'Amour* of Chaucer's *Parlement,*" *Chaucer Review* 18 (1983), p. 27; see also James Dean, "Artistic Conclusiveness," p.
25, n.14.
5. "The Genre of *The Parliament of Fowls,*" in *Chaucer: The Poet as Storyteller* (London:
Macmillan, 1984), p. 7

an "entremes," a game, "an inconclusive trifle, a polished inconsequen-
tiality."[6]

While I share the dissatisfaction that several scholars have expressed
with the available readings of the formel, I argue that the typical invocation of indeterminacy and play too easily obscures both the importance
of the female character and the narrative and ideological problem of
gender difference in this poem. The formel's indecision, I suggest, is
finally neither ambiguous nor inconsequential; it is in fact both explicable
and crucial to serious social and poetic contexts in which this poem can
be situated. The centrality of the female eagle's particular role here is
suggested, from the outset, by the way in which the Chaucerian story
characteristically marshalls and deploys one of its chief sources. As Wil-
lard Farnham has shown, the plot of the *Parliament* is based on the
common folktale of the "contending lovers" type. The fact that the lady
herself (rather than another judge) is asked to choose among rival suitors,
although uncommon in Western versions of the tale, is by no means
original; it is derived from the Oriental form of the story called the
svayamvara. The subsequent failure of the lady or any one else to make
a choice, on the other hand, is not usually found in the *svayamvara* but
is a feature of what Farnham terms all "uncorrupted" Western versions.[7]
The Chaucerian dream-vision thus yokes two elements from different
strains of the folk story in order to bring to the fore and conjoin two
issues in the formel's role: first, the element of "female self-choice";
second, the lady's inability or unwillingness to make that choice. The
formel's indecision, moreover, is made more prominent and troubling
by comparison with the poem's sources. For whereas in other Western
versions textual closure is effected in various ingenious ways (ranging,
according to Farnham, from the stellification of the lady and her suitors
to the woman's decision to marry them all), the formel eagle's choice,
at the end of the Parliament of birds, is merely postponed for a year;
and the poem's openness to interpretation is thereby made to seem the
final point of it all.

6. *Chaucer's Narrators* (Cambridge: D. S. Brewer, 1985), pp. 42–43. If Lawton were to
press his "heavy" interpretation, one could easily point out that as usual women and men
are being held to different moral accounts, for, as I shall suggest in more detail later, the
narrator of the poem is celebrated by many modern readers for claiming precisely what
Lawton would be deploring for a woman: "an escape from love."

7. "The Contending Lovers," *PMLA* 35 (1920), pp. 247–323.

In his study of the "contending lovers" tales, Farnham also observes with some puzzlement that the literary convention of the *svayamvara* seems unrelated to social reality; the representation of female self-choice persists in this Oriental type, he points out, "in spite of the usual belief that woman in the East plays but a small part in the making of her own marriage."[8] This phenomenon is not so hard to account for as Farnham seems to believe, however, and should by no means be construed as evidence of the literary tale's irrelevance to historical reality. Many social codes declare female sexuality more or less illegitimate in a variety of ways, but, as we know, laws serve to define crimes; sometimes the historian's only evidence of subversive behavior may be the statutes against it. The widespread and insistent denial of the female's rights of choice and consent in marriage might suggest that females keep insisting that they do have rights, or that something about those rights is perceived, and not just in "the East," as fundamentally threatening to social order. It should hardly surprise us to find a literary genre reworking a problem that "usual belief" conceals and that the norms of society cannot resolve or contain. In the *Parliament,* the narrator's dream rehearses a conventional plot that turns the attention of fiction to the problem of female desire and consent in a situation where males are fixed in the position of competitors for the scarce resource of the noblewoman's hand in marriage. The Western type of the story also links the problem of female desire to the problem of poetic closure, so that the disruption of the text mimics the disruption of the social order that real female power to choose a marital partner would bring about.

But such a story, like any narrative, may both identify and contain or resolve threats to the dominant ideology, and we see these operations, too, in the *Parliament.* What could more clearly reinforce female silence than to arrange the elements of a familiar tale in the way the Chaucerian dream-vision does, giving the woman a voice that she herself is unable or unwilling to use to bespeak her own desire? Turning from its traditional folk sources to a more detailed consideration of its complex textual and contextual particularities, I suggest that the *Parliament of Fowls* confronts one historical manifestation of the problems of women's choice and Woman's voice by staging a conflict between feudal and courtly matrimonial models that centers on their apparently opposing construc-

8. Ibid., p. 315.

tions of the female subject. In fact, however, these competing ideologies turn out to have one thing in common: their efforts to manage the paradoxical place of female sexuality in medieval culture, to deny and thereby control women's desires at the same time that they compel the myth of natural heterosexuality on which (aristocratic and masculine) identity and discourse alike depend. My reading of this poem will also suggest some possible answers to the question of why female desire is such a frightening, disruptive possibility for masculine identity in the theoretically heterosexual, male-dominated worlds that the poem evokes. In the concluding section of the discussion I shall consider on one hand the narrator's identification, throughout, with the female character and with certain feminine strategies and on the other hand his crucial difference from the formel, through which he continues the task of recuperating the feminization of the poet's position and laying claim to an individual authorial voice.

She / Shal han right hym on whom hire herte is set.
                                    PF 626–7

By these authorities, it is evident that no woman should be coupled to anyone except by her free will.[9]
                                    Gratian, *Decretum in corpus iuris*
                                    canonici, trans. John T. Noonan

Like the *Book of the Duchess,* the *Parliament of Fowls* begins with the retelling of a story from the book that the narrator was reading just before he fell asleep. This time, the text is the *Somnium Scipionis,* the Ciceronian work known to the Middle Ages only through its inclusion in another framing text, Macrobius's commentary. David Aers has recently argued that a female voice or a feminine principle is precisely what has been silenced or suppressed in Scipio's univocal vision, and that this omission is exposed in the narrator's characteristically dialogic, subversive dream. On the face of it, there are good textual grounds for such a reading.[10] If

---

9. "Power to Choose," *Viator* 4 (1973), p. 422.
10. "The *Parliament of Fowls:* Authority, the Knower and the Known," *Chaucer Review* 16 (1981, pp. 1–17). Aers argues that as part of his examination of opposing models of social order, Chaucer challenges the lack of "moral or psychological self-awareness" in the dogmatic claims of "Roman patriots and militarists" and allows us to understand "the

we begin to analyze the dream-within-the-book along the lines that the poem itself proposes (99–105) as a projection or replay of the dreamer's waking preoccupations, we note Scipio's obsession with both his distance from and return to the father and the voice of male authority. The hero's place in the patriarchal state, by virtue of his descent through the male line, is confirmed when he is welcomed joyfully to "Affrik" by his grandfather's friend and ally, Massynisse (see 36–40). In contrast to the source text, this version seems to contain no generational conflict among men.[11] In the dream that follows, the surrogate (grand)father Massynisse is replaced by the true male ancestor, "Affrycan so deere" (41), who also embraces the son with joy. But this model of the felicitous transmission of male authority and the achievement of transcendence depends on the suppression of a female or feminine presence; Scipio's vision of order opens with a glimpse of the destruction and violence it is founded on, when "from a sterry place, / . . . Affrycan hath hym Cartage shewed, / And warnede hym beforn of al his grace" (43–45).

In legend, Carthage is the city ruled by Dido, who represents in Virgilian tradition the lure of the feminine (within and without) that the properly masculine hero and founder, Aeneas, is destined to confront

---

partial and particular views of speakers and authorities." According to Aers, when the dreamer responds to Scipio's dream by dreaming himself of the competing world of Venus, he also "hints at unacknowledged desires, or at least *interests*, in the celestial instructor . . . something Chaucer depicted elsewhere too in the form of moralists' self-deceiving relish for the materials and behavior they are obsessed with condemning, so often sexual." Scipio's dream is, in other words, "eroticized." The juxtaposition of Africanus and Venus may, Aers notes, also reveal something of "the reader-narrator's various personal needs and frustrations," but the main point is that the poem as a whole, in Aers's view, is "thoroughly subversive of all forms of dogmatic thought" or "any totalizing metaphysical stance." This dream-vision thus points the way toward Chaucer's later efforts "to allow yet more voices, in more concrete settings, to enter his poetic works." Aers's reading commends to us a Chaucer very much like the one Jesse Gellrich identifies in the *House of Fame*, a poet subversive of past authorities—or of any authority (save, for Gellrich at least, the authority of the fictive poetic voice); see *The Idea of the Book in the Middle Ages* (Ithaca: Cornell Univ. Press, 1985). In a persuasive essay Louise Fradenburg interprets the birds' inability to distinguish among the rival suitors as a sign that "the lyricism of the royal subject" is defeated in Chaucer's poem ("Spectacular Fictions: The Body Politic in Chaucer and Dunbar," *Poetics Today* 5 [1984], p. 503); in passing she also observes that "the voice of the female other speaks for itself" in the *Parliament*.

11. In this regard, the Chaucerian version omits a detail from the source text that changes the whole tone of things. In Cicero, as preserved in Macrobius, the dreamer is at first frightened by the appearance of the grandfather whom he barely remembers: "My grandfather's appearance was better known to me from his portrait-mask than from my memories of him. Upon recognizing him I shuddered, but he reproved my fears and bade me pay close attention to his words" (Macrobius, *Commentary on the Dream of Scipio*, trans. William Harris Stahl [New York: Columbia University Press, 1952], p. 70).

and overcome. In the dream of Scipio as retold in the *Parliament,* the confrontation is declared over. Male hegemony and patriarchal authority leading to a triumph for the privileged few over both temporality and mortality—"joye . . . that last withouten ende" (49)—are explicitly based on the alleged conquest and destruction of the feminine place, the city ruled by a female who is both ruler and lover. But then two females with precisely these functions reappear undefeated in the narrator's answering, revisionary, subversive dream: Nature and Venus. The vision of the Parliament thus seems to stage quite clearly the return of what Scipio is said to have conquered or repressed; the dreamer wakes up in a garden of love ruled by two powerful female divinities and then witnesses the Parliament in which an alternative version of the quest for "commune profyt," organized under the gracious lady Nature's authoritative control, is centered on and then disrupted by the alluring female for whom three aristocratic males contend.

I submit, however, that the garden of love imagined here cultivates no simple alternative to the *patria*, no essentially female voice or positively feminine counterprinciple that neatly contrasts with, complements, or corrects Scipio's vision. The Chaucerian dream world may be ruled by Venus and Nature and obsessed with the formel's desirability and power, but it is not a matriarchy, and none of these females is unambiguously a figure of authority.[12] The narrator's dream, as I read it, would preserve much that is valued in Scipio's vision. Africanus, after all, is still the narrator's initial guide, the one who pushes him through the forbidding gate and guarantees him immunity from the risks of love. But once inside the gate, what the dreamer sees about female subjectivity and feminine power does indeed subvert the univocal authority of a patriarchal vision such as Scipio's. As in the *House of Fame,* the narrator's contest with the older male generation is thus waged over a familiar issue, with specific historical and literary dimensions: the Woman question. His dream suggests that theories of social organization that claim to subordinate and transcend women and deny the instability of gender are at best oversimplifications. The dream world is a garden of love wherein

12. For a discussion of the complexities of medieval treatments of Nature as a feminine figure that provides an interesting context for the *Parliament's* version of the goddess, see Winthrop Wetherbee, "Some Implications of Nature's Femininity in Medieval Poetry," in *Approaches to Nature in the Middle Ages,* ed. Lawrence D. Roberts (Binghamton, N.Y.: Center for Medieval and Early Renaissance Studies, 1982), pp. 47–62.

heterosexual desire is assumed and even elevated to a religion, or at least the central, inescapable subject of secular poetics, and here females and the feminine are not so easily conquered and left behind; they are a troubling and inescapable aspect of male experience. To some extent, the narrator's dream may even interrogate the possibility of any essential maleness at all, for, as I shall discuss more fully later, if the male poet projects himself into any figure other than the dreamer himself, it is into his heroine, the formel eagle. All this is not to say, however, that the vision that supplants one crude form of patriarchal hierarchy necessarily means to replace it with a feminist utopia in which gender asymmetry is abolished and women are empowered or revalued.

The garden ruled by Venus and Nature cultivates nothing but contra-diction between and within; here, as in all Chaucerian dream worlds, clear relations of difference and similarity constantly dissolve and re-form. At first, for instance, there seems to be an obvious contrast between two parts of the terrain, the area surrounding Venus's temple and the hill on which Nature holds the Parliament. We might expect to be able to read this contrast as a lesson in the difference between illicit lust and marital bliss, or, emphasizing the problem of the female subject, between the two faces of Woman—Venus, a terrifyingly seductive Eve, and Na-ture, a merciful, bodiless Mary.[13] But the truth at once turns out to be more complicated, for the marked opposition of Venus and Nature is laid over contradictions within their respective realms.

Venus's realm is most obviously an unpleasant, disorderly place, and the personifications that the dreamer encounters on the way to her tem-ple are in brazen conflict: "Tho was I war of Plesaunce anon-ryght, / And of Aray, and Lust, and Curteysie" (218–19), and so on. This situation seems troubling to the dreamer, and even his powers of description are beset by contradiction inside the temple, as we see in his contorted depiction of the lack of light in the "prive corner" where the goddess and Richesse are found "in disport" (260): "Derk was that place, but afterward lightnesse / I saw a lyte, unnethe it myghte be lesse" (263–64). The dreamer finds himself with relief returning to the "sote and grene"

---

13. For a clear statement of the argument that Venus represents lust as opposed to Nature's married love, see for instance McDonald, "An Interpretation of Chaucer's *Parle-ment of Foules.*" Lawton, in *Chaucer's Narrators,* notes the problem in seeing an opposition between Nature and Culture here and reformulates the divison as one of good artifice versus bad artifice.

place (296) wherein he thinks to find respite from the paradoxes and oxymorons of Venus: "Forth welk I tho myselven to solace" (297). Here, indeed, the gracious and putatively authoritative voice of Nature, as opposed to the partially visible and oblivious body of Venus, seems to keep order, and for several stanzas the dreamer's catalogue replaces the troubled description of earlier lines and imitates the hierarchical containment of difference and diversity that Nature putatively controls (lines 323–64). The events of the Parliament soon disclose, however, that this ideal of rhetorical and social order is as conflicted as any other this dreamer seems able to imagine. The most deeply embedded, problematic, and elaborated contradiction in the dream world subtends the process by which Nature, in the verbal arena of the Parliament, attempts to resolve the opposition between disruptive individual (male) desire and stabilizing class hierarchy while upholding the fundamental given of both the literary genre and the social context of the poem: the principle of female consent to marriage.

Nature opens the Parliament by calling on the royal eagle, who is given first choice because of his rank, "above yow in degre" (394), and then she describes how the proceedings will continue:

> "And after hym by ordre shul ye chese,
> After youre kynde, everich as yow lyketh,
> And, as youre hap is, shul ye wynne or lese.
> But which of yow that love most entriketh,
> God sende hym hire that sorest for hym syketh!"
> And therwithal the tersel gan she calle,
> And seyde, "My sone, the choys is to the falle.
>
> "But natheles, in this condicioun
> Mot be the choys of everich that is heere,
> That she agre to his eleccioun,
> Whoso he be that shulde be hire feere.
> This is oure usage alwey, fro yer to yeere."
>
> (400–411)

At first glance, these original rules for the Parliament might seem to bespeak, as one critic puts it, "the benevolent and relatively uncomplicated mating system established by Nature."[14] They presuppose a natural heterosexuality that transcends (or underlies) class difference, not to

14. Oruch, "Nature's Limitations," p. 34.

speak of gender difference; within each rank, it is assumed, males and females will properly desire each other, will desire the same thing from each other, and will usually mate. Proper gender difference reconciled by (or, by the reading I suggest, disguised as) mutuality is articulated in the further presupposition that males choose and females consent to be chosen. Reciprocal desire thus assumed and marriage thus made available and orderly at all social levels, neither individual sexual appetite nor the call for female consent need (theoretically, at least) threaten social hierarchy and order. Nature assures her listeners, moreover, that customary practice sanctions her arrangements (411).

But already Nature's decree admits that the orderly mating for every rank of bird may not be so orderly for every individual: by circumstances or "hap," as she notes, some will win; but then some, no matter what their social standing, will lose. There is also an initial disjunction (introduced by "But" in line 403) between the rule of "hap" (402) and the logic of Nature's benediction (403–4), which rewards according to degree of desire. As the second "But" clause further hints (407), female consent, required as either a final obstacle or an afterthought here, actually represents a fundamental adversative in Nature's social syntax and the fatal flaw in her practical efforts to mate her subjects in hierarchical order. This problem becomes manifest when the formel's theoretical right of "eleccioun" is in fact put into practice at the close of the Parliament and of the dream.

Although announced as part of the rules to begin with, the right of female consent is thoroughly ignored until the debate fails to reach a conclusion, even after the birds of other ranks have joined the discussion. Then, when all else has failed and the Parliament cannot determine which of the three contending males desires the lady more and thus deserves to possess her, Nature reinvokes the policy of female election. Now, however, she recasts what she originally proposed as a general rule as a "favour" she is doing for the formel:

> "For sith it may not here discussed be
> Who loveth hire best, as seyde the tercelet,
> Thanne wol I don hire this favour, that she
> Shal han right hym on whom hire herte is set,
> And he hire that his herte hath on hire knet:
> Thus juge I, Nature, for I may not lye;
> To non estat I have non other ye."
>
> (624–30)

It is no longer possible to imagine how Nature's goal in line 628—the gratification of individual male desire—can be universally (or even in most cases) accomplished, since all three royal male birds claim to have their hearts set on possessing the one and only formel. In the very next lines, moreover, Nature contradicts her alleged dedication to the gratification (and reciprocity) of individual desire by suggesting the other "estate" that might have to be taken into account, as she reconfirms her own initial emphasis on the importance of privileging social class above individual desire: "If I were Resoun, certes, thanne wolde I / Conseyle yow the royal tercel take, / As seyde the tercelet ful skylfully" (632–34). Recall that the royal tiercelet's advice that Nature refers to in line 634 was to choose "the worthieste / Of knyghthod, and the lengest had used it, / Most of estat, of blod the gentilleste" (548–50). In this ironic, provisional formulation—"If I were Resoun"—that may in itself open the door for the formel's resistance, Nature goes on to endorse the same choice, and less cryptically identifies just which suitor she means. But the crucial difficulty with this suggestion is that Nature is *not* Reason, and that in retrospect she seems to be trying to accomplish something irrational, perhaps even impossible, on this Saint Valentine's Day.[15] She wants to accommodate incompatible goals; these reflect historically competing matrimonial codes that appear to differ fundamentally in their strategies for containing female desire and their concomitant construction of female subjectivity.

On the one hand, the advice of Nature and the royal tiercelet, which relies on social hierarchy and is aligned with the rational position here, suggests what we might loosely call a feudal model, one designed to sustain the proper rule of aristocratic families and the principle of patrilineal authority. In its starkest formulation, as prefigured in Scipio's dream, such a model denies that women's desires matter at all to the "commune profyt"; or if they do matter, it is because they threaten and so must be conquered and then ignored. The somewhat softer version of this model that Nature and the tiercelet favor holds that the "commune profyt" is best served when female desires are either in harmony with or subordinated to the social principles of "estat" and "blod the

---

15. It is interesting to note that several manuscripts read "If it were resoun," not "If I were Resoun" (see Robinson, textual note on l. 632, p. 903). This reading would of course change the meaning of the line altogether; Nature herself would actually be pointing out precisely what I am claiming here: that to follow the tiercelet's advice is *not* reasonable.

gentilleste."[16] On the other hand, contesting models, which historically challenged feudalism from various vantages, privilege what the feudal code makes illegitimate or of secondary importance: the right of female consent. The particular brand of antifeudalism here invoked is the courtly, which most dramatically elevates the female as a center of value and power.[17]

Called upon at the climactic moment of the poem to resolve the problem and restore social order by stating her preference, the formel refuses to choose, or, more precisely, asks and is allowed to postpone her decision for a year. Her reason for doing so is not stated, but it is not, I submit, ambiguous or indeterminable. The formel does not choose, the evidence of the poem suggests, because female desire, which appears to be construed in opposing ways by the competing matrimonial models I have referred to as feudal and courtly, is actually precluded by both. For the lady to decide on the grounds of social hierarchy and aristocratic precedence, as the formel is counseled to do by authoritative voices, would be to choose by a model that blatantly illegitimates and disenfranchises female desire. She is more covertly but equally blocked from making a free choice by the courtly code as it is represented here. To support the second and less obvious part of this claim, let me turn now to the central event of the Parliament, the tiercels' debate. A closer consideration of the suitors' position reveals how and why the female is in an important sense no more empowered by courtly ideology than by the feudal model it ostensively challenges.[18]

16. For just one somewhat analogous medieval formulation of the position that "estate and degree" are of primary importance in marital choice, see for example *The Book of the Knight of La Tour-Landry*, Chapter 126, "How men ought to love after his estate and degree," ed. G. S. Taylor (London: John Hamilton, n.d.), pp. 257–58. This passage was first drawn to my attention by Margaret Wade Labarge's discussion of how women were educated into submission to legal and moral authority in *A Small Sound of the Trumpet: Women in Medieval Life* (Boston: Beacon Press, 1986), pp. 39–40.

17. Recent scholarship suggests that this conflict in the rules by which Nature vainly tries to organize the Parliament summons up a long-lived contention in the culture at large. For a discussion of the ecclesiastical argument for the right to individual consent, see Noonan, "Power to Choose." Noonan reads the issue as a matter of theological principle and religious conviction, but more recent scholarship stresses the political dimension of the debate. See for example, R. Howard Bloch, *Etymologies and Genealogies: A Literary Anthropology of the French Middle Ages* (Chicago: University of Chicago Press, 1983), pp. 129 et passim, and Georges Duby, *The Knight, the Lady, and the Priest*, trans. Barbara Bray (New York: Pantheon, 1983) and *Medieval Marriage*, trans. Elborg Forster (Baltimore and London: Johns Hopkins Press, 1978).

18. The common assumption about the difference between feudal and courtly modes that I am challenging here is well expressed at the beginning of Chapter 6 of David Aers,

As all commentators inside the poem and most commentators outside the poem agree, the three suitors do not differ adequately in ways that could resolve the Parliament; it is impossible to determine from their arguments who loves the formel more and who therefore might best arouse and meet her desire.[19] The tiercelet who speaks for the birds of ravine, echoing the general response to the day-long debate (496–97), notes that it would be hard to prove " 'by resoun / Who loveth best this gentil formel heere' " (534–35), and he underscores the rhetorical nature of the competition: " 'For everych hath swich replicacioun / That non by skilles may be brought adoun. / I can not se that argumentes avayle . . . ' "(536–38).

The highly similar and predictable courtly sentiments that the three contenders express in fact suggest not only that all three birds are equal or indistinguishable in their protestations of love but also and more importantly, for the formel, that none of them actually feels desire for her. What is most notable about the rivals is what they have in common: their self-interest and their desire to compete in a male homosocial arena. Each talks only about himself, about his own irrational and unswerving devotion to the lady (419–20; 479–81); about the danger or promise that he will die if she refuses her mercy or if *he* is untrue (421–27; 459–62; 469); about his loyalty (428–34; 456–58; 482–83), and increasingly about the superiority of his love to that of other males. The formel's self-centered suitors incrementally reveal their overwhelming interest in outmaneuvering each other; they spend proportionately longer and longer segments of their speeches arguing not so much for their own love as against the claims of the other two. The royal tiercel merely assumes his privileged position and consigns all other contenders to mass anonymity and inferiority: " 'And syn that non loveth hire so wel as I' " (435). The second

---

Chaucer, Langland and the Creative Imagination (London: Routledge and Kegan Paul, 1980). Speaking of Chrétien de Troyes, "the outstanding artist" who preceded Chaucer in the development of courtly literature and of the "important countertendencies to the dominant ideologies and practices" (of orthodox Christian teaching), Aers notes: "The incorporation of passionate, non-coercive mutual and sexually vital love into marriage was a vision which obviously contradicted the power relations of the period and the dominant attitudes to marriage and women propagated by laymen and ecclesiastics alike" (pp. 146–47).

19. For various points of view on this question, compare Brewer, "The Genre of the *Parliament of Fowls,*" p.7, with dissenting opinions expressed by Edith Reichert, "A New Interpretation of the *Parliament of Fowls,*" *Modern Philology* 18 (1920), pp. 3–4, and more recently, H. Marshall Leicester, "The Harmony of Chaucer's *Parliament*: A Dissonant Voice," *Chaucer Review* 9 (1974), p. 25, and Michael R. Near, "Chaucer's *Parliament of Fowls*: Reading as an Act of Will," *Pacific Coast Philology* 20 (1985), pp. 18–24.

tiercel's opening words highlight his primary goal, to contest the claims of the socially superior male—" 'That shal nat be!' " (450)—and so he changes the terms of comparison from qualitative to quantitative ones: " 'I love hire bet than ye don, by seint John, / Or at the leste I love hire as wel as ye, / *And lenger* . . . ' " (451–53, my emphasis). The third tiercel concedes this point but argues for a superlative intensity of experience proved by its self-annihilating and therefore, by familiar illogic, self-affirming quality: I can't boast of long love, he notes, " 'But as possible is me to deye to-day / For wo as he that hath ben languysshyng / This twenty wynter . . . I am hire treweste man' " (471–79).

The third bird's arguments also underscore the even more important point that Nature and the other fowls all indirectly acknowledge: the suitors' motivation is not love or even lust for the formel but entry into a verbal competition with the other rhetoricians. While the first two eagles claim that they will die either if the lady refuses them or if they betray her, the third eagle admits that the really life-threatening possibility is that he will not be able to *speak* of love and enter into the verbal debate: " 'And but I speke, I mot for sorwe deye' " (469).

Finally, it is made clear that at another time, in another dream, this contest might easily become something more than a verbal game, and dying for love might be more than a figure of speech. The potential violence of the suitors' self-centeredness and competitiveness with each other, far more important to them than the formel herself, is glimpsed in the eagerness with which they collectively interrupt the tiercelet of the falcons when he mentions the word "batayle" (539).[20] Perhaps, too, this barely controlled physical aggression of the male suitors retrospectively accounts for the formel's actual response to the first eagle's speech as well as for her subsequent refusal to follow the falcon and Nature in choosing him, or in fact any suitor. When the "foul royal" finishes talking, the formel blushes "for shame" and is rendered speechless, "so sore abasht was she" (444–47). Why is the formel ashamed and afraid to hear of this male desire? J. A. W. Bennett has argued that it is because she is instinctively modest and hence "feminine," while R. W. Frank dismisses her blush as merely conventional.[21] But Nature seems to interpret the

20. Aers, "The *Parliament of Fowls,*" also points out that the aristocratic birds are initially identified as violent "foules of ravyne" (l. 323; see also ll. 334–36 and 339–40); he says that the three tiercels "share a fierce and unreflexive egotism" (p. 11).

21. Bennett, *The Parlement of Foules,* p. 177; Frank, "Structure and Meaning," p. 536. D. W. Robertson has another suggestion: the formel blushes, he argues, "since she has been looking forward to marriage and not to extra-marital indulgence"; the tiercel wants her for his "lady," not his "fer" (*A Preface to Chaucer* [Princeton: Princeton University Press, 1962], p. 377).

formel's blush as a sign of fear, as she consoles her: "Doughter, drede yow nought, I yow assure" (448). The formel's "drede" makes dramatic sense if indeed she hears the ferocity of her would-be lover's self-interest, as I do; she is humiliated and terrified by the thought that she should submit to the egotistical, potentially violent demands of any such lover or read his self-centered and conventional protestations as a sign of concern for her wishes or well-being. (As Bennett points out, moreover, this female knows her choice is crucial to the "commonwealth," and so she may also fear that she will not be allowed to defer or refuse entry into marriage.)[22]

Force, however, will not be exerted in this garden of love; the dream-vision presents alternatives to the way suggested by Scipio's military conquest of Dido's city. The formel will be allowed to postpone her decision, and in doing so she will bring the Parliament (not to speak yet of the poem) to an abrupt and unsatisfying end. This power of postponement is construed, however, as a fundamentally self-negating power. She is caught in what twentieth-century psychology would describe as a classic instance of a double bind, for whatever she does will in some sense work against her self-interest and reinforce male empowerment in the terms in which it is characterized here.

On one hand, as I have argued, neither the feudal model nor the courtly model enables the formel to choose in this situation without acting against her own interests. To the former, her opinion is irrelevant; the female subject is something easily conquered and put behind, as in Scipio's dream, or something quietly subordinated to the demands of class hierarchy, as in Nature's and the falcon's view. The lady is in effect brought into being, desired, and described as desirable only by the conventions of courtly love. But neither does courtly love offer any viable grounds for female choice or desire; the suitors are all alike and all equally undesirable. Her indecision, then, follows from the fact that both models deny the possibility of meaningful female consent, even as the one seems to legitimate it; to elect any of these suitors, on any of the proposed grounds, would be to relinquish power and subjectivity altogether.

On the other hand, the formel's remaining option—to refuse to choose at all—is in an important sense equally self-negating. Power, in the lit-

---

22. Bennett, *The Parlement of Foules,* p. 177.

erary world of the Parliament as in courtly writing, is explicitly equated
with the right to desire and to speak about desire: the courtly male birds
exercise this power over the other ranks quite literally by discoursing for
an entire day on the subject of their alleged love and so in effect blocking
the gratification of the other ranks' desires even as they define and prove
their own nobility. It is the verbal expression of aristocratic male desire,
then, that differentiates between classes and maintains social hierarchy—
male desire that only appears to look outside itself to any referential,
historical female object of desire. In the practice that would be inscribed
and referenced here, desire is male only, and the formel's only power—
the power to deny that she desires at all—in fact confirms this male
exclusivity. We are, after all, in Venus's garden, and here love is an
institution that as usual turns out to be about male competition and
compels female heterosexuality, thus erasing a crucial part of the power
to choose that it allegedly confers on women.

The formel's actual words, when she does speak for the first time at
the very end of the dream, substantiate this argument. She again reveals
fear, as she speaks "with dredful vois" (638); the first (and now obsolete)
meaning of the word "dreadful" is frightened, full of dread.[23] Before
revealing her answer, she both reassures Nature of her subjection—" 'I
am evere under youre yerde' " (640)—and asks for a special "bone" (643).
Assured of Nature's protection, the formel first makes her request for a
year's "respit" (648) to think it over. The perceived enormity of this
"bone" is suggested by her unprovoked insistence that she will say no
more: " 'This al and som that I wol speke and seye. / Ye gete no more,
although ye do me deye!' " (650–51). While by other readings her claim
that she will defend her silence to the death might look overly self-
dramatizing, by my reading this comment is not an idle threat or a
rhetorical pose, but an accurate description of the situation. The formel
has nothing to say except to postpone her desire, to defer her speech;
when she says that she will speak no more, even if she is killed for her
resistance, she is not proclaiming her courage as much as her lack of
subjective power, of self-possession: "ye gete no more" simply because
there is no more.

Before Nature can reply, moreover, the formel speaks two final lines
that emphasize both what she is firmly resisting—conscription into the

---

23. Citing the *Oxford English Dictionary* entry for the adjective "dreadful."

ideology of love—and the temporary nature of her resistance: " 'I wol nat serve Venus ne Cupide, / Forsothe as yit, by no manere weye' " (652–53). The power the formel exerts here, a power that at once frightens and emboldens her, is expressly ephemeral and promises retraction. The "as yit" pledges her to a deferred submission that sits oddly but inevitably with the expressed strength of purpose and conviction that embeds it: "Forsothe . . . by no manere weye." The specifically temporal and temporary nature of her resistance highlights what the formel sees and wants to sustain: the power of being the desired one, which is automatically and paradoxically foreclosed when that desire is reciprocated. It is therefore a power that recognizes and exploits to the lady's ends the real lack of mutuality in courtly ideology, but it cannot formulate a lasting alternative, a narratable story of female subjectivity outside marriage, or an unconstrained form of female desire. Thus we see again the common denominator linking ideologies that seem to be differentiated above all by their treatment of the female and their valuation of the feminine. The narrator's dream, like the courtly model of heterosexuality that it privileges (even as it critiques it), allegedly gives a voice to the woman in direct opposition to Scipio's dream and the feudal, male-dominated model; but like the Wife of Bath and so many others, this voice can speak only of its own silence. The formel's situation in this way also bespeaks what modern scholars tell us about historical reality. There is no secular place outside heterosexual relations for the aristocratic medieval woman; as Ann Haskell puts it, "life for women of the gentry was synonymous with marriage."[24]

Such a reading of the *Parliament of Fowls* may at the same time provide terms for analyzing why no available vision of social order can permit the female to desire and why this prohibition itself constitutes a problem and reveals a frightening possibility, for the courtly model in particular. The formel's voice may be "dredful" (638) in the second and now more familiar sense of the term as well. Full of fear for itself, it is also a formidable voice that terrifies and awes others, striking dread into the hearts of the dominant males; for their maleness, both constituted and constrained by the rules that give the formel the right to choose, is

---

24. "The Paston Women on Marriage in Fifteenth-Century England," *Viator* 4 (1973), p. 459. In a recent essay, Sarah Westphal-Wihl explores how this "fact" is crucial to a German text written almost a century before the *Parliament*; see *"The Ladies' Tournament: Marriage, Sex, and Honor in Thirteenth-Century Germany," Signs* 14 (1989), pp. 371–98.

seriously problematized by the formel's indecision. Essentially undifferentiated as individuals, the three courtly suitors need to define themselves as males and to establish at once their collective similarity and their individual superiority through the possession of the most desirable (because most desired) female. As the double usage of the word suggests, "identity" contains an irresolvable paradox: it means and depends on both a core difference, a uniqueness that is construed as the self, and a similarity with others that situates and directs the individual in the material and social world.[25] Like White, the formel is presented as the only object available that affirms masculine identity, in both senses: individual subjectivity and empowerment articulated (she is mine, not yours, and I am more manly than other men because I possess her), and common manhood proved (I am a man, like all others, because I desire her). Courtly discourse conceals this way in which the female is at once objectified and neglected because to reveal it, it seems, is dreadful; it calls into question both the stability and independence of masculinity, just as the narrator's dream undermines the foundations of Scipio's vision. And so in the suitors' conventional rhetoric we hear the ostensive granting of power to the awesome object of desire: she is "my soverayn lady" (416), and the three vow truly "to serven hire" and her alone forever, to surrender themselves completely to her "whos I am al" and to give her the power of life and death over them.

The formel, backed as it seems unwittingly by her powerful patroness, Nature, calls their bluff. In refusing to choose a lover, the formel simultaneously resists functioning as an object of exchange and prolongs the brief period, before consent is given, during which she is at least temporarily empowered to do what the rhetoric says she can do. By choosing not to exercise the illusory power of consent—by choosing not (as yet) to play her inevitable role in the masculine game of courtly love—the formel momentarily reveals and extends her dreadful power to disrupt the game, to thwart male desire if not indefinitely, in this case, then at least for a substantial period. Courtly love is all but undone, in this plot, by the female subjectivity it has, for other reasons, brought into being.

This power is, as I have said, in the main a "negative" power for the female in that it negates her subjectivity and power, too, in the terms by

25. For one discussion of this "paradoxical" concept of identity with specific reference to female identity, see Judith Kegan Gardiner, "On Female Identity and Writing by Women," *Critical Inquiry* 8 (1981), pp. 347–61.

which subjectivity and power are culturally defined by the courtly code—
it negates her (heterosexual) desire. In order to resist the compulsion to
desire and thus to make a man, she must deny that she desires; she must
speak silence and figure absence. There is, however, another, possibly
more long-lived, threat to masculine identity and power that the formel
and her indecision can suggest: the possibility that women might never
desire men: not that a woman might threaten the male with both the
excess (rampant sexuality) and the lack (castration) that male authorities
from Jerome to Freud are often thought to have feared, but that she
might be indifferent to masculine desire, not loving any man at all.
Nevertheless, she might desire something, might be a speaker, might
have a story. This possibility and the challenge it poses to the ruling
(and otherwise competing) ideologies of love and gender relations are
alluded to earlier in this poem when the dreamer looks further into the
temple of Venus, beyond her reclining body and the two young suppli-
cants kneeling at her bedside, to a wall where the broken bows of former
maidens devoted to chastity are hung "in dispit of Dyane the chaste"
(281). Venus's rule is quite literally backed up by these signs of her
triumph over Diana, who represents the possibility and the threat of
female resistance to the institution of heterosexual desire. The catalogue
of painted stories that the narrator immediately goes on to describe tellingly begins, too, with women who try to be indifferent to the love of
men and succeed only long enough to make Venus's victory worthy of
the name: Callisto, a follower of Diana, and Atalanta, wounder of the
Calydonian boar, "And many a mayde of which the name I wante"
(287).[26] (The sense in which the narrator "wants" the names of resisting
maidens—lacks them or desires them—remains open to discussion.)

It seems highly possible that the formel might indeed be one of Diana's many nameless followers, who wish never to love any man. She
might be satisfied, moreover, by her present preeminent position, presumably a chaste one, as Nature's most beautiful creation. She sits, after
all, on Nature's hand, and is caressed by the goddess: "Nature hireself
hadde blysse / To loke on hire, and ofte hire bek to kysse" (377–78). The

26. So too, in the parliament, the goose indirectly alludes to the possibility that a given
woman might not desire a man: "But she wol love hym, lat hym love another" (567), the
goose advises, and is soundly disparaged by both the sparrowhawk and a number of
modern readers for suggesting this enormity. On the story of Atalanta and its place in
Chaucerian fictions about feminized men, see the next chapter and my discussion of
Cassandra's interpretation of Troilus's dream in Book V of *Troilus and Criseyde.*

wonderful and powerful Nature has trained the formel to believe that she is supremely beautiful, virtuous, and desirable in and for herself, and has showered her with admiring looks and kisses. Why should the formel desire, instead of this divine adoration by one of her own sex, any of the three egotistical, scrappy eagles who care only for themselves, for each other, and for the prestige of possessing her? The likelihood that the formel desires none of her male suitors, that she is indifferent to heterosexual love, implies a more threatening power than the momentary power of postponing a consent that she will eventually have to give. The possibility that women may not desire men undermines the naturalization of heterosexuality and marriage—to a man or to Christ—for all medieval women and is an important part of the problem of Woman that subtends those competing ideologies, the courtly code of ideal love and the aristocratic code of social order, that together bicker and attempt to rule the day.[27]

But this observation gives rise to the further question that I explore in the following section: if the formel's indecision is, as I have argued, both determined by and seriously threatening to the dominant ideologies of gender and class relations, what then is the signficance of the oft-noted and characteristic similarity between the female character and the male narrator, who "has difficulty with decisiveness himself" and has allegedly projected his "state of mind" onto the unlikely figure of a nubile female bird?[28]

To rede forth hit gan me so delite,
That al that day me thoughte but a lyte.
PF 27–28

27. Sarah Kofman, with reference to Freud and René Girard, makes a similar argument: "What is frightening is woman's indifference to man's desire, her self-sufficiency (even if it is based on a fantasy, which is not the same thing as a strategy or a lie): whether this self-sufficiency is real or only supposed to be real, it is what makes woman enigmatic, inaccessible, impenetrable" (*The Enigma of Woman*, trans. Catherine Porter [Ithaca: Cornell University Press, 1985], p. 62). For an analogous conclusion based on a recent feminist reading of the medieval text commonly thought to be most central to Chaucer, see Sylvia Huot, "The Medusa Interpolation in the *Romance of the Rose*: Mythographic Program and Ovidian Intertext," *Speculum* 62 (1987), pp. 865–77. Huot argues that to the God of Love and his followers in the French text, "what is dangerous is neither feminine desire and its effects on men, nor male desire as such, but rather the lack of desire in a woman who refuses to yield. . . . It is the danger of feminine recalcitrance, rather than of bewitching feminine beauty, that is confronted in the myths of Deucalion and Pygmalion" (p. 875).

28. I cite again John Fyler and James Dean here; see note 4 above.

For metonymic deferral, postponement or putting off ironically represents the traditional feminine posture whenever a question of inter(dis)course arises.[29]

Domna C. Stanton,
"Difference on Trial"

In the *Parliament*, the narrator seems less fully or personally characterized than in any of the other dream visions, especially within the dream itself, where he is less a participant than a spectator—or in this case an eavesdropper. Even the little he tells us about the sounds of the dream world and his response to them, however, is highly suggestive; and key elements of this narrator's self-representation are notable, to begin with, in the interplay of two terms, "voice" and "noise," which come to be aligned, respectively, with order, authority, the thing that the narrator seems to want, as opposed to disorder, subversion, the thing that the narrator says he has and doesn't want.[30] When the dreamer describes his first visit to the pleasant part of the garden (where Nature rules, and later the Parliament is held), the key words "voice" and "noise" are not in opposition. Both are at this point associated with the harmony and accord of a Golden Age. A good part of his initial joy in the garden comes from the sounds of literally and figuratively distant, higher, and highly ordered realms and beings. From every branch, for instance, he hears birds sing "with voys of aungel in here armonye" (191). He also perceives what is usually taken to be the music of the spheres, described as "instruments of strenges in acord" (197), and so too elements of nature are in aural accord: the wind in the trees makes "a noyse softe / Acordaunt to the foules song alofte" (202–3). All this evokes in aural terms the possibility of an appealingly transcendent, organized vision like Scipio's; at the outset of the dream we thus see, as I noted before, the narrator's partial attraction and affinity to the dreams of the *patria*.

29. In Nancy Miller, ed., *The Poetics of Gender* (New York: Columbia University Press, 1986), p. 177.

30. Leicester traces out this issue in much more general terms than I do; as he puts it, "The style of Chaucer's allusiveness has the effect of transforming the landscape of the poem from a visual field to an oral/aural one, a landscape treated not in terms of *scenes* (as in Dante) but of voices" ("The Harmony of Chaucer's Parliament" p. 19). For a helpful discussion of "noise" in the *Canterbury Tales*, see also John Ganim, "Chaucer and the Noise of the People," *Exemplaria* 2 (1990), pp. 71–88.

Just as Scipio's vision is problematized, however, so too the dreamer's initial acoustic perceptions of delightful harmony are soon disrupted. In Venus's realm, the only sounds he hears come from below, not from above; they are human, but subverbal and tangible: "sykes hoote as fyr . . . engendered with deseyr" (246–48) or those unheeded cries of the two lovers who kneel before the reclining Venus. When he returns to the "sote and grene" place where Nature holds court and listens to the birds in this garden at closer range, they no longer sing like angels. They can do more than sigh or weep with desire; in fact, they speak (usually) like recognizable types of human beings, and cacophony replaces the music of the spheres.

Notably, once human language enters into the soundtrack of the dream, the original notion of "a noyse softe" becomes oxymoronic; as in most usages of the term "noise," the word henceforth becomes associated with loud, harsh, discordant, and meaningless strains. For instance, when he first hears the birds who have come to Nature's court to choose their mates, their noise literally takes up geographical space and threatens to displace—and perhaps crush—the dreamer himself:

> And that so huge a noyse gan they make
> That erthe, and eyr, and tre, and every lake
> So ful was, that unethe was there space
> For me to stonde, so ful was al the place.
> (312–15)

The next time the birds speak out as a group, immediately after the tiercels' debate, the effect of synesthesia recurs. Their noise again seems to the narrator to have tangible consequences, and his description reveals a sense of widespread violence and fragmentation, as well as personal displacement: "The noyse of foules for to ben delyvered / So loude rong, 'Have don, and lat us wende!' / That wel wende I the wode hadde al toshyvered" (491–93).

In both of the passages I have just quoted, "noyse" as the dreamer uses the term refers to the powerful, even violent clamor of the many for deliverance from a state of oppression identified here as sexual frustration. When Nature subsequently uses the word "noyse," part of her effort to control the power of the crowd's desire entails some semantic shifting, which may clarify what is implicit in the dreamer's response to the forceful din of the group. She authorizes her own univocal judgment by characterizing the noise of desire and class contention as the con-

straining, oppressing force from which she will liberate her subjects—
" 'Hold youre tonges there! / And I shal sone, I hope, a conseyl fynde /
Yow to delyvere, and fro this noyse unbynde' " (521–23)—by delegating
one voice to speak the collective opinion of each group (524–25). The
narrator, moreover, now reserves the term "voice" to describe single,
authoritative speech—Nature speaks "with facound voys" (521). The Falcon also uses "voys" to reaffirm his authority in response to the three
tiercels' interruption, in hopes of battle: " 'Oure is the voys,' " he says in
the royal first person plural, " 'that han the charge in honde' " (545). The
prelinguistic harmony of noise and voice, the many and the one, unruly
desire and meaningful speech, is lost. The single voice (sometimes speaking for a plural class) of authority, supposedly liberating or not, cannot
enforce silence on the crowd; social order keeps dissolving into the noise
of unruly sexual desire, just as alignments within the dream world keep
slipping and reconfiguring, climaxing in the final disquieting anticlimax
of indecision.

A return of harmony and accord—many voices making a pleasant,
polite, cooperative noise—allegedly closes the Parliament with the necessary stability and accord that the failed debate and the formel's indecision threaten. After Nature has given all the other birds "his make /
By evene acord" (667–68) and before the grateful, loving couples depart,
the fowls honor Nature with "a roundel" (675). The sound of the birds'
desire is now organized aesthetically, by convention; the singers are
"chosen" birds, the tune ("note") they sing is "imaked . . . in Fraunce"
and has "wordes" and "vers," and the whole performance restores the
notion of customary rule, the status quo: "As yer by yer was alwey hir
usaunce" (673–79). Some modern readers have been dissatisfied, however, by the closural effect of the rondel.[31] And in fact, modern editorial
practice obscures just how unclosed the poem may be: only one late
manuscript actually includes the complete words of the rondel (lines
680–92), which Skeat first ordered and added to the printed edition and
which all subsequent editions have inserted.[32] Quoted or not, moreover,
the harmonious, artificially ordered and selectively voiced noise of the

31. See, for instance, Aers, who comments thus on the closural effect of the rondel:
"Only a reading determined to dissolve the particulars of Chaucer's art and contexts would
attempt to take this ending as an authoritative image of metaphysical and cosmic harmony
coherently ordering apparent conflict into a unified totality accessible to natural reason"
("The *Parliament of Fowls*," p. 14).

32. See Robinson's textual note on ll. 680–92, p. 903.

rondel does not close the dream. The song is actually followed by the "shoutyng" (693) of the birds as they fly away to mate, and it is this final raucous, nonverbal ejaculation of sound that wakens the dreamer and sends him without further comment back to his literary quest for a certain something—"and yit I rede alwey. / I hope, ywis, to rede so som day / That I shal mete som thyng for to fare / The bet ... " (696–99).[33]

At the end of the poem, then, in the face of all this noise, the narrator's own voice cannot express a single choice or speak a clear verdict. Whether we seek his judgment in what the figure of the poet says or in what the poem does, it is hard to find a certain message; the narrator's last gesture is one of deferral and postponement that appears to provide no definitive solution and that promises only continuation after the end of the story. As other commentators have observed, then, this narrator, who "has difficulty with decisiveness himself," resembles none other than the formel eagle.[34] Once more the figure of the poet aligns his position with that of the female character and thus confronts, even perhaps parades, something feminine in his own makeup. The familiar site of the quest for meaning and certainty is the particular place where the poet and the woman meet: hence the commonality of the narrator's position at the end, in the midst of a nebulous and unsuccessful search for "that thyng that I wolde," "som thyng for to fare / The bet" (698–99) and the formel's, her explicitly unexplained, implicitly overdetermined inability to make a choice. Here the feminization of the writer's position—his inability to be sure, or to act, his disconcerting failure to lay claim to his patrilineal heritage of single truth—is most markedly foregrounded, and here poetic and feminine strategies, delay and indecision, look, as I have said, quite similar.

Like other narrators in similar positions, however, this one finally resists the likeness that threatens to merge into identity with the female character. The narrator's situation, as he seeks to define it, is significantly differentiated from that of the formel in two obvious but crucial respects, and his subversive indecision is thereby modulated, his antiauthoritarian instability restabilized in a characteristic way by these differences. First,

33. For a reading that does focus on the distinction between the rondel, seen to have "a tranquilizing effect," and the rude awakening that leads to the last stanza, see James Wilhelm, "The Narrator and his Narrative in Chaucer's *Parlement*," *Chaucer Review* 1 (1967), 201–6.
34. Dean, "Artistic Inconclusiveness," p. 23.

he himself claims not to be desired; he stands firmly outside the world of love and sexuality, and his lack of difference from women is recuperated as indifference to heterosexual love. Second, he nevertheless feels desire of a particular sort: not sexual desire, he alleges here, but the desire he insistently associates with reading "olde bokes." In concluding this discussion, I want to go over some familiar territory and underscore the salient characteristics of the figure of the poet we see constructed in the *Parliament*. The portrait I examine will not, on the surface, look different from the one most readers observe.[35] But now I want to evaluate the significance of this self-portrait in terms of other questions: how "open" is the poem to the entry of the female voice? If Chaucer is to be read as subversive here, is he critical of *all* dogmas, including dogmatic assumptions about gender difference? What, again, is the function of the narrator's characteristic resemblance to the female character, and if this resemblance breaks down, as it has in the *Wife of Bath's Prologue* and *Tale*, the *Book of the Duchess*, and the *House of Fame*, then where does it do so, specifically, and why?

The narrator situates himself from the beginning in a place explicitly on the margins of the world he ostensibly evokes and celebrates in the dream, even more firmly and willfully outside the institution of heterosexual love than in the *Book of the Duchess* or the *House of Fame*. Only one stanza into the poem, for example, he hastens to point out that his understanding of the conventional oxymorons of love—its "dredful joye"—is not based on any personal experience: "For al be that I knowe nat Love in dede, / Ne wot how that he quiteth folk here hyre . . . " (8–9). The beginning of the dream emphasizes again precisely this point. Africanus brings the dreamer to a gate bearing two inscriptions "of ful gret difference" (125), messages which re-mark the well-known and terrifying paradox within the garden of love; this way lies bliss, this way

---

35. A standard description of the persona who emerges in all the dream-visions and the *Troilus* is available in Dorothy Bethurum's "Chaucer's Point of View as Narrator in the Love Poems," in *Chaucer Criticism*, vol. II, ed. Richard J. Schoeck and Jerome Taylor, pp. 211–31, reprinted from *PMLA* 74 (1959), pp. 511–20. Her study is particularly useful—and neglected—for its opening overview of the way in which Chaucer removes the poet from the frame as a lover, in contrast to all his sources: "The point is that they all adopted a position that demanded identification with the idealistic courtly view of love current from the twelfth to fourteenth centuries" (p. 211); Chaucer's sources assume, then, "an implicated poet." As I point out elsewhere in this study, what I want to interrogate is the myth of the unimplicated poet—the neutral, transcendent observer, compassionate and dispassionate—called into being, in large part, by Chaucer's poetry and its central place in the Western canon.

lies "mortal strokes" (135). As in the first stanza of the poem (see line 7), the narrator at first stresses his unknowingness and paralysis in the face of such a dilemma: "No wit hadde I, for errour, for to chese, / To entre or flen, or me to save or lese" (146–47). His experience obviously prefigures the inability to choose that we will see later in the Parliament, when the formel eagle confronts a true dilemma.[36] But already the confusing message on the gate turns out to represent a false dilemma for the male narrator. The contradiction it signals is not resolved, but simultaneously reinforced and avoided, when Africanus pushes him through the gate with the reassurance that the inscription simply doesn't apply in his case: " 'this writyng nys nothyng ment bi the . . . For thow of love hast lost thy tast, I gesse' " (158–60).[37]

The narrator does not directly claim any particular happiness or power—or any proof of masculinity—for himself as an indifferent man, or a nonlover, and Africanus compares him to a "sek man" (161), a weakling who "may nat stonde a pul" (164). The dreamer's perception of the birds' noise at the beginning of the Parliament, in lines 312–15, aptly sums up his anxious relation to the heterosexual desire assumed by the conventions of *fin amors:* he feels both hemmed in and pushed out, helplessly trapped and isolated inside a violent world where he fears there may be no place for him to stand. But at the same time there are clear benefits, given the nature of love depicted here, to his self-diagnosed disability. Or to put it in another way, at the same time that the poem registers so self-consciously the narrator's liabilities as a man and a lover, other aspects of the work convert them into assets. While he proposes no common bond with the young, aristocratic suitors, whose rhetoric is exposed for the particular illusions and anxieties it covers, he is still able to profit from the protective, educative relation with the male father figure, Africanus, who comes to give him, like Scipio Minor, a vision, or at least a push into the center of the excitement, when he would otherwise be frozen outside by his own fears and incapacities. Inside the garden he finds no single alternative realization of the "commune profyt," but he does find the compensatory thing that Africanus

36. Interestingly, Bethurum also compares him to Criseyde, "not knowing whether to risk it or not" ("Chaucer's Point of View," p. 219).

37. Africanus's remark is somewhat inconsistent with what the narrator himself says in the opening lines, for it suggests a present turning away from past experience in love ("for thow of love hast lost thy tast"), whereas the narrator earlier speaks in the present tense as if of a consistent and continued state of being ("I knowe nat Love in dede").

initially promises him and challenges him, in effect, to use, and that the poem itself represents: a text, a subject matter for writing: " 'And if thow haddest connying for t'endite, / I shal the shewe mater of to wryte' " (167–68).

Both before and after the dream, moreover, the narrator still experiences what he repeatedly represents, here and elsewhere, as perhaps his most prominent characteristic: an odd satisfaction with his ungratified state of arousal, a formative desire yoked above all to his engagement with texts. He has already told us, repeatedly, that he is an eager reader, just like the narrators of the other dream-visions. But in the others, especially in the *Book of the Duchess* and the *House of Fame*, reading old books is presented more plausibly as a compensatory activity, an anodyne for the narrator's own eight-year spell of lovesickness, perhaps, or a substitute for something that might just still be attained. The eagle, for instance, describes the dreamer as one who serves Love "Withoute guerdon ever *yit*" (*HF* 619, my emphasis). By contrast, the *Parliament* presents reading, thematically and structurally, as the primary activity, neither a remedy for nor a distraction from love nor merely analogous to it. When the narrator announces at the very beginning of the poem his own lack of experience in love, he also points out that his alleged obsession with the subject comes from reading: "Yit happeth me ful ofte in bokes reede ... " (10). In the pointedly aimless meandering of the opening stanzas, the narrator veers quickly away from the discussion of love broached in lines 11–14 and back to the subject of his reading: "Of usage—what for lust and what for lore— / On bokes rede I ofte, as I yow tolde. / But wherfore that I speke al this?" (15–17).

Characteristically bemused by his own forgetful ramblings, he answers his question by introducing what he will eventually identify as the particular occasion upon which he read the dream of Scipio:

> ... Nat yoore
> Agon, it happede me for to beholde
> Upon a bok, was write with lettres olde,
> And therupon, a certeyn thing to lerne,
> The longe day ful faste I redde and yerne.
> (17–21)

But still, before we learn the name of the book and find out why this particular reading experience is storyworthy, the narrator loops back to the question of reading in general. In perhaps the most revered and

frequently quoted passage from the poem, he offers an early celebration
of the pleasures of the text, with an emphasis on the radical escape from
temporality that is the cause and effect of his delight. To anticipate a
point I shall make more fully below, note that it is thus an escape that
stands in direct contrast to the formel's contract with time:

> For out of olde feldes, as men seyth,
> Cometh al this newe corn from yer to yere,
> And out of olde bokes, in good feyth,
> Cometh al this newe science that men lere . . .
> To rede forth hit gan me so delite,
> That al that day me thoughte but a lyte.
>
> (22–28)

The pleasure of reading, which makes time fly, is by no means depicted as a frivolous retreat here. When the daylight fails and the reader
must leave his book and go to bed, he falls asleep (after some time) "for
wery of my labour al the day" (93). The first thing that happens in the
dream is that an outside observer confirms the narrator's representation
of himself as a devoted and hard-working reader. Africanus begins by
explaining that the vision he brings will be a reward for toil as a reader,
" 'In lokynge of myn olde bok totorn' " (110). At the end of the dream,
the narrator reaffirms nothing except his serious and all-absorbing commitment to the morally improving task of reading, even where the exact
moral goal remains unstated or ineffable. Providing no summary comment on the significance of his dream, no clue to his own interpretation
of its meaning, he simply describes himself, once again, as a hopeful and
disciplined reader. Consider again the final lines, to which I have referred
earlier:

> And with the shoutyng, whan the song was do
> That foules maden at here flyght awey,
> I wok, and othere bokes tok me to,
> To reede upon, and yit I rede alwey.
> I hope, ywis, to rede so som day
> That I shal mete som thyng for to fare
> The bet, and thus to rede I nyl nat spare.
>
> (693–99)

His parting gesture of deferral is accompanied by a restatement of
what we already know—that the narrator likes to read—and what we
still aren't clearly told—precisely why he is so driven to books, what it

is he is working so hard to find. The state of the ending here recalls the conclusion of the *Book of the Duchess,* with its anticlimactic climax, reiterating the already known ("She ys ded") and at the same time providing no summative message of consolation before or after the dreamer awakes and the poem suddenly ends. Here, too, the narrator seems utterly untroubled by the fact that nothing has apparently been proved by the dream, or by the poem, except his failure to find the definitively indefinite "thyng that I wolde." The apparent incompletion of the *House of Fame* produces much the same effect, a sense that we are both missing something and seeing all there is or ever will be to see, something important, something that signifies in itself.

This odd, characteristically Chaucerian conclusion to the *Parliament* is read by modern critics as either a sign of failure or a mark of political or aesthetic open-endedness.[38] Yet neither explanation is completely satisfactory if we view the enterprise of the poem as not only the putative search for some moral or intellectual authority, but also the ongoing self-inscription and self-authorization of what we have come to know as the individual author of the signed work, the figure of a secular, vernacular poet with both an authoritative public place to stand and a private, individual vision to record, a personal relation to literary convention. This poem is framed by the clearly obscured self-portrait of the fictive author we are coming to know well, one who loves old books even as he resists subjection to their authority and who thereby lays claim to an unfocused desire that makes living and speaking possible: "I redde and yerne" (21); "yit I rede alwey. / I hope . . . " (696–97). The gratification he experiences, the end (the goal and the terminal point) of reading/ writing, is represented here as quest rather than attainment; as in all the dream-visions, the disquieting dream quite literally provides nothing more or less than the original substance of his own speaking. Without

38. Those who take it as a failure of one sort or another include Wilhelm, who emphasizes the heaviness of the narrator's feelings; "they pick up slightly at the end," he observes, "with the narrator's pitiful suggestion that a few more dippings into the *Patrologia Latina* might still produce that miraculously ambivalent thing that he was seeking back in the opening stanza" ("The Narrator," p. 206). Leicester, "The Harmony of Chaucer's *Parliament,*" less bleakly argues that the "project" of the poem—reading the dream in terms of traditional authority—fails because two things get in the way: the multiplicity of authority, and the subjectivity of experience. Readings that stress the open-endedness of the poem range from Bennett's belief in the hopefulness of the narrator's search and his claim that the last stanza "may be construed as holding the promise of all his later works" (*The Parlement of Foules,* p. 186) to Aers's very different (and yet fundamentally similar) construal of the more radical, highly "subversive" Chaucer.

complaint, the narrator postpones, not just for a year but for some explicitly indefinite period of time, the achieving of his quest; finality and certainty are thus both vaguely promised ("som day . . . to fare / The bet") and infinitely deferred ("I rede alwey. / I hope . . . som day . . . "). The ambiguity, the vagueness, and the delay again are posited here as the source of pleasure, not the obstacle to it that they represent in the natural world of the Parliament.

The place where the narrator stands in the *Parliament* is thus the same site for the author that, as Jesse Gellrich observes, is explicitly staked out in the *House of Fame:* a fictive position of real and subversive power that rejects "the Book of the past" for "his own text," to be constructed out of imaginative engagements with old stories of all sorts.[39] Or as David Lawton argues, "The narrator in the final stanza is entirely satisfied and in harmony with his books and his dream." "Nothing," Lawton says, "could be more straightforward or more affirmative than the conclusion that art is superior to love."[40] But such an authorial position and such an aesthetic affirmation entail a clear demarcation of the male narrator's difference from the female character he also resembles. The figure of the poet who yearns with a desire that is not (or not only) heterosexual or erotic is also the figure that at once brackets and occludes the threat to closure that the woman's lack of complicity always poses to both lovers and poets of love.

The difference between the temporally limited postponement sought by the formel and the narrator's more open-ended deferral suggests the crucial distinction between the power claimed for women, on one hand, and for the author, on the other. Unlike the formel, and unlike White, Alcyone, and Dido, the narrator is the unloved one who does not face, either sooner or later, conscription into the ideology of love.[41] A poet looking for a voice, he dreams of the nightmarish noise produced by heterosexual desire, fixed in the dream as a state of suspended frustration, and of the inadequacy of univocal moral or legal models of authority to suppress or control this noise. He also figures for himself a safe place, outside heterosexual love, from which he may at once continue his search for order and, at a comfortable remove from its consequences, actually profit from the inevitable failure of the quest, which spurs on

39. Gellrich, *Idea of the Book,* p. 174.
40. Lawton, *Chaucer's Narrators,* pp. 75 and 44 respectively.
41. Donaldson, *Chaucer's Poetry,* pp. 955–56.

the desires he identifies as useful and gratifying to himself as reader and writer.

By contrast, for all we know, the formel may feel no desire, sexual or textual, at all; she speaks only of deferring desire. Her gesture is thus not one of escape, but one of self-erasure, by the operative definition of selfhood dramatized in the poem, and female desire outside heterosexuality remains only obscurely visible at the edge of representation. Moreover, the woman character cannot forget or transcend temporality; the formel binds herself to time in a way that inevitably cancels her identity. If we project the formel beyond the end of the dream, along the lines she herself lays down, she is contracted to relinquish the power that she has temporarily seized. If we read no further than the closing moment of indecision, she is fixed forever in her indifference, like the images in Venus's temple, and hence ejected from (the) narrative beyond a certain point. Western literature tells stories about indifferent women chiefly if they are subsequently willing or forced to comply—and certainly these are the stories that Chaucerian fiction continues to retell, the stories of defeated Amazons (like the Knight's Emily), happily married victims of rape (like the Merchant's Proserpina), and reluctant paragons who are finally merciful (like White). But for indifferent men, the story is otherwise; Chaucer is one of the first writing in English in that long line of transcendent (male) artists whose moral posture is valued for its supposedly magisterial disinterest and tolerance, its androgyny, possibly, but above all its negative capability.

Both the formel and the narrator confront the impossibility of reciprocal love, which for them at least, chosen or not, represents the unattainability of ideal heterosexual union. The unmanly, unloved male poet constructs in the name of Chaucer a figure of masculine desire on the margins of heterosexuality and is thereby released into a world of resisting reading and the imagination it generates in a quest that many modern critics view as liberating and exemplary. As David Aers sees it, for example, Chaucer's search "is clearly going to be open-ended, finely resistant to authoritative and dogmatic closures of all kinds."[42] By the same confrontation with the impossibility of having anything she might

---

42. Aers, "*Parliament of Fowls,*" p. 14. See also Judith Ferster, in *Chaucer on Interpretation* (London: Cambridge University Press, 1985): "The poem views as a positive decision the narrator's willingness to engage with the world despite uncertainty. It is a sign of good faith and a form of loving" (p. 66).

imaginably want, the desired and desirable female character is in one way or another cast into a troubling silence. What sounds like a female voice again enters and leaves Chaucerian story not as an authoritative speaker, but as a problem. Antecedent systems of thought—in this case, both a classic moment of patriarchal rule and the ongoing discursive tradition of courtly love—are always represented as having failed to solve just this problem, and the narrator's resistance to their authority entails pointing out the errors and omissions in their construction of the female subject. His story nevertheless both rehearses and controls as problem the always unresolved position assigned to Woman, even as it refixes an enabling difference between the male poet and the female character.

6

Troilus and Criseyde:
"Beth war of men, and herkneth what I seye!"

In all of Chaucer's dream-visions, we see highly unnaturalistic female figures: a dead woman, a bird, literary legends considered as such. All are in large part absent, silenced, abandoned, in poems not in some senses about women at all. In what was for hundreds of years Chaucer's most admired poem, *Troilus and Criseyde*, we find a realistic female character whose importance in the text and in modern interpretive debates may appear to contrast sharply with the earlier representations of women and perhaps to pave the way for the creation of a female speaker like the Wife of Bath.[1] But how different is Criseyde from White, the formel, or Dido? Her legendary story served as a popular and consistent anti-feminist exemplum of the fickleness of woman throughout the Middle Ages and into the Renaissance in England; what is the relation of Chaucer's Criseyde to this tradition?

In a reading of the poem that might be assigned to the early feminist stage of Chaucer criticism, David Aers argues that in the character of Criseyde, Chaucer was "exploring the position of woman" and its contradictions. The poem indicts "society," Aers suggests, for its commodification of people and its "appalling destruction of a great human achievement." The achievement in question is specified as "mutual love, involving the total person," as Troilus and Criseyde allegedly experience it in Book III. But is this love truly mutual, and is Criseyde in fact a "total person," according to the poem? Aers's own discussion would suggest not, and in fact he all but sees the objection I would raise when he celebrates Troilus's "compassionate response" to Criseyde in Book V

---

1. See "Table of the Relative Popularity of Chaucer's Poems at Different Times" in Caroline F. E. Spurgeon, *Five Hundred Years of Chaucer Criticism and Allusion, 1357–1900* (Cambridge: Cambridge University Press, 1925), Vol. I., p. lxxix.

(1695–1701): here, Aers says, "Chaucer manifests the quality of love and commitment that has emerged from the relationship, *for the male at any rate*" (my emphasis).[2] But if it is only "for the male," how can it be considered "mutual" or "a great human achievement"? What does "at any rate" ask us not to worry about, not to look into? Must human—or is it male—"love and commitment" always depend, as it does here, on the construction of Woman not as empowered other, but as an object to be excited to love, sympathized with for her weakness and complicity, passed beyond, and judged? If so, how is mutuality possible? The easy slippage from "human achievement" to "for the male at any rate" is characteristic of a great deal of modern Chaucer criticism. What happens when we try to arrest it?

In *Troilus and Criseyde*, I shall argue, the rules of the game are different not only for male and female characters, but also for the figure of the male poet and his fictional heroine, with whom he sympathizes and with whom he shares salient traits. Both the narrator and Criseyde, it seems, live with, recognize, and come to symbolize what we now call the indeterminacy of language, the untrustworthiness and inadequacy of words, but the significance of this fact is read differently by modern critics in each case. For the narrator's alleged unwillingness to resolve the contradictions he sees in his world, for his openness to experience as opposed to dogma, and for his good intentions, at least, toward Criseyde, Chaucer is today often celebrated as a great poet, even by critics who disagree about the meaning of his greatness.[3] If any character in *Troilus and Criseyde* shares some of these signs of greatness, however, surely it is Criseyde. She lives with endless contradictions: as Constance Saintonge was the first, to my knowledge, to point out, she is hated, demeaned, and scorned for the very qualities that her culture tells her are valuable and proper in a woman: obedience, submission, and flexibility.[4] Like the narrator, she is also open to change; when faced with exile among her enemies, she bends to new experience and chooses the

2. "Criseyde: Woman in Medieval Society," *Chaucer Review* 13 (1979), pp. 177–200; the quotations are found, respectively, on pp. 179, 190, 188, and 195.

3. See for example Richard Waswo, "The Narrator of *Troilus and Criseyde*," *ELH* 50 (1983), pp. 1–25; Evan Carton, "Complicity and Responsibility in Pandarus's Bed and Chaucer's Art," *PMLA* 94 (1979), pp. 47–61; Aers, "Criseyde: Woman in Medieval Society," and Barbara Newman, " 'Feynede Loves,' Feigned Lore, and Faith in Trouthe," in *Chaucer's Troilus: Essays in Criticism* (Hamden, CT: Shoestring Press, 1980) pp. 257–75.

4. "In Defense of Criseyde," *Modern Language Quarterly* 15 (1954), pp. 312–20.

only means to survival. Throughout, we are told, her intentions are, or seem to be, good.

But Criseyde, unlike the narrator and/or author, is praised for none of these traits; why not? Is it because she stops reading and risks emotional entanglement, while he stays safely away from any practical involvement in love? Or is it that he knows what he's doing, while Criseyde merely acts as she does out of necessity and is as determined by the discourse that she speaks as by her gender? Aers, again, implies as much in contrasting Criseyde's lack of "adequate consciousness" in Book III (where he says she is not really in control but is enacting "the complex submission of a victim to the dominating groups that control her world") with "Chaucer's own insight and art," which see and reveal the victim's plight as she, the victim, cannot.[5] This is a troubling conclusion, however, for if we are to give Chaucer the credit for aesthetic and moral greatness, then we must assume that it is Chaucer who controls the degree of consciousness that Criseyde exhibits. To what extent does criticism mirror without seeing the fact that the artist's "insight and art," including the illusion that he stands outside discourse and politics himself, depend on portraying a woman as unself-conscious victim, reifying her victimization? When the two are so alike in their material and symbolic relations to the problems of meaning in particular, how is it that the poet becomes a judge of meaning, while this female character remains a figure whose meaning is precisely what must and can be judged?

"Is this a mannes herte?"

III.1098

In Chaucer's version of the opening scene at the Palladian feast, based on stanzas 18–31 of the first part of Il Filostrato, Troilus's sudden capitulation to the love he has previously scorned and mocked is curiously interrupted, and virtually told twice.[6] In the first telling (183–210), Troilus, devoted to no lady himself, appears in the temple leading a group of

---

5. "Criseyde: Woman in Medieval Society," p. 191.
6. For the purposes of analyzing what Chaucer "does" to Il Filostrato, I have found indispensable the parallel text edition by B. A. Windeatt, Troilus and Criseyde: A New Edition of "The Book of Troilus" (London and New York: Longman, 1984). The text of Il Filostrato used by Windeatt, from which I quote in this chapter, is G. Boccaccio, Filostrato and Ninfale fiesolano, ed. V. Pernicone (Bari: Gius, Laterza & Figli, 1937).

young men and busily mocking all those around him whom he sees falling in love. Overhearing this blasphemy, the God of Love takes revenge by shooting Troilus with Love's arrow: "For sodeynly he hitte hym atte fulle; / And yet as proud a pekok kan he pulle" (I.209–10). Here then we see Troilus acted upon by the timeless agency of the male god, Cupid; the proud knight is the victim, the prey, the passive recipient of love's wound. This scene takes place well before Troilus is said to have seen Criseyde; as in so many medieval fictions, the young man falls in love with love even before he has a female object on which to focus his attentions, and it is made clear that he does so because of the agency of a superior male force, the God of Love, whom he has attempted to thwart.

At this point, the narrator interrupts the plot for fifty lines (I.211ff.) with the first of what we come to know as his characteristic, often didactic and self-reflexive digressions. Rehearsing the familiar *doctrina* of love, he observes that proud men must be "subgit" (I.231) to its power; there is no "fredom" (I.235) from this servitude, and he advises willing acceptance of the inevitable. The digression ends with an elaborate, metafictional comment on the need to get back to the story and "leten other thing collateral" (I.262), a concession that alerts readers to the fact that the narrator's pervasive interest in the conventional ideology of love, and its constraining psychological and social implications for men, is anything but collateral.[7]

Then, as the story moves back to the temple and the narrator rejoins his source-text, his description of Troilus's fall seems to start all over again, as we return to a preconversion Troilus:

> Withinne the temple he wente hym forth pleyinge,
> This Troilus, of every wight aboute,
> On this lady, and now on that, lokynge,
> Wher so she were of town or of withoute;
> And upon cas bifel that thorugh a route
> His eye percede, and so depe it wente,
> Til on Criseyde it smot, and ther it stente.
>
> And sodeynly he wax therwith astoned. . . .
>
> (I.267–74)

---

7. For a different discussion of the interpolation, see P. M. Kean, "Chaucer's Dealings with a Stanza of *Il Filostrato* and the Epilogue of *Troilus and Criseyde*," *Medium Aevum* 33 (1964), pp. 36–46.

Where are we, in terms of chronology and perspective, as we read this passage? Are we to assume that Troilus has already been wounded, as we learned earlier, but doesn't feel anything until he sees Criseyde? Or are lines 204–10 to be forgotten—are we starting the story all over again in line 267, this time with a more direct, naturalistic depiction of the episode, one that dispenses with the concealing fiction of Cupid and his arrows, and thereby implies, perhaps, that Cupid is just the little boy in Troilus himself and in every male lover of women? For in lines I.267–74, as in *Il Filostrato* and the literary tradition it follows, it is Troilus who is now actively charged with the responsiblity and agency of the glance that, although it is accidental, seals his fate. With a clear sexual innuendo that contrasts sharply with the narrator's talk of submission and constraint, this male gaze actively penetrates the crowd and smites and fixes (on) Criseyde herself. The consequence of this penetration, however, is explicitly (in Chaucer only) a kind of paralysis for Troilus: after seeing Criseyde, "sodeynly he wax therwith astoned" (I.274).

In this line, the verb "wax," together with the suggestion of stones, or testicles, at least makes possible the understanding that Troilus has an erection at the mere sight of the lady; no knowledge or reciprocal action on her part is necessary or indicated. At the same time, the term "astoned" complicates an understanding of what such independent, even involuntary phallic hardening means. Elsewhere in the poem, it is either Criseyde or a man in a highly feminized position who is "astoned," and always the term or some variant is used not with a verb like "waxen," but with verbs that suggest only minimal motion, such as sitting, standing, or moving "softely" (see, for instance, II.600, IV.354–55, and V.1728–29).[8] In the semantic context of the poem as a whole, then, the tag (or euphemism) in line I.274 not only hints at Troilus's arousal but at the same time reveals what is problematic: the instable, provisional, and uncontrollable quality of what would seem to be an indisputable index of maleness, and the paradoxical powerlessness,

8. But see Chaucer's *Boece* for an apparently innocent use of "wax . . . astoned," describing the speaker after Philosophy casts out the poetical muses in Prosa 1, lines 78–79. In "Chaucer's Continental Inheritance," in *The Cambridge Chaucer Companion*, ed. Jill Mann and Piero Boitano (Cambridge: Cambridge University Press, 1986), David Wallace notes precisely this repeated usage of the romance tag-phrase as an example of his claim that Chaucer "budgets for moments when our concentration may slacken. . . . the reader or listener may nod for a line or two" (p. 32). We *may* nod, of course, but I am suggesting that we may also miss something if we do.

dependence, and perhaps embarrassment of even the most potent male at the mere sight of a woman who does not, as far as we can tell, return his look or know that she has been seen, smitten, and (at least figuratively, for now) penetrated.

Compounding and protracting the representation of male sexuality as a problematic and unstable experience, a few stanzas later the narrator suggests again (harkening back, perhaps, to the earlier telling) that it is in fact *Troilus's*, not Criseyde's, interior parts that have been reflexively penetrated by a thoroughly ambiguous agency. First, as he watches her with pleasure (I.288–89), Troilus sees Criseyde's little "deignous" gesture (I.290) and the brighter look that follows it:

> . . . for she let falle
> Hire look a lite aside in swich manere,
> Ascaunces, "What! may I nat stonden here?"
> And after that hir lokynge gan she lighte,
> That nevere thoughte hym seen so good a syghte.
>
> (I.290–94)

From this moment, Troilus's desire once again is said to be growing, and again a stanza is added in Chaucer's revision of *Il Filostrato:*

> And of hire look in him ther gan to quyken
> So gret desir and such affeccioun,
> That in his hertes botme gan to stiken
> Of hir his fixe and depe impressioun.
> And though he erst hadde poured up and down,
> He was tho glad his hornes in to shrinke;
> Unnethes wiste he how to loke or wynke.
>
> (I.295–301)

Commenting on these lines, Winthrop Wetherbee argues that the verbs "quyken" and "stiken," with grammatical subjects that are not Troilus but his desire and his impressions, indicate that Troilus's experience "happens to him"; his "only action" is to draw in his horns.[9] But the syntactically fronted element here, the putative source and goal of his passion, "hire look in him," in line I.295, is ambiguous with regard to agency—does it refer to Criseyde's appearance, her passive, looked-

---

9. *Chaucer and the Poets: An Essay on "Troilus and Criseyde"* (Ithaca: Cornell University Press, 1984), p. 184. Troilus himself seems to endorse this reading of the power relations in II.533–39.

upon (by Troilus) looks, or to Criseyde's gaze, her active looking? The preceding stanza has made either reading possible, for while Troilus has been watching "hire mevynge and hire chere," her outward appearance, he has also seen the expressive, mobile, possibly seductive look she actively gives in lines I.290–93, which itself prefigures in its movement the appropriate feminine trajectory from aloof disdain to a more welcoming fairness. (At the beginning of the scene in the Temple, moreover, Criseyde stood alone, but "with ful assured *lokyng* and manere" [I.182].) In line I.295, then, "hire look in him" may refer back to her own active, expressive glance, or it may allude to the piercing, smiting gaze of Troilus and what that gaze fixes. The more active role of the male seems to be confirmed in line I.298, for what is both quickening and sticking in the bottom of Troilus's heart is *his* impression of her, which again gives agency (and possession) to his own gaze (and perhaps hints at the gap between "impressioun" and reality). Yet by lines I.300–1, in contrast to his earlier "pouring" up and down, the hero is bashful, frightened, perhaps humble, and confused; even, the metaphor of the shrinking horns might imply, detumescent.[10]

Just a few lines later, the agency only implicitly and possibly attributed to Criseyde in the phrase "hire look" is further qualified by a fairly direct translation of a conventional claim in *Il Filostrato*: "Love hadde his dwellynge / Withinne the subtile stremes of hir yen" (I.304–5; compare "che Amor dimorasse dentro al raggio / di quei vaghi occhi con li dardi sui" [*Il Filostrato*, I.29.3–4]). We clearly return here to the earlier argument for the external agency of love, which seems to imply that neither gender has much control over what is happening. The woman's look, powerful as it may be, is merely the container or site of a power not hers to wield at will; at the same time, the effect on Troilus, now as before (and later), is paralyzing: "sodeynly hym thoughte he felte dyen, / Right with hire look, the spirit in his herte" (I.306–7).

Altogether, this complicated and protracted presentation of Troilus's allegedly precipitous fall into love, interrupted by the narrator's lengthy

10. The reference to Troilus's shrinking or pulling in of his horns is glossed in Fisher "abating his ardor," but given the association of horns with cuckoldry (see *Middle English Dictionary, horn* 1c) we may also suspect the anticipated betrayal of Troilus. Windeatt calls attention to an essay by Siegfried Wenzel, "Chaucer and the Language of Contemporary Preaching," *Studies in Philology* 73 (1976), pp. 138–61, in which Wenzel finds that in addition to the fear or cowardice suggested in many uses of the proverb, one instance also employs the phrase to suggest humility.

aside about the conventional cultural discourse in which he enmeshes
his characters and then elaborately drawn out, raises many more questions than it can answer about gender roles and agency in heterosexual
relations. In interpreting the whole episode, whom should we see as
penetrated by whom or what? Is Criseyde smitten with Troilus's gaze,
as lines I.272–3 suggest? Or is she something even less than a passive
recipient, at this point, if in fact Troilus is struck with his own "impressioun" of Criseyde, as in lines I.295–9, or with the mysterious power in
the wattage she emits, as in lines I.304–5? Does the power of love come
from the God of Love, as in lines I.206–10; or from the (accidental?)
lighting of Troilus's own penetrating gaze on Criseyde, fixing her as the
object of his previously generalized girl-watching, as in lines I.267–73; or
could the power somehow belong to Criseyde's own "lokynge," or at
least to a part of her own self, the lady's eyes and the rays that they
"stick" in Troilus's heart?

Courtly convention, the rhetorical strategy of a quasi-oral telling, or
even authorial or scribal lapse can account for the apparent confusion in
this plethora of possibilities.[11] Those who argue for the mutuality of the
love between Troilus and Criseyde might see it foreshadowed here in
the ambivalence of the situation, for both male and female are given
some agency and some passivity; both are also subjects of the higher
power of love. But to the extent that there is a myth of mutuality in this
poem, we do not see it yet; Book I is clearly about *Troilus's* falling in
love. In light of what subsequently happens, I suggest that the narrative
technique here calls attention from the outset to the question of agency
and power in heterosexual relations, to the confusion within courtly
ideology over precisely this issue, and to the problems of male sexuality
in particular, which the conventions of romantic love both conceal and
exacerbate through the emphasis on role reversal. The problem that we
saw in all the earlier dream-visions is literalized and treated (somewhat)
realistically here, and it becomes a crucial issue that the rest of the poem
addresses. The courtly, aristocratic male lover in the very act of falling
in love is, by convention and by rhetoric, rendered to some degree passive and submissive; he is subject to the God of Love, to the idea, at
least, of the lady, and to his own impression of her; he is, in the terms I

11. On sources in Greek, Arabic, and classical poetry of the notion that "eyes serve
not only as perceivers of beauty but also as agents" see Ruth H. Cline, "Heart and Eyes,"
Romance Philology 25 (1972), pp. 263–97.

am trying to use and examine here, feminized and interiorized by love, or by the language of love. He is nevertheless still ostensively seeking a heterosexual relation; he fixes a real woman in his gaze as the beloved object and so must go outside himself to penetrate her real body in sexual union; in an important sense being a lover is supposed to prove, not undermine, his manhood and his class status. The would-be virtuous nobleman who loves a woman is therefore in at least a theoretical bind from which escape is all but impossible.

The postconversion story substantiates what is suggested by the temple scene. Love is as debilitating for Troilus as he knew it would be, and later Pandarus and even Criseyde are, with good reason, anxious about the threat to his manhood posed by his new status as lover. In the first direct reference to the problem, Troilus thinks to himself that to die of love would be both "unmanhod" (I.824) and sin; it would be tedious to catalogue at this point the ways in which, however, it is living for love, here as in all the dream-visions, that actually threatens to unman the typical male sufferer from lovesickness (in Chaucer, with a few exceptions, a disease specific to men).[12] Troilus's conventional, unmanly behavior reaches new heights in Book III, where the infamous bedroom scene, as Chaucer shapes it, confirms the real difficulty: if the lover is as conventionally submissive, frightened, infantilized, and unmanned by love as he is supposed to be, he will not be able to perform like a man in an actual heterosexual encounter.

In this central scene, Troilus has been hiding in narrow, interior places for a long time.[13] When he finally enters Criseyde's bedroom, he is so stricken by her distress that he goes completely limp: he hangs his head, falls to his knees, and begs forgiveness. Then even his tears (symptomatic of other bodily fluids as well?) dry up, and according to the narrator his "vigour" is seriously diminished:

> Therwith the sorwe so his herte shette,
> That from his eyen fil ther nought a tere,

12. Two exceptions I can think of are May in the *Merchant's Tale* and Dido in the *Legend of Good Women* (see especially lines 1162–67). In other medieval literary texts, men and women often suffer from lovesickness equally; on this subject, see Mary Frances Wack, "The Measure of Pleasure: Peter of Spain on Men, Women, and Lovesickness," *Viator* 17 (1986), pp. 173–96.

13. For a detailed discussion of the probable historical conditions of Troilus's hiding places in Book III, see H. M. Smyser, "The Domestic Background of *Troilus and Criseyde*," *Speculum* 31 (1956), pp. 297–315.

And every spirit his vigour in knette,
So they astoned or oppressed were.
(III.1086–89)

The narrator may further hint, delicately and humorously, at the impotence of premature ejaculation as he describes the catatonic lover: "The felyng of his sorwe, or of his fere, / Or of aught elles, fled was out of towne; / And down he fel al sodeynly a-swowne" (III.1090–92, my emphasis).[14] As Pandarus heaves the flaccid hero into bed, he underscores the problem: " 'O thef, is this a mannes herte?' " (III.1098). When Criseyde joins in the effort to revive Troilus with kisses and caresses, she makes the same point: " 'Is this a mannes game?' " (III.1126).

Before their ideal love can become sexual union, the role reversal of courtly love, the softening and unmanning of Troilus, must be undone; Troilus must be made to feel like a man before he can perform like one. So, after he begs for and receives Criseyde's forgiveness, she in turn asks him to forgive her for the hurt she has supposedly done him, and calls him her "swete herte" (III.1183). Surprised, since courtly ladies customarily grant mercy, rather than ask for it, Troilus begins to act like an aggressor: "He hire in armes faste to hym hente" (III.1187). Pandarus is able to withdraw, and the narrator is able to ask an odd question that further serves to restore Troilus, rhetorically at least, to the role of active male, or even predator: "What myghte or may the sely larke seye, / Whan that the sperhauk hath it in his foot?" (III.1191–2). Although the comment clearly alludes to Criseyde's dream of the eagle in Book II, a reader paying attention to the behavior of the actors in this scene may wonder who is supposed to be the lark and who the hawk. The following stanza confirms that the characters now play the necessary, proper masculine and feminine roles. Criseyde, the equivocally innocent lark, is said to feel herself "itake," and "Right as an aspes leef she gan to quake, / Whan she hym felte hire in his armes folde" (III.1198–1201). Troilus speaks in appropriately combative terms of her capture and necessary surrender as he strains her in his embrace: " 'O swete, as evere mot I gon, / Now be ye kaught, now is ther but we tweyne! / Now yeldeth yow, for other bote is non!' " (1206–8). One effect of the hero's newly hardened, combative stance is to remind us of the realistic imbalance of

14. See also Edward I. Condren, "Transcendent Metaphor or Banal Reality: Three Chaucerian Dilemmas," *Papers in Language and Literature* 21 (1985), pp. 233–57.

power in the lovers' relationship. Troilus, the son of Priam, is in a position of legal and social dominance, soon to be augmented by moral superiority, over the daughter of the traitor Calchas. His unmanly behavior before the consummation serves among other things to gloss over the brutal fact that he gets what he wants, and it allows Criseyde to appear to consent to what would otherwise resemble all too closely the lark's powerless surrender to the sparrowhawk's attack.[15]

Even the stable difference that might seem to be thus revealed and grounded in the biological act of heterosexual intercourse, however, is short-lived in this poem. Before the stanza is out, Criseyde once again unsettles the clear gender difference and asymmetry of power presupposed by orthodox heterosexuality. In response to his command to yield, she offers her infamous answer: " 'Ne hadde I er now, my swete herte deere, / Ben yold, ywis, I were now nought heere!" (III.1210–11). Whatever it means about her own state of mind, her comment undercuts Troilus's play at manliness and reminds us that the apparent return to proper gender hierarchy—female and male, the lark and the hawk—is at this point only apparent and expeditious. The whole bedroom scene, wherein Troilus finally is able to gratify his physical desire, confirms what I suggest is implicated in the temple scene, where all this desire was first aroused: romantic or courtly love, as experienced by these characters and in the conventional code by which they are shaped, is a complex performance in which traditional masculine and feminine roles are confused and the problematic instability and provisionality of gender thereby enacted.

While Troilus's resistance to his feminization begins to take active shape in Book IV, it is not an easy process, and still in Book V his nightmares suggest that he unconsciously recognizes (and wishes for?) his affinity with women; he dreams that he is experiencing precisely what Criseyde is in fact undergoing, "the dredefulleste thynges / That myghte ben":

> . . . as, mete he were allone
> In place horrible, makyng ay his mone,
> Or meten that he was amonges alle
> His enemys, and in hire hondes falle.
> (V.248–52)

---

15. Richard F. Green also sees this as an image of "Troilus's inevitable sexual dominance over Criseyde" ("Troilus and the Game of Love," *Chaucer Review* 13 [1979], p. 216).

Troilus's dream not only evinces his identification with Criseyde but also reminds us that he is living in a beseiged city and is a warrior as well as a lover. A projection of his divided identity, the dream reinforces the fact that this war affords him no alternative, public sphere in which he can develop as a real man, without a taint of the private and the feminine. Theoretically, it might seem that war, in this poem and in the chivalric code, functions in part as an outlet for the aggression that the courtly lover must sublimate, a forum in which the manly behavior that he appears to surrender to Love can be condoned and reaffirmed. War would also seem to allow men to evade the difficulty apparently inherent in the whole sphere of heterosexual relations: with women safely out of the way, men should be able both to bond with each other against a common enemy and to compete. (As we see in the *Parliament of Fowls* and again in the *Knight's Tale*, competition between men is in fact a sanctioned way of bonding within gender and class groupings.) Back in the heterosexual world, there might be yet a further benefit to the warrior, as his prowess may whet the desire of the lady. Indeed, Criseyde's first obvious inclination to love Troilus comes when she spies him riding through the gates of the city, fresh from battle, on his bleeding horse, wearing his battered helmet and shield. The sexual implications of this bloody ride through narrow gates are brought out in her infamous blushing response: " 'Who yaf me drynke?' " (II.651). Here the ideologies of love and war seem to work together, shaping and shaped by male experience and serving men's interests.

But *Troilus and Criseyde* does not so easily restore the problematized manliness of the lover and allow us to understand war simply as a manifestation of or solution to problems of masculine identity. The poem suggests, instead, that even war, an all-male affair in which the narrator claims not to be very interested, poses a threat to the idea of stable gender identity, and hence to the very kind of masculinity that it seems designed to express and confirm. War obviously imperils some male bonds at the same time that it offers a forum in which others may be forged. In war, one side loses and is therefore at least figuratively dominated and unmanned, as Troilus's dream of being alone among his enemies suggests. (The story of the Calydonian boar, alluded to in Cassandra's interpretation of Troilus's later dream, also underlines the point; when Ancaeus of Calydon, stunned and challenged by the manly behavior of the maiden Atalanta, rushes into battle, he is castrated by Diana's avenger.) In the particular war the poem describes, Troy is the losing side, and as other commentators have pointed out, the poem repeatedly affirms the feminized nature of the doomed city: an enclosed space, a city of allegedly brave and lustful men like Paris in thrall to Helen and unmanfully devoting themselves, as the episodes in the temple and at Sarpedoun's palace suggest, to frivolity, the game of love, and other lighthearted pleasures.[16] The way these heroes are unmanned by war is also revealed in the proposed exchange of Antenor for Criseyde, which not only implies her status as a prisoner but at the same time equates the revered martial hero (who turns out to be a traitor) with a mere woman. Finally, everyone knows the reason for this war—an archetypal war, *the* war of Greek mythology and the literary imagination—in the first place: the Greeks have come to Troy because Agamemnon was cuckolded and because they were worried about their failure as men to protect their women from the competing lust of other men. War, like love, is a sphere in which anxiety about the aggressive masculinity it seems to affirm is both cause (for the Greeks) and result (for the Trojans). Whether between men and women or between men alone, any stable relation of culturally gendered oppositions like passive and active, prey and predator, loser and winner, inferior and superior is temporary at best.

The imbrication of lover and warrior that we see here, and the concurrent anxiety about masculinity that men in both positions suffer, retrospectively gives new meaning to the figure of Troilus as he appears at the end of Book I, in the odd tableau that the Chaucerian text arranges after Pandarus vows to help Troilus win Criseyde. One stanza expands the moment in *Il Filostrato* when Troilo hugs and kisses Pandaro thus:

> Tho Troilus gan doun on knees to falle,
> And Pandare in his armes hente faste,
> And seyde, "Now, fy on the Grekes alle!
> Yet, pardee, God shal helpe us atte laste.
> And dredelees, if that my lyf may laste,
> And God toforn, lo, som of hem shal smerte;
> And yet m'athinketh that this avant m'asterte!

16. For other commentaries on the feminization of Troy and Troilus, see John McCall, "The Trojan Scene in Chaucer's 'Troilus,' " in *Chaucer's Troilus*, pp. 101–113; Stephen Barney, "Troilus Bound," *Speculum* 47 (1972), p. 458; Adrienne R. Lockhart, "Semantic, Moral, and Aesthetic Degeneration in *Troilus and Criseyde*," *Chaucer Review* 8 (1973), pp. 100–118; Robert E. Kaske, "The Aube in Chaucer's *Troilus*," in *Chaucer Criticism: Volume II. Troilus and Criseyde and the Minor Poems*, ed. Richard J. Schoeck and Jerome Taylor (Notre Dame: University of Notre Dame Press, 1961), pp. 166–79.

"Now, Pandare, I kan na more seye,
But, thow wis, thow woost, thow maist, thow art al
My lif, my deth, hol in thyn hond I leye.
Help now!" Quod he, "Yis, by my trowthe, I shal."

(I.1044–54)

Troilus's apparently instinctive response here reveals the aggression, nervousness, and ambivalence that accompany his aroused sexuality. He kneels, embodying the feminized position of both the conventional devotee of love and the royal son of a beseiged city—and he thus mimics the position in which we first see Criseyde, "On knees" before Hector (I.106–12), dependent, subservient, and prayerful. But the object of his appeal and his embrace is not the loved one, nor the (potential) enemy, but the male friend with whom he feels (or, in his own interests, pretends to feel) a deeper bond.[17] The homoerotic cast to this scene is intensified not so much when Troilus embraces Pandarus as when he speaks words to Pandarus that are elsewhere directed to the lady, laying his life in Pandarus's hands and seeking his mercy. The boast of a warrior that first escapes his lips even as he kneels in the gesture of a grateful lover—"Now, fy on the Grekes alle!"—both points up the aggressive underpinnings of sexual desire, which he has just denied (in I.1030–36), and suggests that what he hopes to prove in attaining Criseyde is not his gentle subservience but his threatened dominance, his destablized manliness. This confused (for Troilus) and revealing moment symbolizes all that the poem as a whole implies about the interaction of courtly and heroic codes and the problems that beset masculine identity in both spheres. Feminized by, among other things, the inescapable circumstances of the Trojan War, Troilus seeks proof of his masculinity in the love of the most womanly woman; the conventions of love, however, are themselves at least as feminizing as those of war, and the hero is once again represented as a man caught in a vicious circle from which he cannot escape in this life.

Troilus, moreover, is representative: although the focus is on him, he is far from alone in his sufferings either as a private lover or as a male

---

17. For discussions of the topic of male friendship in the poem with widely differing conclusions, see E. E. Slaughter, "Chaucer's Pandarus: Virtuous Uncle and Friend," *Journal of English and Germanic Philology* 48 (1949), pp. 186–95; Alan Gaylord, "Friendship in Chaucer's *Troilus*," *Chaucer Review* 3 (1969), pp. 239–64; Leah Rieber Freiwald, "Swych Love of Frendes: Pandarus and Troilus," *Chaucer Review* 6 (1972), pp. 120–29.

citizen and warrior of Troy, and other men are feminized in similar ways by the densely interwoven circumstances of love and war in this story. Pandarus momentarily escapes from the subjugation and humiliation of both Troy's military situation and his own reportedly unsuccessful love affair into the active, controlling role he plays in bringing Troilus's desire to fruition. His managerial career, however, is short-lived; by the beginning of Book IV, when the exchange is announced, he is unable to devise a successful plan. In the last book, Pandarus for the first time is said to be constrained by political circumstances (see V.281–86); at a loss for words, he can only try to divert Troilus with the unmanly entertainment at Sarpedoun's. The last time we see him he resembles Troilus in Book III, for different reasons silenced—"He nought a word ayeyn to hym answerde" (V.1725)—and paralyzed, not in erect, manly astonishment like Troilus in Book I, but in frustration and speechlessness: "astoned . . . As stille as ston; a word ne kowde he seye" (IV.1728–9).

As Criseyde's uncle, Pandarus also represents the failure of the older male generation to protect Criseyde, a lack of traditional manly virtue portrayed too in Calchas, who abandons his daughter until his renewed interest can do her more harm than good. Calchas's self-serving betrayal of Troy subverts the chief patriarchal virtue of loyalty to the city-state that Troilus later embodies, and his wiliness and prophetic skills suggest traits often assigned inside and outside the poem to women. Even Hector, the older brother and the only man said to be stronger than Troilus himself, is unable to protect Criseyde, although he claims to wish to do so. But no man in the poem can offer the wall of manly steel that a woman as weak and endangered as Criseyde would arguably need and that she herself thinks she has found in Troilus. In the next section, I ask what this means in terms of the figure who is constructed by this story to account for the failure of human love, truth, language itself: Criseyde. For despite the poem's critique of both romantic and martial heroism and its resistance to any simple solution to the problems of manliness, Criseyde as archetype of *wommanhede* is still positioned in the place of, as the figure of, all moral and linguistic error and instability.

She that nyste what was best to rede.
I.96

In an early description of Criseida in the temple, Boccaccio says that she surpasses other ladies in beauty as the rose surpasses the violet.[18] The Chaucerian rendering of the passage substitutes for this conventional poetic figure a comparison that has been described as both "bizarre" and "prosaic": "Right as oure firste lettre is now an A, / In beaute first so stood she, makeles" (I.171–72). To my knowledge, only an historical explanation has been offered to account for this odd revision—Chaucer means to compliment Anne of Bohemia.[19] However, the substitution may better bespeak the specific textuality and conventionality of the Chaucerian Criseyde and of the feminine position in culture and language as it is confronted and constituted in this poem. Criseyde's beauty is first among women, peerless and preeminent, just as A is the first letter of the alphabet; the Western poetic system of signs and symbols in which the story is written begins, as it were, with the character of the beautiful Woman. Like a letter of the alphabet, she incites reading and writing. She is available for use in the composition of infinite numbers of larger units of writing (words and texts); alone she has no meaning, but as part of these larger units she means different things at different times.

Such a comparison begins to suggest, too, what so many modern commentators have described as Criseyde's most important trait: her ambiguity, her slipperiness as both a sign and a represented personality. As Charles Muscatine puts it in an oft-quoted formulation, "The difficulty of assessing the nature of Criseyde is almost proverbial. . . . Her ambiguity is her meaning."[20] Mark Lambert gives credit to Criseyde's ambiguity for the appeal of the poem as a whole: "It is in good part because the reader must keep reinterpreting her that the entire poem shimmers as it does."[21] Both Criseyde's notorious ambiguity and modern readers' pleasure in it, however, merit reconsideration and qualification.

---

18. "la qual, quanto la rosa la viola / di bilta vince, cotanto era questa / piu ch'altra donna, bella" (I.19.3–5).

19. John Livingston Lowes, "The Date of Chaucer's *Troilus and Criseyde*," *PMLA* 23 (1908), pp. 285–306. Lowes cites Sandras, *Etude sur Geoffrey Chaucer* (1859, pp. 45–46), who thought the simile was "bizarre"; Lowes himself calls it "to say the least prosaic" (p. 286).

20. *Chaucer and the French Tradition* (Berkeley: University of California Press, 1957), p. 164. Other recent discussions of this issue include Peter R. Schroeder, "Hidden Depths: Dialogue and Characterization in Chaucer and Malory," *PMLA* 98 (1983), pp. 374–87 and Maureen Fries, " 'Slydynge of Corage': Chaucer's Criseyde as Feminist and Victim," in *The Authority of Experience: Essays in Feminist Criticism*, ed. Arlyn Diamond and Lee R. Edwards (Amherst: University of Massachusetts Press, 1977), pp. 45–59.

21. "*Troilus*, Books I–III," in Mary Salu, ed., *Essays on Troilus and Criseyde* (Cambridge and Totowa, N.J.: D. S. Brewer, Roman and Littlefield, 1979), p. 105.

Following an exhaustive analysis of analogues both previous and subsequent to Chaucer's *Troilus and Criseyde*, another modern scholar, Gretchen Mieszkowski, has argued that Criseyde's "final meaning" is fully fixed: no medieval reader would be fooled into thinking, as many twentieth-century critics have thought, that the apparent sympathy of Chaucer's narrator for his version of Criseyde reflected any true departure from her traditional function as a type of female weakness and unreliability.[22] Two rarely discussed aspects of Chaucer's rendering of this story support Mieszkowski's point and extend its significance: first, Criseyde's characterization as a realistic female personality against a backdrop of mythic women; and second, the ambiguity of the men in the poem, whose words and actions Criseyde is obliged to interpret. Criseyde herself is just ambiguous enough to seem like a real woman, sufficiently in control of her intentions (which we can never fully know) to be held accountable for her behavior, but not strong enough to escape her fate, the meaning imposed on her.

The first strategy I want to explore by which *Troilus and Criseyde* actually fixes Criseyde's final meaning entails consideration of the mythic background that is original to Chaucer's version of this old story. In Criseyde, the central and psychologically developed female character, the narrative embodies one side of the double figure of fallen woman in the Middle Ages—her lack of control over her body, the world around her, and even the inner world of her own beliefs and perceptions—while alluding in embedded stories of other literary women to the other side of the picture—stereotypically feminine powers that prove dangerous to men. To put it another way, we might say that Criseyde is in the psychologically realistic foreground of the poem; but her meaning and function are shaped in part by the deployment of her character against a well-developed literary tradition that offers sharply contrasting images of women.

Early in the poem, this background intersects the foreground in the allusion to the Ovidian tale of Procne and Philomela that frames the long opening scene of Book II, wherein Pandarus first speaks to Criseyde

22. "The Reputation of Criseyde: 1155–1500," *Transactions of the Connecticut Academy of Arts and Sciences* 43 (1971), pp. 71–153; see also J. D. Burnley, "Criseyde's Heart and the Weakness of Women: An Essay in Lexical Interpretation," *Studia Neophilologica* 54 (1982), pp. 25–38.

on Troilus's behalf.[23] Initially, Pandarus is wakened from his own love-sick half-sleep by "The swalowe Proigne, with a sorowful lay" (II.64), who "so neigh hym made hire cheterynge / How Tereus gan forth hire suster take" (II.68–69), and he sets off forthwith for his niece's palace (II.77).[24] The valence of the brief allusion at this point is not clear, or at least not single. There may be an indirect parallel, for example, between Tereus's betrayal of a sister-in-law in the myth and Pandarus's betrayal of a niece; or it may be Troilus, the hero who actually becomes Criseyde's lover, who is made analogous to Tereus the rapist in an early moment of dark foreshadowing. If the interpretive emphasis is laid instead on the correspondence between Criseyde and the female characters in the myth, however, the beginnings of a pattern in the representation of Criseyde emerge. Criseyde, like Procne and Philomela, is in some sense victimized by circumstances; and yet no matter how sympathetically we construe Criseyde in order to call attention to her victimization, she seems very unlike the two Athenian sisters. Where Philomela is without question raped, for instance, Criseyde, by most legal and lay definitions of this crime, is not, for in the bedroom scene in Book III and elsewhere she declares herself to be a willing, and, some would say, initiating partner.

At the same time, Criseyde ironically differs in another way from the mythic sisters: she turns out to be far less powerful, in the not very long run, than the betrayed Procne and the raped, brutalized, and silenced Philomela. In Ovid, the latter manages to break the silence Tereus sought to impose on her when he brutally cut out her tongue by using her archetypally feminine skills at the loom, making a weaving that tells the truth without words—a mode of communication to which, as we shall see, Criseyde in vain aspires. The wordless work of this female artist is sent to Procne, who can instantly read the text(ile) correctly and act on her own understanding—whereas Criseyde, as we shall also see, is ever

23. The Ovidian story is found in VI.438–674 of the *Metamorphoses*, ed. Frank J. Miller (London: Heinemann, 1928), Vol I.

24. It is perhaps telling that John V. Fleming, in defending Chaucer's brand of "feminism," mistakes the bird that wakes Pandarus: there is a "whiff of incest," Fleming observes, "in the song of the nightingale that wakens Pandarus to his pimp's errand" ("Deiphoebus Betrayed: Virgilian Decorum, Chaucerian Feminism," *Chaucer Review* 21 [1986], p. 188). The nightingale, however, is later associated not with Pandarus but with Criseyde. The force of the allusion depends, I think, on the initial evocation of the swallow, reinforced by the indication in lines II.68–69 of precisely why her song is sorrowful. Fleming's slip is particularly interesting, however, in light of the association (in tales like Marie de France's *Laustic*) of the nightingale and the go-between.

the misreader. In a rage, Procne rescues her sister and then avenges her by killing her own son, ignoring his cries of "Mater! Mater!" and serving his flesh to his father, Tereus. The Ovidian story seems to say that women will not be silenced by even the most extreme means, that female victims of the most brutal male violence can collectively punish men by turning their womanly skills of weaving, mothering, and feeding against them.

Criseyde, on the other hand, cannot bear witness in the same way as Procne and Philomela to the power of women to tell their wrongs, to the force of sisterhood, or to mythical male fears of women as sexual partners and mothers. She never complains (or seems to perceive) that, as some modern readers believe, she has been abandoned and victimized, or at least taken advantage of, by a series of men—her father, her uncle, and the military leaders of Troy, including Troilus himself—who, like the brother-in-law Tereus, ought to protect her. She never actually threatens the well-being of any of these men; Pandarus's and Troilus's warnings that she will be responsible for their deaths if she does not love Troilus are reiterated so often that the idle and conventional nature of this charge is apparent.[25] Notably, Criseyde is not represented, like Procne and Philomela, as anyone's sister (although she does have a niece), and she gets anything but support from other women in the poem. Other female characters only appear in the poem when Criseyde's isolation from them is crucial: when, wittingly or not, they encourage her to accept the ideology of love that dooms her (like her niece Antigone), when they fail to guard her virtue (like the women who accompany her to Pandarus's house), or when they misunderstand her (like those who come to console her for the exchange and think she is weeping for the loss of their friendship).

Criseyde's dissimilarity to Procne and Philomela is underlined when the myth resurfaces to bracket the scene of her first arousal to love. In a mirror image of Pandarus's awakening to the chatter of the swallow, Criseyde, with her new problem, falls asleep to the song of the nightingale (II.918–24). The noise of one bird-sister rouses Pandarus from his

---

25. The foolishness and hollowness of Pandarus's death threats are exemplified in II.444ff., as he pretends to leave Criseyde with a vow that he and Troilus will both die soon. She pulls him back, and the narrator emphasizes that *she* is the one who is almost scared to death—and highly unlikely to become a murderess: "Criseyde, which that wel neigh starf for fre, / So as she was the ferfulleste wyght / That myghte be" (II.449–51).

own sexually frustrated torpor to the possibility of vicariously indulging male lust, while the song of the other—coming *after* Pandarus's scene of persuasion—lulls Criseyde to a sleep in which her wavering guard can slip. In between Pandarus's awakening and Criseyde's falling asleep, courtly rhetoric has inserted itself to disguise the violence of the original myth.[26] For when Criseyde hears the nightingale, he does not sing, as Philomela wove, of betrayal and brutality; like the nightingales in most poetry of the Middle Ages and later, he warbles instead "a lay / Of love, that made hire herte fressh and gay" (II.921–22). Immediately after his song, Criseyde dreams her dream of painless violation, in which the white eagle tears out her heart and replaces it with his own, "Of which she nought agroos, ne nothyng smerte" (II.930). This dream thus evokes and contains, like the poem as a whole, the sexual violence and mutilation that the myth of Procne and Philomela, the song of the swallow and the nightingale, brings to mind and then sets in contrast to Criseyde's story.

Criseyde is also set beside and against another mythic woman who is frightening and dangerous to men in a different way: Helen of Troy. Both Criseyde and Helen are actual characters in this poem, women living inside the gates of Troy, and both have significant relations to men in the enemy camp (a father and a husband, respectively), bonds which suggest the feared alliance of beautiful women and enemy forces. Both Helen and Criseyde are so enchanting that they unintentionally, at least at first, tempt the sons of Priam to put love of a woman before patriotic duty, and both thus represent the myth of potent female sexuality that holds in sway the strongest of men and the nations they form and defend. The legendary power of Helen is apparently still in full force; Deiphebus notes, for instance, that Helen " 'may leden Paris as hire leste' " (II.1449). Criseyde is inscribed into a very different kind of legend. By the end of the poem we might say that she has, ironically, lost her sexual hold over Troilus because she is in turn equally attractive to

26. The complexities of nightingale symbolism are too numerous for me to broach here, although it is tempting to suggest at least that the framing allusions to the swallow and the nightingale, as used in Book II, raise the whole problem of how it is that the Greek myth, a story about male lust and female vengeance, is lost or transmuted in medieval and later poetic references to the nightingale. For a recent survey of some of these complexities, see Wendy Pfeffer, *The Change of Philomel: The Nightingale in Medieval Literature* (New York: Peter Lang, 1985). The nightingale in its non-Ovidian signification appears again in Book III, associated with Criseyde when she loves Troilus (III.1233–39).

Diomede, and her threatening feminine beauty is vitiated and made into an inevitable moral failing.[27]

Still other aspects of those legendary powers of women that the womanly Criseyde does not exhibit are evoked near the end of the poem, where another mythic reference added to the Chaucerian version of the story both sums up and expands the point I have been making. Asked to interpret Troilus's dream of the boar in Book V, his sister Cassandra launches into "a fewe of olde stories" (V.1459), offering a highly abbreviated version of Ovid's tale of the Calydonian boar (*Metamorphoses* VIII.270–525) in order to link the boar in Troilus's dream with Diomede by tracing his ancestry through the male line, through his father, Tideus, to Meleager, slayer of the Calydonian boar. There are many interesting intertextual effects here, but most important to my argument are the parts of the story that Cassandra pointedly foreshortens or omits (as in V.1482–84), especially as they allude to the figures of Atalanta and Althaea. In Ovid, Atalanta is an ambiguously gendered huntress: "As for her face, it was one which you could truly say was maidenly for a boy or boyish for a maiden," obsessively beloved by Meleager and fiercely resented by other men, especially after her spear is the first to wound the boar.[28] The men are subsequently unmanned in their efforts to show her up; as Ancaeus, vowing vengeance, rushes into battle, "the boar . . . fiercely struck at the upper part of the groins with his two tusks."[29] In the fight that ensues when he attempts to give the spoils of the hunt to Atalanta, Meleager kills his maternal uncles. His mother Althaea then murders her son, as Procne does, to avenge her own kin.

In Chaucer, yet again, Criseyde's dissimilarity to frighteningly powerful mythic women, manly Atalanta and maternal Althaea, stands out. As if even the appearance of any possibly masculine traits needs to be firmly interpreted, the narrator early on glosses Criseyde's tallness, noted in *Il Filostrato*, by insisting that there is no ambiguity about her womanly looks: "creature / Was nevere lasse mannyssh in semynge" (I.283–84). Later Troilus, too, harps on Criseyde's womanliness, choosing epithets and endearments that stress her exemplary femininity (e.g., III.106, 1296,

27. For a comprehensive study of Helen in medieval mythography and iconography and in Chaucer's poem, see Christopher C. Baswell and Paul Beekman Taylor, "The Faire Queene Eleyne in Chaucer's *Troilus*," *Speculum* 63 (1988), pp. 293–311.

28. "facies, quam dicere vere / virgineam in puero, puerilem in virgine possis" (VIII.322–23).

29. "summa ferus geminos direxit ad inguina dentes" (VIII.400).

1302, 1740–41, V.244, 473–44). The possibility that Criseyde is a mother simply never comes up in the sources, but the Chaucerian narrator simultaneously alludes to and dismisses it in his seemingly gratuitous claim of ignorance and indifference: "But wheither that she children hadde or noon, / I rede it naught, therfore I late it goon" (I.132–33). Criseyde might be a mother, and therefore like Althaea or Procne dangerous to more men than Troilus; but we can let that fear go, the poem as a whole confirms. True womanhood, as inexorably defined in the person of the realistic, attractive heroine, does not entail the frightening, maternal vengeance against father and son alike of Procne and Althaea any more than it involves the competitive, manly prowess and ambivalent appearance of Atalanta, or even the more subtle and appropriately feminine skills of the speechless weaver, Philomela, or the beautiful and politically savvy Helen. These manifold powers for which the men of Western myth seem to fear women—their mothers, the unattainable ladies of their dreams, and their actual female sexual partners and victims—are densely and deftly embedded in the mythic substratum in which the Chaucerian story of Troilus and Criseyde is grounded. For all its infamous ambiguity, the representation of Criseyde denies these powers to the central, verisimilitudinous, and psychologically vivid female character in the poem. As the salient features of Criseyde constructed by the interaction of foreground and background in the poem offset the very threats of femininity to which the text repeatedly alludes, Criseyde's "final meaning" is fixed as both real and paradigmatic.

Criseyde's presumed ambiguity can also be more directly and complexly interrogated from a second direction. The modern critical emphasis on this aspect of her depiction, and on the linguistic and interpretive problem she is thereby thought to represent, would seem to be supported by a commonplace of much medieval theorizing about the relation of readers and texts: the reader is a man, and the text—especially the problematic fictive text—a woman who may seduce him with her heady wiles, her beautiful duplicity, and her fleshy presence, unless he penetrates and masters her.[30] Troilus accepts and reiterates this trope in his view of Criseyde at many points, and most markedly in conjunction with the consummation of their sexual relationship, when he speaks of Criseyde's eyes as "nettes" (III.1355) and adds: " 'Though ther be mercy writen in

30. For a comprehensive and persuasive discussion of this long tradition, see especially Carolyn Dinshaw, *Chaucer's Sexual Poetics* (Madison: University of Wisconsin Press, 1989).

youre cheere, / God woot, the text ful hard is, soth, to fynde!' " (III.1356–57). But neither Troilus's conventional reading of Criseyde as the mysterious, mystical, and entrapping body of the female text nor the modern critical consensus about her titillating ambiguity tells the whole story. The emphasis on the enigmatic and equivocal nature of Criseyde as, paradoxically, a site of crucial meaning, occludes something equally important, although harder to assimilate, about the poem's representation of this female character. Criseyde is not only, like the letter *A*, a cipher for men to manipulate and a symbol to the readers, both inside and outside the text, who can construct meaning out of ambiguity and thus redeem the infidelity of women and words. She is also characterized as an unsuccessful and relentless interpreter of the words and intentions of others. At the level of dramatic interaction, Criseyde is at the very most no more ambiguous than the people and events around her: that is, no more ambivalent and disingenuous as a represented personality, and no harder to interpret as a character. If we look quite closely at the Chaucerian telling, it is indeed she who is most often cast as the reader of hard texts, and her seductions are quite literally shown to be abetted by her response to a variety of male-authored discourses, both spoken and written.[31]

Books II and III tell us initially that reading is a fraught and gender-differentiated activity in which the woman character is baffled and ma-

31. As will become evident, when I speak of Criseyde as a reader I am not entering into the question of Criseyde's literacy, or the related, important, and highly complicated question of the literacy of the women in Chaucer's possible audience. All we can say for sure is that the poem presupposes that Criseyde can read and write; although she is being read to at the beginning of Book II, later she takes Troilus's letter away to read in private, and she writes back in private. She says then that "this is the firste lettre / That evere I wroot, ye, al or any del," II.1213–14. In Book V she seems to be a much more frequent writer, although of course her letters to Troilus need not be written by her own hand. For discussions of female literacy in the period, see Norman Davis's introduction to *Paston Letters and Papers of the Fifteenth Century* (Oxford: Oxford University Press, 1971), vol. I, pp. xxxvii–xxxviii; M. B. Parkes, "The Literacy of the Laity," in *The Medieval World*, ed. David Daiches and Anthony Thorlby (London: Albus Books, 1973); Joan M. Ferrante, "The Education of Women in the Middle Ages in Theory, Fact, and Fantasy," in *Beyond Their Sex: Learned Women of the European Past*, ed. Patricia H. Labalme (New York: New York University Press, 1980), pp. 9–42; and Susan Schibanoff, "The Art of Reading as a Woman," in *Gender and Reading*, ed. Elizabeth A. Flynn and Patrocinio P. Schweickart (Baltimore: Johns Hopkins University Press, 1986), pp. 83–106. For a study of female book ownership that argues for the cultural influence of women, through the knowledge acquired from vernacular works and translations owned and inherited by women, see Susan Groag Bell, "Medieval Women Book Owners: Arbiters of Lay Piety and Ambassadors of Culture," *Signs* 7 (1982), pp. 742–68.

nipulated by the concealed intentions of male speakers and the dominant cultural discourses, none of which serve either her personal or her positional interests. As if to situate Criseyde even more firmly in the highly textualized reality of this poem and to identify her as a reader in a narrow as well as a broad sense, the drama of interpretation in which Criseyde so often plays the role of inept and unempowered audience opens in Book II, in an episode once again original to Chaucer's version of the story, on a scene of actual reading. Come to woo his niece for his friend, Pandarus finds her in "a paved parlour" with two other women, listening to a third woman reading from a book, "the geste / Of the siege of Thebes" (II.83–84). Before Pandarus begins to put his own plan into action, he and Criseyde briefly discuss the story as she has heard it read so far; Pandarus says he knows it well, all twelve books. The gendered difference here is suggestive. Reading in this instance is an activity that we see women doing together, in a private place, until they are interrupted. Pandarus, the male intruder, establishes himself as one who has elsewhere already read and therefore knows the whole story, just as he will control the plot in the rest of Books II and III.[32]

The failure or futility of Criseyde's efforts to control events, moreover, is blatantly underscored by the content of the reading here, for, as Cassandra later tells Troilus, Diomedes is a son of Tideus, a hero killed in the siege of Thebes (see V.1485ff.). In the poem, the Theban story is only later implicated in the Trojan one, but the early allusion reminds us that from the beginning the plot is in fact fixed, and Criseyde, entering part way through the story, can neither know this nor escape the part she is destined to play. For the poem's archetype of *wommanhede*, then, reading in old books is defined both as a personally significant, even determining activity—she is hearing the beginnings of the story in which she is already caught up—and a passive, unself-conscious one, in which the reader hears her own fate read, just as she falls into her place in an already written text, without knowing it: "al unwist" (I.93).[33]

32. Windeatt notes an interesting gender distinction in this passage, although he does not comment on it as such: Criseyde speaks of the "romaunce" of Thebes (II.100), suggesting that she reads the vernacular *Roman de Thebes*, whereas Pandarus's "rather superior reference" to twelve books (II.108) implies that he has read the Latin epic, Statius's *Thebaid* (p. 157, note on lines 100–108). For a discussion of the enormous popularity of the *Roman de Thebes* in the Middle Ages, and its part in establishing the figure of Criseyde as the type of female inconstancy, see Mieszkowski, "The Reputation of Criseyde."

33. Compare Criseyde in this regard to the "immasculated" reader discussed by Schibanoff, "The Art of Reading as a Woman."

Following up on the implications of this literal scene of reading, in which we see Criseyde enmeshed at several levels in old stories, we find that the problem of reading the meaning of others' words and actions continues to be foregrounded in the repetition of the terms "mean/meaning" and "intend/intention" throughout the poem, in another pattern created only in Chaucer's telling. This pattern begins with Criseyde's efforts in Book II to understand precisely what Pandarus wants from her. On his first visit, he characteristically and strategically obfuscates the suggestion he has come to make by hinting at a wonderful secret and then refusing to tell it. He thus sets Criseyde up to ask, for the first of many, many times, a crucial question: " 'Shal I nat witen what ye meene of this?' " (II.226). " 'No,' " he says, " 'this thing axeth leyser' " (II.227). Pandarus's answer is typically equivocal: false in one way, true in another. He intends to tell her of Troilus's secret passion quite soon; at the same time, however, a real answer to her question is "no." She will never know for sure what Pandarus means, or at least her suspicions or her understanding can never be openly acknowledged or confirmed. Pandarus's method is to tease and to deceive, and moreover the rules of the courtly love game forbid talk that is too direct or too frank. The situation described here and throughout this part of the poem (see, for further instances, II.267–73, 386–87, 473, 665; III.124–26) seems to bear witness to R. F. Green's suggestion that the ambiguity of courtly men's discourse was the problem any historical fourteenth-century noblewoman confronted as she struggled to interpret "luf-talkynge" and protect her honor: "The social reflexes of the medieval noble woman, at least in the later Middle Ages, needed to be far sharper than her modern counterpart's if she were to maintain the precarious balance between courtesy and propriety."[34]

Criseyde's insistent, repetitious, quite possibly arch and yet apparently futile attempt to discover the deliberately obscured meaning and intentions of Pandarus and Troilus is met by their even more insistent claims that whatever she may suspect, they mean well. Pandarus peppers his discourse in Book II with direct protestations of goodwill that can only call our attention to his evasion and bad faith (see, for example, II.295, 360, 363–64, 437–38, 580–81, 592–93). Readers are licensed to see that he protests too much and that he intends precisely the "vilenye" and

34. Green, "Troilus and the Game of Love," p. 202.

"yvel"—those are his own terms—that he keeps indicting as a false interpretation of his words.[35] As Pandarus speaks, the possibility that
words faithfully convey (good) intentions is incrementally undermined,
even as the fact is established that Pandarus has clear and conscious
intentions to hide from Criseyde.

Already in Book III, moreover, the integrity of Troilus's own speech
is compromised by the scene in which for once he does not merely follow
Pandarus, but takes the lead in controlling and concealing meaning and
using wordplay to acquit himself and his friend of wrongdoing. Here we
see again not only that Pandarus and Troilus spend the night together
more frequently than Criseyde and Troilus do, but also that the two men
truly understand each other's desires and meaning, clearly and without
the need of words. (See, for example, Pandarus's assurance to Troilus:
" 'For wel I woot, thow menest wel, parde,' " III.337). The depth and
centrality of the homosocial bond and its intended impact on the semantic system itself is confirmed in Troilus's substitution of the words
"gentilesse, / Compassioun, and felawship, and trist" for the term that
Pandarus dares not speak to him: "bauderye" (III.397). His rationale for
the semantic play, "for wyde-wher is wist / How that ther is diversite
requered / Bytwixen thynges like . . . " (III.404–6), sounds like a scho-
lastic quibble, the use of logic to support a private, personally beneficial
reinterpretation of communally authorized meaning and to lay claim to
the power to make and revise convention as necessary. His high-minded
interpretation of the nobility of Pandarus's actions is problematized, and
again the priority of the homosocial alliance is confirmed, in the offer he
makes in the very next lines. So that you will know I do not think your
service "a shame . . . or jape," he says, just tell me which of the women
I control you want, and she's yours, " 'my faire suster Polixene, / Cas-
sandre, Eleyne, or any of the frape' " (III.408–10).[36]

This scene encapsulates the efforts of Troilus and Pandarus to have
and act on intentions, to retain power over the meaning of words, and

35. My reading of this scene might be accused, like many feminist readings, of lacking
a sense of humor. For an interpretation of Pandarus's first visit to Criseyde as "one of the
most delightful comic scenes that Chaucer ever wrote," see Alfred David, "Chaucerian
Comedy and Criseyde," in Salu, *Essays on Troilus and Criseyde*, pp. 90–104.

36. For different readings of this scene, see Myra Stokes, "Wordes White: Disingenuity
in *Troilus and Criseyde*," *English Studies* 64 (1984), pp. 18–29, and Donald Howard (who
says this is "an avowal of good intentions and loyalty, not of depravity"), *The Three
Temptations: Medieval Man in Search of the World* (Princeton: Princeton University Press,
1966), p. 137, n. 86.

the ambiguities of their position. The equation of Criseyde with "any of the frape" of women should seem inconsistent with Troilus's other protestations of love; later, for instance, he rebukes Pandarus for suggesting that since there are lots of lovely ladies in Troy, the exchange of Criseyde is a minor problem. What the apparent inconsistency reveals, however, is a single underlying assumption about women. All that keeps Criseyde from crossing the fine but fatal line between a Mary and an Eve, a White and a Dido, an otherwordly ideal and "any of the frape," is her relation to Troilus, whose perception of her, his "fixe and depe impressioun," is what defines her (most of the time) as innocent, trustworthy, and good, and in turn defines him as loving, trusting, and noble. As we shall see, however, he too is a misreader, especially when the text is Criseyde.

Criseyde is not represented as blind to this problem of reading, the fact that she is obliged to interpret the intentions of men who do not say what they mean or mean what they say. She is characterized as worried about Pandarus's meaning from the outset, and ironically it is her awareness that (his, and perhaps her) words can deceive that leads her to invest herself in the false hope of something that can transcend language—that is, love. She yearns to overcome both the unreliability of men's words and her own uncertainty, her incapacity as a woman and as a reader to control or know for sure what people mean and intend. Consequently, she works hard to convince herself that it is possible to do so and that Troilus, unlike any other man she knows, can be trusted (see, for instance, III.162–66). Explaining Criseyde's conversion to love even before the physical culmination, the narrator affirms that what attracts her to Troilus is his apparent ability to bridge altogether the gap between utterance and intention, words and meanings, that as a struggling reader, a betrayed daughter, and a solicited niece, she has felt and feared from the beginning: "It semed hire he wiste what she thoughte / Withouten word, so that it was no nede / To bidde hym ought to doon, or ought forbeede" (III.465–67, my emphasis).

In the story's first mention of Criseyde, before she is named, she is described as a daughter that the traitor Calchas has left behind, "Al unwist" (I.93) and in fear for her life, "As she that nyste what was best to rede" (I.96). Repeated twice more in the last two books (IV.679, with minor syntactic variation, and V.18), this line might serve as a motto for the role of Criseyde as an unknowing, necessarily persistent but ineffectual reader of deliberately obscure texts, authored by men with intentions that they cannot admit (even perhaps, in Troilus's case, to themselves).

In this phrase, the verb *reden* does not literally refer to the reading of (written) words. In the fourteenth-century lexicon, as elsewhere in this poem, *reden* carries, along with its chief modern meaning, one of several earlier senses, some of which survive into Modern English and probably pertain in I.96: to give advice or counsel; to take charge, govern, or control; to interpret, perceive, or understand something obscure.[37] In the context of *Troilus and Criseyde* as a whole, nevertheless, *reden*, in this phrase repeatedly used to describe the heroine, invokes and links the whole range of possible meanings. "She (that) nyste what was best to rede" encapsulates the complex of social, political, and linguistic activities that the female character wants to but cannot do and at the same time figures the relation between a woman's reading (a book, a cultural text, a man's social and sexual intentions) and holding responsibility and power (over one's own and others' actions).

Love brings Criseyde "joie" (III.469), then, when it seems to minimize the difficulty of knowing "what was best to rede" by simply making reading and interpretation unnecessary, short-circuiting the deceptiveness and ambiguity of fallen language, doing "withouten word." But neither Troilus nor the version of ideal love he represents can so easily resolve the problem of language for Criseyde or for any other reader. Love, unlike reading, is supposedly the sphere in which desire masters reason and words are redundant; the poem affirms, however, that despite Criseyde's hopes it is reading, an activity so far at least controlled by men, that directs love and fuels desire.

Why not conclude, as other readers have done, that the representation of Criseyde as a woman trying her best to exert control in a world where no man can be trusted reveals the narrator's (and/or the author's) sympathy for women in general and for this victim of ideology in particular? One problem that such a reading elides returns us precisely to the point at which we began: the problem of Criseyde's own ambiguity, which is not erased when we sketch in the fuller picture, as I have tried to do here, of her uncertainty in the face of other characters' ambiguities. Any discussion of Pandarus's and Troilus's deliberate obfuscation of an intention that knows itself to be illicit, for instance, also entails a further question that readers are directly impelled by this narrative to ask: when does Criseyde realize what Pandarus wants her to do with or for Troilus?

37. See *Middle English Dictionary*, R.2, *reden* v.(1), pp. 280–90.

The narrator characteristically hints that Criseyde understands precisely what Pandarus has in mind at least as early as II.589–90, when she responds to his slip of the tongue with a giggle: " 'Nay, therof spak I nought, ha, ha!' quod she; / 'As helpe me God, ye shenden every deel!' " At the very end of Book II, however, she is still described as "Al innocent of Pandarus entente" (II.1723), ignorant at least of his specific plan to lead her into the bedroom at Deiphebus's, where Troilus is pretending to be sick. Hints that she knows nothing or that she knows everything, throughout Books II and III, are always only hints, not clear proof of either Criseyde's ignorance and victimization or her knowledge and agency.

Augmenting rather than resolving this conjunction of innocence and complicity, particularly in Book II, Chaucer either adds to or revises *Il Filostrato* significantly, and we see Criseyde both as subject to discourses that she either encounters by chance or has thrust upon her and as participant in the process of internalizing the beguiling meanings on which Pandarus and the ideology of romantic love insist. Take, again, the moment when Criseyde glimpses that icon of love and masculine sexuality, the battle-bloodied Troilus, from her window. In Boccaccio, Troiolo is seen after her internal debate; the repositioning of this scene in Chaucer, so that it precedes Criseyde's solitary deliberations, seems to emphasize the importance to her subsequent decision of what and how Criseyde sees. Criseyde, we are told, looks at the hero's bloodied horse and battered armor, "And leet it so softe in hire herte synke, / That to hireself she seyde, 'Who yaf me drynke?' " (II.650–51). The formulation succinctly suggests that Criseyde is both responsible for the impression that the visual text makes on her—she "let it" sink into her heart—and acted upon by an intentionally intrusive, penetrating, but obscure force; her own sense that she is acted upon by an unknown outside agent is reflected in the question she asks.

So too when Criseyde overhears her niece Antigone sing a "Troian song" (II.825) about the bliss of love and when she is forced by Pandarus to read a written and, though formulaic, more personally directed text, Troilus's letter (II.1093ff.), we see that Pandarus's plot and Troilus's desire are aided and abetted by the direct, sensory impact of a cultural discourse that Criseyde on one hand resists, or at least hesitates to rely on, and on the other hand wants to believe and so willfully internalizes. The emphasis in Book II on Pandarus's control over a meaning that he artfully conceals from Criseyde is summed up in the cliff-hanging close of the book, as we see Criseyde about to be led into Troilus's sickroom: "Al innocent of Pandarus entente . . . arm in arm inward with hym she wente" (II.1723–25). Criseyde is literally, physically drawn further into the plot, and towards the bedside, at once without complete understanding—"al innocent"—and yet, and therefore with complicity, "arm in arm" with Pandarus.[38]

We cannot, in short, view Criseyde's position as misreader as a position of either full innocence or full complicity, and the effects of her carefully constructed ambiguity are multiple and critical to the situation of characters and readers alike. Most obviously, the meaning of Criseyde and her representative womanhood is again solidified. The protracted and wavering course of arousal for the female staged in Book II and then continued into Book III reinforces the notion that whereas Troilus falls in love instantaneously, and despite his conscious intentions, Criseyde ponders at great length, hesitates, resists, and at some point chooses to consent. The difference suggests not only a physiological distinction but also, more interestingly, the discursive nature of female sexuality and the common notion that although a man cannot help himself, a woman can. In puzzling over Criseyde's claim that she has already yielded to Troilus, in lines II.1210–11, A. C. Spearing brings out another effect. "When exactly was the moment of yielding?" Spearing wonders, and then answers his own question: "We cannot tell: it seems to have happened in one of the gaps between scenes (perhaps after Criseyde awoke from her dream in Book II?) rather than in any specific scene."[39] What does it mean, however, when a narrative locates the moment of female consent in "the gaps between scenes"? It may mean, I suggest, that we can never determine exactly when—or even if—Criseyde "yielded," because her consent is a fiction, one that she is forced to invent, believe in, invoke, and revise at crucial points in order to save face and survive. As Catharine A. MacKinnon has noted in studying modern legal definitions of female consent in cases of rape, given Western cultural constructions of gender, the very notion of a woman's consent is illusory.[40] In yet

---

38. The road to the completion of Pandarus's plot is clear, and the narrator confirms its achievement in the morning after scene of Book III. Again the end ryhme (with the terms reversed) appears as Criseyde is dismissed, once Pandarus is satisfied: "hom to hire hous she wente, / And Pandarus hath fully his entente" (III.1581–82).

39. *Chaucer: Troilus and Criseyde* (London: Edward Arnold, 1976), p. 19.

40. "Feminism, Marxism, Method, and the State: Toward a Feminist Jurisprudence," *Signs* 8 (1983), pp. 635–58.

another way, the represented ambiguity of Criseyde's feelings and intentions serves to vitiate her power as either complicitous agent or innocent victim: as a woman and a reader, Criseyde in Books II and III is not allowed to be either unequivocally desirous (like a Criseida or a Helen) or completely indifferent (like an Atalanta, say, or like the formel eagle in the *Parliament of Fowls*). Both unswerving desire and utter indifference are women's powers that *Troilus and Criseyde* alludes to but discharges, here as before, in the representation of Criseyde.

Effects of Criseyde's ambiguity that go beyond her character and the representation of femininity it enables emerge, moreover, when we consider what happens to the position of the reader and the problem of reading in Books IV and V. Through its insistent connection of the ambiguities of male meaning and intention with the story of Criseyde's seduction in Books I–III, I have suggested, the poem initially establishes an equation between (mis)reading and the feminine position. In that last, original scene in Book II, however, we already see that other characters, too, may be beguiled by the act of reading. Two others are cast as literal readers here: Eleyne and Deiphebus, who both "nothyng knewe of his entente" (II.1665). These guilty innocents, too, are manipulated and blinded by reading; Pandarus asks their advice about a letter from Hector, which they go off to ponder at some length. In Book III, after he leads Troilus to Criseyde's bedside for the first time, Pandarus too reads, or pretends to, as he withdraws to the fireside with the light, "and fond his contenaunce, / As for to looke upon an old romaunce" (III.979–80). Here, as throughout the poem, the reality of love is both contrasted with and intersected by the fiction of love. As in the final scene of Book II, moreover, (the pretence of) reading enables (the fiction of) privacy; so too Criseyde's intermittent sense of her private selfhood—"I am myn owene womman" (II.750)—is brought out by her struggle to read.

In Books IV and V, however, even Troilus and Pandarus are suddenly stripped by circumstances of their apparent power to establish meaning and stage events, and this shift returns attention to the general feminization of male experience that is at issue in the poem as a whole. The two men are explicitly reduced to the passive, constrained position as readers that they previously played with, feared, and resisted. Troilus is perhaps most notably put into the uncomfortable position of a reader confronting a difficult text whose meaning does not serve his interests or desires during his long wait for Criseyde's return. As he stares at the closed facade of Criseyde's empty house and rides by the places where he has seen Criseyde dance, laugh, or sing, he now reads the story of their former love, and he seems to relish the textual, fictive quality of that past experience as he remembers it: " 'Men myght a book make of it, lik a storie' " (V.585). Although the story of Troilus and Criseyde is in fact ended, Troilus keeps trying to read against the set, closed text, but the only way to resist the meaning that frustrates him is to be a bad, self-deluding reader. But that strategy fails, and we see the error and finally the impossibility of his attempted misreading. When he decides he has miscounted the ten days during which he awaits Criseyde, his self-deluding comment has ironic force: " 'I understonde have al amys' " (V.1186). Troilus's misapprehensions reach a kind of comic, debasing na-dir—debasing for Criseyde, above all—when he mistakes a "fare-carte" for his lady (V.1158–62). Even when Troilus finally understands and ac-cepts the true meaning of Criseyde's absence, he still misreads: he de-duces, for instance, that Criseyde deliberately gave Diomede the brooch that was a gift from Troilus, " 'for despit, and ek for that ye mente / Al outrely to shewen youre entente' " (V.1693–94). Several hundred lines earlier, however, we were directly shown Criseyde giving that brooch to Diomede, with no suggestion that she did it in "despit" (see V.1037–50) or that she has any such clear or deliberately motivated intentions.

Throughout Books IV and V, Pandarus and Troilus repeatedly make this critical misreading: they assume that Criseyde can control meaning and have intentions (see, for instance, IV.173, 656–57, 853, 1416–18), but the poem suggests otherwise and insists that the archetypal misreader of others cannot suddenly become an author of her own intentions and acts. The assumption that Criseyde has intentions to be consulted and even relied upon cannot by itself bring into being what was never before imagined or allowed. If the Criseyde we read of has any intentions other than to survive in a hostile world, they are presented as no more than intentions; she cannot act on them now any more than she could earlier, or any more than Pandarus and Troilus can, when larger forces take over. She cannot single-handedly solve the problem of language and wield the power that would fuse word and deed, wish and fulfillment. In Book V, any hope that Criseyde had of trusting to the good intentions behind men's words, or of transcending words altogether, is even more emphatically dashed, and in the Greek camp Criseyde's role as misreader is replayed in a different place; but only the names, not the gender relations, have changed. Another male speaker, Diomede, takes over; he successfully reads the meaning that others try to conceal while obscuring his own intentions in order to revise Criseyde's.

The reappearance of the man who at once conceals and controls meaning, for the time being, confirms the point that to be a (desirable) woman is in some sense to be a poor, submissive reader (see for example V.88–89, 105, 150–51, 775–76). Criseyde is thus right back where she started, trying to interpret the intentions of a single man now who combines the roles of lover and intriguer that Troilus and Pandarus separately embodied.[41] She tries to answer Diomede's questions, and the lines might be taken word for word from Book II: "but, as of his entente, / It semed nat she wiste what he mente" (V.867–68). The "semed nat" directly raises the by now tired question of how much Criseyde knows, and how much she herself, the narrator, and the audience are all invested in her unknowingness. Although she perceives herself at this point as becoming more clearly a text—" 'O, rolled shal I ben on many a tonge!' " (V.1061)—she is also forced to remain a reader, and as such she is still and always "she that nyste what was best to rede." By the end of the poem, Criseyde embodies for Troilus (as she has for so many modern readers) the original corruption of all faith in words, in verbal protestations of good intentions and meaning well: " 'Who shal now trowe on any othes mo?' " (V.1263). Here we see in Troilus, and in the traditional interpretation of Criseyde he voices, the attempt, so familiar in Western culture, to locate the cause of human error in one gender so that the other may contemplate and subdue, if not avoid, error incarnate. But this reading of Criseyde, like Troilus's other misreadings, is not only false to the facts as we are shown them elsewhere; again, it also gives the woman more credit, in an odd way, than the poem as a whole does.

According to *Troilus and Criseyde*, the problem of the untrustworthiness of words is not actually a problem that any woman causes, although she may embody it and certainly suffers from it. The heroine in this story is not a wily manipulator of words and an agent of bad faith any more than she is an innocent victim, an agent of seduction, a mother or sister to be feared, or a hard text to read, although men may sometimes be put in positions where they believe in one or more of these assumptions about women. Criseyde is, rather, a powerless, self-blinding reader, like most people, who perforce accepts the meanings of those who have

41. As Stokes points out, Diomede "thinks like Pandarus, but speaks like Troilus" ("Wordes White," p. 22).

social power over her. As in the mythic program, traditional fears about women's powers, specifically now their textual or discursive capacities, are here denied. Troilus voices some of those fears in conventional terms, but the poem as a whole dismisses them.

As usual, moreover, the problem is not just (or even, in this case) the woman outside, but rather the woman inside. Pandarus and Troilus make Criseyde the scapegoat for their own incapacities, and if we care to look, we see how and why misogyny works at one level. But they are just as powerless to control meaning, to act out their own intentions, or to have power as readers over the already written text as is Criseyde. Revising, then, the trope of the text as a woman to be penetrated by the male reader, the poem suggests that the act of reading, as performed by any of these characters, involves a relation to power that is commonly viewed in the Middle Ages as feminine and is specifically associated by the time we have finished the first half of the poem with the main, unreliable female character; but it is a relation from which males in the text are never immune. Readers of the poem, unsure of Criseyde's meaning and intentions, may also be implicated in these problems. In a relation to Criseyde that is analogous to her relation to Pandarus and Troilus, they too may yearn for a clear answer, a definitive reading, a moral appraisal of "poor Criseyde" by an open-minded, friendly judge. And this is where a sense of Criseyde's ambiguity, the narrator's and readers' foregrounded inability to know with any certainty what she thinks or why she acts as she does, serves another fundamental purpose, at once complicating and reinforcing moral judgments against her and tempering the narrator's putative sympathy so that he can finally control her meaning as a character. Only the figure of the poet can (mis)read in a self-constructive way in this poem, and as I shall suggest in the next and final section, his uniquely empowered position rests in large part on his resolution of Criseyde's ambiguity and his direct confrontation, from the characteristic position of the unreliable Chaucerian narrator, with the instability of gender and power in heterosexual relations.

N'y sey nat this al oonly for thise men,
But moost for wommen that bitraised be
Thorough false folk; God yeve hem sorwe, amen!
That with hire grete wit and subtilte
Bytraise yow! And this commeveth me

To speke, and in effect yow alle I preye,
Beth war of men, and herkneth what I seye!
                    V.1779–85

The narrator of *Troilus and Criseyde* interrupts his story for one last time with five stanzas of self-conscious commentary and conversation near the end of Book V (1765–99). Abandoning once more the Boccaccian text he has been following relatively closely for the past several stanzas, he seems ready to close the poem even before the hero's death and final transcendent vision. He begins to speak self-reflexively about the text in history, about his own relation as a poet to other great poets of the past, and about the poem's uses and possible abuses by present and future readers, who are conceived of initially as distinctly male and female. Like others in the poem, this excursus begins (V.1765–71) as if in answer to real or anticipated complaints, in this case unstated objections, perhaps, that his male characters are not manly and his portrayal of Troilus not heroic enough, not sufficiently or accurately interested in or expressive of the hero's masculine prowess. It is because his initial topic was love, the narrator argues, that he has purposefully not written about Troilus's "worthi dedes" in battle; dismissively, he sends readers interested in martial matters, "whoso list hem heere," to "Dares" (V.1770–71). In the next stanza he turns directly to an alleged female readership, "Bysechyng every lady bright of hewe, / And every gentil womman, what she be" (V.1772–73). He asks women not to be angry with him on account of his representation of Criseyde's guilt, which, as he has so often noted, is already written "in other bokes" (V.1776). In lines usually taken to allude to the upcoming *Legend of Good Women*, he adds that he will more happily write stories, "yf yow leste," about a different kind of woman, celebrating "Penelopees trouthe and good Alceste" (V.1777–78).

In the third and, I think, pivotal stanza of the passage (V.1779–85), quoted in full above, the narrator seems to continue speaking to women, although he manages at the same time to suggest a certain loyalty to his own sex by explaining that he has written his poem "nat . . . al oonly for thise men" (V.1779)—presupposing, then, that it is to some extent written for men—"But moost for wommen that bitraised be" by men of "grete wit and subtilte," whom he curses (V.1780–83). The obfuscation of both his didactic intention and his allegiances along lines of gender is indicated by the odd correlative construction in V.1779–80, *not only* for men, . . . *but most* for women. He concludes this stanza with the claim that his sympathy for women motivates his speaking and with an en-

treaty (or warning) to the ladies that also sounds like what will come in
the *Legend*: "Beth war of men, and herkneth what I seye!" (V.1785).

At first glance, this central stanza and particularly its closing line seem
highly inappropriate to the story of *Troilus and Criseyde*, the legendary
tale of a faithful man and the woman who betrays him. But the implications of this passage in fact befit and highlight what I have argued
about the poem thus far. The narrator's reminder that it is more often
women who are betrayed by men may serve to reinforce the perception
that Troilus, from his early sufferings as a lovesick male to his final
posture as the abandoned lover, is tragically feminized. Alternatively, or
even at the same time, it may imply that Criseyde, the real woman, is
in fact, in some senses, the betrayed one in this story. The attribution of
"grete wit and subtilte" to those "false folk" who betray women is also
in accord with the diminution of women's powers, for good or bad, that
I have traced throughout the poem. As the presaged *Legend of Good
Women* will confirm through its treatment of women known elsewhere
for their great power, the narrator here implies that in fact females rarely
have the strength to be so wicked, to be agents rather than victims of
betrayal.

The imperatives in the last line of this stanza—"Beth war of men, and
herkneth what I seye"—might also seem odd in at least a couple of ways.
First, they raise the question of the narrator's gender. Isn't he, as we all
assume, a man? If so, his first command contradicts or at least problematizes his second: if women follow his advice and are wary of men in
general, as members of a fixed category, (how) can they rely on the male
author's putative words of wisdom? Second, just what does this narrator
intend to say to women, exactly? The second imperative, "herkneth,"
suggests that a clear (re)statement of some pertinent advice, in addition
to the warning to be wary of men, will follow; otherwise, it is not at all
obvious what a woman reader can take away as some positively useful
moral of this story. But the narrator does not go on to give women
anything to hearken to; instead, he jumps in the next two stanzas to a
seemingly unrelated topic.

Suddenly, starting in V. 1786, he speaks about his poem not as a
didactic piece for gendered readers troubled by the actual and imaginary
difficulties of heterosexual relations, but as a literary artifact related to
the work of past writers and endangered by the incompetence of future
scribes and (mis)readers. In the well-known and highly traditional apos-
trophe to the text—"Go, litel bok, go, litel myn tragedye" (V.1786)—the

narrator (moving most overtly into a position that is usually associated with Chaucer's) at once expresses his humble subjection to tradition and audaciously claims a place for his work in the canon of great narrative poetry here represented by the catalogue of masterpoets: "And kis the steppes, where as thow seest pace / Virgile, Ovide, Omer, Lucan, and Stace" (V.1791–92). Then with a suspicious tone, reminiscent of the one heard at the beginning of the *House of Fame* or in "To Adam Scriveyn," he closes with a prayer for accurate transmission and correct interpretation of his text (V.1793–98).

The oddities and ambiguities of this whole digression, like those of its central stanza, are characteristic and telling; and the apparent disjunction between the problems of love and the problems of literature, between what we might call gender politics on one hand and the question of literary authority and the anxieties of authorship (in a manuscript age), on the other, is only apparent. Focusing on the situation of the narrator, as we are invited to do by his persistent self-representation and self-reflection, we see how the gender relations he so markedly puts into play among himself, his literary antecedents, his characters, and his readers are crucial to his fears and claims for the status and integrity of his "litel bok" and its author among literary forebears and future interpreters. I take the digression in V.1765–99 as an explicit closing metacommentary on the whole poem (and possibly on Chaucer's career as a poet to date). In it, we see the narrator's ultimate interest in empowering the figure of the secular poet and addressing familiar worries about the indeterminacy and instability of words, and the consequent difficulties of interpretation and the risks of being (mis)read. His strategy for serving this interest is grounded in the characteristic sympathy with women as characters and as readers he alleges here, together with the critique of (most) men who love women and (other) male authors who write about women that this sympathy implies. The Chaucerian version of the Trojan story thus openly interrogates and deeply complicates the misogyny it imputes to other men and prior tellings. But it does so, I shall argue, in a way that not only retains and even reinforces a proper difference between male and female, masculine and feminine, but also inscribes a notion of literary authority entailing a controlled engagement with women and the problem of Woman (inside and outside the masculine subject) said to be unavailable to other men.

The narrator of *Troilus and Criseyde*, like other Chaucerian storytellers, prominently displays both an attraction to and an affinity with his central female character, that "ferfulest wight." Evidence of this special relation to Criseyde has been offered by a number of modern critics, many of whom take it as a sign of the author's exceptional understanding of the feminine plight and possibly his close, personal identification with the heroine. Donald Howard, for instance, praises Chaucer for his rare ability, as a male author, to see "into the mind of a woman," and even argues that the male reader is similarly privileged: "I have *been* Criseyde."[42] Lambert concludes that "she [Criseyde] and not the poem's hero may be the more profoundly autobiographical creation."[43] Other critics describe and evaluate the narrator's or Chaucer's putative identification with Criseyde differently. Eugene Vance, for example, calls attention to one specific and problematic similarity between character and author when he observes that "sincerity is no more Criseyde's trademark than it is Chaucer's."[44] Barbara Newman sees the narrator's apologies for Criseyde as "disturbing" because he "so nearly succumbs to her ethic."[45] But however they evaluate the fact, most modern readers seem to share the fundamental assumption that the narrator (and usually the author too) at once likes and is like Criseyde in particular and women in general.

As I have suggested in preceding chapters, however, the Chaucerian narrator's apparent affinity with women and similarities to his female characters may mark and respond to both the feminization of the position of the male court poet and his alignment in this regard with the feminized male lovers he so often writes about, and in this case the city-state they live in. Specifically, the narrator himself here displays precisely those feminine characteristics that Troilus and Pandarus respectively embody. Like the courtly lover, he is by convention humble, passive, timid, dominated, and devoted; like the go-between and artist figure, he is of necessity evasive, ingenious, a good storyteller, and a liar.[46] However, the feminization of Troy and the leading Trojans, as we have seen, by

42. Donald R. Howard, "Experience, Language, and Consciousness: 'Troilus and Criseyde,' II, 596–931," *Chaucer's Troilus*, pp. 159–80.

43. "*Troilus*, Books I–III," p. 125.

44. *Mervelous Signals: Poetics and Sign Theory in the Middle Ages* (Lincoln: University of Nebraska Press, 1986), p. 301.

45. " 'Feynede Loves,' Feigned Lore, and Faith in Trouthe," p. 261.

46. Scholarship on the poem offers many analyses of the similarities between Pandarus and the narrator; for discussion and some bibliography, see for example Fyler, *Chaucer and Ovid*, p. 129 and Chapter 5, note 6; and Adrienne Lockhart, "Semantic, Moral, and Aesthetic Degeneration," pp. 114ff.

no means brings with it any particular understanding of women or effective concern for their well-being; on the contrary, the men in the poem exhibit both blatant and subtle forms of antifeminism, and Troilus and Pandarus in particular reveal their common devaluation of the female and the feminine as they struggle in different ways to be more manly, to resist the position in which they find themselves. I argue that the narrator, too, resists his feminization. But if we compare his strategies of resistance as a man in a feminized position with those of Pandarus and Troilus, we discover crucial distinctions between the figure of the poet and the two central male characters.

Pandarus's most notable way of resisting, or at least railing against, his own feminization is to take the active role in seducing Criseyde for the gratification of another man. The advantages of such a strategy might seem multiple: he not only avenges himself against women as a group but also solidifies his relationship with one of his king's sons; and he distances himself from the risks of actually loving a woman, from which he has apparently suffered in the past. But he is not as safe, after all, as it may seem, and the misogyny implicit in his behavior throughout the poem simply backfires at the end. He overtly acknowledges this misogyny in his last brief speech: " 'My brother deer . . . I hate, ywys, Cryseyde; / And, God woot, I wol hate hire evermore!' " (V.1731–33). The Chaucerian version of the story departs from *Il Filostrato* here to intensify this response; in Boccaccio, Pandarus merely wishes never to see his niece again. Chaucer's Pandarus evinces a familiar motive for misogyny. He hates Criseyde and devalues all women, we can infer from the poem as a whole, because even the weakest of females has such power over men; Criseyde has not only changed the whole course of Troilus's life, but now, due to the same instabilities he once exploited, she has also predictably spoiled Pandarus's game and brought him face to face again with his own actual powerlessness. Worst of all, her behavior has called into question the authority of Pandarus's words and fictions; she has, in effect, however unwittingly, silenced the most garrulous, inventive of men. His proclamation of eternal hatred underscores this point; it is framed by a rhetorical question, " 'What sholde I seyen?' " (V.1732), and ends with an admission of defeat, " 'I kan namore seye' " (V.1743). Once he has admitted his misogyny, Pandarus quite literally has no more words; such forthright hatred of women does not, after all, generate much original discourse. Despite his many affinities with the narrator, then, as a manipulator and mediator of words and women, Pandarus is finally very different in his attitude toward women. The narrator never hates Criseyde, and he doesn't let her spoil his game, or silence him. Instead, in fact, she becomes his game, and the poem as a whole testifies to his understanding that writing about this woman is the only game in town—for serious authors.

Troilus's way of resisting his feminization seems more subtle and complex than Pandarus's, and to many readers he is finally more effective in demonstrating his proper manliness and superiority to Criseyde, (even) in love—his integrity, his large soul and his important thoughts, his nobility of spirit, even his beatitude.[47] Despite Pandarus's cynical urgings that he either ravish or abandon Criseyde, Troilus refuses; he retains his love and sympathy for her well beyond the point where he might reasonably start hating. Even when he sees the brooch on Diomede's collar and finally admits his lady's perfidy, he says he cannot find it in his heart to "unloven" her (V.1698): " 'yow, that doon me al this wo endure, / Yet love I best of any creature!' " (V.1700–1). Troilus's refusal to hate Criseyde is an important step in proving his worth in the very arena where he has reluctantly risked entry, and where women are usually allowed to excel: fidelity to love.

In the third book of *The Art of Courtly Loving*, Andreas Capellanus explains why it is useful for noblemen like Troilus to learn how to love women. Andreas instructs his male readers: "Read this little book, then, not as one seeking to take up the life of a lover, but that, invigorated by the theory and trained to excite the minds of women to love you may, by refraining from so doing win an eternal recompense and thereby deserve a greater reward from God." And Andreas concludes: "For God is more pleased with a man who is able to sin and does not, than with a man who has no opportunity to sin."[48] This passage suggests quite

---

47. It would be impossible to cite even a small proportion of the studies that conclude that Troilus, however flawed, is still the hero, still the man to be admired. The terms I have used to describe this assessment of Troilus here are taken respectively from: Barney, "Troilus Bound," p. 458; Lambert, "Troilus, Books I–III," p. 122; Lee Patterson, "Ambiguity and Interpretation: A Fifteenth-Century Reading of *Troilus and Criseyde*," in *Negotiating the Past* (Madison: University of Wisconsin Press, 1987), p. 149; and Peter Dronke, "The Conclusion of *Troilus and Criseyde*," *Medium Aevum* 33 (1974), p. 49.

48. Andreas Capellanus, *The Art of Courtly Love*, trans. John Jay Parry (New York: Frederick Ungar, 1941), p. 187. The original text reads: "Taliter igitur praesentem lege libellum, non quasi per ipsum quaerens amantium tibi assumere vitam, sed ut eius doctrina refectus et mulierum edoctus ad amandum animos provocare a tali provocatione abstinendo praemium consequaris aeternum et maiori ex hoc apud Deum merearis munere gloriari. Magis enim Deo placet qui opportunitate non utitur concessa peccandi, quam cui delinquendi non est attributa potestas," (*Andreas Capellanus on Love*, ed. and trans. P. G. Walsh [London: Duckworth, 1982], p. 286).

clearly how the apparently conflicting points of view in *The Art of Courtly Loving* seriously cohere, and why Andreas's interest in courtly rules does not sit as oddly with his antifeminism as scholars have often thought; it also reads like a gloss on Troilus's experience, in Chaucer's telling. "Invigorated by the theory" [*eius doctrina refectus*] of Love at the very beginning of the poem, the hero is then "trained [by teacher Pandarus] to excite" the mind of Criseyde to love in Books II and III, and Troilus learns his lesson well. But his fidelity to love, however praiseworthy, cannot in itself serve to designate proper manliness or moral worth; it is, as Andreas says, indulging so far and then refraining from what is so delightful that matters.

One of the first signs that Troilus can move on, can learn to rise above the love of women, appears in his response to the news of the exchange of prisoners. In Book IV, separated from the lady whom he has excited to love, he begins to recover the manly spirit that he often lost when he was with her in Books II and III, as he conceals his "affeccioun": "*With mannes herte* he gan his sorwes drye" (IV.154, my emphasis).[49] Similarly, his first reaction to Pandarus's suggestion that he abduct Criseyde, thus acting " 'with thy manhod. . . . To take a womman which that loveth the' " (IV.529–34), is to remind Pandarus that Troy is at war because of this false sense that manliness can ever prove itself when taking (or keeping) a woman is the goal. Now Troilus reverses his earlier position and shows his aspiration toward better manhood by aligning his own honor with a sense of the "townes goode": " 'I sholde han also blame of every wight, / My fadres graunt if that I so withstoode, / Syn she is chaunged for the townes goode' " (IV.551–53).[50]

At the end of the poem, moreover, Troilus is at last able to see that even his supposedly selfless adoration of Criseyde is a delusion, and it is then that he rises above both love and hate in his transcendent, Christianized, and conclusive vision that scorns and laughs at the "vanite"

49. It is notable that Chaucer adds the notion of "mannes herte" here; in Boccaccio, Troilus merely restrains himself with difficulty, "come si convenne" (IV.14.8).

50. Many critics take this new resolve on Troilus's part as proof of his growing virtue; see, for instance, P. M. Kean, "Chaucer's Dealings," p. 46. I am not sure whether this is the kind of argument that Green has in mind when he comments on Troilus's refusal to ravish Criseyde: "Though we may find the aspersions which are cast on Troilus' manliness . . . comic in the context of the bedroom scene, there is a certain pathos in his later inability, in the face of a far more serious challenge, to 'manly sette the world on six and sevene' (IV.622)." He acts, Green says, "with a short-sightedness that is almost admirable" ("Troilus and the Game of Love," p. 216).

and "blynde lust" of all earthly passion. In this vision, if not before, Troilus might be said to vitiate the feminization he has endured: he is no longer passive and submissive, subject to Criseyde and imprisoned in his desire for her or for what he thinks she represents; he no longer misreads what he sees. Instead, he has lost interest in the woman altogether and hence freed himself from subjugation to her power to provoke strong emotion; his vision surveys and then, with proper Boethian scorn, dismisses the earth he sees beneath him. Criseyde, then, affords Troilus the soul-saving opportunity to go wrong. Male virtue is made possible in this rendition of an old story by the improper, inevitable, and instable female desire the hero learns to arouse and then is strong enough to shun.

In modern criticism of the poem, however, a crucial question has emerged: should Troilus's eschatological vision be taken as the correct one, the one that satisfies the narrator and/or author completely and serves without further comment as the moral of the poem? Some readers defend Troilus's final judgment as one that the text approves, arguing not only that the sentiment is suitably Christian, Boethian, or Dantesque, but that the narrator himself has demonstrated from the beginning something of Troilus's final detachment. Others, by contrast, contend that Troilus's last position is undermined or qualified by the poem as a whole and fails to offer a sufficient conclusion to what they perceive as its meaning or Chaucer's intention.[51] The critical debate, I suggest, reflects the importance of the characteristic ambiguities of closure in this poem, especially as they entail, here as elsewhere, the question of the narrator's gender and his alliances in the putatively timeless antagonism of the sexes in which he embeds his story.

There is certainly evidence to support both sides of this argument. On one hand, the narrator does anticipate and perhaps thereby sanctions

51. It is impossible to represent here the range of opinion on the ending of this poem, or to engage in any rigorous way in the variety of problems it raises, but critics who see the ending as unstable or problematic in some way include Richard Waswo, "The Narrator of *Troilus and Criseyde*"; Thomas H. Bestul, "Chaucer's *Troilus and Criseyde*: The Passionate Epic and Its Narrator," *Chaucer Review* 14 (1980), pp. 366–78; Burlin, *Chaucerian Fiction* (Princeton: Princeton University Press, 1977), pp. 132ff.; Peter Dronke, "The Conclusion"; Murray J. Evans, " 'Making Strange': The Narrator (?), the Ending (?), and Chaucer's 'Troilus,' " *Neuphilologische Mitteilungen* 87 (1986), pp. 218–28; Wetherbee, *Chaucer and the Poets,* especially p. 234; and, for a more complete summary of criticism on the ending, Monica E. McAlpine, *The Genre of "Troilus and Criseyde"* (Ithaca: Cornell University Press, 1978), p. 237, n. 19.

his hero's final transcendent distance and detachment from experience in his own attitude throughout the poem. He has insistently presented himself as someone outside the system of heterosexual love, and while he does not claim to have chosen this marginalized position, it means that he is already free, from the beginning, of the blind lust for a woman for which he, unlike Troilus, refused to risk his soul. The narrator's professed distance, submissiveness, inadequacy, and fear in the face of love is pointedly replicated in his (sometimes) detached, subordinate, deferential relation to the alleged literary sources of his story, a higher authority to whom he willingly submits. He repeatedly presents himself as a translator only, writing not from his own experience and feeling ("of no sentement I this endite" [II.13]), but merely taking the story "out of Latyn in my tonge" (II.14; see also I.394). Again and again, he expresses an ostensive and highly conventional humility and compliance with authority: "Myn auctour shal I folwen, if I konne" (II.49).

On the other hand, the narrator's brand of distance, detachment, and submission to higher forces remains fortified and enriched by the problematic, equivocal, characteristic interest he retains and admits in Criseyde and Woman, an interest that he never directly scorns or completely recants. While this apparently meek, acquiescent narrator quietly revises the traditional story extensively and pervasively, he becomes openly resentful, suspicious, and possibly even subversive of authority only when he speaks of his unfortunate obligation, because he is following his "auctours," to tell the sad truth about Criseyde. At the beginning of Book IV, to cite just one prominent instance, he signals an emotional investment in Criseyde in conventional terms, noting that his heart bleeds and his pen quakes "for drede of that I moste endite" (IV.14). He goes on to mention the allegedly painful subject of Criseyde's betrayal of Troilus in these interesting terms:

> For how Criseyde Troilus forsook,
> Or at the leeste, how that she was unkynde,
> Moot hennesforth ben matere of my book,
> As writen folk thorugh which it is in mynde.
> Allas! that they sholde evere cause fynde
> To speke hire harm, and if they on hire lye,
> Iwis, hemself sholde han the vilanye.
>   (IV.15–21)

In his comments on this passage, E. Talbot Donaldson reads line 15 as "a *manful* stroke, restating unambiguously for the last time the basic fact on which the whole action depends" (my emphasis); lines 16–18, by contrast, suggest the narrator's characteristic effort "to soften" the harsh reality about Criseyde.[52] In this formulation, Donaldson accurately (if unwittingly) points out the narrator's shifting assumption, here almost within the same breath, of masculine and feminine positions. The weight of the stanza as a whole seems to provide a typical show of sympathy with the female character, carried to the point of speaking, as the narrator so often does, to "soften" the harsh treatment of Criseyde by his literary precursors and even to impugn their honesty. This sympathy with Criseyde and dissent from the allegedly traditional and authoritative treatment of her character first inscribes that traditional opinion, however, as the hard fact on which the whole poem turns, restated here as elsewhere with a "manful" avoidance of ambiguity.

Furthermore, the narrator's insistence that his sources oblige him against his will to disparage a woman whom he is attracted to and pities is qualified by the fact that departures from the "auctours" he claims to follow frequently raise at least as many doubts about Criseyde's innocence as they do about her guilt, giving rise to those critical commonplaces about Criseyde's ambiguity, which as we have seen is so carefully and purposively constructed. Donaldson, again, finds proof in this phenomenon of the narrator's "wildly emotional attitude" toward Criseyde, his "avuncular" love of the heroine; Chaucer, on the other hand, he views as the unambivalent author "standing behind" this narrator, creating such an earnest but unreliable narrator in order to give us a different light on Criseyde—and to demonstrate his own impartiality. The strategy, according to Donaldson, leads to the following judgement of Chaucer, on one hand, and Criseyde, on the other: "We could never convict him [Chaucer] of having brought Criseyde's sincerity into question; on the other hand, as readers we may tend to feel that she bears some responsibility for having become the victim of the narrator's incompetence."[53]

---

52. *Speaking of Chaucer*, p. 70.

53. Ibid., p. 73. If Donaldson seems again too obvious a target or too convenient a straw man, it should be kept in mind that his eagerness to blame the victim is hardly unique. For just one other example, see Alfred David, "Chaucerian Comedy." Noting Criseyde's melodramatic response to the (false) story of Troilus's jealousy of Horaste, David argues that Pandarus is exploiting her "instinctive fears," but adds: "perhaps he also understands that the crises he invents fulfil an emotional need for Criseyde and that she *wants* to be deceived. She cannot yield to Troilus except in the course of some high drama in which she is the innocent victim of false accusations" (p. 98).

But if we are trying both to understand and resist the temptation to blame the female victim—even the victim of so figurative a crime as willful narrative incompetence—we are obliged to ask harder questions about the narrator's complicated self-representation and self-division and about the special relation to Criseyde and Woman that he claims for the figure of the male author. In the first place, it has been repeatedly shown that the separation of the unreliable narrator and the wise author is never as easy to make or agree upon as those who would argue for and from their knowledge of Chaucer and his intentions must assume. While many critics wish to hear the author at the end of the poem rising with or above Troilus, rejecting all that has gone before, the difficulty of knowing precisely where the voice of Chaucer kicks in can never be satisfactorily addressed. Throughout this study I have assumed, as I noted in my introductory remarks, that it is not possible to dismantle the complex fiction of Chaucer, if that means discovering for sure he who is "standing behind," pulling the strings. What we do and do not know about the historical contexts of the text, and what we assume about the function of language, should oblige us to avoid any such leap without a great deal of care, to concentrate instead on analyzing the positions that the narrating persona occupies and invokes and the effects that can thereby be generated.

Here those positions are, as I have said, substantially defined by the palpable ambiguity of the narrator's feelings and intentions concerning the female character. Unlike Pandarus, as we have seen, the narrator does not simply hate (and fear) Criseyde. Unlike Troilus, moreover, he does not directly claim to be able to forget or transcend her or the weaknesses she as Woman represents. To some if not all critics, indeed, the last lines of the poem, where the narrator too may leave women behind, can only be read as "diversionary," and what matters is the larger body of the narrative, wherein he repeatedly sympathizes with his heroine.[54] At the same time, as we have seen, he draws his own life, his own voice, from the story that dramatizes, complicates, analyzes, and thus all the more richly reinscribes her betrayal, her weakness, her "crime." He hates the sin, and loves the sinner—from a safe distance.

In this finely wrought, thoroughly equivocal distance from and sympathy with Criseyde, the narrator of *Troilus and Criseyde* takes up a stance that manages the problems of the feminization of the poet and the self-reflexive, self-destructive misogyny of the literary tradition: he simultaneously accommodates and resists the instability of gender and the problems of masculine identity from which his male characters suffer. Above all, he creates for the figure of the poet an empowering ambiguity not only about Criseyde but also (and hence) about his own gender alliances and his own intentions—an ambiguity first developed in and then denied to his characters. The compellingly lifelike characters are, within the story as told, full of contradictions, and nowhere are these clearer than in the depiction of their gender traits. The womanliest of women, Criseyde, is at times sexually aggressive; the proud and strong Troilus is often timid and weepy; the controlling, godlike Pandarus of Books II and III is also gossipy throughout, and in Book V he is helpless and speechless. The plot of the story, however, finally refixes the characters in positions that flatten ambiguities and restore proper gender alignments. Pandarus is frozen in the role of the all-too-clever male misogynist, while both the lovers find themselves in their original positions: archetypally and fictively masculine and feminine. Following a heroic death in battle, Troilus dwells in an abstract realm, detached from and scornful of life, free of self-interest, and closer to God; still alive, Criseyde is only more aware of her endless and inevitable subjection and error. He finally reads correctly, according to certain orthodoxies, and resists the seductive text of the female body and the love story. She finally takes her proper place not as the earnest, complicitous, and shortsighted reader she has been earlier but as text that can be mastered by character, author, and reader; as Davis Taylor puts it, "She becomes the subject of our judgment, not, like Troilus, judging us from heaven."[55]

As I have argued, the narrator also feminizes the position of the reader by presenting Criseyde as the archetypal interpreter who cannot decipher, let alone control, the intentions of those whose texts she reads. Pandarus and Troilus, in the second half of the story, turn out to be equally poor readers. The narrator himself may be a "bad reader" too, but the result of his (mis)reading is that he rewrites the story, and in doing so writes in the uniquely empowered position of the equivocal, evasive, marginalized poet.[56] The narrator alone is able to transcend the limits of both masculine and feminine genders by at once "understand-

55. "The Terms of Love: A Study of Troilus' Style," *Speculum* 51 (1976), pp. 69–90.
56. This point is made by Vance, *Mervelous Signals*, p. 283.

ing" both and adopting, it seems, neither position. "Beth war of men, and herkneth what I seye": I am not a man like other men, but (and therefore) I have the authority over women (and myself) that they ought to but fail to have.

In recent comments on the French sociologist Jean Baudrillard's book *De la séduction*, American feminist Jane Gallop critiques the author in terms that would serve equally well to describe my view of the position of the poet inscribed and celebrated in Chaucer's *Troilus and Criseyde*. Baudrillard speaks, Gallop argues,

> not from the masculine or masculinist position (which he identifies as against appearances and for profundities) but from a position that knows the truth of the feminine and the masculine and can thus, from this privileged position beyond sexual difference, advise women how best to combat masculine power. It is his assumption of this position of superiority, of speaking the truth—more than any content of "truth" that he may utter—which offends me. Women, he warns, are in danger of losing their power, but if they would only let themselves be seduced by what he says. . . . A line if ever I heard one.[57]

To Gallop's observation, I just want to add: a remarkably old line, it seems.

57. "French Theory and the Seduction of Feminism," in *Men in Feminism*, ed. Alice Jardine and Paul Smith (New York: Methuen, 1987), p. 114.

7

The Powers of Silence:
The Case of the Clerk's Griselda

> To take a stand would be to upset the beautiful
> balance of the game.
>
> > Richard A. Lanham,
> > "Chaucer's *Clerk's Tale:*
> > The Poem Not the Myth"

To most Chaucerians, it is by now either commonplace or irrelevant to point out that the *Clerk's Tale*, like so many of Chaucer's poems, situates a strong female character in what one modern editor describes as "a context of masculine authoritarianism."[1] Recognizing this situation does not seem to resolve the interpreters' fundamental confusion about the Tale's meaning. This confusion, in fact, is one of the few things that a number of critics can agree upon: whatever its specific significance, this poem appears to many to be bound up with its ambiguities and contradictions, the insolubility of its many problems.[2] The force of gender conflict in the Tale is thus at once recognized and neutralized; if Chaucer takes no definitive position on the victimization of women that he so clearly depicts, then we need not raise charged and difficult questions about misogyny and great Western art, and we can instead contemplate

---

1. John H. Fisher, ed., *The Complete Poetry and Prose of Geoffrey Chaucer* (New York: Holt, Rinehart and Winston, 1977), p. 145. The article from which the epigraph is drawn appears in *Literature and Psychology*, 16 (1966), pp. 157–65.

2. For other readings like Richard Lanham's (cited in note 1) that locate meaning in the contradictions and tensions that the Clerk brings to his story, see Dolores Warwick Frese, "Chaucer's *Clerk's Tale:* The Monsters and the Critics Reconsidered," *Chaucer Review*, 8 (1973), pp. 133–46; Warren Ginsberg, " 'And Speketh so Pleyn': The Clerk's Tale and its Teller," *Criticism* 20 (1978), pp. 307–23; Lloyd N. Jeffrey, "Chaucer's Walter: A Study in Emotional Immaturity," *Journal of Humanistic Psychology* 3 (1963), pp. 112–19; Patrick Morrow, "The Ambivalence of Truth," *Bucknell Review* 16 (1968), pp. 74–90; J. Mitchell Morse, "The Philosophy of the Clerk of Oxenford," *Modern Language Quarterly* 19 (1958), pp. 3–20; and Robert Stepsis, "*Potentia Absoluta* and the *Clerk's Tale*," *Chaucer Review*, 10 (1975–76), pp. 129–42.

"the beautiful balance of the game," a playful, aesthetic foreclosure of the problems of sexual politics and gendered poetics.

Here I want to recharge the question of the impenetrability of the *Clerk's Tale* with further consideration of the nature of "masculine authoritarianism" in the poem. The text offers readers a fundamentally equivocal—and hence rich and compelling—confrontation with patriarchal power, a confrontation necessitated and implicated by the literary project foregrounded in all the Chaucerian fiction I have examined thus far: the representation of a male author telling, with great verbal skill and studied, multivalent ambiguities, the story of a female character. In the first part of my discussion, focusing on the female character and her multiple, slippery significations, I argue that the tale of patient Griselda addresses central questions about women and power and articulates a clear paradox. Woman's insubordination is, as our lexicon suggests, a derivative of her subordination. In the second half of the chapter, focusing on the representation of the male author, I ask again what kind of men, in Chaucerian fiction, choose to tell such stories about women, and why and how such men might well prefer to play games and make jokes rather than take a stand.

"This is ynogh, Grisilde myn."
IV.365, 1051

From one point of view, the plot of Griselda's story demonstrates how a woman may rise to the highest position of hegemonic power, becoming the honored wife of a wealthy lord and a coruler of his kingdom, through her archetypally acceptable behavior: utter submissiveness and essential silence. Griselda is a complicated figure of both class mobility and the classless (or cross-class), feminized ideals of Christian thinking. She succeeds in rising from poorest peasant to ruling aristocrat—and at another level even serves, the Clerk reminds us, as an allegorical figure for the patient Christian soul—by living up to her culture's image of perfect femininity, by willfully accepting and even reveling in the powerlessness of her position.[3] To some modern readers, of course, Griselda may not

---

3. See Caroline Walker Bynum, *Holy Feast and Holy Fast* (Berkeley: University of California Press, 1987), for a discussion of the feminization of medieval Christian practice and theory, and especially Chapter 10, "Women's Symbols."

in this way represent a positive model of female power, but rather the kind of prescriptive antifeminist propaganda for which the medieval period is well known.[4] Even from the naturalistic point of view that the Clerk sometimes at least insists on, the happy ending brings the heroine the dubious reward of permanent union with a man whom the Clerk, embellishing his sources, has characterized as a sadistic tyrant, worst of men and cruelest of husbands (although not, he suggests, unrealistic or atypical in this regard). The Clerk's peculiar handling of the Griselda story both supports and complicates such responses by exploring the implications of Griselda's paradoxical position as a woman: the fact that she attains certain kinds of power by embracing powerlessness; the fact that she is strong, in other words, because she is so perfectly weak. The Tale suggests on one hand that Griselda is not really empowered by her acceptable behavior, because the feminine virtue she embodies in welcoming her subordination is by definition both punitive and self-destructive. On the other hand, the Tale reveals that the perfectly good woman *is* powerful, or at least potentially so, insofar as her suffering and submission are fundamentally insubordinate and deeply threatening to men and to the concepts of power and gender identity upon which patriarchal culture is premised.

The *Clerk's Tale* specifies early in the plot that even legitimate exercises of direct power only endanger a woman's well-being. Immediately after his description of Walter and Griselda's marriage, the Clerk, following his sources, points out how swiftly and remarkably the good peasant girl is transformed into the perfect noblewoman. In the space of a few stanzas (393–441), we learn that after her marriage Griselda is beloved by Walter's people and famed in many regions; people travel to Saluzzo, we are told, just to see her. Not merely a paragon of "wyfly hoomlinesse," she also serves the public interest (the "commune profit," 431) by acting in her husband's absence as a peerless adjudicator who settles all disputes with her "wise and rype wordes" (438). The passage seems in its own right to document Griselda's innate "virtue"—but the root of the word "virtue" itself, from the Latin for "male person," signals what

4. For a discussion of Chaucer's relation to the antifeminist tradition as it emerges in "images . . . which celebrate, with a precision often subtle rather than apparent, the forms a woman's goodness is to take," see Hope Phyllis Weissman, "Antifeminism and Chaucer's Characterizations of Women," in *Geoffrey Chaucer: A Collection of Original Articles*, ed. George D. Economou (New York: McGraw-Hill, 1975), pp. 93–110.

the *Clerk's Tale* subsequently affirms: a *virtuous woman*, the stuff of folk tales and saints' legends, is a contradiction, a semantic anomaly, a threat to the social order and to the stability of gender difference and hierarchy.

Walter, it appears, recognizes part of this threat right away. Griselda's public virtue, her ability to exert a power at once masculine in kind and superhuman in degree, would seem to vindicate the sovereign's willful choice of an unsuitable bride beyond his wildest dreams; people soon say, according to the Clerk, that Griselda is literally a godsend. But Walter's decision to torture and humiliate her as a wife and mother comes, according to the narrative, after she has been acclaimed as a saintly ruler, and so the narrative sequence implies on the contrary that such virtue in a woman only provokes male aggression. A woman's public powers, even if they are conferred upon her through her husband and divinely sanctioned, cannot be integrated with her proper identity as a female and a wife. Griselda's supposedly unusual and seemingly innate ability to rule wisely and well, to pass good judgments and speak in ways that men admire and respect, to assume, that is, the power and position normally assigned to the best of men, fails to empower her or enable her to escape her subordinate gendered status. Her situation may in this way remind us of a point made by modern feminist analyses of history: the occasional existence of a strong, wise, and successful female in a position of power is the exception that proves the rule; the token Virgin Mother or queen or bourgeois female entrepreneur does not alter the material position of most women or the conventional definition of the feminine. To prove her "wommanhede," Griselda must suffer and submit; the more obviously unsuitable part of her virtue—her allegedly inherent but nevertheless unnatural manliness and power—must be punished and contained.

One reason why Griselda's public virtues must be controlled, why the good woman of any social class must be defined as silent and submissive, seems patent. If a peasant woman can so easily rule as well as a noble man—or even better—then Walter's birthright and the whole feudal system on which it depends are seriously threatened. This realization is surely part of the Clerk's meaning when he remarks, near the end of the tale, that it would be "inportable," or intolerable, unbearable, if real wives behaved like Griselda. His comment seems intended to heighten the pathos and abstraction of his portrait of Griselda and to express yet again his alleged sympathy with her situation as a woman; it also suggests, however, his sympathy with Walter and his understanding that it is precisely Griselda's saintliness, her superhuman—or inhuman—goodness, her feminine ability to be just what he asks her to be, that (rightly, or at least understandably) enrages her husband. For as the tale goes on to disclose, if Walter is at first shown up, defeated, and made powerless by the position and authority he hands his wife, which she so effortlessly and successfully wields, he is again all but undone by the self-abasement that he then demands and that she, ever obedient and adaptable to her situation, so easily and successfully performs. Galled by the unbearable way in which this woman eludes his tyranny by refusing to resist and define it, he can only torture her again and again, seeking to determine her elusive identity as well as his own, to find the Other in Griselda, someone he can master in order to find himself.

The series of seemingly unmotivated trials proving Griselda's worth also emphasizes that the better Griselda is, the more she must suffer, or that the more she suffers the better she must be. While this principle is consistent with medieval Christian thought, we shall see at the close of the tale that one logical conclusion of this potentially fatal prescription for female virtue proves troubling. The end of the heroine's suffering must in a sense spell the end of her virtue, and what voice Griselda has is silenced, her story finished, when Walter finally stops torturing her. And what makes Walter stop, after the third trial, may be his eventual understanding of the paradoxical sense in which this woman continues to win, in venerable Christian fashion, by losing so fully and graciously to a tyrannical man.

The last scene of the tale becomes crucial to our understanding of the complex interaction of the subordination and insubordination of the female; Griselda almost beats Walter to the draw. She has been called back to the palace to clean it up for Walter's second wedding, and, as the nobles sit down to dinner, Walter calls the old wife over to ask how she likes his beautiful new one. But in the preceding stanza we have learned that Griselda is already busy praising the girl and her brother "So wel that no man koude hir prise amende" (1026). When Walter, who hasn't apparently noticed what she's up to, foolishly invites her to come center stage for a moment, in her rags, Griselda seizes the opportunity to protest and celebrate, at the same time, her own treatment at Walter's hands. First she wishes him well of his lovely young bride; at the same time that she once again accepts and cooperates in her own abasement here, she subtly praises herself, born again into better circumstances, and engages in the competition between women, even between mother and daughter, that her culture enforces. She goes on to warn Walter not to torment the maiden as he has tormented "mo" ("others"), as she tactfully puts it; Griselda predicts that the well-born creature could not endure what the poor one could. Her strategy recalls her earlier move when she responded to banishment with the longest, most pathetic speech in the poem (814–89), but this time Walter knows better than to let his patient wife have the floor for more than one stanza. He is at this point said to "rewen upon hire wyfly stedfastnesse" (1050), and while the chief sense of "rewen upon" is "to feel pity or compassion for," we may also think of the more familiar sense of the verb, one which was also current in Middle English: "to regard or think of . . . with sorrow or regret, to wish that (something) had never taken place or existed."[5]

Walter must indeed regret Griselda's surpassing wifely steadfastness, because whichever way he turns, it all but defeats his lordly urge to dominate. When in the next stanza he tells Griselda, " 'This is ynogh, Grisilde myn,' " we are reminded that he said this once before, when she gave her initial promise (365), and in retrospect the repetition may underline for Walter the dangers inherent in the way Griselda from the beginning sought to exceed his demands for wifely subordination. In setting the conditions for their marriage, he asked only that she would do what he wished, and never contradict his will. She promised far more: a perilous merging of wills ("But as ye wole youreself, right so wol I" [361]), which would in fact imply her full knowledge of his will and thus destabilize the power differential and difference between them; and a surrender of her own life ("In werk ne thoght, I nyl yow disobeye, / For to be deed, though me were looth to deye, "[363–64]), which again would defeat his intention to keep her, alive, under his thumb. When, at the end of the story, he sets the limit to her excessive self-abasement, which is beginning to be coupled with the self-assertion it always entails, we cannot be sure whether he intends to call a halt to her suffering or to her emergent powers of subversive speech—powers paradoxically dependent on his continued oppression of her. When he goes on to seal Griselda's lips with kisses, her reaction is telling. She is so stunned, the Clerk says, that for a moment she cannot hear Walter's astonishing concession that she has finally proved herself in his eyes: "She herde nat what thyng he to hire seyde; / She ferde as she had stert out of a sleep" (1059–60). Griselda's temporary deafness and stupor represent, I suggest, her unwillingness to hear that the nightmare is over. She knows

5. See Oxford English Dictionary, *rue*, v.1, sense 1.

that any power she has lies only in continuing to excel at suffering, that she can speak only to assent to being silenced, and that the promise of a happy ending precludes her potential for martyred apotheosis, and forces her to awaken into the reality of her material, gendered power-lessness.

In the second half of this chapter I shall explore what happens after this climactic moment, in the multiple endings of the *Clerk's Tale*, as the Clerk himself confirms Griselda's powerlessness at many levels, but let me conclude this section by underscoring some implications of the read-ing I have just offered. Griselda has threatened to escape Walter's tyranny by willfully refusing to resist it, and it is possible to argue that he keeps testing her because given his view of selfhood and power, her behavior can only seem to him unmotivated, implausible, irritating, and even inhuman. As the Clerk says after the second trial, Walter "wondred" at his wife's patience; if he hadn't known better, he would have thought that she took some perverse or treacherous delight in seeing her children murdered (687–95), and modern readers have frequently complained that Griselda was not a good enough mother. In one way Griselda's behavior is certainly both perverse and treacherous, not because she fails to protect her children against paternal infanticide and thus to live up to ideals (and realities) of motherhood, but because she lives up all too well to certain ideals of womanhood and thus makes manifest their latent pow-ers. Walter cannot and does not solve the mystery or negate the threat that her perfect womanly behavior poses; he merely stops trying to do so and stops giving his wife the chance to act in ways that he cannot understand or control.

Just as she remains a mystery and a threat to Walter, so too Griselda remains an unresolved problem for the Clerk and for his audiences. The *Clerk's Tale* suggests, and generations of modern interpreters confirm, that Griselda is a "humanly unintelligible" entity, as one critic puts it, comprehensible and coherent only at the allegorical level that the Clerk at once entertains and undermines.[6] In an unusual way, the inhumanity and perhaps inhumaneness of Griselda's perfect femininity confirms that the human is often posited as equivalent to the masculine in the symbolic order that reaches from the western European Middle Ages into more recent centuries. At the same time, the problem she presents—the un-

6. Marsha Siegel, "Placing Griselda's Exemplary Value by way of the *Franklin's Tale*," paper presented at International Congress on Medieval Studies, Kalamazoo, MI, May 1982.

intelligibility of the perfectly good woman, or perhaps of any woman—
is the most threatening thing about her. Griselda's embodiment of the
archetypally feminine position thus not only insists on the absence and
silence and powerlessness of real women in history but also marks again
the limits of power for masculine authority (Walter), for the male author
(the Clerk), and for the audience attempting to fix the meaning of the
female character in the tale.

Grisilde is deed, and eek hire pacience.

IV.1177

Viewed as a poem about either a woman's subversive silence or her
silenced subversion, the *Clerk's Tale* thus affirms two conclusions about
the history of masculine and feminine power in Western culture. It suggests that "maleness," as Catharine MacKinnon has put it, has often
been perceived as "a form of power that is both omnipotent and nonexistent, an unreal thing with very real consequences."[7] It also explains
why Woman, identified as absence, is a fearsome ideal for both real
women and masculine presence. Turning the focus of my reading to the
Clerk now, I want to suggest that the oft-noted and characteristic ambiguity of the tale is most fruitfully read as a reflex of his position as a
male storyteller, which turns out to be much the same here, where the
narrator is an unbeneficed cleric writing in a specifically religious mode
and explicitly translating from Latin, as when he is a secular court poet
translating from the vernacular. To support and flesh out this claim, it is
possible to compare the subtle Clerk of the *Canterbury Tales* with one
narrator who exemplifies the coyness, insecurity, and playful evasiveness
that we see in the narrators of all the earlier dream-visions and *Troilus
and Criseyde:* the poet of the *Legend of Good Women.*

The *Clerk's Tale* and the *Legend of Good Women* are not, as far as I
know, frequently compared, but the comparison is in fact indirectly suggested within the *Canterbury Tales,* where the Legends are invoked in
the preface to the *Man of Law's Tale,* a poem that, in the most common
ordering of the Tales, comes right before the *Wife of Bath's Tale,* to which
the Clerk in turn is responding. The link between the *Man of Law's Tale*

7. Catharine A. MacKinnon, "Feminism, Marxism, Method, and the State: An Agenda
for Theory," *Signs* 7 (1982), p. 543.

and the *Clerk's Tale* is reinforced by the fact that both are female saints' lives, potentially or actually bracketing the Wife's monstrous tale of feminine misrule. The Clerk may emphasize this point with his two allusions to the Man of Law's heroine, Constance: one when Walter finally admits that Griselda is "constant as a wal" (1047), and one when the Clerk says that we should all be, like Griselda, "constant in adversitee" (1146). And even if we read the tales in another order, or discount the dramatic interaction between tellers altogether, the analogies between Griselda in the *Canterbury Tales* and the female saints of the *Legend of Good Women* are obvious. All these women are represented as archetypally passive. They put the love of a man above all other responsibilities, even above life itself. As a direct consequence of this love they endure great suffering. (The heroines of the earlier poem almost all die; Griselda's survival, at least until the *Lenvoy de Chaucer* proclaims her demise, may thus indicate either a flaw in her goodness, or the story's need, like Walter's, to keep her alive in order to punish and contain her perfection.) The unremarked similarities between the men who tell this kind of story, the narrator of the *Legend* and the Clerk of Oxenford, are equally obvious and perhaps more subtly interesting, and three prominent features of their performances warrant comparison: the ostensive circumstances under which they tell their stories, the changes they make in their sources, and their closural strategies.

In both the *Legend of Good Women* and in the *Canterbury Tales*, the audience is made privy to specific circumstances or preconditions, outside and prior to the narratives of good women, that occasion each act of storytelling and hence oblige us to speculate about the dramatized motives and attitudes of both the poet/dreamer of the earlier poem and the Clerk of Oxenford, and to see each narrator's voiced personality as part of the meaning of his fiction. In the *Canterbury Tales*, not in a dream but in the framing matter of his tale, the Clerk, like the narrator of the *Legend*, is commanded to tell a story—"Telle us som murie thyng of aventures" (15)—by the Host, a figure who like Cupid in the dream assumes godlike powers of judgment and behaves like a tyrant. The Host first makes fun of the Clerk's unaggressive, even effeminate behavior: "Ye ryde as coy and stille as dooth a mayde / Were newe spoused, sittynge at the bord" (2–3). He reminds the Clerk that he agreed to submit to the Host's authority when he entered into the "pley" (10). The Clerk's professional status is also underscored by the Host's prohibitions against an overly didactic or boring tale in the "heigh style" associated with learned clerks (18). In the *Wife of Bath's Prologue* (separated from the *Clerk's Tale* only by the *Friar's* and *Summoner's Tales*), clerks in general, again like the poet/dreamer of the *Legend of Good Women,* have already been associated with and castigated for their literary antifeminism. The Clerk appears to accede more meekly to the tyrant's commands than the dreamer does, just as we would expect from the quiet, virtuous, willing learner introduced in the *General Prologue.* But even before the tale proper begins, the coy Clerk also quietly defies the Host's orders by translating, within an ostensibly disparaging framework ("Me thynketh it a thyng impertinent"[54]) almost all of Petrarch's "prohemye" to the story. This is presumably just the kind of elevated, clerkly fare that the Host hoped to forestall, and its inclusion clearly suggests that this Clerk has his own share of the impertinence he displaces onto Petrarch, that crafty impudence associated with others of his profession throughout the *Canterbury Tales.*

If we are obliged to recognize even before we begin to listen to their stories that both the Clerk and the poet/dreamer of the *Legend of Good Women* have somewhat comparable axes to grind with specific reference to a male figure of alleged sexual and literary authority, then their subsequent representations of good women confirm the wary reader's suspicions that, as in all literature, bias and resentment and special pleading color the stories. The Clerk, as we shall see, disguises himself and his motives more cleverly than the poet/dreamer of the *Legend* (or other storytellers, like the Wife of Bath and the Pardoner); he is so discreet, in fact, that at least one modern critic sees his performance as "a rarefied act of literary-critical wit," executed not in the "voiced style" of the other Canterbury pilgrims but in the manner of Petrarch himself, as "man *of letters,* a posited ideal character, created, displayed, and caught only in the act of writing."[8] This argument may disclose the Clerk's intentions quite accurately, but the alleged neutrality of the man of letters does not stand up under close inspection of the minor additions and revisions the Clerk makes to his two apparent sources, Petrarch's Latin version of Boccaccio's Griselda story and an anonymous French translation of Petrarch. In one early addition, for instance, the Clerk aims a direct blow at the Wife of Bath by supplementing the original description of Griselda with these lines: "No likerous lust was thurgh hire herte yronne. / Wel

8. Anne Middleton, "The Clerk and His Tale: Some Literary Contexts," *Studies in the Age of Chaucer* 2 (1980), p. 149.

ofter of the welle than of the tonne / She drank . . . " (214–16). No such
comment is found in either the Latin or French version of the story; it
recalls to attentive listeners or readers the Wife's self-proclaimed drinking
and sexual habits and her memorable observation that "A likerous
mouth moste han a likerous tayl" (III.466). In light of the insults that the
Wife hurled at clerks as a profession and at her Janekyn in particular,
the Clerk's allusion cannot be accidental or innocent; and so too the
subject of his tale—a patient, submissive married woman who is faithful
to one husband despite his insufferable exercise of *maistrie*—must be
interpreted by the audiences of the *Tales* as a central part of the inter-
personal, voiced drama of the poem as a whole.

In another set of additions and revisions, the Clerk's strategy may
again be profitably compared to the narrator's in the *Legend of Good
Women*. As I have argued elsewhere, alterations in all of the legends
consistently reshape the heroines into figures like the narrator's Cleopatra, less active, aggressive, and passionate, or like his Thisbe, less
noble, more flawed, and more feminine.[9] So too, as J. Burke Severs has
documented, Walter in the Chaucerian version is "more obstinately wil-
ful, more heartlessly cruel," while Griselda's "gentleness, her meekness,
her submissiveness" are more pronounced.[10] Together, these changes,
like many of the alternations in the Legends, call attention to the heroine's feminine powerlessness with respect to a ruthless, self-centered, all
but omnipotent man with whom she herself purports to be in love, and
hence to her victimization; Griselda's suffering, no matter how we view
its signification, arises specifically from the actions of a cruel, deliberate,
and decidedly male oppressor, and the war between the sexes is on
again. At the same time, the Clerk's version of the Griselda story, like
the poet/dreamer's treatments of his good women (and his bad ones),
stresses the heroine's archetypal femaleness, as Petrarch certainly does
not. Note, for instance, this minor change in Walter's motivation: according to the Clerk, what he is seeking and testing in his wife is not
her patience or obedience or ability to live up to her vows but her
"wommanhede." Whereas in Petrarch (as in the anonymous French

---

9. For a more complete discussion of this point and others in the Legends, see my
"Irony and the Antifeminist Narrator in Chaucer's *Legend of Good Women*," *Journal of
English and Germanic Philology* 82 (1983), pp. 11–31, as well as the discussion in Chapter 1
of this study.

10. *The Literary Relationships of Chaucer's Clerk's Tale* (New Haven: Yale University
Press, 1942), pp. 231, 233.

version) Walter is said to admire her *virtutem eximiam supra sexum sup-raque etatem* (a virtue beyond her sex and age),[11] the Clerk gives us Walter (here like Troilus) "Commendynge in his herte hir wommanhede, / And eek hir vertu, passynge any wight / Of so yong age" (239–41). The translation effectively alters the entire thrust of the passage; Griselda still transcends her youth, but notably she does not transcend the expected limitations of gender. Instead, she exemplifies, first and foremost, what has become an almost holy (or mock-holy) ideal in the *Clerk's Tale* as in the *Legend of Good Women*: the abstraction of certain gender-specific characteristics into the ideal state of "wommanhede." After Griselda passes her last test, Walter reiterates his motivation: " 'I have doon this deede / For no malice, ne for no crueltee, / But for t'assaye in thee thy wommanheede' " (1073–75). Again his self-justifying claim, original to the Clerk's version (and in defiance of the Clerk's subsequent injunctions), brings Griselda into line with the heroines of the Legends as type and embodiment, if not caricature, of the idealized medieval good woman.

In another set of even more obvious additions to his source materials, his own intrusive comments on the characters' behavior, the Clerk also underscores the issues of gender difference and marital conflict so central to the *Legend of Good Women* and so common in the *Canterbury Tales*. Just as Walter celebrates Griselda for her "wommanhede," the Clerk repeatedly notes that Walter's behavior is typical of a certain type of "housbonde" or "wedded" man (698, 622) who needlessly tries his "wyf" (452, 461) and her "wyfhod" (699; note that in this line "wyfhod" is mentioned before "stedefastnesse," just as in lines 239–40 "wommanhede" comes before "vertu"). In another original comment, after drawing the standard analogy between Griselda and Job in line 932, the Clerk observes:

> . . . but as in soothfastnesse,
> Though clerkes preise wommen but a lite,
> Ther kan no man in humblesse hym acquite
> As womman kan, ne kan been half so trewe
> As wommen been, but it be falle of newe.
> (934–38)

11. I take the Latin quotation from the convenient edition of Petrarch's *Epistolae Seniles*, Book XVII, Letter III (with a facing edition of *Le Livre Griseldis*) in *Sources and Analogues of Chaucer's Canterbury Tales*, ed. W. F. Bryan and Germaine Dempster (Chicago: University of Chicago Press, 1941), pp. 296–331. The text of Petrarch's version is translated in Robert Dudley French, *A Chaucer Handbook* (New York: F. S. Crofts, 1927), pp. 291–311.

This particular moral to the story, just one of many we will be offered, is found nowhere in Chaucer's sources, but the superiority of women to men, especially in terms of humility and fidelity, is the same highly unoriginal point that the narrator of the *Legend of Good Women* has been commanded to make. The qualifying, tonally odd turn at the end of the Clerk's comment—no man can be as humble or half as true as woman can, unless it has just happened recently—is also reminiscent of the odd jokes that the poet/dreamer often throws off at the end of his legends. Here and there such jests may indicate, like a knowing wink of the eye, the speaker's amused distance from the *querelle des femmes* and/or his actual loyalties. Moreover, the Clerk's implicit separation of himself from those other clerks who "preise wommen but a lite" is, I suggest, part of his attempt to show himself sympathetic to the cause of women, even at the expense of professional solidarity. So too in an earlier intrusion he poses a rhetorical question to the female members of his audience: "But now of wommen wolde I axen fayn / If thise assayes myghte nat suffise?" (696–97; compare the narrator of the *Legend*'s "And trusteth, as in love, no man but me," 2561). The Clerk's strategy in this kind of commentary is remarkably similar to the poet/dreamer's attempts in the *Legend of Good Women* to ingratiate himself with supposed women listeners and demonstrate his unique sympathy with their gender. But despite his efforts to deny that he is the epitome of "clerkhede," to condemn needless male cruelty and to sympathize with Griselda as archvictim of patriarchal tyranny, the Clerk is finally not able or willing to distance himself from a specifically masculine attitude toward feminine virtue.

The fact that the Clerk's perspective is not morally universal, as many modern critics have assumed, not actually sympathetic to women, and not artistically neutral is dramatically confirmed at the conclusion of the tale, where what we might call the excess of endings has the same effect as the apparent incompletion of the *Legend of Good Women*.[12] Although

12. For a sampling of different approaches and conclusions all based on the fundamental premise that the Clerk's answer to the Wife of Bath presents the obviously sensible, beautiful, "universal" refutation of her equally obviously monstrous and ridiculous perversion, see S. K. Heninger, Jr., "The Concept of Order in Chaucer's *Clerk's Tale*," *Journal of English and Germanic Philology* 56 (1957), pp 382–395; Thomas H. Jameson, "One Up for Clerks," *Arts and Sciences* (Winter 1964–65), pp. 10–13; Lynn Staley Johnson, "The Prince and His People: A Study of the Two Covenants in the *Clerk's Tale*," *Chaucer Review* 10 (1975–76), pp.17–29; Alfred Kellogg, "The Evolution of the *Clerk's Tale*," in *Chaucer, Langland, Arthur: Essays in Middle English Literature* (New Brunswick, N.J.: Rutgers University

they appear to close in such radically different ways, both endings are definitely and strategically equivocal, designed to compound readers' uncertainties about the meaning of the narratives, about the narrators' respective attitudes toward the purposes of stories and storytelling, and especially about Chaucer's attitudes toward the problematic issues of gender and marital conflict. In the case of the *Clerk's Tale*, the storyteller addresses the problem for men that he has discerned in the story of the good woman by shifting his ground, dismantling the fiction of feminine virtue by at once denying in various ways that Griselda is a woman and reaffirming that he is a man.

There are several endings to the *Clerk's Tale*. The narrative itself first concludes with a completely closed and happy ending: Walter and Griselda live "Ful many a yeer in heigh prosperitee"; their daughter is married to one of the worthiest lords in Italy; Walter brings Griselda's old father to court and takes care of him for the rest of his days; and Walter's son succeeds to the lordship of the land and makes a fortunate marriage (1128–37). At this point, the Clerk departs briefly from Petrarch to add that Walter's son, however, did not test his noble wife, and that "This world is nat so strong . . . As it hath been in olde tymes yoore" (1139–40). This comparison between the hardiness of wives then and now, between the fabular or literary and the real, implies that Griselda is not like real women, and this point will be picked up three stanzas later, where it leads directly to the Clerk's reference to the Wife of Bath and then to the envoy.

First, however, another possible ending to the story, a religious moral, is offered, prefaced by a closing call to attention, "And herkneth what this auctour seith therfoore" (1141). The subsequent moral is found in both Petrarch and the French versions; the point is not that wives should adopt Griselda's humility but that all human beings should be as "constant in adversitee" as she is: again, then, Griselda is not really a woman. Following this, a third conclusion to the tale is initiated with a second closing formula, "But o word, lordynges, herkneth er I go" (1163), and in

---

Press, 1972), pp. 276–329; Morrow, "The Ambivalence of Truth"; Irving N. Rothman, "Humility and Obedience in the *Clerk's Tale*, with the Envoy Considered as an Ironic Affirmation," *Papers in Language and Literature* 9 (1973), pp. 115–27; Jerome Taylor, "Fraunceys Petrak." For readings that stress the Clerk's (or Chaucer's) sympathy with women, see for example Harriet Hawkin, "The Victim's Side: Chaucer's *Clerk's Tale* and Webster's *Duchess of Malfi*," *Signs* 1 (1975), 339–61; Velma Richmond, "Pacience in Adversitee: Chaucer's Presentation of Marriage," *Viator* 10 (1979), pp. 323–54; and Morse, "The Philosophy of the Clerk".

the next two stanzas the Clerk playfully does precisely what he has just told his audience not to do. Returning to the notion that it would be hard "now-a-dayes" to find two or three live Griseldas in a town, he de-allegorizes the notion of "assay" from the religious interpretation of Griselda's trials to offer this comment on material women, who fall so short of the ideal female malleability that his tale prescribes:

> For if that they were put to swiche assays,
> The gold of hem hath now so badde alayes
> With bras, that thogh the coyne be fair at ye,
> It wolde rather breste a-two than plye.
>
> (1166–69)

He then goes on to dedicate a blessing (in contrast to the Wife's parting curse) to the Wife of Bath and "al hire secte," who are implicitly presented as the real, living examples of that superficially fair coin that will not bend.

With a third parting call to attention—"Herkneth my song that seith in this manere" (1176)—as if he realized that our minds may well be wandering or at least confused by this plethora of contradictory conclusions and applications of his tale, the Clerk offers what now stands as the last ending to the text, titled in many manuscripts *Lenvoy de Chaucer*. Here, as in the preceding two stanzas, the speaker interacts directly with the other pilgrims and links the story we have just heard to the question of marital sovereignty. Now reading the heroine not as a paradigm for all humanity but as an historically real character, dissociable from her ideal virtue, the speaker replicates Walter's move, saying, in effect, "This is enough": "Grisilde is deed, and eek hire pacience, / And bothe atones buryed in Ytaille" (1177–78). He warns husbands that they will fail if they try to test their wives. Turning to "noble wyves," he advises them not to let any clerks tell a story about them like the story of Griselda; and in the remaining stanzas he presents advice couched as the most extreme version possible of the Wife's already extreme philosophy of female dominance.

The Clerk's disclaimer two lines before the beginning of the Envoy—"And lat us stynte of ernestful matere" (1175)—has encouraged modern readers to see the ending as comic play that protects the seriousness of the tale. In a frequently cited appraisal of this "concessionary comedy," for example, Charles Muscatine argues: "The Clerk admits the opposition purposely, so willingly and extravagantly as to make safe from vulgar questioning the finer matter that has gone before."[13] Such a reading is consistent with Freud's view of humor as a healthy, even precious, defense mechanism wherein the humorist takes on the psychic part of both father and child; the superego speaks like a parent to the frightened ego, saying " 'Look here! This is all that this seemingly dangerous world amounts to. Child's play—the very thing to jest about.' "[14] But what, exactly, is the young male ego of the Clerk so frightened of? And how is it the "finer matter" of Griselda's story that the envoy makes safe?[15] As Freud further suggests, the humorist always repudiates suffering and affirms the ego's invulnerability; humor, then, would seem far more likely to trivialize, even undercut, a heroine whose power is equivalent to her capacity to embrace suffering and who can subordinate her own ego so completely to the cultural superego (the Law of the Father, the domination of Walter).

Given the similarity of the Clerk and the narrator of the *Legend of Good Women*, I conclude from the nature of the jest attempted in the envoy that the Clerk is simultaneously afraid of women and afraid of being (like) a woman. What frightens the Clerk so much that he has to joke about it is, first, the power of Griselda, the silenced woman, and her inhuman, celebrated capacity to suffer. This power, within the tale, has also frightened her husband Walter, in ways I have suggested; the envoy reveals that it is, moreover, paradoxically reminiscent of the power attributed by the Clerk to women like the Wife of Bath. What Griselda and the Wife seem to have in common is their capacity, manifested in opposite ways, to escape or at least lay bare the operation of male tyranny by exceeding, in different directions, its enunciated limits. Second, I submit, the Clerk may be frightened by his own likeness to Griselda, a parallel often drawn by readers.[16] As a youth whose manhood is openly questioned by the Host, as an unbeneficed young cleric, and as a storyteller translating a renowned author, the Clerk occupies a marginal and insecure position in the culture that wants to rule the day, the hearty

---

13. *Chaucer and the French Tradition* (Berkeley: University of California Press, 1957), p. 197.

14. "Humour" (1928), in *Collected Papers*, vol. 5, ed. James Strachey (New York: Basic Books, 1959), p. 220.

15. The term "purity" is one Muscatine insists on; see *Chaucer and the French Tradition*, p. 196.

16. For a good analysis of the similarities between narrator and female character in this case, see Carolyn Dinshaw, *Chaucer's Sexual Poetics* (Madison: University of Wisconsin Press, 1989), pp. 135–37.

manly world organized and policed both by the menacing Host of the *Canterbury Tales* and by the literary tradition embodied in the authority vested in Petrarch and the Latin source text. If Griselda exceeds the demands of her husband, so too the Clerk exceeds the demands of translation, and nowhere more than in the excess of endings to his tale. While the Clerk's sympathy with women may be suspect, then, his identification with the feminine position and hence his insight into the nature of a certain kind of psychic oppression is plausible, and it is as frightening to him as it is to a woman like the Wife.

The Clerk's strategy at the end of his tale suggests both his fears and his defense against them. By playing in the envoy at taking the shrew's part, he continues to dissociate himself—now, however, with tongue quite obviously in cheek—from the crude antifeminism of men like Walter, who seriously and mistakenly expect women to submit to masculine dominance and who underestimate the powers of their victims. At the same time, he implies that after all he has managed to transcend the merely literal response to the tale's pathos that his ostensive sympathy with Griselda might indicate and that he is in fact distanced by his superior learning and wit from the whole field of sexual warfare. Like the narrator of the *Legend of Good Women*, the Clerk finally signals that he is neither for real women nor against them; he is just playing a game, not the courtly cult of the marguerite but something not very different, a game played for and about men, and one that entails the transmission of the patriarchy's values, courtly or religious, through stories about idealized female figures. Griselda, then, is not finally unintelligible and threatening, she is just implausible; her suffering and its finer meanings can be forgotten. This is all there really is, the comic ending says, to the seemingly dangerous world of women and the war between lordly husbands and long-suffering wives—the very thing to jest about.

Freud, again like many modern Chaucerians, values humor for its "liberating" element and sees something "fine and elevating" in what he calls "the triumph of the ego": "It refuses to be hurt by the arrows of reality or to be compelled to suffer."[17] But as humor liberates the humorist, does it liberate everyone? What about people who cannot laugh off the arrows of reality, who cannot refuse to be compelled to suffer—what about people like Griselda, whose only power lies in suffering?

17. "Humour," p. 217.

What about those who are the targets of real arrows, the butts of jokes, like the Wife of Bath? The Clerk's humorous ending deflates rather than protects Griselda's virtue, surely, and deflects us from both the real experience and the figurative value of her suffering and endurance; in liberating and elevating himself, then, he devalues and dismisses the feminine power of silence without liberating women from the complementary myths of absence or excess. The envoy in particular not only trivializes but also preempts the voice of a woman like the Wife of Bath, exaggerating just the sort of "vulgar" response—something short of throwing his books into the fire—that she might indeed offer to a story like the Clerk's. Griselda, I have suggested, is made temporarily deaf, like the Wife, when Walter suddenly undergoes a dramatic reversal and agrees that she has proved her worth and can stop being tested; her story ends and her voice is silenced when the misogyny and fear that brings her into being finally comprehends how dangerous it is to let her suffer so visibly and well. In the same way, the Wife's position is silenced and disarmed by the Clerk's reversal when he impersonates her voice and takes up in jest precisely the kind of argument she might make.

The tale's reception, moreover, suggests that the vocal men on the pilgrimage have not been fooled into thinking that the Clerk is really on women's side in all this, or that the telling of this tale could possibly serve to liberate any wives from the domination of husbands that they are compelled to suffer outside the worlds of story and jest. In the link between the *Clerk's Tale* and the *Merchant's Tale*, we hear the Host's enthusiastic response to the story of Griselda, which he wishes his wife could hear. The Merchant, another manly man, begins the next tale in the series by comparing his own shrewish wife to Griselda. Disguised, but not completely so, as sympathetic to women, the Clerk nevertheless affirms to other men his proper maleness by offering them a comforting example of how both virtuous and vicious women alike may be silenced, and Griselda's meaning is reduced to its most minimal and least threatening level. The Host and Merchant have been accused of distorting the tale, and indeed they simply ignore the Clerk's half-hearted, clearly ambivalent and finally subverted warning that we should view Griselda not as a woman, but as a figure for the human soul.[18] But their response, biased as it may be, is invited by the Clerk's presentation.

18. Middleton, "The Clerk and His Tale." The Host's words, lines 1212a–g, are found in only one family of manuscripts, including the Ellesmere manuscript and

The audience outside the poem may be more alert to the tale's sub-tleties, but modern critics at least have not been able to agree on its significance in a persuasive way either. And one of the problems that plagues more skillful interpreters outside the pilgrimage is the identity, not to mention the intentions, of the speaker in this poem, and especially in the envoy. Apart from the teller of the tales of *Melibee* and *Sir Thopas*, the Clerk is the character most often associated with Chaucer and his point of view, one of the few pilgrims usually thought to be treated with little irony and left in control of his own story. At the same time, the voicing of the envoy is particularly problematized by the scribal heading, *Lenvoy de Chaucer*, invoking the author's name at just the point where the joke is made. Robinson's explanatory note seems either obvious (aren't all the dramatically appropriate tales finally composed by Chau-cer?) or confounding: "The song . . . is Chaucer's independent compo-sition. But it belongs dramatically to the Clerk, and is entirely appropriate."[19] It points, however, to the importance of the fact that insofar as Chaucer speaks, it is only through the dramatic composition of other characters and other voices. Here, as in all the earlier dream-visions (and perhaps again with special relation to the *Legend of Good Women*, whose narrator also likes to make obscure little jokes about the ladies), the poet develops and plays on both the proximity and the dis-tance between himself and the narrator of the story. To the extent that both proximity and distance remain in evidence, he creates the possibility of writing about his own limitations and biases with a penetrating self-scrutiny and an ironic self-reflexivity, and hence at the same time im-plying that he has in some sense escaped these limits and can be caught only in the equivocal act of writing and the liberating gesture of humor. Like Griselda, again, the figure of Chaucer transcends ostensive limits because he admits in play to perceiving and accepting them. In his marked equivocation, so central to the game, he figures himself in and

---

Hengwrt 154. Robinson identifies them as "without doubt genuine," perhaps part of a canceled job. See also Eleanor Hammond, *Chaucer: A Bibliographical Manual* (New York: MacMillan, 1908), pp. 302–3, and Aage Brusendorff, *The Chaucer Tradition* (Lon-don: Oxford University Press, 1925), p. 76.

19. *The Works of Geoffrey Chaucer*, note to line 1177, p. 712; John Koch argues, however, that the Envoy is spoken by the author; ("'Nochmals zur Frage des Prologs in Chaucers 'Legend of Good Women,' " *Anglia* 50 [1926], p. 65); for recent comment that supports Robinson's view, see Thomas J. Farrell, "The 'Envoy de Chaucer' and the *Clerk's Tale*" *Chaucer Review* 24 (1990), pp. 329–36.

as one who realizes the powers of silence and unintelligibility that he usurps from and finally denies to his female heroines.

Whereas many modern readers have posited a radical break between early and late Chaucerian fictions, one of my aims in discussing selected *Canterbury Tales* is to underscore some lines of thematic and rhetorical continuity that are especially visible to a feminist criticism interested in the problem of masculine identity and authority. The *Clerk's Tale* highlights such continuity, and we see how the evasiveness of the narrator and his position, so characteristic of all the early poems, manifests itself in an even more emphatic way in the *Tales:* through the creation of other fictive speakers altogether, with their own proper, fictive names, at different degrees of distance from the author, in the fiction of the framed collection. Here the functional moves toward the self-disguise, self-division, ambiguity, and resistance that I trace as empowering strategies in all the earlier poems proceed a logical step further toward the position of "negative capability" and aesthetic transcendence that becomes the hallmark of the humanist artist and earns Chaucer his status as Father of English poetry, even as he plays the child and perhaps identifies with children.[20] Through this further step in self-effacement, brought out so clearly in the Clerk's performance, the figure of the poet avoids precisely the predicament that the remaining male storytellers I am interested in here—the Miller, Knight, Merchant, and Franklin—to varying degrees reflect: any representation of Woman seems to entail a revelation of the male speaker's anxiety about his manliness, his status and identity. Again, this revelation goes hand in hand with a discourse that is thoroughly misogynistic, but the strategic intersection of the present, impersonated male narrator and the absent author has served to liberate Chaucer from the self-revealing, self-destructive side of the misogyny that powers the literary canon.

20. For the argument that Chaucer identifies with children and plays the childish role in the *Canterbury Tales* in particular, see Lee Patterson, " 'What Man Artow?' Authorial Self-Definition in *The Tale of Sir Thopas* and *The Tale of Melibee*," *Studies in the Age of Chaucer* 11 (1989), pp. 117–75.

8

"Women-as-the-Same" in the A-Fragment

> Probably no male human being is spared the terrifying shock of threatened castration at the sight of the female genitals.
>
> Freud, "Fetishism"

> The misdirected kiss reminds us that Emily and Alisoun are no different under their clothes.
>
> Edward C. Schweitzer,
> "The Misdirected Kiss"

The general understanding that the Miller's story comments on the Knight's from another class and generic perspective is unexceptionable, and many critical readings of the interaction between these first two offerings in the Canterbury sequence are available. Here, I want to inflect the critical discussion of both literary and class relations between Knight and Miller, romance and fabliau, with the category of gender.[1] The *Knight's Tale*, like the *Miller's Tale*, takes the problem of male rivalry as its (unromantic) topic, and through its specific articulation and resolution of the problem seeks to consolidate aristocratic masculine identity. As Jerome Mandel points out in his study of courtly love in the *Canterbury Tales*, the tale that is apparently most courtly of all, the *Knight's Tale*, differs from other literary treatments of courtly passion, from Chretien to Malory, in a prominent structural regard: the two courtly lovers in the tale are both men. Such male rivalry, he notes, is generically atypical of romance and epic and more commonly associated with fabliaux. According to Mandel, this alteration of generic expectations identifies the

---

1. The epigraphs are taken, respectively, from Freud's *Collected Papers*, vols. 1–5, ed. James Strachey (New York: Basic Books, 1959), Vol. 5, p. 201, and Edward C. Schweitzer, "The Misdirected Kiss and the Lover's Malady in Chaucer's *Miller's Tale*," in Julian Wasserman and Robert J. Blanch, eds., *Chaucer in the Eighties* (Syracuse: Syracuse University Press, 1986), p. 227.

real subject of the A-fragment as a whole: "The central issue is still *amicitia*. . . . Questions of order, power, loyalty, and friendship were far more pressing and more momentous to Chaucer's audience, the nobility and intellectuals of Ricardian England, than were delicate matters of a decayed literary convention that no one took seriously any longer."[2] But "delicate matters," insofar as the phrase suggests among other things the place and interests of the female and the feminine, may not be as readily erased from either the romance or the fabliaux of the A-fragment as such a reading suggests. The Knight's assumptions about women are not, on careful inspection, so different from the Miller's. A certain common ground between men of different classes is available and necessary, it seems, to the formation of their gender identity and their literary voices, and Emily and Alisoun together represent, I shall argue, a kind of shared terrain whereon knight and peasant talk to each other across their differences.[3]

THE *KNIGHT'S TALE*

The central narrative of the *Knight's Tale* begins with the discovery and imprisonment of Arcite and Palamon, and it is in their relation to each other and to Theseus that the tale imagines what is both desirable and difficult about relations between noblemen. The introduction of the two young knights underscores not their rivalry, which becomes the main focus of the story, but their sameness and intimacy. Their wounded bodies are discovered by pillagers among the victims of Theseus's victory over Creon, "liggynge by and by / Boothe in oon armes . . . of sustren two yborn" (1011–12,1019). The common heraldic decoration they wear, marking them as the same, is their only identity at this liminal moment. As a sign of their shared class identity, it spares them from the death suffered by the nameless masses of defeated Thebans (1005–8), but at the same time it condemns them to remain side by side in Theseus's prison, where they are barred from the mutually interactive exercises in

---

2. "Courtly Love in the *Canterbury Tales*," *Chaucer Review* 19 (1985), pp. 286–87.

3. For a recent reading of male rivalry in the A-fragment that comes to quite different conclusions about the treatment of women in the sequence, see Emily Jensen, "Male Competition as a Unifying Motif in Fragment A of the *Canterbury Tales*," *Chaucer Review* 24 (1990), pp. 320–28.

love and war that should give each noble youth an opportunity to claim his own name, to forge an identity that negotiates his necessary similarity to and difference from other noblemen. Modern commentators have repeatedly disputed whether subsequently the two characters can be adequately distinguished.[4] The interpretive debate defies resolution because it replicates precisely what it is that Arcite and Palamon themselves are trying to work out and what the Knight presents as the dramatic heart of his tale: how can noblemen be both identifiably discrete heroes and yet true chivalric types, models, and brothers?[5]

The (eventual) solution to their problem lies in the (apparent) cause of the main plot, the woman they spy from their prison window. The two cousins are spoiling for a fight that can simultaneously unite them in their common goals and divide them adequately, and Emily is the only "bone," as Arcite puts it, in sight. Like the aristocratic eagles in the *Parliament*, in their initial dispute over the same lady Palamon and Arcite show predictably little interest in the beloved; instead they quibble, just like the birds, over conventional, unanswerable questions such as who "loved hire first" (1146, 1155). In their early verbal disputes, moreover, each knight fairly clearly and coherently represents one side of the chivalric code. Palamon speaks for the value of sworn brotherhood among noble kinsmen and recites the proper pledge they have made "ech of us til oother" (1132), while Arcite articulates their equally pressing need to be individual heroes: " 'Ech man for hymself, ther is noon oother' " (1182). As Arcite also points out (1172ff.), that neither of them looks to stand a chance of actually winning the lady's hand is irrelevant; the competition is all.

As storyteller, the Knight intrudes at the end of Part I to underscore the comforting illusion of individual difference between men that unattainable love can sustain by posing the concluding, again necessarily undecidable question, the *demande d'amour*: which of the knights suffers more from his ungratified desire (1348)? In Book II, moreover, a deus ex

4. For discussions of the problem and references to the scholarship on this topic, see Robert B. Burlin, *Chaucerian Fiction* (Princeton: Princeton University Press, 1977), pp. 100ff. and p. 262, n. 6; also, Lorraine Kochanske Stock, "The Two Mayings in Chaucer's *Knight's Tale*: Convention and Invention," *Journal of English and Germanic Philology*, 85 (1986), p. 218 and p. 217, n. 40.

5. Judith Ferster, in *Chaucer on Interpretation* (Cambridge: Cambridge University Press, 1985), makes the same point from a different perspective when she argues that in this tale, and in the relation of Palamon and Arcite, "solidarity and separation are linked" (p. 28).

machina of sorts offers Arcite an experience that will materially separate
and distinguish him from Palamon, but the sudden twist of the plot also
underscores in its own right the power, endurance, and complexity of
male bonds. Perotheus, "felawe . . . unto Duc Theseus / Syn thilke day
that they were children lite" (1192–93), comes to Athens for a visit, and,
with a characteristic gesture, the Knight digresses for a moment to celebrate what looks peripheral to his narrative, but actually lies at its very
heart: the lifelong love of two boyhood friends who, as grown men, still
play together. Perotheus comes to Theseus

> . . . for to pleye as he was wont to do;
> For in this world he loved no man so,
> And he loved hym als tendrely agayn.
> So wel they lovede, as olde bookes sayn,
> That whan that oon was deed, soothly to telle,
> His felawe wente and soughte hym doun in helle—
> But of that storie list me nat to write.
>
> (1195–1201)

Perotheus also, however, "loved wel Arcite," and so he is able to go
between the older ruler and the youthful enemy and persuade Theseus
to honor male friendship over male rivalry by letting Arcite go.

Arcite's behavior in the rest of Part II further dramatizes the entan-
glements of aristocratic masculine identity in a way that at once antici-
pates and resists the Miller's subsequent challenge. The transformation
that Arcite suffers when he is exiled to Thebes—his enervation, his weeping, and the alteration in his speech and voice, "that no man koude
knowe" (1370)—suggests the threat to selfhood and manhood, to both
class and gender identity, that love of a woman (even when that means
merely talking about and gazing at her) inevitably poses. As Schweitzer
has noted, the correspondence between the martial Arcite and the effeminate Absolon of the Miller's Tale is made clear at this point,[6] and the
dream that follows underscores that it is Arcite's yet unproven manhood
that is at risk: Mercury comes to tell him to go back to Athens, and he
bears the emblem of the elusive, promised phallus: "His slepy yerde in
hond he bar uprighte" (1387). The disguise Arcite adopts defines the
implicated class concern: love has so disrupted his identity—"turned was
al up so doun" (1377)—that the royal youth can appear "as a povre

6. Schweitzer, "The Misdirected Kiss," p. 223.

laborer" (1409), willing to hew wood and bear water, to become a servant in Theseus's household, just to see Emily.

Later, in both the Miller's and the Reeve's tales, the dangers inherent in taking single young men into households become apparent, and retrospectively it is possible to note in Arcite a model of the subversive potential of gender and class fluidity. But the truly disruptive possibilities of Arcite's situation are thoroughly rejected by what happens next in this story. Arcite profits from his disguise as a servant of the lord, assigned to the lady's chamber, not to woo Emily but to win the love of Theseus. He spends three years in the position of servant, but his inborn nobility shines through and establishes a critical bond between former enemies— or else Theseus prefers men of lower ranks. At any rate, Arcite bears himself so well that "ther was no man that Theseus hath derre" (1448).

But to win the ultimate prize, the lady, the knight must still reclaim his true name and, most important, must fight and be reconciled with his sworn brother, Palamon, under Theseus's close supervision, and reenacting precisely the move from enemy to dear friend that Arcite has already made in his relations with Theseus. As a servant, apart from Palamon and acting in secret disobedience to Theseus, no matter how close to Emily he may come and how much "renoun" he may win under his false identity, Arcite cannot develop into a noble, manly hero. This limitation is clear in his lament in the grove where Palamon is hiding. Sounding now more like Palamon in the beginning, because he has recognized the price paid by a man who betrays male bonds in order to pursue (uselessly) his identity through heterosexual love, Arcite bemoans the confusion of both lineage and personal selfhood that plagues him: " 'Allas, ybroght is to confusioun / The blood roial of Cadme and Amphioun . . . I dar noght biknowe myn owene name' " (1545–46,1556). Palamon's first words to Arcite, when he comes out of hiding, accuse his cousin of having "byjaped" Theseus, " 'and falsly chaunged hast thy name thus!' " (1586). In ironic contrast, he who has upheld the priority of sworn brotherly bonds is able to proclaim with pride his own name and identity as male rival: " 'For I am Palamon, thy mortal foo' " (1590).[7]

7. Lorraine Stock observes that Chaucer's changes in the story stress the importance of "the familial and national mortification" that the winning of Emily will help Arcite to overcome ("The Two Mayings," p. 219).

Just as Palamon and Arcite have a necessarily oscillating association as antagonists and comrades, so too Theseus has an essentially conflicted relation to the single position of aristocratic young male that the two represent. No motive is supplied for Theseus's original decision to imprison Arcite and Palamon "perpetuelly" (1024), instead of simply killing them or allowing them to be ransomed; subsequently, he seems to set Arcite free quite as easily as he made him stay. Theseus's willingness to release his prisoner may testify to the strength of his love for Perotheus, as I suggested earlier; it also enables the plot to clarify that it is love, not war, that really imprisons a man "perpetuelly" (cf. 1458). Furthermore, his change of heart is congruent with the shifting, somewhat mysterious feelings that Theseus seems to have for Palamon and Arcite. This instability is again prominent in his attitude toward his prisoners when he finds them fighting illicitly in the grove: although "he first for ire quook and sterte" (1762) and pronounces a death sentence, in the next line Theseus "shortly" accedes to the ladies' request that he spare the younger men. It might be simplest to assume that he acts out of "pitee" (1761) or "resoun" (1766), or that they just are not all that important to Theseus, but elsewhere the poem suggests otherwise. The disguised Arcite, as we have seen, is taken "so neer" by Theseus in Part II, and in Parts III and IV Theseus goes to extraordinary lengths first for the tournament and then for Arcite's funeral. The tears he weeps for the dead hero register an investment in his young erstwhile enemy that goes beyond "pitee" and "resoun," and when he subsequently makes Palamon his brother-in-law, multiple motives seem to be in play.

Theseus's behavior is only superficially inconsistent; it actually reconfirms and extends the concern of the tale with the fraught ties between powerful men. More specifically, his relations with Arcite and Palamon enact the complex relations of older and younger males, in local, temporary, and transitional competition and in larger concert. Theseus, we might imagine, imprisons the young men for two good reasons: because he must control the threat they represent to the Athenian state and to Theseus's own position within the kingdom and the household; and because he wants to hold onto and protect them and the youth and promise they embody (and his identification with them is made clear in the grove scene, as he recalls "in my tyme a servant was I oon" [1814]). In the plot that follows, Theseus experiences and manages the dual demands of the patriarch, who must dominate his sons while teaching and allowing (one of) them, eventually, to dominate in turn. The otherwise gratuitous and innovative appearance of Egeus, Theseus's father (2837–52), emphasizes the divided nature of masculine identity: Theseus, like every patriarch, is also a son, and his behavior here models the narrative of generations of ruling men coexisting under one roof. The father's philosophy is superannuated by Theseus's more enlightened (Boethian) views, but the father himself is honored, not supplanted, and he offers crucial emotional support when precious male bonds within and across class distinctions are severed: he is said to be the only one who can comfort Theseus (2837–38) and "the peple" (2852) for the death of Arcite.[8]

For the duration of the *Knight's Tale*, Theseus's elaborate, artificial arrangements hold potentially disruptive generational conflict in bounds, and the symmetry of the temples, the equality of the competing sides of the tournament, and even the outcome of the fighting all reveal the paradoxical return to a certain sameness that unites different men in harmony and affection. There is indeed a winner in battle, to prove that a fight has taken place, but both Theseus and the Knight take pains to establish the seemingly illogical but essential claim that there is not really a loser. There is no "cowardye" in a proper defeat (2719–30), Theseus insists; wounds are all healed, and Theseus makes revelry and feast and decrees that the competition is now over (2731ff.). With the help of the gods, too, both sides can triumph: Arcite fights a heroic fight and receives a splendid funeral, and Palamon gets Emily. The obsessive symmetry of the poem equates funeral and wedding as the two halves of Part IV, at the end of which we might expect the Knight to pose a final question: who has it best, now, the dead hero or the living husband?

The truly decisive winner is the aristocratic ideal of manhood, whereby a man can compete with and still be brother, son, and/or father to other men, an ideal proven by the quarrel over Emily, the ritual sacrifice of Arcite, and the belated marriage of Palamon to Theseus's sister-in-law. It is interesting that Arcite, the initial spokesman for individual heroism, is killed, while Palamon, who valued brotherhood, survives and inherits. But the lines of difference between the two cousins cross and recross too frequently to distinguish them or their signifying fates so firmly. Even before the tournament, Arcite's vital will to differ-

---

8. The lines given to Egeus are spoken much later by Theseus in the *Teseida;* see *The Book of Theseus,* trans. Bernadette Marie McCoy (New York: Medieval Text Association, 1974), 12.6 (p. 314).

entiate himself from Palamon coexists, thanks to the chivalric code, with his care for his "felawe," as he brings his rival food, drink, and proper weapons. By line 2762, Palamon is "his cosyn deere" again, and in what most critics view as his most generous act, Arcite is reconciled on his deathbed to Palamon and recommends that Emily marry his ex-rival.[9] He thereby enacts the virtuous repudiation of love and the lady that we witness in Troilus, and this is just the notion of male generosity, as we shall see, that resurfaces to close the Franklin's Tale.

Just as Palamon and Arcite's differences are both proved and erased, or written over by their common concerns, so too Theseus's conflicted relations to the young men are fortuitously resolved by the plot. He retains his position as lord by organizing the tournament, the funeral, and the marriage, and yet he moves easily from tyrannical enemy to mournful friend and father-in-law. But subsequently the Miller's Tale, if nothing else, may make us wonder what will happen, or whether it is really possible for the older man to take the younger one into his household without risking his own manhood and inviting humiliation and betrayal. The scalding of Nicholas's "toute," as other commentators have noted,[10] restages and foreshortens the tournament in the Knight's Tale, and thus we may be led to reconsider the homosocial and homosexual undertones of chivalry as the Knight presents it. I suggest, moreover, that the integrity of the Knight's ideals is more seriously called into question by the fact that despite his apparent disagreement with the Miller about how men are made and how they bond, the two actually reveal a common attitude toward women.

Woman in the Knight's Tale looks at first glance like the inverse of Woman in the Miller's Tale: we can hardly imagine the courtly heroine, Emily, playing even a polite joke, let alone exposing her backside for a kiss from whichever one of her rival suitors she isn't sleeping with at the moment. Emily is usually presented to readers as the idealized lady, just as she appears to Palamon to be a goddess. If Emily and Alisoun have anything in common, it would seem to be that they are both peripheral to the main concerns of the male characters and storytellers who

---

9. Kurt Olsson, in "Securitas and Chaucer's Knight," Studies in the Age of Chaucer 9 (1987), speaks of this as Arcite's "noblest act" (p. 143); Ferster, in Chaucer on Interpretation, describes it as "the most generous action in the Tale" (p. 38).

10. Such as Donald Howard, in The Idea of the Canterbury Tales (Berkeley: University of California Press, 1976), pp. 238–39.

ostensively desire them. While Alisoun's marginality is less obvious and
will be discussed at length later in this chapter, Emily's exclusion from
the *Knight's Tale* seems to require no subtle reading and has been affirmed by many modern critics. As one early twentieth-century scholar
says, we have in Emily "a heroine who is merely a name."[11] Mandel
points out that "For all courtly intents and purposes of love, Emily does
not exist in this tale."[12] Charles Muscatine views Emily as "merely a
symbol of the noble man's desires"; E. Talbot Donaldson stresses that
"she has no character," and Donald Howard notes that "the lady herself
is a distant and unreal figure."[13] I submit, however, that while all these
observations are accurate, and while the poem is, in the ways I have
already argued, about male rivalry and the reconciliation it affords, the
representation of women in the *Knight's Tale*, especially when viewed in
the context of the A-fragment as a whole, is not quite as simple or simply
exclusionary as it seems. We need not take the Knight's representation
of Emily at face value, nor is Emily the only female figure in the poem.

The tale actually begins not with the love triangle—Palamon, Arcite,
and Emily—but with another triad of characters that has a different gender ratio, in which Emily is the only common factor: Theseus, Hippolyta,
and her "yonge suster Emelye" (871) on the way back to Athens after
Theseus has conquered the Amazons and married their queen. Shortly
after he has begun, the Knight interrupts his story to describe this pro-
cession with a characteristic use of *occupatio* (875–94) in which he speaks
of what he will not, he says, have time to represent fully:

> And certes, if it nere to long to heere,
> I wolde have toold yow fully the manere
> How wonnen was the regne of Femenye
> By Theseus and by his chivalrye;
> And of the grete bataille for the nones
> Bitwixen Atthenes and Amazones;
> And how asseged was Ypolita,
> The faire, hardy queene of Scithia;
> And of the feste that was at hir weddynge,
> And of the tempest at hir hoom-comynge;
> But al that thyng I moot as now forbere.
>
> (875–85)

---

11. This is J. R. Hulbert's assessment, cited in Charles Muscatine, *Chaucer and the
French Tradition* (Berkeley: University of California Press, 1957), p. 176.

12. "Courtly Love in the Canterbury Tales," *Chaucer Review* 19 (1985), p. 286.

13. See, respectively, *Chaucer and the French Tradition*, p. 185; *Speaking of Chaucer* (London: Athlone Press, 1970), pp. 48–49; and *The Idea of the Canterbury Tales*, p. 234.

What he forbears to speak of, here and elsewhere, calls attention to itself as something that the Knight consciously views and treats as incidental, corollary, or distracting, but which audiences are invited to perceive as bearing a deeper significance. What the Knight can't help talking about, and yet doesn't want to talk about, is an odd conjunction of events that suggests both cyclical and progressive movement: a battle, a wedding, and a stormy homecoming. The relevance of these events, in this sequence, becomes clearer only as the story progresses.

When the plot is picked up again in line 893, Theseus is almost home; Emily and Hippolyta are not mentioned at this point, but Theseus interacts with another group of women associated with military defeat and subservience to Athenian rule, the Theban widows. Theseus thus appears in the beginning in conjunction with two sets of women, not with men: throughout the tale, he is always described with a female entourage or audience for his actions and words, even as those actions and words are directed almost exclusively toward other men. From the outset, the male ruler and the problems of masculine authority are situated in contexts that always include women. Most important to my reading, moreover, is the particular way that the presence of women in these contexts is redefined so that it looks like absence and is thereby managed in conventional ways by both Theseus and the male storyteller.

In the first passage in the poem, Emily is associated with Hippolyta, that "hardy" queen of what the Knight refers to twice as "the regne of Femenye" (866, 877). (The *Middle English Dictionary* defines *hardy* as "strong in battle"; the term is also used to describe Turnus [1945] and Arcite [2649].) The term "Femenye" is interesting: John Fisher notes that "this place name (from Latin *femina*, woman) was evidently invented by Chaucer."[14] Whether or not Chaucer invented it, it seems to have been rarely enough used to be striking, and its generalizing, abstracting quality equates Amazons with women in general and with Woman as an idea and a territory.[15] The name Femenye reminds us, too, that Hippolyta

14. *The Complete Poetry and Prose of Geoffrey Chaucer* (New York: Holt, Rinehart and Winston, 1977), note to line 866, p. 25.

15. The *Middle English Dictionary* cites only three other uses of the term, one by Gower and two by Lydgate. In the background of the story, as Fisher also notes, we may think of Boccaccio's suggestion in the Teseida that Theseus's war against the Amazons is an attack on their sin of what Fisher calls "feminism." As Hippolyta puts it, when she hears that Theseus is coming, he finds them "troublesome because we are not satisfied with remaining subject to men and obedient to their whims like other women" (*McCoy, Book of Theseus*, p. 24).

and Emily are not to be seen (yet) as courtly ladies in their initial appearance; they are described as Amazons, mythical, fighting, manlike
women who have waged "grete bataille" with Theseus. They are being
brought from a distant land into the court of Athens; notably, Theseus
has not just conquered them but is also marrying their queen. In their
first appearance, then, women in the poem are erstwhile powerful sep-
aratists, rivals to the hero who first defeats them with martial violence
and then domesticates them through marital union.

The "tempest at hir hoom-comynge" about which the Knight does
not speak is original to Chaucer's version of this story; in the *Teseida*, the
return journey is notably easy and pleasant. The tempest might well
allude to the untold story of stormy early days in Theseus and Hippolyta's marriage; in any naturalistic account, the transformation of an Amazonian queen into a proper wife for the Athenian king would probably
be difficult and protracted.[16] The Knight, however, both acknowledges
and eclipses that presumably tempestuous taming of the wild woman
and then embodies the success of Theseus's policy in those females who
stand in the place of Hippolyta and Emily in the second part of the
opening: the Theban widows, who are represented as proper, submissive, defeated, and dependent and who thus serve as a crucial part of
the narrative strategy that defines Woman. The widows appears in pairs,
suggesting the Amazon royal sisters (and the sister-mothers of Palamon
and Arcite), but unlike Hippolyta and Emily, they are nameless, part of
a group, kneeling, dressed all alike in clothes that symbolize their status
in relation to (dead) men: "A compaignye of ladyes, tweye and
tweye, / Ech after oother, clad in clothes blake" (898–99). In gestures that
hint at their simultaneously passive and yet demanding and intrusive
nature, they wail superlatively and seize the bridle of Theseus's horse.

Theseus's odd double response to these female petitioners suggests
that he is himself making a transition from challenging women as enemies and rivals to pitying them as dependents. He speaks first to wonder
if these strange females are complaining because they are jealous of him:
" 'Have ye so greet envye / Of myn honour' " (907–8). On second
thought, he becomes more chivalrous and asks if someone has hurt them

16. The additional reference to a storm at homecoming has been read as an allusion
to a historical tempest, one that destroyed the ship bringing Queen Anne to England (see
John Livingston Lowes, "The Tempest at Hir Hoom-Cominge," *Modern Language Notes*
19 [1904], pp. 240–43); this reading does not exclude the possibility that I am suggesting.

and whether he can help (909–11). The oldest lady speaks for the group—after she swoons—and clarifies how they represent the proper narrative of aristocratic, cultivated womanhood. She stresses that each one of them was once "a duchesse or a queene" (923); now they are a collective of feminine misery ("us wrecched wommen," 921). She goes on to explain that they want Theseus to help them bury the bodies of their husbands, whom Creon has defeated and thrown in "an heep" (944) without funeral rites—negating their individual identity as men, which it is the function of wives to help sustain, and prefiguring the fate of Theban men, who will be treated by Theseus just as Creon treats his enemies. The Theban women thus serve to incite the main plot of a story that has nothing to do with them. The imprisonment of Arcite and Palamon and all that follows is generated by Theseus's eagerness to best Creon ("That al the peple of Grece sholde speke / How Creon was of Theseus yserved," 963–64), under the guise of polite service to a domesticated female honor that actually serves to define and aggrandize Theseus's personal reputation and the collective values of aristocratic men.

Taken together, Theseus's appearances in the first hundred lines of the poem with two sets of foreign women—first his new wife and sister-in-law, former Amazons, and then the Theban widows—suggest that although Emily may not be a "fully-rounded" character, but "merely a name," still the haunting subject of Theseus's relation to the female Other is fundamental to the rest of the story and to our understanding of the Athenian ruler's character. The opening scenes tell us, quite literally, where Theseus is coming from: from the apprehension that women somewhere, on the margins of culture and historical or narrative reality, are powerful rivals, martial and manlike, whom the proper male hero must first conquer with superior violence and then domesticate. Theseus's rule, like Scipio's vision in the first part of the *Parliament of Fowls*, is founded on a martial conquest of Femenye that is reportedly complete and, in this telling, unproblematized by the feminine qualities of the hero himself. To this end, the Knight omits a crucial episode in Boccaccio's version, wherein Theseus dallies in Scythia after his marriage to Hippolyta and is summoned back to manly fame and glory in a dream that links immaturity with a comfortable life among foreign women.[17]

17. In the dream, Theseus thinks Pirithous speaks to him (although later he decides that the warning came from the gods): "Have you slid back shamefully into immaturity? As you live among a crowd of women, have you consigned to oblivion on the bosom of Hippolyta that prowess of yours which every kingdom has already experienced?" (*McCoy, Book of Theseus*, p. 54).

The appearance of the Theban widows suggests what the *Parliament* also sees as somewhat more problematic or as yet unimaginable: that the conquest can and will be continued, and won, on the domestic front. For, among other things, these widows represent the destiny and proper destination of the Amazonian sisters, Hippolyta and Emily. This point is reaffirmed in the center of the poem, in a scene that neatly matches the opening one, when the royal ladies intercede to spare Palamon and Arcite from the wrath of Theseus. Here Hippolyta, now referred to only as "the queene," weeps "for verray wommanhede" (1748); she is joined by Emily and other ladies who collectively cry for mercy "upon us wommen alle" (1757), fall down on their bare knees, and even, the Knight says, "wolde have kist his feet ther as he stood" (1759).

Emily's function in the rest of the story corroborates and develops the repressed narrative about Woman upon which the aristocratic story is founded. She is an unattached Amazon in Athens, and her position here can be compared to Alisoun's in the *Miller's Tale* in one salient way. Alisoun represents the excessive female sexuality that the Miller, as we shall see, presupposes in his prefatory remarks to the Reeve. So too Emily, as Hippolyta's younger sister, represents an extra female whom Theseus himself cannot marry, but whose sexuality—clearly deadly to at least one knight, and symbolically threatening to the bonds that unify and identify aristocratic men—must be contained by marriage. (Does the story of Theseus's mythic involvement with another pair of sisters, Phaedra and Ariadne, which Chaucer tells in the *Legend of Good Women,* have any bearing on a reading of the Knight's Theseus? If it does, Emily's meaning in relation to Theseus and the problem of male rivalry is more complicated than I have suggested here.)

The Knight's treatment of Emily plays out both the latent threat of Femenye and the control that Theseus manages, through the elaborate artifice of the tournament, to maintain. The sense that there is something dangerous and (therefore) titillating about Emily is made explicit at least once, however, in the Knight's obscure attraction and resistance to representing her ritual cleansing at the temple of Diana:

> This Emelye, with herte debonaire,
> Hir body wessh with water of a welle.
> But hou she dide hir ryte I dar nat telle,
> But it be any thing in general;
> And yet it were a game to heeren al.

> To hym that meneth wel it were no charge;
> But it is good a man been at his large.
>   (2282–88)

This passage has puzzled many modern readers, but seen in the context of this study, it confirms the Knight's wishful and somewhat guilty participation in the old game of trading stories about women that he thinks he is too polite to play, as well as his investment in avoiding the frightening sight of the female body.

Another crucial aspect of the threat that the female body poses to masculine identity and dominance, as we saw in the *Parliament of Fowls*, is the possibility of a woman's indifference to heterosexual relations. That possibility is prominently added to the Knight's version of this story— added, however, in order to be foreclosed. As other commentators have noted, the Chaucerian Emily differs from her counterpart in Boccaccio in her ignorance of the lovers' interest in her; whereas the Boccaccian lady knows she is being watched, and responds immediately by playing to her audience, Emily is apparently oblivious to the gaze of Palamon and Arcite that seals her fate. Her indifference is sustained, moreover, in her devotions to Diana and her prayer that she may remain chaste. But this indifference is from the beginning of the poem eroded in various ways; Emily's heterosexual desire is constructed so that it can be channeled into marriage.

From the outset, for instance, there are hints that Emily is not quite as resolutely devoted to chastity as she appears to be. When she first appears in the garden, her conventional and necessary susceptibility to romance is suggested by the Knight's indication that this Amazon has been aroused from sleep and led to the garden by her own response to May, the season that "priketh every gentil herte" (1043). May is the traditional time of courtly love, and critics have often suggested that Emily's association with May simply confirms that she is the perfect romance heroine: Donaldson waxes lyrical over Emily as "not only the embodiment of all pretty young girls in the Spring, but a proof that the Spring of pretty young girls is a permanent thing, and that May in their persons will always warm the masculine heart as May warms their hearts and sends them out among the flowers."[18] But Natalie Davis reminds us that in the festive tradition of the Middle Ages in nearby

18. *Speaking of Chaucer*, p. 49.

parts of Europe that she studied, May is also the time of disorder and of female sexual excess. In folk traditions, Davis points out, "Generally May . . . was thought to be a period in which women were powerful, their desires at their most immoderate. As the old saying went, a May bride would keep her husband in yoke all year round. And in fact marriages were not frequent in May."[19] The final turn of Emily's prayer to Diana, similarly, suggests her practical understanding that chastity is only an ideal, not a plausible destiny for a woman, and that it is in her interests to believe that these men want her, that her value is proportional to the male desire she can arouse: if I must marry, she begs, " 'Sende me hym that moost desireth me' " (2325).

Another strategy for controlling and eroding Emily's indifference involves a series of comments by both the male characters and the story-teller that devalue or question the sincerity of her indifference even as they remark on it. Theseus makes the point most directly and callously in the speech where he forgives Palamon and Arcite for their folly in loving and then observes that the joke is on them. Emily could care less: " 'She woot namoore of al this hoote fare, / By God, than woot a cokkow or an hare!' " (1809–10). Theseus's low tone absorbs Emily's potentially disruptive indifference into the game here, presumes its irrelevance to the fact that men will keep on falling in love whether women know it or not, and compares the courtly lady to small birds known for their low-mindedness and selfishness or to minor animals of prey known for their timidity.

One of the Knight's own asides similarly works to call into question the sincerity of Emily's devotion to Diana. Just before his fatal fall, Arcite looks up at his prize, and Emily returns his look: "And she agayn hym caste a freendlich ye / (For wommen, as to speken in comune, / Thei folwen alle the favour of Fortune)" (2679–82). The Knight, like Theseus and Arcite, resorts to the "comune" register when he wants to constitute Emily in terms of her representative status and at the same time suggest her willingness to respond to male desire, her opportunism, and her subjection to Fortune. In effect he is only saying that Emily, like all women, acts on Theseus's dictum and makes a virtue of necessity, but the effect of this policy when enacted by a woman is, in the context of

19. "Women on Top," in *Society and Culture in Early Modern France* (Stanford: Stanford University Press, 1975), p. 141. For another discussion of the significance of May arguing that Chaucer conflates contradictory aspects of Flora and Diana, carnal and innocent sexualities, see Stock, "The Two Mayings."

this tale, quite different. Several lines later, the Knight for once lets women speak for themselves, but in a way that reauthorizes both their status as male property and their own foolish incomprehension of the higher ideals that men serve: the women of Athens, bemoaning Arcite's loss, ask the corpse, " 'Why woldestow be deed . . . And haddest gold ynough, and Emelye?' " (2835–36).

The indifference that might be threatening or at least disruptive in a poem like the *Parliament of Fowls* is thoroughly disallowed by the end of the *Knight's Tale*, as the conquest of Femenye that we were told we were not going to hear about is actually reenacted inside the gates of Athens through the narrative strategies I have examined. Emily's marriage at the end of the poem not only allies Athens and Thebes but also contains and domesticates the dangerous female excess that an Amazon sister-in-law might represent in Theseus's royal household. Moving on to the *Miller's Tale* from this vantage, we shall see that Alisoun's response to Nicholas, moving from perfunctory resistance to lusty acquiescence in six lines, restages with all the force of comic foreshortening much the same course that the lengthy *Knight's Tale* charts, and thus underscores the inevitability of Emily's conquest and the fundamental similarity of the polite and churlish views of Woman.

THE *MILLER'S TALE*

> Just as (the Manciple reminds us) a countess can be laid as low
> as a peasant girl, a miller (or, at least, Chaucer's Miller) can
> make a tale to match a knight.
>
> Carl Lindahl, *Ernest Games*

When Absolon begs Alisoun for a kiss in the dark of the night, she offers him not her mouth, "sweete as bragot or the meeth" (3261), but "hir hole" (3732).[20] Alisoun's substitution of what is perceived as foul for what is described as sweet is a revealing gesture; in more ways than one, it exposes what is usually kept hidden by polite discourse. It seems to confirm what the churlish male storyteller has already suggested: this female character's frank sexuality and animal nature, that "free, instinc-

---

20. The epigraph appears in *Ernest Games: Folkloric Patterns in the Canterbury Tales* (Bloomington: Indiana University Press, 1987), p. 13.

tive, sensual, untamed" brand of femininity depicted earlier in the Miller's opening barrage of similes comparing Alisoun to animals and other natural or material objects.[21] The Miller expresses this same view of women from the moment he first speaks, even before the tale begins, in the linking matter. In response to the Reeve's objections, he clarifies the presupposition that women's sexual desires are in fact naturally excessive, and the only sure way for a man to avoid being humiliated by female promiscuity is to forgo marriage: "Who hath no wyf, he is no cokewold" (3152). For those with wives, like the Miller himself, he goes on to suggest another strategy. A man may simply close his eyes to the likelihood that he has been cuckolded; "I wol bileve wel that I am noon" (3162). His final generalization reiterates the principle that the inevitable excess of female sexuality should not be looked at too closely by men whose own needs are adequately satisfied (or who wish to believe that that is the case):

> An housbonde shal nat been inquisityf
> Of Goddes pryvetee, nor of his wyf.
> So he may fynde Goddes foyson there,
> Of the remenant nedeth nat enquere.
> (3163–66)

Here, it could be argued, the Miller seems happy enough to accord women not only sexual desire and experience but also the freedom and privacy to enjoy their sexuality, powers most often denied to women in the plots of Chaucer's fictions as in the authoritative discourse of the Middle Ages in general. Bearing out this unusual attitude, the tale that follows punishes the three male characters for their sensuality and blindness, while Alisoun teases and frolics and giggles and is "swyved" but not hurt in the final fray.[22] Modern critics have almost unanimously relished and praised this "triumph of Alisoun's fresh and lusty animal-

---

21. The quoted adjectives are taken from V. A. Kolve, *Chaucer and the Imagery of Narrative: The First Five Canterbury Tales* (Stanford: Stanford University Press, 1984), p. 163. See, too, Kolve's analysis of the portrait of Alisoun for his suggestion that her clothing symbolizes the constraints of her position as a bourgeois wife.

22. I am following here the traditional assumption that Alisoun is not punished, although one might read the ending differently if one were to emphasize, as I will later, the change in Alisoun's status from agent to passive object. But usually the fact that Alisoun is pronounced "swyved" at the end is read as part of *John's* punishment. Lee Patterson, for instance, lists her fate as the first (perhaps least, perhaps most important?) of three ways in which John is "most severely punished" at the end of the Tale: "his wife is 'swyved,' his arm is broken, and his reputation as a man of probity is ruined" (" 'No man his reson herde': Peasant Consciousness, Chaucer's Miller, and the Structure of the *Canterbury Tales*," *South Atlantic Quarterly* 86 [1987], p. 479).

ity," the "entirely successful" performance of "Nature's female."[23] The story has been judged "not only funny but also oddly innocent and imaginatively gay."[24] And Alisoun, like her namesake the Wife of Bath, may represent to many readers Chaucer's unprecedented understanding, defense, and even celebration of female desire.

There is a darker, less liberal and innocent side, however, to the Miller's tolerant, churlish, frank view. What is odd about this tale is not its innocence, but the modern critical insistence on its innocence; and at the risk of displaying that poor sense of humor often attributed to feminist scholars, I want to take this poem seriously by considering what is revealed by Alisoun's prank that is not so funny and not so openly treated by the Miller, this tale, or many of its readers. Most obviously, Alisoun's freedom from punishment, like the Miller's tolerant injunction not to inquire too far into the natural and uncontrollable excess—the "remenant"—of female sexuality, may reflect the familiar judgment that Woman is not immoral but amoral.[25] Her animality is all there is; it is not worth examining a woman's moral or spiritual qualities, the tale implies, because she has none that are available to either correction or representation by husband or storyteller. One recent critic describes Alisoun as "the good they [the three men] have chosen, as innocent in herself as gold or rich food or drink. The choice, not the object, is punished."[26] As this formulation unintentionally (I assume) reveals, Alisoun's "triumph" only further clarifies her objectification and guarantees her erasure. By such a reading, the male characters are, as we might expect, the subjects and agents of the tale and its morality; and they, like their counterparts in the *Knight's Tale* and like the Miller and the Reeve, are less interested in Alisoun than in besting each other and proving their threatened manliness in ways I shall explore. If I find it hard to see Alisoun, therefore, as a triumphant or liberating or harmless sign of female desire, I find it even more difficult to praise or enjoy, as so many

23. See, respectively, Burlin, *Chaucerian Fiction*, p. 156, and Earle Birney, "The Inhibited and the Uninhibited: Ironic Structure in the *Miller's Tale*," *Neophilologus* 44 (1960), p. 337.

24. Kolve, *Imagery of Narrative*, p. 161.

25. Kolve argues that all three younger characters in the tale are not even amoral, but just quintessentially young and therefore unjudged; "the condition is too transitory, and *some* lessons are learned" (p. 173). My point is to investigate more fully which lessons are learned by whom. In doing so, I suggest that the two young men are regarded very differently from the young woman, that in the question of age and its cultural meanings we again see gender asymmetry.

26. Schweitzer, "The Misdirected Kiss," p. 227.

critics do, the "wholesome sexuality"[27] of a tale in which the more polite of the two male rivals intends and attempts to assault the "pryvetee" of the woman he claims to adore with a red-hot iron blade. I also want to open up for discussion the fact that it is only an accident, a side-effect of Nicholas's intervention in Alisoun's prank, that saves the female from punishment of a particularly vicious sort and ask again the question raised in the *Clerk's Tale:* Who can be liberated by humor, and at whose expense?

At the same time that I interrogate the significance of the female character's (alleged) freedom to desire and (narrow) escape from judgment, I also want to suggest that this tale does not in fact let the topics of female sexuality and imperiled manhood go quite as easily or lightly as the Miller himself recommends to the Reeve, or as most critics have been eager to do. Reexamining Alisoun's final self-exposure of her "hole," I submit that the Miller's description of her gesture reveals not so much a straightforward representation of a woman's desire, which we might read as either celebratory or dismissive, but the actual and strategic vagueness, or obfuscation, in his portrayal of female "pryvetee," as he at once focuses on and just fails to bring into focus Alisoun's genitals, in a rhetorical move subtly comparable to the Knight's elaborate refusal to say more about Emily's rites in the temple of Diana. In the beginning of the Tale, the Miller speaks quite frankly and unambiguously, it seems, about Alisoun's "queynte," the "woman's external organ" (as the *Middle English Dictionary* puts it) that Nicholas grabs.[28] What Alisoun exposes to Absolon at the end, however, is referred to as her "hole," a term that may refer either to her anus or to her vaginal orifice.[29]

---

27. Howard, *Idea of the Canterbury Tales*, p. 241.

28. See entry for *queint(e)* n., *Middle English Dictionary* Q, p. 37.

29. The *Middle English Dictionary* suggests this possibility under *hol*(e n.2, sense 2 (a) (H.4) without specifying whether the quotation from the *Miller's Tale*, which it cites, refers to the anus or "the orifice of the female pudendum." There are more instances of the term "hole" referring to anus, although often there is a specifying modifier such as "hinder hole" or "hole of the ars." In line 3852, as the Miller sums up what has happened to each character, he says that Absolon kissed Alisoun's "nether ye"; this phrase is unambiguously glossed "anus" by the *MED* and taken as a variant of "nether ende" (see *nether*(e adj.," N.2). However, since the only example cited for "nether ye" is the Miller's usage in this line, the dictionary does not offer the confirming evidence we might seek. (It also cites the Wife's reference to her husband's "nether purs," which pushes the sense of the phrase slightly at least toward a genital interpretation.) Again, under "*eie* n," the phrase "nether ye" is glossed "the anus"; again, the only example of this usage is line 3852 of the *Miller's Tale.* The specification of Alisoun's "naked ers" as the part of the body he kisses in line 3734 may seem to confirm that the hole in question is her anus, but the ambiguity still

Reflecting the absence of nomenclature for female sexual organs in the lexicon, the Miller does not distinguish between these two proximate parts of the female anatomy, and it actually remains unclear what Alisoun intends Absolon to kiss, what Absolon does kiss, and what he thinks he has kissed.[30] As far as I know, Chaucer scholars have not pursued this particularly rich case of semantic and structural ambiguity; to do so, however, proves instructive.

Insofar as the word "hole" may refer to Alisoun's vaginal orifice, the Miller seems to be moving onward and inward in his examination of female sexuality, progressing from the "external" organ, the pudendum, to the gateway to internal organs. Most readers seem to have assumed that the "hole" in question, however, is Alisoun's anus. And since this assumption is at once likely and unverifiable, the word "hole" suggests both that the Miller as inspector of woman's private parts is actually in retreat, moving here and in the tale as a whole away from the female genitals, and that his move, moreover, effects the conventional association or conflation of (female) genital and anal functions, of women's sex (or sex with a woman) and dirt, decay, and dissolution.

This association has in fact been assumed, however unself-consciously, by many modern critics. Derek Brewer, for instance, in expressing sympathy for Absolon, notes in the *Miller's Tale* the "injustice" typical of fabliaux: "They rub the nose of a young man in the *dirt*, simply because he is fastidious in love" (my emphasis).[31] Earle Birney writes that Absolon "offers up his sweetened effeminate lips to the unsavory bearded female *fact*" (my emphasis); and V. A. Kolve (reading the pun in line 3754) notes that "though fastidious Absolon may . . . have missed his mark by a few millimeters, the *real nature* of what he sought has been made unmistakably clear to him" (my emphasis).[32] It is assumed by these scholars that the "fact," the "real nature" of female sexuality is

---

persists in determining what she meant to offer him, since her gesture would be the same in either case, and the possibility that he has kissed the vaginal opening is reinforced by his reference to her pubic hair. In any event, of course, what I see as important is both the ambiguity and the clear shift of focus from genitals (the "queynte") to the anus, possibly of Alisoun and certainly of Nicholas.

30. For discussion of the lack of names for various female organs of reproduction, see Thomas Laqueur, "Orgasm, Generation, and the Politics of Reproductive Biology," in *The Making of the Modern Body* (Berkeley: University of California Press, 1987), pp. 1–41.

31. "The Poetry of Chaucer's Fabliaux," in *Chaucer: The Poet as Storyteller* (London: MacMillan, 1984), p. 110.

32. Birney, "The Inhibited and the Uninhibited," p. 336; Kolve, *Imagery of Narrative*, p. 196.

what Alisoun exposes—that is, its "dirt." By this quite traditional view, the anal and the genital have been confused and hence connected. The reference to Alisoun's "hole" thus succinctly performs the contagious magic at the center of the tale's plot, whereby exposure to the desired "queynte" entails a shocking encounter with female dirt and danger that both sickens and (therefore) heals the lovesick man.[33] Or as the Miller puts it in a pun that semantically pulls "hole" away from the anus and back to the female organ: "His hoote love was coold and al yqueynt" (3754).

The tried and true cure that the Miller provides for lovesick Absolon, however, may be as painful as the disease. For the use of the term "hole" also shifts attention from something that is anatomically female, the "queynte," to something that men have too, something that is anatomically undifferentiated in males and females, the anus. This shift sets up and is writ large by the subsequent substitution of Nicholas's body for Alisoun's, a maneuver that returns agency to the male but in doing so also exposes the humiliating and frightening lack of difference between male and female bodies.[34] While the Miller's semantic strategy realizes an implicitly and conventionally hostile view of women and of sex with women, then, it also returns attention simultaneously to men, to the instability of gender difference, and hence to the particular problem that the Knight's Tale, from a different angle, also tackles: the vulnerability of masculine identity.

Nicholas and Absolon compete with each other and with John for sexual access to Alisoun, and, true to type, the male rivals actually demonstrate less interest in the female object of their alleged desire than in their own gender and class identity and hence their relations to each other in a closed sphere of male activity. Alisoun herself may seem most important to the uxorious John, whose first thought, when he believes the second flood is coming, is "Allas, my wyf!" (3522). John, however, is the least developed of the male characters and the biggest fool of the three; moreover, his explicit motivation for cherishing Alisoun (and therefore keeping her "narwe in cage," 3224), according to the beginning of the tale, is his jealousy and his expectation that other men will makee

---

33. Schweitzer, in "The Misdirected Kiss," notes that Absolon's cure, his contact with Alisoun's "hole," accords with actual medieval medical prescriptions for (male) sufferers from the lover's malady.

34. Britton J. Harwood also points out the "failure of differentiation in both sexual and cosmological codes" in "The 'Nether Ye' and its Antithesis: A Structuralist Reading of 'The Miller's Tale,' " Annuale Mediaevale 21 (1981), pp. 5–30.

him into a cuckold (3224–26) and thus disprove the manhood that the old man's possession of the young wife is meant to confirm.[35] Absolon and Nicholas, the more fully characterized males in the story, are in their respective roles of bachelor and clerk excluded from the possession of a wife and so even more in need of proving their manhood through Alisoun, and it is possible to see in some detail how and why they struggle— with only partial success—to do so.

Absolon is the more obviously worried about his manliness, for he is the effeminate man par excellence. Other critical studies have already detailed the ways in which Absolon is "too ladylike" and have located the sources of his characterization in patristic readings of the biblical Absalom and in the figure of Mirth in *Le Roman de la Rose*.[36] Most often such studies suggest that the purpose of Chaucer's emphasis on Absolon's effeminacy is both humor and "organic unity"; his squeamishness, it is thought, makes Alisoun's joke all the more fitting.[37] Attention to the carefully narrated details of his response to actual contact with Alisoun's "hole"—with the general neighborhood, at least, of the female parts he presumably desires—suggests, however, that Absolon figures underlying issues that make effeminacy a source of both masculine humor and masculine anxiety: in general the fluidity and instability of gender difference, and in particular the possibilities of homosexuality and castration.

After kissing Alisoun's "naked ers / Ful savourly" (3734–35), the kneeling Absolon jumps up:

> Abak he stirte, and thoughte it was amys,
> For wel he wiste a womman hath no berd.
> He felte a thyng al rough and long yherd,
> And seyde, "Fy! allas! what have I do?"
> (3736–39)

35. Brewer, in "The Poetry of Chaucer's Fabliaux," suggests that his broken arm at the end symbolizes his sexual impotency.

36. Studies include Paul E. Beichner, "Absolon's Hair," *Mediaeval Studies* 12 (1950), pp. 222–33, and "Characterization in the *Miller's Tale*," in *Chaucer Criticism*, vol. I, ed. Richard Schoeck and Jerome Taylor (Notre Dame: University of Notre Dame Press, 1960). Many commentators note in passing Absolon's effeminacy; see Donaldson's comment on his "rode" complexion in "Idiom of Popular Poetry in the Miller's Tale," in *Speaking of Chaucer*, pp. 20–21, and Macklin Smith's discussion of the parallels between Absolon and the adulterous woman in "Or I Wol Caste a Ston," *Studies in the Age of Chaucer* 8 (1986), p. 16. Smith observes: "For all his fantasizing, I can only with difficulty imagine him paired with a real woman" (p. 18).

37. This is Beichner's conclusion in "Characterization."

His first vague thought that something is wrong, because he knows women don't have beards, suggests that what's immediately upsetting is the apparent displacement of what he thought was a certain and visible sign of fixed sexual difference; it may also suggest that he hasn't had much experience with certain parts of the female body. It may imply, too, that Absolon wonders initially whether he has kissed a man's face, rather than a woman's—that the fear of homoerotic experience is uppermost in his mind. At another level the subsequent actuality of an unwitting homosexual exchange—the branding of Nicholas—is also anticipated by the initial reference to the secondary male sex characteristic.

Then Absolon overhears Alisoun sniggering and Nicholas repeating the word that most directly indicts Absolon's confusion: " 'A berd, a berd!' quod hende Nicholas" (3742). At this point Absolon seems to realize whom, or at least what, he has in fact kissed, and he responds by furiously biting and scouring his polluted lips: "Who rubbeth now, who froteth now his lippes / With dust, with sond, with straw, with clooth, with chippes" (3747–48). This hysterical response indicates his deep sense of the foulness of Alisoun's "hole" and the self-scourging that contact with this dirt demands. After he vows revenge (3744–52)— using precisely the term that the Host and Miller have used, in the linking matter, to speak of the verbal competition, " 'I shal thee quyte' " (3746)— the narrator tells us he has been "heeled of his maladie" (3757) and that he weeps "as dooth a child that is ybete" (3759).

This last simile is particularly telling, for it suggests that Absolon feels both infantilized and punished by oral contact with female "pryvetee." The Freudian fiction seems to be anticipated here. Absolon is like the putatively generic little boy who sees female genitals for the first time (and his childishness has already been suggested in line 3704, in his parody of the Song of Solomon: " 'I moorne as dooth a lamb after the tete' "). The boy-child has in this case felt, although not seen, the lack that seems to mark the place of women's sexual organs, and his response indicates both guilt and fear for his own as yet unproven difference and dominance, his phallus. Like his initial confusion (and like the subsequent interchangeability of male and female posteriors), this reaction identifies what is most disturbing: the actual and feared lack of distinction between women and men, which in turn suggests the related possibilities of castration and homosexuality.

A relation between (the fear of) castration, homosexual behavior, and the rape or mutilation of the female (who is presented in this tale as definitely asking for it) is equally clearly brought out in the revenge Absolon hastens to enact. Absolon borrows a hot "kultour"—the iron blade at the front of a plough—from his friend Gervase, the blacksmith, and his own professional skills, we may remember, include barbering (and hence surgery). Gervase has been taken as a figure of "plain masculinity" who serves to confirm that Absolon may be effeminate, but not homosexual: according to Cornelius Novelli, "one never supposes that Absolon has anything but a masculine desire for women."[38] But what happens afterwards problematizes modern efforts to distinguish homosexual desire so clearly from "masculine desire." It seems plausible that Absolon urgently, stealthily, and seriously seeks out the masculinity represented by the smith, who swears and makes jokes about Absolon's lovemaking, because this masculinity is indeed what was already at risk in his squeamishness and parodic courtly behavior and what Alisoun's gesture has openly challenged. He borrows the violent maleness, the phallus-as-weapon, that the coulter symbolizes simultaneously to avenge and display his vulnerable manhood.[39] The choice of instruments, incidentally, also takes us back to the sexualized terminology used both to differentiate and to link as gendered male the approaches and motives to narrative taken by the Miller and the Knight. Absolon realigns himself with the phallic Miller, who ambiguously swears that he won't believe he's a cuckold "for the oxen in my plogh" (3159), instead of with the "gentil" knight whose first use of *occupatio* ends with the allegation that "wayke been the oxen in my plough" (887).

But what Absolon does with the borrowed blade of the plough is not exactly what he apparently intends to do; he is fooled again in a second moment of even more explicit gender confusion and cross-undressing. His reaction to the first substitution of Alisoun's "hole" for her mouth indicates that Absolon's effeminacy is an outward sign of the precariousness of masculine desire in the ways I have suggested; the second substitution of Nicholas's private parts for Alisoun's blocks Absolon from

---

38. "Absolon's 'Freend So Deere': A Pivotal Point in the *Miller's Tale*," *Neophilologus* 52 (1968), pp. 65–69.

39. Harwood also suggests that "the disjointed male part may show itself in the colter and the symbolic anal intercourse," "The 'Nether Ye,' " p. 16.

affirming his masculinity through violence against the woman who has humiliated him. It is no accident that the actual recipient of Absolon's blade—the surrogate of his imagined, frustrated desire for a woman—is a man, and a man in a social position very similar to his own in many ways; and this turn of events has several interesting consequences. It frustrates the effort to prove manliness and emphasizes the ambiguities of gender difference, and it further unmans and humiliates the effeminate male both by demonstrating that he is not even capable of taking revenge against a woman and by forcing him to engage unwittingly in an act that must suggest sodomy.[40] At the same time, the substitution of Nicholas for Alisoun, together with the tale's humorous treatment of the episode, covers up the will to violence against women that is represented in Absolon's case as an effect of male fear and sexual anxiety.

It should be emphasized, however, that such violence, as in the *Knight's Tale*, is occluded but never denied or condemned. Because nothing happens to Alisoun, readers never seem to notice what Absolon intended to do with the hot coulter, and Absolon's cruel and exaggerated retribution for the woman's practical joke is both presented and read as a normal, appropriate response by a man whose masculinity has not been able to express itself honestly and naturally: as Kolve, for instance, puts it, "The hairy kiss restores him to his *proper* person, ending the make-believe and role playing . . . " (my emphasis).[41] Finally, the inefficacy of the effeminate man's sudden conversion to violent misogyny also indicates one aspect of the actual illogic of extreme woman-hating, for the more women are the overt target of male hatred, the more their centrality and power over men is implied. (This point is quite overtly addressed, as we shall see, in the *Merchant's Tale*.) Nicholas's intervention in the plot allows the tale to sidestep this issue, however, and to reaffirm that the only real social and moral agents are male.

In arguing for the importance of the fact that the actual recipient of Absolon's blade is male, however, I do not want to lose sight of the fact

---

40. What Absolon does to Nicholas also imputes to homosexual acts the displacement of violence against women, and this perception might be explored more fully in a discussion of representations of the complicated relations between misogyny, male homosexuality, and homophobia.

41. *Imagery of Narrative*, p. 197. One of the rare exceptions to my claim that readers do not seem to notice what Absolon intended is Raymond Tripp, "The Darker Side to Absolon's Dawn Visit," *Chaucer Review* 20 (1986), pp. 207–12; Tripp notes the "ugliness of Absolon's intentions" but does not pursue the point much further.

that Nicholas's part in the joke foregrounds the way in which his own masculinity is also put into question by this tale. Nicholas has often been taken as the antithesis of Absolon, a type even of "uncomplicated male maturity."[42] But in fact the "hende" clerk reflects the same complicated lack of certain manliness that Absolon flaunts. Most dramatically, the substitution of his body for Alisoun's discloses that the region of the female's private parts is, in the dark night of this tale, interchangeable with the male's: what might seem to be a grounding line of gender difference is thus blurred. When Nicholas puts himself literally in the woman's exposed position here, he may intend to tap into her power and her immunity to one-up his rival, and, as I have said, he certainly reappropriates the role of prankster and agent that Alisoun has momentarily played. But at the same time he acts out the feminization he too, only slightly less obviously than and in different ways from Absolon, has displayed throughout the tale.

"Hende Nicholas" is first described as "sleigh and ful privee" (3201), with a wiliness and secrecy more often associated, in other fabliaux as in the Miller's opening comments on women's "pryvetee," with women.[43] In the same couplet, he is, like other clerks, literally described as feminine and/or virginal in demeanor: "lyk a mayden meke for to see" (3202; compare the last words that Absolon speaks before he is cured: " 'I may nat ete na moore than a mayde' "[3707]).[44] His unequivocal and direct lust for Alisoun would seem designed to contradict this maidenly appearance: the first words he speaks, while grabbing his land-

42. Birney, "The Inhibited and the Uninhibited," p. 336. For a discussion of the two men in another respect, focusing on Absolon's dancing and discussing the all-male folk dances evoked by the tale, see Margaret Jennings, "Ironic Dancing: Absolon in the *Miller's Tale,*" *Florilegium* 5 (1983), pp. 78–88. Jennings notes that in the dances alluded to in lines 3328–30, "the dividing line for participation was not between peasantry and gentry but between old and young," and thus she implies the similarity or common factor between Absolon and Nicholas.

43. For evidence of this claim see R. Howard Bloch, *The Scandal of the Fabliaux* (Chicago and London: University of Chicago Press, 1986).

44. The fact that "maiden" could mean "virginal man" in the period in question (see *Middle English Dictionary*, M.1, *maiden n.* 2(d), "a man who abstains from sexual experience for religious reasons; also, a man lacking sexual experience") does not vitiate my point but rather extends it beyond the tale into the lexicon. The appropriation of the term for an unmarried woman to describe the sexually chaste or uninitiated man reflects the perceived feminization of the celibate position and suggests too that the most important thing about a woman—so important that it floats free of her historical specificity as a woman—is her sexual status. The asymmetry in gender is also telling: the corresponding term "boy" or "bachelor," for instance, is never borrowed for an unmarried woman or used to represent gender-free celibacy.

lord's wife "by the queynte," are: " 'Ywis, but if ich have my wille, / For deerne love of thee, lemman, I spille' " (3277–78). The action and texture of the tale, like the formulaic nature of his words, reveal, however, that his real interest lies elsewhere, in his own "queynte" skills, his clever tricks. When an intrusively parenthetical reference interrupts the narrative of his first approach to Alisoun, the conflation of female genitals and clerkly ingenuity is blatantly signaled in the dissolution of rhyming difference into mere repetition and synonymity:

> . . . this hende Nicholas
> Fil with this yonge wyf to rage and pleye,
> Whil that hir housbonde was at Oseneye,
> As clerkes ben ful subtile and ful queynte;
> And prively he caughte hire by the queynte . . .
>
> (3273–76)

Note, moreover, that the ruse Nicholas cooks up will not provide him with what he professes to want, gratification of his alleged desire for Alisoun, on a routine basis. In fact, his cleverness is bound to be found out, or at best to work only once, and to destroy John's dim-witted faith in the "queynte" clerk as completely as it verifies his instinctive distrust of his wife's "queynte."

What Nicholas's scheming does offer him, more than a single night in possession of Alisoun's "queynte," is the chance to prove that he is "queynte," that he can play the parts of both actor and director in this once-in-a-lifetime performance of an elaborate and supremely tellable, highly formulaic drama, in which the "hende" clerk once more outwits the old married fool. The energy of the narration in the tale matches and defines the energy of Nicholas not as sexual but as authorial. He plans in splendid detail and complication for an actual sexual encounter that is itself described in less than ten lines (3650–56). By one reading, then, what is excessive in this story is neither female sexuality nor sex itself, but fiction-making.

Fiction-making, moreover, is not a gender-neutral activity, and both the benefits and risks of authorial daring and excess are clearly (re)attached to questions of gender, sexuality, and power at the end of the tale. While Nicholas is literally feminized, and literalizes his feminization in the ways I have suggested, he also does his best to reaffirm gender hierarchy and restore the action to a competition between men. His substitution of his male body for Alisoun's female body, his "ers" exposed instead of hers, preempts the woman's initiative, just as it seems to disambiguate the earlier reference to Alisoun's "hole." Even in play, or perhaps especially in play, it seems that the female cannot be left in the unsuitable role of agent for long; what is exposed, whether it is the similarity or difference between *queynte* (n.) and *queynte* (adj.), is too dangerous.[45] As a result of his appropriation of her attempted joke, Alisoun escapes the retribution that would too clearly mark the fact that women can't defend themselves with humor, as men can, that they can't merely refuse to suffer. She is also refixed in a position that is clearly marginal to the action and the message of the tale and that is now even passive. For when she is referred to in the closing recapitulation—"Thus swyved was this carpenteris wyf" (3850)—Nature's female has suddenly become the grammatical object of the verb and a nameless possession of her husband in a way that does not seem to reflect what we saw earlier of Alisoun any more than it supports a reading of her as "triumphant."[46]

Nicholas's punishment is in part the price he pays for reasserting his control and firmly ousting the woman from the position of visible importance and potential liberation she momentarily occupies; however, the price might have been higher. He is merely "scalded in the towte" (3853), and while it hurts so much that "he wende for to dye" (3813), a few lines later he is perfectly capable of more self-defensive jesting, running into the street to make everyone in town laugh at John. Just as the near miss of Absolon's attack on Alisoun obscures the reality and the horror of male violence against women, so too Nicholas has a near miss, if we think about it, one that suggests that if he is not really like a maiden to begin with, he comes close to being like one in the end. If the hot iron of Absolon "brende . . . his toute," then those same few millimeters that separate (and connect) Alisoun's two holes save him from castration, the fate of so many other promiscuous medieval clerks, real and fictional.

Nicholas's potential castration, like Alisoun's rape or mutilation or the sodomy of Absolon's attack, lurks not at some deep level in this tale but quite close to the surface, where it clarifies part of the threat to masculine

45. Smith also points out that Alisoun's remark, "Or I wol caste a ston," might be a threat of castration ("Or I wol Caste a Ston," p. 19).

46. Smith, again, says that the Miller's grammar at the end puts Alisoun "among the victimized"; "she has been done to, screwed, and her pleasure is passive past perfect" (Ibid., p. 28).

identity that the Miller's story recognizes and averts; and yet no castration, rape, or sodomy is literally said to take place. The humorous substitution of the male body for the female body, again, together with the sudden, tightly closed denouement, occludes the consequences for women of male anger and anxiety, and for men of the vicious circle of feminization. The Miller has warned against inquiring into a woman's "pryvytee," and the tale follows and proves the wisdom of his counsel. By deflecting attention from Alisoun's threatening self-exposure as he does—blurring the focus to begin with by the use of the word "hole," and then replacing Alisoun altogether—he mystifies and averts the threats that any representation of female sexuality seems to entail: the feminization of the man who tells "queynte" stories, as well as both the homoerotic and self-mutilating aspects of male competition for the "queynte" of a woman.

But God forbede that we stynte heere.
The *Cook's Prologue*, 4339

At first glance, the Knight and the Miller might appear to be as different in their attitudes toward women as the pairs of male rivals within their tales—Palamon, devoted to Venus, and Arcite, follower of Mars; courteous Absolon and "hende" Nicholas—are different. In other words, disagreement within each tale between men who view Woman as goddess and those who view her as "creature" seems to be restaged between the two tales. But the differences between antithetical discourses about Woman are flattened out by the narratives in which they are embedded, in the respective tales and in the meta-tale in which each storyteller also takes part. Palamon and Arcite, never as far apart as the other rivals, are elaborately yet easily reconciled, and on his deathbed the latter putatively proves his nobility and his true bond with his brother through the generous transmission of Emily. Absolon and Nicholas, at the end of the *Miller's Tale*, parody the consolidating exchange of a gift, whereby Emily is equated with a fart, and their perspectives on Alisoun also draw literally and figuratively closer and perhaps even cross. So too the taletellers, the Knight and the Miller, are not as different as they seem; in fact, when we look more closely at their representations of women and their definitions of Woman in the ways I have suggested here, we may see their common interests and the collective effect of their two tales, the first two blows exchanged in the Canterbury tournament.

Most prominently, the first two tales similarly inscribe violence against women at the margins of their respective plots—in what happens just before Arcite and Palamon's story begins, and in what nearly happens at the end of the Miller's—so that this violence frames the tales as a pair. Moreover, what the Knight doesn't have time to talk about, like Emily's rites in the temple of Diana, is often equivalent to what the Miller doesn't want to inquire too closely into, like Alisoun's (or his wife's) sexuality: again, women are thereby characterized in divers ways as fundamentally dangerous in the world just outside or narrowly averted by each narrative. The ideals that contain women in the polite genre and the joke that lets women go in the churlish genre direct attention away from the remote violence and the threats it brackets. In each tale, moreover, women's initially marked presence—in the foreshortened story of the conquest of Femenye and in the prefatory encounter with the Theban widows, as in the rhetorically rich opening portrait of Alisoun—is gradually recast as absence. At the same time, each narrative moves to confirm the most orthodox medieval view of Woman, her fleshly, fallen reality; and, given the ordering of the tales, the progressive movement from the apparent idealism of the Knight's treatment of Emily to the apparent, although equally formulaic, realism of the Miller's representation of Alisoun also validates the Miller's highly conventional view as real, as frank and open and natural.[47] This reiterated movement, from presence to absence and from ideal to real, accounts for the seemingly paradoxical cultural alignment of female absence and reality, of Woman as both marginal and material.

At the same time that the contrast between the paired, sequentially presented genres thus effects a sense of what is true about women, the way each of these tales also defies certain generic conventions and interacts with the other manages the potential for female presence and power more securely than either genre might in isolation. Fabliau elements in the courtly tale, including the rivalry of the two male courtly lovers and the tone of some of Arcite's, Theseus's, and the narrator's remarks, establish both the marginalization and the lack of spirituality in Woman. Courtly elements in the fabliau, such as the narrator's long

---

47. I have already cited above several references to the "reality" of Alisoun; to add just one more clear statement of this position, note Patrick J. Gallagher's comment: "Alison . . . brings us uniquely into contact with what is real" ("Perception and Reality in the *Miller's Tale*," *Chaucer Review* 18 (1983), p. 40).

portrait of his heroine or the language of Absolon's wooing, parody the
rhetorical elevation of Woman to confirm that Emily and Alisoun are not
so different "under their clothes."

Taking the tales together, however, it is also possible to see the instability in both genres or positions that is opened up by the topic of Woman
and the hazardous, irresistible urge to inquire into (and thus try to control) female sexuality. The importance of the idealized lady for whom
men fight and die in the courtly model, for instance, calls into question
the Miller's claim that the problem is so easily solved by looking the
other way, that women can be "swyved" and disregarded as moral or
legal agents. When Alisoun takes the initiative to trick and humiliate
Absolon, it is telling that she is called to the window by his own pseu-
docourtly summoning: polite love in fiction grants women just the kind
of power that Alisoun perversely wields, momentarily at least. The churlish view—again, appearing by virtue of its contrasting tone and content
as well as its place in the sequence to offer the real, natural view—thus
provides a pervasive exposure of what the *Knight's Tale* might on its own
cover up more successfully. The character of Absolon, in particular, focuses attention on what the Knight really does refuse to talk about, the
risk of effeminacy for men in polite attitudes toward women and in
excessively courtly behavior. Absolon follows the logic of a Palamon, as
it were, to its logical absurdity, and he is both punished and apparently
locked out of the heterosexual gratification that is made available, at last,
to the patient yet stalwart nobleman. Nicholas's feminization suggests
the more successful usurpation of feminine strategies, the substitution of
his "queynte" wits for her "queynte," to return moral agency to males.
But in creating Nicholas as a type of storyteller, the *Miller's Tale* firmly
and irrevocably destabilizes the clear gender difference and the possibility of unstrained male bonds that were reinforced by the *Knight's Tale.*

Such destabilization and play with the fluidity of gender need not,
and in this case does not, empower women or alter the fundamental
drive to define Woman in a familiar way. The function of misogyny in
the fourteenth-century literary text may thus be comparable to what
Peter Stallybrass finds over two centuries later in English court drama.
Stallybrass argues that contradictory conceptions of woman's body in
early modern England reflect "the contradictory formation of woman
["women-as-the-same" and "women-as-different"] within the categories
of gender and of class." In the interests of differentiating among classes,
Stallybrass argues, women may also be differentiated, so that "those in

the dominant social classes are allocated privileges they can confer (status, wealth) . . . back on *men.*" Oppressed groups, on the other hand, may attack aristocratic privilege by denying the class differentiation of women, constructing "women-as-the-same." But the potentially subversive conflation of women as different into "a single undifferentiated group," such as I see in the Miller's and Knight's tales, is, Stallybrass adds, "commonly articulated within misogynistic discourse."[48]

The Miller's challenge to certain aspects of the Knight's vision of men and the social order they make tends to open up the fictions of aristocratic masculine identity to discourse (between men) across class divisions on the question of women. Despite the Miller's unchivalric view of what male bonds might amount to, then, the possibility of male bonding across class lines is precisely what is affirmed by the first two tales. And the Miller explicitly introduces Alisoun, taken as "Nature's female," as the woman for whom men of different ranks can feel common masculine desire, even as they have sexual relations with her in class-specific ways: "She was a prymerole, a piggesnye, / For any lord to leggen in his bedde, / Or yet for any good yeman to wedde" (3268–70). The gender disorder and feminization of the storyteller subsequently imagined by the Miller makes possible class satire and sustains the leveling discourse about women that enables these genres to interpenetrate so easily and these two stories to cohere so neatly.

For potentially divergent reasons, both genres and both tales seem to wish profoundly that it were as they try to say it is: that masculine identity and male bonds were possible without the problematics of what I have called the woman outside—the overt markedness and power, in different specific articulations, of the feminine position in both courtly romance and fabliaux—and the woman inside—the covert universalization of the negative feminine position that we see throughout the *Canterbury Tales.* What predictably seems to horrify and titillate men in both the *Knight's Tale* and the *Miller's Tale* is the thought, and/or the sight, of what women look like "under their clothes": we can call this, as Freud does, "the fright of castration," or, as I have been calling it, the perception and fear of gender instability, a lack not of the phallus but of stable sexual differentiation, and the consequent charges, for men, of male

---

48. "Patriarchal Territories: The Body Enclosed," in *Rewriting the Renaissance: The Discourses of Sexual Difference in Early Modern Europe,* ed. Margaret W. Ferguson, Maureen Quilligan, and Nancy J. Vickers (Chicago: University of Chicago Press, 1986), p. 133.

homosexuality and feminization. In the *Canterbury Tales* men loathe, fear, and deny Woman because their efforts to construct masculine identity and discursive authority on the ground of Woman as Other, as properly and stably different, are constantly necessitated and undermined by the experience of both Woman and women as the same, of their own femininity as a function of both external circumstances and inherent, unruly nature. Concomitantly, what is really excessive is not (only) female sexuality but (also) authorial energy—the elaborateness of the Knight's rhetoric or of Nicholas's scheme—which displaces but does not finally conceal the anxiety about manliness that any representation of Woman entails.

Such excessiveness reappears in the remaining tales of the A-fragment, the *Reeve's Tale* and fragmentary *Cook's Tale*, and in closing I would like to sketch out some ways in which these works might be more fully explored along the lines I have laid out here. Although the Reeve says that he is out to "quite" the Miller, in several respects his tale resembles and rewrites the Knight's offering more than it does the Miller's, while at the same time it sustains the Miller's interest in what men of different classes have in common.[49] The Reeve's story of (yet again) three male characters—the miller Symkyn, and the two clerks, John and Aleyn—restages the familiar contest between the old man who legitimately possesses a woman and the young men who don't; readers of the tales as a sequence might at this point begin to wonder if there were any other plot. The Reeve himself and the Knight's Theseus share a common trait, their "ire" (compare, for example, 1762 and 3862), and the Reeve's miller of Trumpyngtoun more closely resembles the Duke of Athens than old John the carpenter. Both Symkyn and Theseus have legal control over two women, in the miller's case a wife and a daughter, in the Duke's case a wife and a sister-in-law. Just as Theseus's marriage to Hippolyta represents proof of his aristocratic male prowess, Symkyn's marriage, in keeping with his far lower rank, is intended "To saven his estaat of

49. Lee Patterson argues that the *Reeve's Tale* subverts the Miller's subversion first by revealing "disunity within the peasant class itself" and second by "requiring us to read the *Reeve's Tale* as the expression of an individual psyche" (*Negotiating the Past* [Madison: University of Wisconsin Press, 1987], p. 182). But I am not convinced that we must read the Reeve's narrative as only "psychological and spiritual"; in comparing it here to the *Knight's Tale*, I am sketching out a meaning that is also political and social, once gender and the representation of women are seen, as feminism insists they be seen, as political and social issues.

yomanrye" (3949); and in his later concern for the shame of his daughter, "that is come of swich lynage" (4272), the Reeve's miller also replicates the dynastic anxieties of Arcite and Palamon. Theseus's use of Emily to stabilize his patriarchal rule is further parodied by the *Reeve's Tale* in the otherwise extraneous character of the miller's father-in-law, a parson about whom we know nothing except that his corruption extends to his ludicrous desire to arrange his granddaughter's marriage "for to bistowe hire hye / Into som worthy blood of auncetrye; . . . Therfore he wolde his hooly blood honoure, / Though that he hooly chirche sholde devoure" (3981–86).

Theseus's reputation for martial prowess, born out by the beginning of the tale, is also matched and defined, in a reductive sense, by the portrait of formidable Symkyn that opens the *Reeve's Tale*. Never to be caught like Absolon without a blade, this miller bears a profusion of swords and knives on his belt and in his pouch and hose:

> Ay by his belt he baar a long panade,
> And of a swerd ful trenchant was the blade.
> A joly poppere baar he in his pouche;
> Ther was no man, for peril, dorste hym touche.
> A Sheffeld thwitel baar he in his hose.
>
> (3929–33)

And the tournament Theseus arranges is patently reenacted in the struggle with staves at the end of the tale.

More like Arcite and Palamon than like Nicholas and Absolon, too, the young men in the triangular schema of the Reeve's plot, the "testif" (4004) John and Aleyn, come from "o toun" (4014). They are related through both a kind of brotherhood, an alliance of age and class interests in the hope of besting the miller (and representing the all-male institution, a college at Canterbury, whose rights they hope to protect, just as Arcite and Palamon represent Thebes), and a competitive engagement to each other. John openly casts this low form of chivalric rivalry as a jealous concern for his own reputation, " 'when this jape is tald another day' " (4207), and thus implicates storytelling and masculine sexual adventure. So too it is precisely the urge to tell—comparable to Palamon's odd confession to Theseus in the grove—that initiates the final pseudo-tournament/brawl, when Aleyn cannot resist boasting of his conquest of the miller's daughter to the wrong bedfellow.

The female characters in the *Reeve's Tale* may also recall Emily in that they are much less realistic than Alisoun appears to be, and the extent of their interest in sexual play is at least slightly ambiguous, like Emily's. Symkyn's unnamed wife and his daughter, Malyne, are more overtly than ever the means by which men compete and prove their masculinity and power over each other; the initial conflict between the clerks and the Miller, notably, is about grain, and the thieving Symkyn's wife and daughter are explicitly referred to as the "esement" (4179) to which the cheated clerks claim a legal right. Male sexual gratification is subordinated to and conflated with other male entitlements: money, possessions, and professional honor. The women do seem to enjoy sex, although Mrs. Symkyn's pleasure is referred to only in a line that clearly serves to cast aspersions on the husband's sexual capacity: "So myrie a fit ne hadde she nat ful yoore" (4230). The Reeve's description of the rape of Malyne, who is presumably a virgin, hints at her unseemly, instantaneous pleasure, but speaks of her potential pain in a way that both reminds us of it and belittles it: "This wenche . . . faste slepte / Til he so ny was, er she myghte espie, / That it had been to late for to crie, / And shortly for to seyn, they were aton" (4194–97). Malyne also recalls the romance heroine more than Alisoun when she almost weeps in saying farewell to her "goode lemman" (4247); in this same speech, however, her effective purpose is to betray her father by telling the clerk where to find the cake that has been made out of his stolen meal. So too, when the more well-intentioned wife mistakes her husband's bald head for a clerk's nightcap and smites Symkyn "at the fulle" (4305), we see most clearly of all what both the Knight and the Miller have been able to obscure but not overcome in their tales: women are literally as well as metaphorically dangerous, wittingly or unwittingly, because even very different men sometimes look too much alike.

Were we to go on in this vein, moreover, to the *Cook's Prologue* and *Tale*, we would be able to see the only possible outcome that the tales can imagine to all this quiting and requiting among male storytellers. The Cook's response to the *Reeve's Tale* acknowledges the bonds of pleasure, mutual irritation, and reciprocal service between male comrades that such tale-telling affords: "For joye him thoughte he clawed him on the bak" (4326). And when the Cook encapsulates and focuses what he sees as the moral of the Reeve's story, using a proverb from Solomon, his comment in fact spells out the link between all three preceding tales:

"Ne bryng nat every man into thyn hous";
For herberwynge by nyghte is perilous.
Wel oghte a man avysed for to be
Whom that he broghte into his pryvetee.
(4331–34)

In these very different versions of the domestic crisis, all three older men have found it threatening to bring younger men into their houses (or their prison towers) at night. The Cook refocuses attention on what is at stake: not only access to the women's "pryvetee" that is guarded within the domestic walls, and from which Knight and Miller both explicitly avert their eyes even as they wish to take a quick, thrilling peep, but also men's "pryvetee"; and when the gender changes, "privacy" also changes from a question of sexuality to a matter of place and property.

The Cook wants more of the same back-scratching—"But God forbede that we stynte heere" (4339)—and his call for an endless proliferation of authorial voices, all saying the same thing, reminds us as in the *Miller's Tale* and the *Knight's Tale* that what is excessive is a certain kind of masculine fiction-making, in which Woman is both quintessential fiction and inescapable, unspeakable reality. What we have of his own tale also suggests endless repetition of the same thing, the joke about the cuck-olded husband, as the Cook sets up the story of a riotous servant— something of a cross, if possible, between Absolon and Symkyn—who is going to be taken into another man's house by night. These are the last five lines of the A-fragment:

Anon he sente his bed and his array
Unto a compeer of his owene sort,
That lovede dys, and revel, and disport,
And hadde a wyf that heeld for contenance
A shoppe, and swyved for hir sustenance.
(4418–22)

The last line leaves us with another strong verbal echo of (the end of) the *Miller's Tale*—"Thus swyved was this carpenteris wyf . . . ," al-though "swyved" in the *Cook's Tale* is an intransitive verb, rather than a participle, of which the wife is the subject. The Cook doesn't want to stop, and the literal fact that there is no end to this degenerative sequence of tales must be read as accidental. The repetition seems at the same time to effect a kind of curtailment that is highly appropriate. The incompletion of the tale and thus of the sequence as a whole implies on one hand that there can be no end to such tale-telling and on the other hand that we have finally reached natural closure in this hardly newsworthy vision of the real truth that underlies men's dreams and jokes, that unifies and divides them across age and class differences: women are prostitutes. This is the common denominator, the familiar, traditional definition of Woman that is exchanged and fixed by the opening voices of the *Canterbury Tales,* as they look away from the violence against women on which the sequence is founded and instead lead the way into reality, defined here as the inevitable and progressive disillusioning of Palamon's painfully naive view that the woman in the garden is a goddess.

9

The *Merchant's Tale,*
or Another Poor Worm

God of his grete goodnesse seyde than,
"Lat us now make an helpe unto this man
Lyk to himself"; and thanne he made him Eve.
The Merchant's Tale 1327–29

[The *Merchant's Tale*] transcends the traditional medieval criticism of women for their seductive powers and inconstancy
in love; equally important is the tale's demonstration of the
reprehensible folly and lechery of men.

Karl P. Wentersdorf, "Imagery, Structure,
and Theme in Chaucer's *Merchant's Tale*"

Why has the *Merchant's Tale* seemed so much more horrifying to modern
readers than other tales in which characters are similarly ignoble and
deluded, actions by certain standards equally if not more obscene, and
storytellers just as fixated on the failure of all ideals and the success of a
kind of rude justice?[1] Compare, for instance, interpretations of the *Miller's
Tale.* As I noted in the preceding chapter, critics have held that this tale
of adultery and deceit, with its undertones of rape or genital mutilation,
sodomy, and castration, is just wholesome good fun, that courtliness in
it is "harmlessly misplaced," and that the unfaithful wife, Alisoun, is a
symbol of "healthy animality."[2] The *Merchant's Tale,* on the other hand,
is only rarely seen as humorous; most often it is noted for its darkness,
its "unrelieved acidity"; it is said to offer a "perversion" of the courtly

---

1. The article from which the epigraph is drawn appears in *Chaucer and the Craft of
Fiction,* ed. Leigh A. Arrathoon (Rochester, MI: Solaris Press, 1986), pp. 35–36.
2. Charles Muscatine, *Chaucer and the French Tradition* (Berkeley: University of California Press, 1966), p. 231; E. Talbot Donaldson, "The Effect of the *Merchant's Tale,*" *Speaking
of Chaucer* (London: Athlone, 1970), p. 35.

code.[3] For committing the same sin that Alisoun commits—without the accompanying prank, and, as far as we know, with none of the "myrthe" and "solas" that she is said to enjoy—May is deemed "a completely unfeeling wife."[4] What happens to May in the tree is not at all funny but a "culminating outrage," "high and horrible fantasy," and presumably the source of what is to me an otherwise inexplicable critical judgment that this tale contains "greater obscenity than any of the other Canterbury Tales."[5]

Scholars convinced that this is a "brutal, bitter, and hence un-Chaucerian" piece have imputed to Chaucer divers motives for writing it, all of which depend on separating the author from the ostensive teller, the Merchant, to varying degrees and in various directions.[6] The only critical approach that seems sure about this distance, and hence about the tale's meaning and merits, is one that confidently finds a higher message in all this obscenity, discounting what is troubling by reading it as a negative exemplum. But many other readers have been unsatisfied with such a solution; E. Talbot Donaldson, one of those most disturbed by the tale, maintains that the *Merchant's Tale* gives rise to "a state of nervousness from which only the most resolutely unflappable reader can free himself," and Jay Schleusner observes that the apparent absence of Chaucer's usual wit and good nature makes the tale "a critical embarrassment."[7]

A key to understanding both these feelings of nervousness and embarrassment that the tale has engendered in many modern readers and its place in the patterns of Chaucerian fiction that I am exploring here lies in the Merchant's early evocation of the biblical myth of human creation. Genesis 1–3 was a frequent topic of commentary throughout the Middle Ages, often analyzed in theological debates about proper

3. J. S. P. Tatlock, "Chaucer's *Merchant's Tale*," in *Chaucer Criticism: The Canterbury Tales*, ed. Richard Schoeck and Jerome Taylor (Notre Dame: University of Notre Dame Press, 1960), p. 175; Muscatine, *Chaucer and the French Tradition*, p. 231.

4. Muscatine, *Chaucer and the French Tradition*, p. 236.

5. Donaldson, "The Effect of the *Merchant's Tale*," p. 42; Tatlock, "Chaucer's *Merchant's Tale*," p. 175.

6. John Elliott, "The Two Tellers of the *Merchant's Tale*," *Tennessee Studies in Literature* 9 (1964), p. 12.

7. Donaldson, "The Effect of the *Merchant's Tale*," p. 43; Jay Schleusner, "The Conduct of the *Merchant's Tale*," *Chaucer Review* 14 (1980), p. 237. Schleusner's essay provides an interesting discussion of the problem of distance between Merchant and Chaucer that interrogates "the author's complicity" in the teller's position. A review of the problem of accepting the "exegetical" approach mentioned earlier in this paragraph is offered in Emerson Brown, Jr., "Biblical Women in the *Merchant's Tale*: Feminism, Antifeminism, and Beyond," *Viator* 5 (1974), pp. 389–98.

gender relations and the religious meaning and value of human sexuality. The Bible tells two quite different stories about creation. The first, found in Genesis 1:26–28, seems to indicate that male and female human beings were originally created together, at the same time, or perhaps even that human nature was in the beginning androgynous: "to the image of God he created him: male and female he created them." Chapter 2, however, posits instead that Adam was created first and alone; after he named all the animals, God saw and pitied his solitude and so created Eve second, out of and for the lonely male.[8] In the ironic encomium on the married state near the beginning of the *Merchant's Tale*, it is the second version of creation, taken from Genesis 2:20–24, that is cited:

> The hye God, whan he hadde Adam maked,
> And saugh him al allone, bely-naked,
> God of his grete goodnesse seyde than,
> "Lat us now make an help unto this man
> Lyk to himself"; and thanne he made him Eve.
> Heere may ye se, and heerby may ye preve,
> That wyf is mannes helpe and his confort . . .
> . . . .
> O flessh they been, and o flessh, as I gesse,
> Hath but oon herte, in wele and in distresse.
>   (1325–36)

In Donaldson's view, the Merchant here degrades and "vulgarizes" the creation of Adam and Eve—and especially Adam. When the first man is described as "bely-naked," we feel that God was moved, Donaldson observes, by "cynical pity" for "the poor naked thing . . . there is no *imago Dei* here." While the story of Genesis 2 is usually used to differentiate and rank Adam and Eve, the Merchant's version of it, especially in the context of the tale that follows, actually implies their similarity, the failure from the beginning of a reassuring difference between male and female. Eve was made for Adam "lyk to hymself," Donaldson observes: "And Eve, another poor worm, is as like Adam as May turns out to be like January. It is a depressing thought."[9]

---

8. Recent discussions of the two-part creation story and its interpretive legacy can be found in Phyllis Trible, "Eve and Adam, Genesis 2–3 Reread," in *Womanspirit Rising: A Feminist Reader in Religion,* ed. Carol P. Christ and Judith Plaskow (San Francisco: Harper and Row, 1979), pp. 74–83, and in several essays included in *Genesis 1–3 in the History of Exegesis: Intrigue in the Garden,* ed. Gregory Allen Robbins (Lewiston, N.Y. and Queenston, Ontario: Edwin Mellen Press, 1988).

9. Donaldson, *Speaking of Chaucer,* p. 40.

Donaldson might also have commented on how the poetics of God's speech as formulated by this narrator reinforces his reading. The crucial phrase, "lyk to hymself," is underscored by its prominence at the beginning of line 1329. Furthermore, syntactic ambiguity in the second half of the line, "he made him Eve," suggests the possibility that in making the woman *for* the man, God made the man *into* a woman. Making two out of "O flessh," God transformed human nature from solitary (and in Genesis 2 expressly linguistic) preeminence over all other creatures to uneasy, silencing doubleness, leaving Adam desirous of a former unity and wholeness still recalled and promised in the ideal of "O flessh" but tempted and prevented by the equivocal nature, "as I gesse," of gender difference. In the *Book of the Duchess*, the oneness of man and woman, "Oo blysse, and eke oo sorwe bothe," was represented as just such an impossible, or lost, dream. Firmly treated as lost to both narrator and characters, it could become the generative matter of an allegory in which masculine identity and access to the power of language was positively reinscribed. In the *Merchant's Tale*, oneness in more tangible and present senses—oneness as common (fallen) humanity and as depraved, illicit (re)union in the flesh—is all too possible, and the stuff of nightmares, or at least of brutal fabliaux.

Lines 1325–36 evoke, then, the problems of gender difference, sexuality, and male domination that the creation myth embodies to the Middle Ages, and the tale as a whole goes on to explore a particularly troubling issue for patriarchal Christian thinking: what is the source of allegedly innate, natural feminine inferiority? If Eve is made "lyk to hymself," of Adam's "bely-naked" flesh, why is she instinctively deceitful, untrustworthy, and carnal? The tale contains without reconciling two possible answers to this question, neither of which is supportive of claims for the legitimacy or even possibility of masculine dominance. On one hand, the matter that Eve is made of, Adam's flesh itself, might be pervasively corrupt; this idea is a commonplace of medieval world-hating, and a truism, as readers have noted, of the Merchant's characterization of both men and women. It is also a "depressing thought," as Donaldson says, that not only problematizes the notion of inherent male superiority but also denies men the ability to resist the self-reflexive trap of womanhating in two ways attempted by characters and narrators in other Chaucerian fictions: through sympathizing with innocent female victims or by positing the existence, always in absentia, of a good woman to be worshipped. On the other hand, it might be argued that Woman has some

quality not derived from Adam, some carnal drive of her own that jus-
tifies the need for male mastery. But this possibility opens the door to a
radical female difference and hence a distinctly female subjectivity—like
May's—that needs to be punished and controlled but will always manage
to outwit the sons of Adam.[10]

Reading the *Merchant's Tale* in this way accounts for both the horror
that most modern critics have seen in it and the "nervousness" that it
exhibits in its narrating voice and seems to generate in some readers.
The *Merchant's Tale* is, I agree, brutal and bitter: brutal in its attitude
toward domestic and narrative violence against women and bitter in its
confrontation with the fact that even violence cannot guarantee masculine difference and dominance. I read the tale not, however, as "un-
Chaucerian" in this regard but as quintessentially Chaucerian in its concentration on familiar questions about the intersection of gender difference, the representation of women, and poetic or narrative authority.
Perhaps more rawly than most, this tale exposes and turns on an unre-
solvable dilemma inherent in orthodox medieval assumptions about
gender relations. In struggling with this dilemma, it shifts from one uncomfortable account of Woman to another in ways that I shall explore
in some detail. First, I consider the tale's emphasis on the facts that May
is made in the image of both January and her maker, and that when
men bring Woman into being, they both see themselves more truly and
induce or reveal their own feminization. I then argue that the tale at the
same time gradually introduces the "horrifying" second possibility: May
is different and has something that cannot be fully known or seen or
controlled. The nature of the female character's difference here does not
enable the would-be manly storyteller in the *Merchant's Tale*, as it often
did the figure of the poet of Chaucer's dream-visions, but hoists him
very visibly on the petard of his own unrelieved, unhappy antifeminism.

10. The "crooked rib" theory, of course, negotiates precisely the dilemma I am speaking of by positing that Eve was made out of a part of Adam but that that part—a rib from
the breast—was naturally "bent" away from the man. One discussion of this theory is
found in the fifteenth-century *Malleus Maleficarum*, by Heinrich Kramer and James
Springer, trans. Montague Summers (London: Pushkin Press, 1948), p. 44.

JANUARY'S FANTASY

The *Merchant's Tale* reproduces the first of the two unsettling possibilities
that might account for the putatively natural and invariable corruption
of the female: May is made in the image of both January and her maker,
the Merchant, and both project themselves and their base desires all too
clearly onto the creature they bring into being. At the narrative level,
there is literally no May before January marries her; that is to say, she
enters the story quite explicitly as the product of the old man's warped
imagination, the "heigh fantasie" of a male who is anxious about his
waning manliness and wants to see his own lost youth and powers of
discernment reflected in the image of a young wife.[11] The production of
May herself out of January's clichéd anxieties is most explicitly brought
out in the long passage in which the old knight chooses his future wife
from "Many fair shap and many a fair visage" (1580). The narrator first
uses a simile to suggest that January looks at women from a distance,
seeing the superficial image and gazing through the eyes of public opinion, and also in a way that will show him more of himself (whom he
also misconceives) than of the objects he gazes at:

> As whoso tooke a mirour, polisshed bryght,
> And sette it in a commune market-place,
> Thanne sholde he se ful many a figure pace
> By his mirour; and in the same wyse
> Gan Januarie inwith his thoght devyse
> Of maydens whiche that dwelten hym bisyde.
> (1582–87)

What one sees in a mirror is a reflection, an image, not the thing itself;
as much scholarly discussion of this passage already suggests, it reminds
us of the acknowledged vanity and imperfection of human sight.[12] Moreover, if January is looking as if in a mirror, he is likely at some point to
see a part of himself; hence the figure confirms the way in which May,

---

11. For a helpful discussion focusing on the critique of January in this regard, rather
than on the construction of May, which is my interest, see Robert B. Burlin, *Chaucerian
Fiction* (Princeton: Princeton University Press, 1977) pp. 207ff.

12. See, for instance, Arrathoon, " 'For Craft is al, whoso that do it kan': The Genre
of the *Merchant's Tale*," in *Chaucer and the Craft of Fiction*, pp. 253ff.

the woman, is at the beginning at least a sharp reflection of January's problematic, erring, threatened masculine perception. May is, in the terms of this narrative, devised out of January's thoughts just as Eve is made out of Adam.

But January, in turn, is made out of an equally determining discourse; the man whose distorted fantasies create May is in no way a free(r) agent here, and what I have referred to as "his" imagination is as derivative and stereotypical, produced as much by antifeminist discourse, as May herself is. As the narrator dwells on January's initial inability to choose in the marketplace where women are exchanged, for instance, he describes the neighboring maidens' competing attractions—and reciprocal liabilities—thus:

> He wiste nat wher that he myghte abyde.
> For if that oon have beaute in hir face,
> Another stant so in the peples grace
> For hire sadnesse and hire benyngnytee
> That of the peple grettest voys hath she;
> And somme were riche, and hadden badde name.
>
> (1588–93)

What the narrator presents here as if it were January's experience is, like so much of this tale, drawn from standard and well-known antifeminist material (and as if to make sure that this is clear, a similar citation appears in that compendium of misogynist lore, the *Wife of Bath's Prologue*, lines 248ff.).[13] The ideology out of which January's experience is made thus determines that January must choose among an imperfect set of options and hence close his eyes to imperfection; to love a woman is always already to err—even as it is to love (what is worst in) oneself, as the mirror simile reveals.

Finally, despite the difficulties of making a choice, and the impossibility of making a correct choice, when confronted with the dilemma that women are said to present, the narrator tells us that "bitwixe ernest and game" (1594), in that infamous site of Chaucerian expertise where accountability, like identity and intention, is so consistently up for grabs, January chooses one. The voice of the narrator (clearly distinct at this point from January's inner speech) underscores the predetermined fault-

---

13. Modern editors of the Wife's *Prologue* have noted that this particular antifeminist motif is taken from Theophrastus's *Liber Aureolus de Nuptiis,* Deschamps' *Miroir de Mariage,* and *Le Roman de la Rose;* see Robinson, *Works of Chaucer,* p. 698.

iness of the choice—"For love is blynd alday, and may nat see" (1598)—
and then offers what might appear to be, at last, a description of May.
It turns out, however, to be not only a highly abstract and conventional
portrait but also a depiction of what January sees in his mind's eye as
he lies in bed thinking of May:

> He purtreyed in his herte and in his thoght . . .
> Hir myddel smal, hire armes longe and sklendre,
> Hir wise governaunce, hir gentillesse,
> Hir wommanly berynge, and hire sadnesse.
>
> (1600–4)

It hardly bears repeating that these lines do not represent some "actual"
May. We see once more how January visualizes what medieval literary
texts repeatedly say that men admire. Moreover (and I shall return to
the significance of this point), the May of January's imagination is made
to seem not only predictable but also implausible in this passage, since
she combines the abstract qualities of ideal physical beauty and sober
moral virtue that were earlier said to be mutually exclusive in women.

The narrator closes this discussion of how January chooses a wife by
emphasizing once more that what January seeks to prove by selecting
May is his place in an all-male pecking order. Recalling the earlier and
by now thoroughly undermined assertion that the old man "chees hire
of his owene auctoritee" (1597), the narrator reminds us that January is
less interested in a real woman than in laying claim to authority and
defending his own wisdom:

> And whan that he on hire was condescended,
> Hym thoughte his choys myghte nat ben amended.
> For whan that he hymself concluded hadde,
> Hym thoughte ech oother mannes wit so badde
> That inpossible it were to repplye
> Agayn his choys, this was his fantasye.
>
> (1605–10)

Here we learn still more about what we already must know of January—
his lack of "auctoritee," perception, or free choice, and his stubborn
investment in mis-seeing—and nothing about the woman he mistakenly
expects will prove his superiority to other men, not even her name. Both
the importance and inefficacy of his attempt to compete through May
in a homosocial arena is underscored in the narrator's attention to January's conferences with his menfriends, including the long, fruitless de-

bates between Placebo and Justinus. When the proper name of the bride is finally given, it is still syntactically postponed and embedded—"she, this mayden, which that Mayus highte" (1693)—in a sentence describing the more or less reluctant exertions of January's friends to arrange the marriage quickly, "whan they saughe that it moste nedes be" (1691).

What little we are told about the marriage ceremony itself suggests that May is also derived from another traditional discourse about women, somewhat different from and even older than the conventional medieval misogyny that January echoes earlier. Performing the traditional marriage service, the priest enjoins May to "be lyk Sarra and Rebekke" (1704), and the allusions reinvoke the earlier ironically voiced catalogue praising a series of Old Testament types of the *mulier fortis*: Rebecca, who helped her son Jacob trick his blind old father into giving him his brother's birthright; Judith, who beheaded Holofernes; Abigail, who saved her husband Nabal from David's wrath and then, when Nabal's "heart died within him," married David; and Esther, who married King Ahasuerus to achieve her own ends (1362–74).[14] As Emerson Brown has pointed out, positive readings of these stories were also common in medieval exegesis; these strong women were often viewed typologically as figures, like the Virgin Mary, of the triumph of truth, Christ, the true Church, over evil, and the use of bad means (deceit, betrayal, murder) justified by good ends. Although Brown notes that the *Merchant's Tale* emphasizes the literal, pejorative side of these stories, the audience, Brown believes, learns to distrust the Merchant sufficiently to find the "positive level of meaning" that rises above the literal level on which the Merchant focuses. As Brown observes, however, the Merchant still obliges the audience to sink to his level, to remember also the literal truth of these stories.[15]

There are two other effects of citing this double, divided tradition about female duplicity, these two apparently contradictory ways of read-

---

14. The reference to the story of Abigail and Nabal is taken from the Douay Bible, 1 Kings 25:37 (in the King James version, 1 Samuel). The full verse reads, "But early in the morning when Nabal had digested his wine, his wife told him these words (her judicious speech which tempered the wrath of David towards her foolish husband), and his heart died within him, and he became as a stone." The *Merchant's Tale* may allude to this story again, ironically, when it is May who is brought to January's bed "as stille as stone." The catalogue also of course sets the *Merchant's Tale* in interesting dialogue with the *Tale of Melibee*, where Dame Prudence cites Rebecca, Judith, Abigail, and Esther as apparently unironic evidence that women can be "ful discret and wis in conseillynge" (1096ff.).

15. "Biblical Women in the *Merchant's Tale*," especially pp. 410–12.

ing the same stories of powerful women, and of foregrounding the tensions within and between traditional strains of thinking about women. First, at either level, literal or figurative, negative or positive, the allusions underscore the tale's thematic interest in the feminization of men. The type of the strong woman, viewed as good or evil, available to pro- or antifeminist interpretation, exposes and punishes the unmanliness of (some) men, and particularly, as Brown says, men's sensuality: the way in which many males are too feminine, too much like the normative conception of fleshly, sinning Woman. Second, the narrator's revisionary deployment of the catalogue *against* more orthodox religious readings of biblical history suggests how, through his reading and writing about women, he, like January, attempts to best other men and assert his own authority. Specifically, his use of the catalogue implies that figurative readings "cover up" something: they conceal the strength and power of women as they reassert masculine domination and difference in the face of blatant counterevidence. That is, by turning these historical or mythical women into types of Christ, the exegetical reading subsumes stories of castrated men into the teleology of salvation history. The *Merchant's Tale*, responsive to the hermeneutic traditions in which it may be read, problematizes this easy way of avoiding the internal or symbolic threats that women pose. By evoking a discourse and a way of knowing in which literal is so clearly set against figurative, the tale validates itself and its depiction of "women on top" *as* the literal: that is, as the true, the real, the unglossed, the impolite and undisguised. (Thus, as I noted earlier, the effect on the definition of Woman is similar to the effect generated by following the polite *Knight's Tale* with the frank *Miller's Tale*.)

May's sanctioned, even enforced entry into the scriptural tradition of castrating, manipulative, deceitful wives is confirmed in the narrator's characteristically sly description of the bride at the wedding feast, which includes a third reference to a type of the *mulier fortis:*

> Mayus, that sit with so benyngne a chiere,
> Hire to biholde it semed fayerye.
> Queene Ester looked nevere with swich an ye
> On Assuer, so meke a look hath she.
> I may yow nat devyse al hir beautee.
> But thus muche of hire beautee telle I may,
> That she was lyk the brighte morwe of May,
> Fulfild of alle beautee and plesaunce.
>
> (1742–49)

Once again the rhetoric implies that May is made of masculine fantasy; and here, more clearly than ever, as the use of the first-person pronoun suggests, it is partly the narrator's fantasy as well, so that the picture of May is at once both more obscured and more reflective of masculine ways of seeing. May is described by what it "semed" like to behold her "chiere" and her "look"; by the contorted negative comparison to Esther, whose own story can be read two ways and keeps intruding on this tale; by the narrator's use of the ineffability topos; and finally by the formulaic simile that incidentally reminds us of the conventional status of May's name itself. The effect of the narrator's strategy is to tell us more about himself and his discursive heritage than to clarify the object of his dubious praise; May remains a function of (slippery) figuration, of (not quite accurate or adequate) allusion and trope.

I have been arguing thus far that the narrative in which May is introduced and the rhetorical devices out of which she is made suggest quite relentlessly that a woman is created by the men who look at her and talk about her. One problem for men in this explanation becomes increasingly obvious as the tale unfolds. If the female is a projection of the husband and storyteller—if Eve is made of precisely the same stuff as Adam—then the antifeminist tradition, as it seeks to naturalize and essentialize Woman's sin and guilt, confronts a profoundly disturbing crisis, problematizing proper difference at two levels, first between male and female and second within the category of men. In the *Merchant's Tale*, the more obvious of these problems, the denial of proper difference between the sexes, is explicitly developed as May, acting on the illicit sexual desires imputed to her, and like the strong women she has been compared to, comes both to dominate and to resemble the men who foolishly desire to be "o flessh" with her.

The predictable entry into the story of the young man who easily seduces the older lord's wife might be somewhat reassuring to the manliness threatened in the feeble figure of January and in the Merchant's literal-minded reading of the Bible, if like "hende" Nicholas the squire here were at least cleverer than May and more at the center of the story. But he is not. Damyan is essentially just like January, only younger; both are "ravysshed" by May (cf. 1750, 1774). Six lines after he is introduced, Damyan as parodic courtly lover almost faints and "hastily" takes to his bed (1775–79). After he gives May the initial signal (the letter), she takes the lead and, true to the type with which she has been identified, plays the man's part.[16] The proverb cited from the *Knight's Tale* in speaking of her swift decision to commit adultery—"Lo, pitee renneth soone in gentil herte!" (1986)—referred there, notably, to Theseus and his mercy. Here, like Theseus, May is the one who pities, and she becomes the stage manager of the affair. So too when May writes to Damyan, the narrator describes her frustrated love as that of a typical (Chaucerian) male lover:[17]

> [May] loveth Damyan so benyngnely
> That she moot outher dyen sodeynly,
> Or elles she moot han hym as hir leste.
> She wayteth whan hir herte wolde breste.
>
> (2093–96)

As their love affair progresses, the tale focuses less on role reversal and more on the essential similarity of May and Damyan, female and male. These two lovers are so alike, so interchangeable, that they understand each other as readily as most other courtly couples in Chaucerian fiction misunderstand. They communicate easily in both verbal and nonverbal ways, and so just as Criseyde (falsely) hoped and believed Troilus knew her thoughts without words, Damyan and May truly know and act on each other's every wish: "But nathelees, by writyng to and fro, / And privee signes, wiste he what she mente, / And she knew eek the fyn of his entente" (2104–6). To drive the point home we find a repetition of this idea—with emphasis on the central term, "entente"— twice more. First, May and Damyan cooperate in forging the key to the garden. She initially imprints its shape in "warm wex" (2117), thus doing to the key what January planned to do to her (" 'a yong thyng may men gye, / Right as men may warm wex with handes plye,' " as he puts it in 1429–30). Then "Damyan, that knew al hire entente, / The cliket countrefeted pryvely" (2120–21). Once they are all in the garden, May signs to Damyan to climb up the pear tree,

---

16. Roy Pearcy, "The Genre of Chaucer's Fabliau," in Arrathoon, *Chaucer and the Craft of Fiction,* pp. 329–84, compares the *Merchant's Tale* with twelfth-century Latin comedy and points out that May usurps the role of the son or his agent in comedy, while the young man is transformed in Chaucer "into a strangely langerous lover."

17. Lovesickness of the kind May experiences was attributed at times to both genders in the literature of the Middle Ages. Chaucer, however, more commonly adheres to the tradition that assigns the disease only to males. For a discussion of the problem of the sex-specificity of lovesickness, see Mary Wack, "The Measure of Pleasure: Peter of Spain on Men, Women, and Lovesickness," *Viator* 17 (1986), pp. 173–96.

> ... and up he wente.
> For verraily he knew al hire entente,
> And every signe that she koude make,
> Wel bet than Januarie, hir owene make.
>   (2211–14)

Between these lovers, as between even the oldest husband and the youngest wife, there is thus no mystery, no tantalizing, erotic, face-saving difference, no distance between the sexual appetite or sign-making capacity of male and female. The female, putatively, is as much the possessor of "entente" as the male, and her intention and his are both one and the same and mutually intelligible. Both men and women use words and other signs in the same way, to advance their equally pressing sexual desires. And so the tree bearing tempting pears, the fruit known in the Middle Ages as an ambiguous symbol for both male genitals and female breasts, stands as an apt icon at the end of the tale for part at least of what has been perceived as the "culminating outrage" of this story: the blurring or failure of gender differences at the moment of heterosexual climax, when they ought to be most natural and secure.[18]

Difference in a second, less blatant way—difference within the category of men, between males of dissimilar age, status, and kind—is also problematized by this plot: there is little distinction, other than age and sexual competence, between January and Damyan; and Pluto, elsewhere god of the underworld, is here treated by his shrewish wife Proserpina just as January is treated by May. At another level, the similarity between the narrator himself and his character, January, as type of the naive, uxorious husband is clear from the outset of the tale. In the infamous praise of marriage with which it begins, the narrator establishes the tongue-in-cheek stance he will maintain, however unevenly, for the rest of the tale. If there are doubts about the sarcasm intended in this compendium of both pro- and antifeminist citation, what happens later removes them; retrospectively, at least, we can only assume a pervasive irony that condemns January and all other blinded men (including, possibly, the Merchant before he married; see the prologue to the tale, 1233ff.) who believe that "A wyf is Goddes yifte verraily" (1311). Yet at the same time, the ironic voicing of the lines in itself highlights the interpenetra-

---

18. For this understanding of the pear's symbolic doubleness, I am indebted to Wentersdorf, "Imagery, Structure, and Theme," pp. 51–52; he points out that the pear was also known to the Middle Ages as a sign of infamy and effeminacy.

bility of storyteller and character, of January's naive enthusiasm for marriage and the narrator's misogynist cynicism. And just as January's self-deluded choice of May backfires and fails to prove his superiority to other men, so too, I will argue, the narrator's insistence that he now reads and writes women more authoritatively than other men rebounds on him and on the relentless misogyny in which he participates. Above all, the rhetorical strategies by which the narrator condemns January and other men for their foolishly naive or idealizing views of women, in an effort to differentiate himself from them in their blindness, presuppose another disturbing possibility inherent in medieval misogyny: May has a subjectivity and a sexuality that is something more than a projection of male fantasy and can therefore never be fully known or controlled.

<hr />

MAY'S AWAKENING

From the beginning, the development of May might at crucial moments suggest that she has a problematic, uncontrollable selfhood that escapes the narrator's mastery and understanding as easily as the wife escapes her husband's most jealous attempts to control and confine her. As we have seen, for example, in order to indict January's blindness in choosing a bride, the narrator insists that the May January thinks he sees is merely a reflection of the old man's pathetic needs. Yet if January is wrong about May's innocence and malleability, as he soon turns out to be, must there not be another May, a true May, a May who is precisely *not* what she looks like in the mirror of January's eye? The narrator's recurring use of *occupatio* frequently suggests precisely this; what he usually doesn't have time to look at and talk about is the real May. In lines 1697–98, for instance, he says that it would take too long to tell us "of every scrit and bond / By which that she was feffed in his lond"; and thus he hints that the maiden has her own socioeconomic interests, or that marriage allows a woman to enter, however marginally, into material and legal being. Like other instances of irony, the sarcasm in the description of May at the wedding feast (1742–49) not only confuses the gaze of the narrator and the character but also imples the existence of a terrifying female subjectivity. The narrator superficially describes May as a (false) male fantasy, telling us only what it "semed" like to behold her, what kind of "look" she had, what she was "lyk." But the presupposition of sarcasm and irony of all sorts, again, is always that there is a truth behind the false appearance, a reality that someone, presumably the storyteller and audience, as opposed to the duped male character, can see. Because of his own insistent misogyny, the putatively true or actual May that this undeluded narrator must claim to discern predictably turns out to be the obscenity that therefore seems both shocking and inevitable to so many modern readers: a woman getting away with it, escaping male mastery and going unpunished.

I do not mean to argue that the picture of May that we begin to glimpse through the narrator's irony and sarcasm, or in what he can't or won't say about May, is any more accurate a representation of some historical female experience or position than January's mental image; my point is that the narrator's strategy inevitably raises the *possibility* of a female subjectivity, and what I want to emphasize now are the ways that he more fully both realizes and resists this frightening possibility as the tale progresses. Indirectly implicated by early irony, allusion, *occupatio* and simile, the awakening, so to speak, of an independent female consciousness appears with something of a sudden lurch in the narrator's representation of May on her wedding night. First, after January has consumed his aphrodisiacs and sent his friends home, the narrator glances at May, predictably, in a simile: "The bryde was broght abedde as stille as stoon" (1818). The cliché continues to fix May at a distance, in rhetoric and conventional figure, all feelings undisclosed. But if she is *like* stone, something about her is not stone; her properly inexpressive demeanor may cover fear, repulsion, innocence, indifference, passivity, stoicism. After thirty or so lines devoted to describing January's physical and mental repulsiveness in bed, the narrator returns to the question of what May felt:

> But God woot what that May thoughte in hir herte,
> Whan she hym saugh up sittynge in his sherte,
> In his nyght-cappe, and with his nekke lene;
> She preyseth nat his pleyyng worth a bene.
> (1851–54)

Like the earlier simile, the narrator's initial claim here of ignorance and distance from May's feelings—"God woot"—could indicate that May is as yet sexually uninitiated, (hence) undeveloped as a female (character), and, perhaps, pitiable. It may seem strained to suggest that the conventional phrase also implies that God, at least, knows what May thinks: that is, that she has thoughts of her own, even if no human male can hope to understand them. But this possibility is precisely what is reinforced in the final line in the passage, when the narrator contradicts himself and offers for the first time a clear, apparently frank and therefore true statement about the allegedly divine mystery of May's feelings. And what does this astonishing about-face tell us? The negative formulation—she didn't find his lovemaking worth a bean—discovers a maiden who is already making judgments about men's "pleyyng," instead of just silently and stonily enduring her fate; it reveals that she can already compare and verbalize her evaluation of male sexual performance, that she might praise another man's playing as worth a few beans at least. The diction obviously lowers the tone of May's thoughts to a less than innocent level. It also continues to imply, in some sense, that she is a reflection of January and in fact a good match, despite her youth, for the old man, who uses this same expression in the very first line he utters in the tale, praising wedlock: " 'Noon oother lyf . . . is worth a bene' " (1263). May, like the Wife of Bath, quite literally borrows her husband's idiom as she enters into selfhood. For the reader who might seek to find female experience or a feminine voice recorded here, this may be just another troubling but unsurprising confirmation of female absence and silence. For the antifeminist tradition, however, May's imputed judgment is analogously but inversely problematic, for it disturbs the notion that January's language *is* men's idiom, that it is only men who speak, and only men who can desire and appreciate praiseworthy "pleyyng."

The third and last time the narrator alludes to May's feelings about January's sexual demands (or lack thereof), his strategy and its effects reinforce this perception. The passage comes immediately after May has taken Damyan's love letter into the privy, read it, and disposed of the evidence. The act recalls the *Miller's Tale* as it equates women's privacy, her private parts, her unknowable subjective self, with the dirt and decay of the site of her reading, the privy. A few lines later, we see her obliged once more to take off her clothes for January. The narrator underscores that May acts under compulsion, and he again overtly refuses to tell us what she felt:

> And she obeyeth, be hire lief or looth.
> But lest that precious folk be with me wrooth,
> How that he wroghte, I dar nat to yow telle;
> Or wheither hire thoughte it paradys or helle.
> (1961–64)

The first line reminds us that May is January's wife, legally and mor- ally bound to obey his will, and the next three lines may occasion readers to guess what the narrator only teases us with, to imagine how repulsive the constrained sexual service of January might be for May. In passages like this that refer to May's sexual life with January, some modern readers have found a trace of sympathy on someone's part.[19] But if sympathy for May is even remotely possible here, why then does the narrator say that polite folk would be offended to hear not only what January did to May, but also what May thought of the old man's sexual fumblings? The narrator has already told us a great deal about January's performance in bed that "precious folk" may presumably not wish to hear, but he has not told us—he has said before, and demonstrated on all but one occa- sion, that he cannot tell us—what May thinks. The emphasis on what he dares not say about May, however, can in no way suggest, as her stoniness might, that she has no feelings or that she has feelings of distaste under the kind of virtuous control that could be imputed, say, to a stony woman like Constance. It confirms, rather, that she has them, and that they are in fact impolite. What is so unutterably offensive that the narrator himself cannot risk speaking it, these lines indicate, is not that the young wife is compelled, which he says she is; or that the old man is impotent and repulsive, which he has repeatedly told us; but that the woman would have any thoughts about the situation at all: that she might even (although not in this case) enjoy it.

Attributing sympathy to the Merchant or the implied author, then, is an unsatisfactory and naive—or maybe nervous—reading of both the narrator's imputed intention and the actual effect of his words. For even as May "awakens" in the ways I have suggested, strategies for resisting and managing her potential power and her difference are at work, and one such strategy that is prominent in these passages where the narrator looks at her sexual life with January is the sadistic pleasure he takes in imagining May's discomfort and distaste. When the audience is invited, after lengthy descriptions of January's aging male body, to think about May's feelings in bed, there is undoubtedly for some an element of titillation; as I suggested in reading the *Legend of Good Women* and other Chaucerian fictions, victimized and suffering women arouse a certain kind of masculine desire. Even more important is the way in which the

19. Donaldson, for example, in "The Effect of the *Merchant's Tale*," bemoans the even- tual loss of "our natural sympathy" for May (p. 42).

lawful husband's violence against an innocent woman is alluded to and then dismissed. In the context of the tale as a whole, this cavalier dismissal cannot stem from the narrator's desire to cover over the history of male violence (as the Knight and the Miller do in very different ways); clearly, the main point is that women don't suffer for long, if at all. On her wedding night, for example, May endures whatever January manages to inflict in silent stoniness for only about thirty lines before expressing colloquial disgust at an inadequate male sexual performance and hence, in the only way available, getting her own back.

The same conclusion may be drawn from Proserpina's characterization in the garden scene; her rape is alluded to, but the reader is sent to "Claudyan" for details of that story. Other glancing allusions to rape appear in January's hopeful reference to the way he will "manace" May "Harder than evere Parys dide Eleyne" (1752–4); the narrator's invocation of Priapus (who raped Lotis [2034]); the mention of Wade's boat (linked by one recent scholar to the capture of an Irish princess [1424]); and of Argus (set to guard Io, who is raped by Jove [2111–13]).[20] In the *Merchant's Tale*, we find in this set of allusions a subtext of violence against the virginal woman so minimal that it can hardly be taken too seriously and yet so persistent that it cannot be ignored. Rape, I suggest, is thus invoked again as a kind of wishful thinking, in the no man's land "betwixe erneste and game," to remind us that men are (they hope) capable of it; it is part and parcel of both the narrator's and January's way of thinking about their role in heterosexual relations. The main point here, however, is, as Pluto says, recalling the allusions to the *mulier fortis*, "The tresons whiche that wommen doon to man" (2239), proving that male violence is much exaggerated as a subject matter and thoroughly deserved. The tale may then remain "depressing" because rape, like Absolon's foiled attack on Alisoun in the *Miller's Tale*, doesn't work and is not even the proof of manhood it might seem to be, if the domestication of Pluto, arch-rapist, is any evidence of the efficacy of sexual violence in maintaining normative male domination over female speaking as well as over the female body. Even the most egregious cases of rape are normalized and trivialized, and sympathy with the lawfully bound wife who suffers nothing

20. For useful elaboration on the allusions to Priapus and the story of the rape of Lotis and to Wade's boat and the abduction of an Irish princess, see Wentersdorf, "Imagery, Structure and Theme," pp. 40–41. On Argus as guard of Io, raped by Jove, see Arrathoon, " 'For Craft is al,' " pp. 252–53.

worse than the prickles of her husband's beard is hardly the point of the *Merchant's Tale.*

In the last scene, too, the narrator at once follows the antifeminist vision of woman to one inexorable conclusion and yet continues to resist the logical implication that if women have illicit desires and can always fool their husbands with a good story, then they have a certain agency that not only resembles a man's but also escapes its control. In her final speech, with a self-protective twist, May borrows the notion of a contagious magic that operates in the *Miller's Tale,* as she claims that her "strugle with a man upon a tree" (2374) was intended to restore January's sight. And she is in a sense right. Both Absolon and January are cured of their analogous, age-appropriate diseases—youthful *hereos*[21] and effeminacy, senile uxoriousness and blindness—by the contact, tactile or visual, with the female genitals that they thought they desired and needed to attain or sustain the status of adult male. But Absolon's cure is far more complete; he knows he has been tricked, although Nicholas's intervention in the joke subsequently covers over both Absolon's attempted revenge and its failure—or its unexpected, unconscious success. January's cure, by contrast, is only literal, and the narrator's unflinching representation of the old man's moral and emotional blindness at the end of the *Merchant's Tale* suggests that finally there is no way either to transcend or laugh off this fate, this obscenity, this knowledge, this end to all narrative. For a man to marry or love a woman, or to narrate a woman, is to discover both his own lack of difference and her true difference, her private parts: to discover that she has genitals, and sexual desire, and hence, by the logic of masculine dominance and Christian thought, subjectivity that cannot be controlled. This, I think, is what Donaldson means when he speaks vaguely but forcefully of the exposure in the tale of "the *ugly muck* that formerly lay hidden beneath the surface" and the disturbing "force *and truth* of the Merchant's hatred" (my emphasis; again, the truth is dirty feminine sexuality).[22] As the Miller knew, it is better not to inquire into a woman's "pryvetee"; to do so, as the hateful voyeurism of the *Merchant's Tale* discloses, is to run the risk

---

21. The diagnosis suggested by Edward C. Schweitzer in "The Misdirected Kiss and the Lover's Malady in Chaucer's *Miller's Tale,*" in *Chaucer in the Eighties,* eds. Julian Wasserman and Robert J. Blanch (Syracuse: Syracuse University Press, 1986), pp. 223–33.

22. *Speaking of Chaucer,* pp. 30, 45; the first quotation also appears in *Chaucer's Poetry,* p. 921. Donaldson also worries about his inability to laugh at this tale as heartily as other male critics have done.

of Absolon's fate or of January's horrifying vision of the strong woman in the pear tree.

At the same time, the narrator's treatment of this final vision of May's "pryvetee" actually works to protect him from the ugly sight of her privacy and to undercut and contain the woman's agency in a couple of ways. First, the quick-witted stratagem by which she thinks of a good story to fool her husband is not of her own devising; she is the passive vehicle for the words of another mythic victim, Proserpina, who in response to Pluto's standard antifeminist diatribe becomes in this telling the oddest example yet of the *mulier fortis.* Second, and more important, the narrator, in a time-honored way, refuses to represent May as enjoying any actual sexual pleasure. Here his strategy recalls what happens to Alisoun as Nicholas substitutes his body for hers, so that she becomes merely another "swyved" wife at the end of the tale. After all the tale's emphasis on May's urgency and agency in arranging the tryst with Damyan, her actual intercourse with her lover in the pear tree is oddly truncated in the narration and described exclusively from the males' point of view. Her last reported act is an unmistakable gesture of female dominance: "He stoupeth doun, and on his bak she stood" (2348). At this painful, humiliating moment for the poor old husband, the narrator interrupts: "Ladyes, I prey yow that ye be nat wrooth; / I kan nat glose, I am a rude man" (2350–51). But what his rude literalness actually proceeds to show us is not May, for he suddenly shifts the focus from what she is doing to what the men are doing. First Damyan takes over: "And sodeynly anon *this Damyan* / Gan pullen up the smok, and in *he* throng" (2352–53, my emphasis). Then, at the very moment of Damyan's thrust, and thanks to the divine intervention of another male subject, Pluto (2354–56), the blind January suddenly regains his vision and syntactically becomes once again agent and possessor:

> Up to the tree *he* caste *his* eyen two,
> And saugh that Damyan *his* wyf had dressed
> In swich manere it may nat been expressed,
> But if I wolde speke uncurteisly.
> (2360–63, my emphasis)

In his effort to handle his tricky climax, the narrator veers from confessions of rudeness to protestations of politeness, and impotence is implied in both positions: "Ladyes ... I kan nat glose ... ; it may nat been expressed." So too, as we saw in the A-fragment, in both fabliau and romance modes men may avert their eyes to the crude fact of female sexuality with gestures that at once inscribe, shrink from, and resist that fact. Here, according to the narrator, the denouement of his tale, the wife's expected, generically required adultery, is in some way ineffable; and again the part that may not be expressed is not what Damyan did, or what January saw, but what May felt in the pear tree. In the glimpse of this scene that the narrator offers, May herself is represented first, metonymically, by the clothing that Damyan, as agent, must displace ("Gan pullen up the smok"), and then as the wife of January (2359), who resumes the role of viewer and possessor. A few lines later May does reappear in the position of an agent (or at least mouthpiece) to speak the words that Proserpina gives her (2368ff.). But the words are not her own, and she sounds completely cool and calculating as she speaks them, giving no indication that she was just interrupted in a moment of adulterous passion with the man she was allegedly dying to have (2092–6). Although she has been granted the power of (deceitful) language, then, we are right back where we started in our understanding of May: only God knows what she thought of Damyan's playing, or of January's. At the moment of her putative sexual gratification, the narrator closes his eyes; as far as her human creator and his audience know, May's sexual feelings were and are a contradiction in terms, nonexistent and unspeakable.

The tale's insistence on the similarity, and by certain standards common depravity, of men and women has been read by some modern critics as proof that Chaucer here "takes a more balanced view of human sexual relationships and responsibilities than many other writers of his age."[23] On the contrary, the condemnation of men for the feminine part of their nature and behavior—a condemnation that is also part of orthodox discourse—cannot logically and does not in the tale's unfolding either redeem human corruptibility or subvert the asymmetrical and internally contradictory alignment of Woman and women with blindness, sensuality, fleshly corruption, and absence. In fact, the characterization of (evil) men as weak, sensual, and therefore unmanly, which reaches a new and unmistakable peak in this tale, uses and hence reinforces the standard hierarchy rather than opens the way to "a more balanced view" or to the possibility of human salvation. What the *Merchant's Tale*, like

---

23. Wentersdorf, "Imagery, Structure, and Theme," p. 55.

so much Chaucerian fiction, does confront is the lack of proper gender difference and the concomitantly feminized position of many men, and what is even more thoroughly problematized through the Merchant's performance is the possibility of narrating Woman without exposing the provisionality and instability of masculine identity for the narrator and for the misogynistic discourses he is drawn to and from. In one of the clichés that January spouts so that the tale can neatly ironize it, the deluded man claims that women are safe weapons for men to use to their own ends: " 'A man may do no synne with his wyf, / Ne hurte hymselven with his owene knyf' " (1839–40). In disproving this claim, the *Merchant's Tale* runs the risk of affirming that the sharp wife has a life of her own and that she uses her cutting edge to just one end.

This threat to the identity and adult manhood of any male narrator who undertakes the project of representing Woman is also figured both in the identification of the narrator and January, as I have suggested, and in the oft-noted slipperiness of knowing whose tale this is, or who speaks here. To explain the tale, most readers find it necessary to posit the existence of the Merchant, and to use the framing matter, including the portrait in the *General Prologue* and the headlink, to justify or naturalize his misogyny and to distinguish it from a more palatable authorial position. But as recent critiques of the dramatic approach warn us, this too is particularly risky business for both internal and external reasons. The voicing of much of the tale, as we have seen, contains its own warning to the same effect; and yet, however cautiously, we must continue to imagine the Merchant, or speak of the narrator, as distinct from both author and character, in order to discuss the tale. Characters and narrator alike are at once constituted and deconstructed by the misogynistic discourses that they use, and so again the *Merchant's Tale* reminds us that the fused problems of identity and writing cannot be divorced from the fundamental problems of gender difference and gender relations. No one escapes into the position of asexuality and nonrepresentability, here—except, more visibly than ever, perhaps, the Chaucer that modern criticism has nervously attempted to discern.

10

Making Ernest of Game:
The Franklin's Tale *and Some Partial Conclusions*

> Game-playing, rule-breaking, are a function of
> the confidence of legitimate status, of knowledge
> of the game and of its rules.
> > Terry Lovell, "Writing Like a
> > Woman: A Question of Politics"

> Like the members of the male elite, the class aspirant has an
> interest in preserving social closure, since without it there
> would be nothing to aspire *to*. But, at the same time, that
> closure must be sufficiently flexible to incorporate *him*. His
> conceptualization of woman will as a result be radically un-
> stable: she will be perceived as oscillating between the en-
> closed body (the purity of the elite to which he aspires) and
> the open body (or else how could he attain her?), between
> being "too coy" and "too common."
> > Peter Stallybrass, "Patriarchal
> > Territories"

The *Merchant's Tale* seems particularly "bitter" and "dark" to so many modern readers, I have argued, because it fundamentally doubts the proper difference between male and female upon which various ortho-doxies depend.[1] Both the Squire and the Franklin feel that same ner-vousness in the face of the Merchant's performance that some modern critics have felt. Both tellers, first the figure of the son and then the figure of the more experienced and sagacious surrogate father, try to take up the task of representing Woman in a way that avoids the consequences,

---

1. The epigraphs are drawn from articles in, respectively, *The Politics of Theory*, ed. Francis Barker et al. (Colchester: University of Sussex, 1983), p. 22, and *Rewriting the Renaissance: The Discourses of Sexual Difference in Early Modern Europe*, ed. Margaret W. Ferguson, Maureen Quilligan, and Nancy J. Vickers (Chicago and London: University of Chicago Press, 1986), p. 134.

for the male storyteller, of the Merchant's self-destructive, self-reflexive misogyny.[2]

The *Squire's Tale* can be viewed as a response to the Merchant's questioning of both gender difference and the possibility of feminine virtue; as an antidote, it attempts to restore one familiar version of the ideal heroine, a victimized female, in the abandoned, self-mutilating falcon in Part II of the Squire's incomplete romance. But as the *Legend of Good Women* attests, one difficulty with this worn-out strategy is that it too inscribes a troubling image of the male. Like Aeneas, Theseus, Jason, and all those other false men, the tiercelet who abandons the falcon in the *Squire's Tale* is, according to the lady's description, a typical lover who "semed welle of alle gentillesse" but turns out to be "ful of treson and falsnesse . . . so wrapped under humble cheere, / And under hewe of trouthe . . . " (505–8). If the Franklin in turn is anxious about his own "gentillesse," or his son's, this will never do. If he is made uncomfortable by the implications of the Merchant's allegedly unvarnished vision, the Squire's fantastic alternative will not soothe. His own tale attempts in an earnest way to lighten the darkness of the Merchant's and to correct the immature efforts of the Squire by restoring proper gender difference and affirming a more positive ideal of proper masculinity.

Susan Crane has offered persuasive evidence that the Franklin's anxiety about his social rank, his "liminal" position, is crucial to our understanding of his offering: he is, she argues, "of a rank not quite common but not securely gentle either."[3] Furthermore, Crane makes a strong case for the homology of the Franklin's marginal status, which is based on

---

2. The assumption that Fragment IV (F), containing the *Clerk's Tale* and the *Merchant's Tale,* and Fragment V (G), the *Squire's Tale* and the *Franklin's Tale,* "might be regarded as one group" (see Robinson's note, *Works of Chaucer,* p. 708) is consistent with and supported by this argument. Studies like David Lawton's on the literary history of the *Squire's Tale* have given great weight to the textual uncertainties that are particularly rife in the sequence of which the *Squire's Tale* is thought to be part and have persuasively interrogated any oversimplified connection of the tales by way of the tellers' psychology. From my perspective, it is also interesting to note, however, that in the fictive continuation of the *Squire's Tale* that Lawton offers as pure "speculation," he too reads the story of the victimized and abandoned female bird as I shall suggest the *Franklin's Tale* does: "Canace's sympathy with the falcon may have led her to a general distrust of all men, from which she has to be won" (*Chaucer's Narrators* [Cambridge: D. S. Brewer, 1985], p. 117). Thus Lawton implicitly interprets the central problem of the tale as one of excessive sympathy for women and concomitant distrust of men.

3. "The Franklin as Dorigen," *Chaucer Review* 24 (1990), p. 236. For a discussion of the class anxiety of both the narrator and Arveragus, see John M. Fyler, "Love and Degree in the *Franklin's Tale," Chaucer Review* 21 (1987), pp. 321–37.

class, and Dorigen's status, which is marginalized by her position as romance heroine and conventionally feminine figure. Both narrator and heroine, Crane points out, are constrained by their social position; through either rank or gender, each is simultaneously dominant and subordinate in both socioeconomic and discursive systems, while both are to some extent constrained by the romance genre. The Franklin and Dorigen are aware of their marginalization in aristocratic and clerical discourse, too, but their attempts to resist their subjection fail. Crane concludes that "Both vavasour and lady can inhabit romance but do not control its events," and that both finally give in to the reassuring dominance of the hero, Arveragus.[4]

Crane's work highlights what we have seen throughout this study: the *Franklin's Tale* offers yet another example of a male narrator's perceived feminization, represented in part by the familiar depiction of striking affinities between the position of Dorigen, the female character, and the Franklin, the man who tells her story. At the same time, I would note again, it is precisely the homology between male and female, between the figure of the storyteller/class aspirant and the figure of the woman, that requires the male narrator to distance himself so clearly from the female character—and to do so, in this case, so successfully that generations of critics fundamentally uninterested in Dorigen and questions of gender have been able to avoid seeing the similarities that Crane makes so visible. In the following discussion I want to bring out the ways in which the *Franklin's Tale* identifies its feminized narrator with male interests and male characters, promises in a more affirmative way than the Miller does the possibility of male bonding across class and discursive boundaries, and reaffirms at the end of the tale what the Merchant has discredited, both proper gender difference and a positive notion of masculine virtue.

The tale early on concedes quite explicitly that what the Merchant says is true. In at least one important regard, men and women are alike: "Wommen, of kynde, desiren libertee, / And nat to been constreyned as a thral; / *And so doon men*, if I sooth seyen shal" (768–770, emphasis added). The general sentiment expressed in these lines might be assented to by the Merchant (and, in fact, by most of the pilgrims). But his tale, harking back to the *Wife of Bath's Prologue*, set out to say the grim "sooth"

4. Crane, "Franklin as Dorigen," p. 246.

about what *women* naturally desire. The truth emphasized in the *Franklin's Tale* is by contrast *men's* desire, which turns out to be proper and beneficial to all, to be "free" in the most noble senses of the word.[5] Men and women are alike in their desire for liberty, the *Franklin's Tale* demonstrates, but men are this narrator's true interest, and the story suggests that only men can truly achieve and use freedom so that no harm actually befalls anyone.

To negotiate the complex problem for men that representing Woman and loving women entails without admitting, as the Merchant does, a kind of defeat, it is above all necessary in the *Franklin's Tale* to give Dorigen enough rope to hang herself and then to effect her rescue at the last moment, through the combined pity and generosity of the men for whom her potential desire has been so threatening. The tale's characterization of Dorigen is meaningfully unstable in a way that specifically and thoroughly cancels out the implications of May's characterization in the *Merchant's Tale*. Dorigen begins in a position of power, theoretically, at least, "on top," as free of her husband's direct control as May is subject to it. From this position Dorigen moves (partly because of the desire to do so that is imputed to her, partly because of circumstances beyond anyone's control except the magician's) to a welcomed or at least silently accepted submission to male fantasy. She is no longer cast in the role of an agent who either takes pity or heaps shame and abuse on those men who desire her but instead is represented as subject to the pity of men and as much a pliable victim as May seemed to be at the outset.[6]

DORIGEN'S POWER

Dorigen's freedom—her generosity, power, and subjectivity—is initially an effect of generic convention; she is introduced as the fair and highborn

---

5. An ironic statement early in the *Merchant's Tale* suggests both the similarity and difference between the tales in this regard: "They [a husband and his wife] been so knyt ther may noon harm bityde, / *And namely upon the wyves syde*" (1391–92, my emphasis).
6. Like so many of Chaucer's interesting female characters, Dorigen is controversial and ambiguous to modern critics. To one recent reader she is both the "most important, sympathetic, and convincing" character in the tale and a uniquely "good, loving, and lovable woman"—unlike anything else in Chaucer's or other medieval writings (Anne Thompson Lee, " 'A Woman True and Fair': Chaucer's Portrayal of Dorigen in the *Franklin's Tale*," *Chaucer Review* 19 [1984], p. 169). To many others, she is far from perfect; to

lady of courtly romance who causes Arveragus's subjection and "wo" and then takes "pitee" on him explicitly because he has submitted so decisively and properly to her. Their marriage, which in reality would undermine the lady's dominance and "libertee," is described as something to which *she* actively consents because of her lover's theoretically proper self-subordination:

> But atte laste she, for his worthynesse,
> And namely for his meke obeysaunce,
> Hath swich a pitee caught of his penaunce
> That pryvely she fil of his accord
> To take hym for hir housbonde and hir lord,
> Of swich lordshipe as men han over hir wyves.
>
> (738–43)

At first glance, this passage inscribes the female complicity that supports patriarchal ideals; it affirms the reconciliation of the ideologies of courtly love and medieval marriage through Dorigen's generous, willing endorsement of normative marital hierarchy. As an opening, it unmistakably picks up from the happy ending that closed the *Wife of Bath's Tale*, wherein the powerful figure of the Hag, because of her husband's "obeysaunce," transforms herself into the wife "bothe fair and good" (III.1241) who in turn "obeyed hym in every thyng" (III.1255). But only fifteen lines into a story that seems to begin where other romances must leave off, with this ideal and implausible complementarity of love and marriage, sovereign lady and submissive wife, the vagueness of the formulation in line 743 invites the crucial question that the tale will answer: Just what is Dorigen "pryvely" agreeing to, and why "pryvely"? What is the valence of "swich" here—what kind of "lordshipe" *do* worthy, obedient noblemen privately have over the courtly ladies they marry? The line also sounds a lot like those other passages, sprinkled throughout Chaucerian fictions, that record the nervous innuendo of allegedly polite discourse. Compare, for instance, the narrator's salacious reference to the holy woman's necessary sexual submission to her husband in the *Man*

---

some, she must be taught a lesson by her husband (see R. E. Kaske, "Chaucer's Marriage Group," in *Chaucer the Love Poet*, ed. Jerome Mitchell and William Provost [Athens: Univ. of Georgia Press, 1973], pp. 45–65); to some, she is "almost giddy femininity" embodied (Robert B. Burlin, *Chaucerian Fiction* [Princeton: Princeton University Press, 1977], p. 200); to some, she is even unfaithful to her husband at least "in words" (Wolfgang E. H. Rudat, "*Gentillesse* and the Marriage Debate in the *Franklin's Tale:* Chaucer's Squires and the Question of Nobility," *Neophilologus* 68 [1984], p. 465).

of Law's Tale (II.708–14). Even this early in the *Franklin's Tale*, readers familiar with Chaucerian idiom may well hear euphemistic allusion to one central aspect of male "lordshipe" that the *Franklin's Tale* soon focuses on: the sexual rights that husbands have, or should have, over their wives' bodies.

The ambiguity and instability of the arrangements between Dorigen and Arveragus are also subtly suggested in the digression that follows the opening description of their harmonious union, in the narrator's vague and prolix discussion of how happy marriages negotiate the conflict between freedom and obedience (761–805). The narrator shifts abruptly in this passage from the specific story he started telling to the general and abstract social issues it raises. This move from narrative to commentary quite clearly indicates that a realistic tale of Arveragus's divided life as a husband—"Servant in love, and lord in mariage" (793)—like that of the Black Knight's married life with White, lacks tellability or defies credibility. It is only when the husband departs for England that a plot can emerge, for it is the man's prolonged absence that clarifies and confirms both the nature and the necessity, to social and narrative systems, of the "lordshipe" that husbands have over the sexuality of their wives.

Alone, unguarded by the repressions of domestic bliss, Dorigen has dangerous and storyworthy powers. The very devotion to Arveragus that she so passionately expresses in his absence carries with it the possibility of something as improper in a wife as the power that courtly love would impute to the lady. When the narrator says, for instance, that "Desir of his presence hire so destreyneth / That al this wyde world she sette at noght" (820–21), he implies not only excessive but even inappropriate desire, insofar as he suggests that the lady too has a public self, a responsibility to "this wyde world," which she willfully sets aside for love. Elsewhere in Chaucerian fiction, it is men who set the world aside for love: Troilus, who has the will and the power to put Criseyde over the interests of state, or the Antony of the *Legend of Good Women* who loves Cleopatra so much "That al the world he sette at no value" (*LGW* 602). Like Antony, too, Dorigen is "in swich rage" for her husband (compare *FT* 836, *LGW* 599). Dorigen's questioning of God's wisdom and the order of Nature itself in her long protest against "the grisly rokkes blake" (865–93) also suggests the inappropriateness and irrationality of such intense desire in a woman.

Above all, however, it is her complicated, three-part response to the importunities of Aurelius (980–1005) that brings the implicit dangers of ungoverned female subjectivity and sexuality to the crisis that the tale can proceed to resolve.[7] When he tells her of his love, the young squire, like Arveragus before him, calls the idealized fictional powers of the beloved lady to the realistic narrative fore. At first, in lines 980–87, Dorigen uses her power to avow clearly and firmly her fidelity to Arveragus. She says this is her "fynal answere," but if it were, Dorigen's goodness and subjection would be already complete; without the excess that follows, there would no story and no demonstrable need for Arveragus's return. The second phase of her response is the well-known "rash promise" (989–98); explicitly offered "in pley," it exemplifies the many dangerous dimensions of Dorigen's precarious position as both lady and wife. It is instructive to compare Dorigen at this point with another female jokester in the *Canterbury Tales*, another woman who "plays": Alisoun of the *Miller's Tale*. Alisoun gets away with her joke (even if, as I have said, her escape is a narrow, accidental one), but Dorigen does not. The latter is not violated or dishonored at the end; instead, she is alleged to suffer great emotional distress from which she can be released only by male decisions that clearly put her in her place.[8] She is not to be excluded from punishment, like Alisoun, for this treatment would be churlish and too obviously misogynist. Instead, she is to be chivalrously rescued from humiliation and abasement by the proper intervention of her husband and the chain reaction of male virtue he sets in motion. What is it about Dorigen's joke, and the context in which it is made, that necessitates both punishment and reprieve? Why doesn't her play lib-

---

7. As in the case of the *Parliament of Fowls*, comparison with possible sources of the Chaucerian story underscores the tale's interest in questions of female subjectivity and sexuality. Bruce A. Rosenberg, in "The Bari Widow and the *Franklin's Tale*," *Chaucer Review* 14 (1980), pp. 344–52, points out that the episode of the rash boon is made much more prominent in Chaucer; Rosenberg sees it as "the central episode and symbol of the narrative" and "the very symbol of Dorigen's shallowness, foolishness, or frail reason" (pp. 351–52).

8. Compare Roberta L. Krueger's discussion of four thirteenth-century French romances from the wager cycle, "Double Jeopardy: The Appropriation of Woman in Four Old French Romances of the 'Cycle de la Gageure,' " in *Seeking the Woman in Late Medieval and Renaissance Writings*, eds. Sheila Fisher and Janet E. Halley (Knoxville: University of Tennessee Press, 1989), pp. 21–50. The pattern that Krueger observes closely resembles what happens in the *Franklin's Tale*: male characters and narrators (and the implied audience) "use the figure of woman to test the honor of their courtly discourse" (p. 26) in stories of the "good" woman which become "a vindication of the knight who rescues the helpless women he has endangered" (p. 31).

erate her—as it does, for example, the Clerk? Why and to whom is a woman's game-playing, as opposed to a man's, so threatening that the polite tale must teach her this earnest kind of lesson?

Most obviously, Dorigen's pledge to Aurelius—I'll love you if you get rid of the rocks that keep my husband from me—is a potential threat to Arveragus and both the "lordshipe . . . men han over hir wyves" and "the name of soveraynetee, / That wolde he have for shame of his degree" (751–52). Challenging the fundamental rights of the aristocratic husband to the coterminous purities of wife and name, Dorigen's little joke signals the possibility at least of that excess of desire also indicated in her passion for Arveragus; it moreover asserts, for a moment, "in pley," her right to control her own body, to give where she will her love and, even more importantly, the sign that marks such control, her word. As Terry Lovell suggests, game-playing is "a function of confidence of legitimate status, of knowledge of the game and of its rules"[9] ; so too Dorigen's joke implies her (misplaced) confidence in her status, her right to play games with the power she thinks she has.

Dorigen's joke also threatens Arveragus by revealing the similarity between men in putatively very different positions: the ideal husband and the young rival.[10] Aurelius's conventional adoration of Dorigen mimics and fleshes out Arveragus's presumed relationship to her before their marriage, and she exercises the same (highly conventional) power over both men, conditionally granting her love because she pities Aurelius, just as she pitied Arveragus: "Syn I yow se so pitously complayne" (991; cf. 740). Her joke threatens Aurelius, too, because it plays with and makes light of the predictable passion, so much like Arveragus's, that he claims to experience; it may be even more disturbing to Aurelius because, like the reader, he must decide whether she means it or not. Is Dorigen really saying no and emphasizing her rejection of Aurelius with a graphic example of its impossibility—not until hell freezes over, so to speak? Or is she revealing, as some critics allege, her subconscious desire to be unfaithful to Arveragus? How can a man tell whether a woman really means it when she says no, especially if she makes a joke of her refusal?

---

9. Lovell, "Writing Like a Woman," p. 22.

10. Lee, " 'A Woman True and Fair,' " describes Aurelius's portrait as "distressingly similar to that of Arveragus" (p. 172). As others have pointed out, however, Aurelius is also very similar to Dorigen (for details, see A. M. Kearney, "Truth and Illusion in the *Franklin's Tale*," *Essays in Criticism* 19 [1969], pp. 245–53); the problem here, as usual, is that the very possibility of female sexuality collapses gender boundaries and alignments.

And which in fact would be more disastrous for Aurelius's position: to have Dorigen or not? To want a woman who is unattainable or to want one who might just want him back? Dorigen manages, through her equivocation and play, to represent both disquieting possibilities and hence to embody the dilemma that masculine identity confronts in romantic love.

Dorigen's playfulness also imperils the class and generic distinctions that the Franklin seems eager to maintain. She acts in part on the power of sovereign lady that her marriage has not yet fully contained, and so her joke imagines the possibility that the ostensive right of a woman, under the courtly code, to grant or deny sexual access might be real. At the same time, as the comparison with Alisoun underscores, it also suggests that as the folk or fabliau tradition insists, a woman just might have rampant, illicit sexual desires and might act to gratify them. Her game-playing threatens not only to lay claim to her "legitimate status," then, but also to lay bare some of the covert rules of the game as we saw them in the play of the A-fragment: for instance, the stipulations that differences of age and rank between men may be leveled or crossed by discourse about women and that common male fears about female powers also transcend differences in genre, style, and class. And in a recent discussion of the tale, R. A. Shoaf parenthetically alludes to another aspect of the problem, for a male storyteller, that Dorigen's joke brings out: "(a lady who loves 'in pley' [F 988] is no Beatrice, no begetter of the great poet)."[11]

Dorigen's joke is thus troubling enough; even worse, however, is the third phase of her response, the violent retraction (1000–5) in which she maintains that she is just kidding. As if she realizes that she has gone too far "in pley" and revealed too much, Dorigen herself tries to cancel out or seal off the implications of her joke by following it up with a firm, unplayful rebuke of Aurelius, including a reminder that she only dares to make her roguish promise because Aurelius cannot possibly meet its terms: " 'For wel I woot that it shal never bityde' " (1001). She adds a question, moreover, that puts the reality of the situation in surprisingly frank, even churlish terms that can only make matters worse for everyone involved: " 'What deyntee sholde a man han in his lyf / For to go love another mannes wyf, / That hath hir body whan so that hym liketh?' " (1003–5).

---

11. In "The *Franklin's Tale:* Chaucer and Medusa," *Chaucer Review* 21 (1986), p. 285.

Here Dorigen articulates as directly as possible her blunt, impolite, and impolitic understanding of everyone's actual position. She exposes the illusory nature of the empowerment that courtly fictions seem to cede to her and of the lover's claim that she is the object of his desire. Dorigen's serious, sensible, knowledgeable, unseemly observation discloses that indeed she knows the real rules: what is proper, who is in control, and precisely what "swich lordshipe as men han over hir wyves" actually amounts to. Such excessive knowledge, however, can hardly reinstall her in the position of the perfect, bodiless courtly lady whose devotion to Arveragus is altogether self-chosen, nor can it reassure Aurelius that he knows how to act the part of the proper courtly lover in this tricky situation. Her rebuke is intended, presumably, to have a dampening effect on Aurelius's ardor, but while it calls his motives (and sexual tastes) into question, it may at the same time work in just the opposite way, whetting his appetite for Dorigen: not only by reminding him that she has a body but also by fanning the flames of his jealousy. Worse yet, it clarifies the real stakes here. Dorigen makes it clear that in his attempt to seduce a married woman, Aurelius, the very type of the courtly lover as that type is repeatedly defined in the *Tales,* is seeking what one modern critic has referred to as "seconds": a woman whose body is not his exclusively, nor his by rights.[12] A good part of the "deyntee" he derives from this effort, then, must be the pleasure of challenging and supplanting the male rival, as much as or more than loving the woman. And what Dorigen blurts out, the crude, unvarnished reading of the situation, turns out to be the gist of the tale as a whole.

Dorigen has been described as a misreader, but at this moment she is reading all too well.[13] She reveals a "knowledge of the game and of

12. See Rudat, "*Gentillesse* and the Marriage Debate," pp. 454–55. Rudat argues that Dorigen is figuratively or psychologically castrating Aurelius in this scene (p. 456); see also "Aurelius's Quest for Grace: Sexuality and the Marriage Debate in the *Franklin's Tale,*" *The CEA Critic* 45 (1982), pp. 16–21.

13. Shoaf has argued that when Dorigen is "astoned" by Aurelius's words, we are meant to see that she is the figure of the literal reader; Aurelius and the Clerk have fooled her into accepting the deceptive letter without bothering to "rend the veil," to see for herself the illusion that lies beneath the literal ("Chaucer and Medusa," pp. 275ff.). The tale as a whole, then, is about how not to read and write; literalism is opposed to the power of metaphor (i.e., poetry) to disclose the truth. Shoaf's argument goes on in interesting directions, but I want to stop here and just raise a couple of obvious questions. If Dorigen is a figure of the reader who misreads, we have another example of what we saw in *Troilus and Criseyde.* And once again I would want to ask why the misreader is a

its rules" that contradicts the illusion of female power to which she also lays claim when she tries to play, and thus she at once exposes and confirms the paradox of the feminine position in the social game: consciousness of self is consciousness of the negation of self. For her excessively accurate reading, for her overt statement of the covert rules, as much as for the possibility that she has desires, she must be corrected. The rest of the tale validates her interpretation of the situation by the very strength of its efforts both to reaffirm and to conceal what Dorigen has divulged.

DORIGEN'S PUNISHMENT

As I noted in Chapter 18, the Miller's Alisoun is not directly punished for her threatening playfulness, which serves to uncover all sorts of things that polite literature must conceal, but her freedom from punishment does not empower her; instead, Nicholas appropriates her jest, and the close of the *Miller's Tale* excludes Alisoun from the possession of a moral stature worth punishing. Dorigen, however, cannot so easily escape, in part because Arveragus and the genre in which the tale begins both have already ceded her a kind of authority that she has unfortunately, for a moment, almost used; she has, at the same time, temporarily shattered the illusion that the tale is explicitly devoted to perpetuating. It is, after all, belief in the fiction of Dorigen's bodiless, nonthreatening power and subjectivity, the possibility of female "libertee" without female sexuality, that is the "inpossible" (1009), the great feat of magic that the tale performs. The black rocks are a multivalent symbol that may be taken as, among other possibilities, an objective correlative of masculine fantasies about the monstrosity of female sexuality, another version of Scylla and Charybdis, and the dangers embodied in Dorigen as heroine that stand in the way of Arveragus's return to a chaste wife. Like the clerk/magician's removal of the rocks, this illusion must be understood by reasonable people as no more than an illusion, something unreal, temporary, unnatural, something too threatening to masculine domi-

woman, or why is (mis)reading feminized? Whose interests does the definition of reading here serve? And what about the sex change, if indeed Chaucer alludes to Dante's reading of the Medusa myth? The Medusa is explicitly a woman; what happens in a story where two men become Medusa, the castrating woman?

nance—to reality, as it were—to sustain, something belonging to and contained by make-believe. Dorigen obsessively sees the rocks for what they are, barriers to her powers as romance heroine, just as in the moment of her response to Aurelius she is not taken in by the part she plays. Even as she speaks, she becomes the agent of disillusionment, first teasing Aurelius and Arveragus with the possibility that she might both have the power they pretend to confer on her and not be the ideal they worship, then deflating them with her blunt acknowledgment of the crude facts, reified as fact by her frankness, of masculine dominance and homosocial desire. Appropriately enough, then, it is only a counter-illusion—the removal of those rocks—that can (re)turn Dorigen to a proper feminine position: stunned, terrified, all but hopeless, in retreat from sexual desire and afraid for her only remaining asset, her sexual virtue, and desperately in need of the pity and corrective guidance of both her husband and her lover.

To reassert control over Dorigen without admitting to anything too crudely controlling, and to suppress her apparent ability to penetrate, however fleetingly, the discursive illusions that have created her in the first place, the *Franklin's Tale* literally and pointedly must reverse the trajectory of the female character's development that we saw in the characterization of May in the *Merchant's Tale*. In the first moment in which she is attributed some feelings, May is brought to January's bed "as stille as a stoon." By the end of the tale, however, she is anything but paralyzed by her situation; she is busy reading and writing letters, stealing keys, climbing trees, and (however stereotypically) blinding her husband with feminine wiles. Dorigen begins with more active freedom than she says she wants and access to both playful and serious speech. However temporary or illusory, the possibility of female liberty and mobility is imaged in the power granted to her by Arveragus, in her restless roaming by the sea, and in the psychological realism of those contradictory and self-canceling moves in her response to Aurelius. She subsequently suffers, however, precisely the kind of paralysis in which we first saw May: quite literally, after Aurelius tells her that the rocks are gone, "she astoned stood" (1339; compare too Griselda's astonishment when she is temporarily stunned by Walter's change of heart at the end of the *Clerk's Tale*). The efforts (and financial promises) of the courtly rival and the tricks of the clever clerk have together returned her to her proper place and decorously covered over the exposure of her latent, potential sexuality; henceforth, she enacts male meaning and

makes possible male bonds that defy economic reality. In the denouement of the tale, she quite literally functions to restore one paradigm by
which female characters are contained, the paradigm of homosocial exchange, the so-called traffic in women, on which the *Canterbury Tales*
insists so relentlessly and which the Franklin manages much more successfully than most.

Moreover, Dorigen is kept in place even as she is passed around, by
a familiar strategy: violence against women, both by men and, even more
effectively, perhaps, by the victims themselves, is threatened and then
averted because both the husband and the lover in this story are generous, and the wife is obedient. Sympathy with Dorigen as a victim of
any such violence is prevented because she herself imagines that it ought
properly to take place and because the male characters show so much
pity for her themselves that the audience can feel little or no need to do
so.

After Dorigen's "a-stone-ishment," two passages serve simultaneously to raise and avert the familiar specter of violence against women.
The first of these is Dorigen's lament, with its exceedingly long catalogue
(1355–1456) of famous female suicides. Much has been written about this
catalogue, and while critics vary in their opinions of its significance, it is
considered by the majority to be "a failure," the Franklin's "most serious
rhetorical blunder."[14] A few readers have already suggested, however,
that it is anything but a blunder.[15] Stephen Knight argues that the irrelevance to her own situation of most of the *exempla* Dorigen offers is
actually purposive and effective in suggesting her self-image. Her citation
of so many virgins, for instance, indicates to Knight her "recoil" from
sexual relationships into self-destruction. (This would certainly accord
with the revealingly hot denial of sexual initative implicit in her rebuke
to Aurelius, when she describes herself as "another mannes wyf.") Moreover, "the challenge she has presented as a woman with a viewpoint is
foreclosed," Knight observes, "as she imagines that very viewpoint as
manless, nameless, lifeless."[16]

The point is, I would add, that even self-destruction and willing victimization impute to a female a possible power, certainly ambiguous but

14. These comments are taken from, respectively, Lee, " 'A Woman True and Fair,' "
p. 169, and Burlin, *Chaucerian Fiction*, p. 199.

15. For a strong and interesting defense of the catalogue, see Gerald Morgan, "A
Defence of Dorigen's Complaint," *Medium Aevum* 46 (1977), pp. 77–97.

16. "Ideology in 'The Franklin's Tale,' " *Parergon* 28 (1980), p. 27.

nevertheless real, and a discursive life, as we see so clearly in the case of the Clerk's Griselda and her powers of silence. The *Franklin's Tale* therefore cannot sustain Dorigen's tragic self-image as manless martyr to virtue any more than Criseyde can be allowed to follow the path of a tragic heroine in Book IV of *Troilus and Criseyde*. Even more importantly, the catalogue serves to remind us of what might, in another context, be Dorigen's fate; it therefore functions as a necessary background in establishing the atypical but exemplary generosity, tolerance, and sympathy for women of these male characters, including Arveragus, who does not ask his wife to die for him, and the Franklin as narrator, who does not add to the literary tradition of female self-destruction.

This function becomes clearer when the catalogue is read in the context of another less frequently annotated moment in which violence against Dorigen herself is threatened but not (yet) enacted. In the second half of Arveragus's double response to Dorigen's confession, after he grants her the privilege of keeping her "trouthe," he orders her perpetual future silence thus: " 'I yow forbede, up peyne of deeth, / That nevere, whil thee lasteth lyf ne breeth, / To no wight telle thou of this aventure' " (1481–83). Dorigen is here expressly forbidden to make a story out of her experience, to tell her own tale. There is an obvious irony in the fact that she is told in the same breath to keep her all-important word and to keep her mouth shut about doing so; this is another instance where the woman is constituted to bespeak her own silence. But in the logic of the tale, this is also an appropriate command, since it was Dorigen's excessive speech—the reopening of her "final answer" with the joke and then the rebuke—that set the disturbing events in motion. While many critics simply avoid this moment, those who find it jarring for the loving husband to threaten his wife with death if she disobeys him have provided some interesting suggestions. Anne Thompson Lee has observed, for instance, that Arveragus may indeed be doing just what Dorigen wants him to, consciously or unconsciously, taking over his rightful masculine identity, "acting like a man," and thereby serving to "assure Chaucer's pilgrims that he is not the willing cuckold they would have scorned, but a 'proper man.' "[17] But this reading only confirms that Arveragus's problem, like Aurelius's, is one we have come to know so well in this study

17. Quoted comments in this sentence are from Lee, " 'A Woman True and Fair,' " p. 174; and Kathryn Jacobs, "The Marriage Contract of the *Franklin's Tale*: The Remaking of Society," *Chaucer Review* 20 (1985), pp. 132–43.

that I hardly need reiterate it here: as courtly lovers, and as either husband or sexual partner, these men have been paradoxically unmanned.[18] The way to begin correcting this situation, to restore proper manhood to those who would love Dorigen, is for the husband to remind his wife of the death that he could legitimately impose, the violence that is averted in this case, as in her failure to commit suicide, by wifely patience and obedience rather than potentially subversive self-sacrifice—by male generosity and female complicity.

It is interesting to note, moreover, that just as most critics overlook Arveragus's threat, neither is it repeated in Aurelius's version of the story as he tells it to the clerk-magician. The young rival calls attention, instead, to the *husband's* willing self-sacrifice (which, as the catalogue of female suicides reminds us, would actually put him in an unseemly position for a man): " 'Arveragus, of gentillesse, / Hadde levere dye in sorwe and in distresse / Than that his wyf were of hir trouthe fals' " (1595–97). Presumably the reference is to Arveragus's comment in lines 1476–78 that he would rather be "ystiked" than have Dorigen betray her "trouthe," although we never hear Dorigen repeat this to Aurelius, and there is certainly a great deal more textual emphasis on her possible death than on Arveragus's. Whether the omission or alteration is knowing or not, Aurelius needs to foreground Arveragus's generosity and to occlude the threat of force that backs it up.

Aurelius's part in the closing action also specifically reclaims the power that Dorigen originally exerted over both her husband and her would-be lover: the power of pity so frequently assigned to women. When he meets Dorigen by chance as she rushes to the garden to keep her word, she is a pitiable object. The rhyme underscores the direct relation between the wife's obedience and her derangement: when Aurelius asks her where she is going, "she answerde, half as she were mad, / 'Unto the gardyn, as myn housbonde bad' " (1511–12). Aurelius is said to feel "compassioun" (1515) and "routhe" (1520, which rhymes with "hir trouthe" in 1519) for both her and Arveragus, and this pity moves him to reconsider the "cherlyssh" (1523) nature of his own lust. What is actually quoted of Aurelius's repetition of the story to the magician emphasizes, again, that the point is the empowering

18. Again, see the studies cited in the preceding footnote for the assumption that Arveragus needs re-manning, and see Kearney, "Truth and Illusion," for a discussion of the parallels between Aurelius and Dorigen that support a reading of his feminization.

nature of a *man's* pity, which resolves all problems and brings the story
to its end:

> "That made me han of hire so greet pitee;
> And right as frely as he sente hire me,
> As frely sente I hire to hym ageyn.
> This al and som; ther is namoore to seyn."
>
> (1603–6)

Depending on how one reads the chain of events that Arveragus's
founding, patriarchal generosity sets off, either one or all of the males in
the story, the husband, the courtly lover, and/or the clerk, are thus made
"fre": noble, independent, generous, frank, privileged, and exempt.[19] The
two men lower in the social hierarchy, the younger squire and the clerk/
magician, are allowed to exhibit their equality, if not superiority, to the
knight. The Franklin's admonition, spoken to Dorigen in the third person
and to all the wives she represents, links her exemplary value quite
explicitly with the virtue and upward social mobility of men:

> But every wyf be war of hire biheeste!
> On Dorigen remembreth, atte leeste.
> Thus kan a squier doon a gentil dede
> As wel as kan a knyght, withouten drede.
>
> (1541–44)

Again, space for the social interaction among male ranks is opened up
by their similar, and similarly unstable, treatment of a woman at the
same time that any threat of a common denominator of churlishness,
such as we saw in the A-fragment, is routed. Male subjectivity and
individual aspiration, on one hand, and male bonding both across and
within classes, on the other, is enabled by a transaction in which the
dangers of trafficking in women are safely averted as desire for or control
over the woman's body is made secondary to a higher good, the "gentil"
ideal of keeping one's word. Like the story of Troilus, in a way, this is
the story of two (or more) men who learn the rules of love in order to
excite a woman's desire; then they master their own womanlike passions
and let her body go, earning for themselves the greater reward.[20]

---

19. For the crucial range of meanings, see *Middle English Dictionary, fre* adj., F.4, pp.
868–73.

20. It could be argued, however, that in the third "letting go," when the magician
releases Aurelius from his financial obligation, Aurelius is not only one-upped but also
feminized, for his position is then precisely analogous to Dorigen's. This point is in no
way developed, of course; the abrupt closure of the tale seals off any such problematic.

Freed of the feminizing consequences of lust or love for a woman by their adherence to this ideal, males in the story thus lay claim to proper manhood in a way that is seldom possible in other tales. In the judgment of modern critics, Arveragus shows "moral courage" and "manly fortitude," and the triumph of masculinity and the masculine imagination is taken as evidence of the highest human achievement: "Fantasy and magic," says one recent reader, ". . . come finally to allow for acts of generosity that show *human beings* at their best" (my emphasis).[21] Readings are found in the literature in which one or all of these men are flawed, but not fatally, and the debate about who is *more* manly in this tale is still often taken as a serious question. This concern arises in part, I suggest, because manly courage and fortitude are not stable virtues but precisely those that must be constructed and reconstructed in the face of counterevidence, and in part because the debate itself positions male characters, author(s), and audiences as judges and unifies them in an apparently disinterested quest for moral understanding. No matter how the debate is answered or not answered, no matter how the Franklin's motives are assessed or declared irrelevant, no one reads the *Franklin's Tale* as the "acidulous" work of a man as bitter as we are told the Merchant must be. When they control women—whether by assuming proper lordship over the most ideal of wives, by making sure that the female jokester is corrected, by threatening a woman, or by rescuing her from the fate they have actually brought upon her themselves—men control themselves (and the woman inside themselves), or at least conceal from themselves their own baser emotions and their own anxiety about manliness. Such a trick indeed requires, as the tale confirms, the services of an unnamed master magician, who can enable readers, in turn, to name Chaucer: one critic sums up the express position of many in claiming that Dorigen is "treated with the amused sympathy and understanding that are Chaucer's hallmarks."[22]

I kan namoore; my tale is at an ende.
Franklin's Tale, 1624

---

21. See, respectively, Mary J. Carruthers, "The Gentilesse of Chaucer's Franklin," *Criticism* 23 (1981), pp. 283–300; Kearney, "Truth and Illusion," p. 250; and Lee Patterson, " 'What Man Artow?': Authorial Self-Definition in *The Tale of Sir Thopas* and *The Tale of Melibee*," *Studies in the Age of Chaucer* 11 (1989), pp. 117–75.

22. Gertrude White, *"The Franklin's Tale*: Chaucer or the Critics," *PMLA* 89 (1974), p. 461.

The knowing self is partial in all its guises, never finished, whole, simply there and original. . . . Only those occupying the positions of the dominators are self-identical, unmarked, disembodied, unmediated, transcendent, born again. It is unfortunately possible for the subjugated to lust for and even scramble into that subject position—and then disappear from view. Knowledge from the point of view of the unmarked is truly fantastic, distorted, and irrational. The only position from which objectivity could not possibly be practiced and honored is the standpoint of the master, the Man, the One God, whose Eye produces, appropriates, and orders all difference. No one ever accused the God of monotheism of objectivity, only of indifference. The god trick is self-identical, and we have mistaken that for creativity and knowledge, omniscience even.[23]

> Donna Haraway, "Situated
> Knowledges"

In performing what Donna Haraway calls "the god trick" and in bearing those "hallmarks" of the master author, in the *Franklin's Tale* as in the other poems I have considered here, Chaucer stands as both a special case and a paradigmatic one for feminist analysis. One thing that makes Chaucerian fictions special is that they have been an enduring part of the British literary canon for the past six hundred years in a way that no other texts written before 1500 (and only a handful before 1800) have been. Chaucer has been known and valued differently in different ages, but he has always been read, talked about, and more often than not singled out for praise as the precursor to be emulated, the forebear to be revered, the Father of English poetry.[24] Up to the age of the great modern editions, when professional scholars made Chaucer part of the academic industry, his reputation was sustained by readers we recognize today as themselves major or prominent minor figures in the pantheon of British writers, including Spenser and Dryden before 1800 and thereafter authors as various and influential as Blake, Wordsworth, Barrett Browning, Ten-

---

23. Donna Haraway, "Situated Knowledges: The Science Question in Feminism and the Privilege of Partial Perspective," *Feminist Studies* 14 (1988), pp. 575–99.

24. Hoccleve seems to have been the first to speak of the paternity of Chaucer, his "maister deere, and fadir reuerent" (in *The Regement of Princes*, cited in Caroline F. E. Spurgeon, *Five Hundred Years of Chaucer Criticism, 1357–1900* (Cambridge: Cambridge University Press, 1925), vol. I, p. 21; Patterson seems to be one of the latest, as he argues that "As the Father of English poetry, Chaucer was surely right to choose it [the figure of the child] for his emblem" (" 'What Man Artow?' " p. 175).

nyson, Ruskin, and Keats.[25] In most current English departments, Chaucer still stands as one of only two or three premodern authors (with Shakespeare, and maybe Milton) almost always taught in both broad survey courses and single-author courses. In their recent research, Ellen Rose and Corey Kaplan point out that since 1970 *PMLA* has published more articles on Chaucer (seventeen, to be exact) than on any other single author except Shakespeare (twenty-five) and Milton (twenty). (They also compare these figures to "two each on Emily Dickinson . . . and Ralph Ellison, and one each on Gertrude Stein, Jane Austen, Doris Lessing, Richard Wright, African tribal literature and Asian poetry.")[26] And in the present institutional organization of literary studies, Chaucer is the preeminent figure who defines everything else in the Middle Ages in England: the Modern Language Association sorts about four hundred years of literary history into two divisions that both depend on naming this potent author: "Chaucer" and "Middle English Language and Literature, excluding Chaucer." Present or absent, Chaucer matters.

Another thing that has made Chaucer special—although as a mark of his importance it may be more visible and open to investigation now than in previous eras—is his representation of women characters and speakers. So rare is this, particularly in the period before 1800, that a character like his Wife of Bath has transcended both her status as character and her historical context. As I noted in Chapter 2, historians, even feminist historians, have repeatedly used the Wife as empirical evidence to support conclusions about the experience of real women in the Middle Ages.[27] So too, in the pioneering feminist theorizing of the late 1970s, *The Madwoman in the Attic,* Sandra Gilbert and Susan Gubar take Anne Eliot and the Wife of Bath as direct spokeswomen for the literary theories of their respective authors, Jane Austen and Chaucer, and cite the Wife's words as evidence of the same order as Anne Finch's poetry.[28] But this is to misread the Wife, as I have argued, and to base an understanding of both history and feminism on false assumptions about women as

---

25. An interesting overview of the pre–twentieth-century reception of Chaucer is provided in the introduction to Spurgeon's invaluable *Five Hundred Years of Chaucer Criticism.*

26. Research conducted in the course of writing *The Canon and the Common Reader* (Knoxville: University of Tennessee Press, 1990), from unpublished materials generously made available to me.

27. A classic instance is Eileen Power's study. "The Position of Women," in *The Legacy of the Middle Ages,* ed. C. G. Crump and E. F. Jacobs (Oxford: Clarendon Press, 1926), especially pp. 403, 408, 412–13.

28. *The Madwoman in the Attic* (New Haven: Yale University Press, 1979), pp. 11–12.

agents and speakers. The two things that seem to make Chaucer special, the uniqueness of his status as the medieval author who transcends his own age and is most read and written about by modern scholars and their students, and his virtuoso representation of women characters and speakers, are not coincidentally related, but together define the ways in which he is also paradigmatic. This is not because modern audiences, having left behind the misogyny of earlier times, canonize only those authors who are friendly to women. Rather, it is because Chaucer stands prominently at the beginning, in English, of the story that literary humanism in various guises has been writing for hundreds of years to negotiate the history and implications of that misogyny, in ways that the preceding chapters of this book have sought to specify.

When Roland Barthes describes "writing" in "The Death of the Author," he might be describing the space that Chaucer, I have argued, preeminently works to occupy, but he denies that this space has a temporal dimension: "Writing is that neutral, composite, oblique space where our subject slips away, the negative where all identity is lost, starting with the very identity of the body writing. No doubt it has always been that way."[29] But has it always been that way?[30] Or, as some feminists now ask, is it ever that way?[31] Reading Chaucer, I believe, actually suggests otherwise and enables us to study not the death but, to continue the metaphor of a single individual's development, the alleged birth or infancy perhaps of "the author"—recognized from the beginning, paradoxically, as already a father figure—as an individual and a personality who seeks to enjoy all the material and symbolic privileges of maleness while transcending the constraints of "the body writing" to grasp the

---

29. I quote from Stephen Heath's translation in *Image, Music, Text* (New York: Hill and Wang, 1977), p. 142. For a brilliant analysis of the contradictory senses in which Barthes speaks of "the death of the author" in this famous essay—in a nonhistorical sense, on one hand, and in a historical sense on the other—see Peggy Kamuf, *Signature Pieces: On the Institution of Authorship* (Ithaca: Cornell University Press, 1988), pp. 5–12.

30. This is one way of formulating Foucault's claim, for instance, that the "author-function" is not "universal or constant in all discourse" ("What Is an Author?" in *Language, Counter-Memory, Practice* (Ithaca: Cornell University Press, 1977), p. 125; see also *The Archaeology of Knowledge*, trans. A. M. Sheridan Smith [London: Tavistock, 1972]).

31. Compare Biddy Martin and Chandre Talpade Mohanty's argument: "The claim to a lack of identity or positionality is itself based on privilege, on a refusal to accept responsibility for one's implication in actual historical or social relations, on a denial that positionalities exist or that they matter, the denial of one's own personal history and the claim to a total separation from it" ("Feminist Politics: What's Home Got to Do with It?" in *Feminist Studies/Critical Studies*, ed. Teresa de Lauretis [Bloomington: Indiana University Press, 1986] p. 208).

otherwise unavailable, to take a neutral or universally human position. As "the author," Chaucer is paradigmatic, then, of just those problems that modern feminist criticisms face in theorizing and historicizing the representation of women by male authors in many periods and the implications of the historically gendered subjectivity of both readers and writers.

Reading Chaucer in the way I propose here can make a difference to the general scholarly perception that the most interesting problems for feminist and other current theorists spring up in the late eighteenth or nineteenth century. There are so many examples of this assumption that it is hard to choose a representative one, but this claim from Stephen Heath's "Male Feminism" is typical: "Because . . . [sic] women have been men's problem, the question; and the historical reality of literature and theory over the last hundred and fifty years has been crucially bound up with that, a problematic of sexuality and sexual identity in which the pressure of women's struggles against the given definitions produced men's concern with that question."[32] By no means do I want to suggest that there is no difference between the ways in which women in the fourteenth century and women in the nineteenth and twentieth centuries are men's problem. My aim in writing this book has been, on the contrary, to articulate with some degree of care and specificity the particularities of the problem in a local instance that is far more often taken to be a universal or transcendent one. But I hope this articulation demonstrates that there is a history to present discussions about gender and sexuality that goes back far more than a hundred and fifty years, a perceivable continuity to the intersecting questions of literature, sex, and gender that we ought to be examining and historicizing more extensively. The assumption that the medieval period was a monolithic block of placid submission to orthodox authorities is belied by closer examination on many fronts, and the problematics of gender difference did not spring up, as a modern ideological formation, at whatever moment we begin the history of modernity. (Why else did Freud turn to ancient Greek drama for his metaphors? Why would the nineteenth-century romantic and post-romantic poets revere Chaucer?) The pressure of women's resistance to definition is different in different ages, just as the definition of Woman has been both different and in some ways the same across

32. "Male Feminism," in *Men in Feminism*, ed. Alice Jardine and Paul Smith (New York and London: Methuen, 1987), pp. 17–18.

the centuries. But the history of "women's struggles" surely entails the late fourteenth century, when Christine de Pisan, it has been argued, resisted antifeminist definition and initiated the age of the *querelle des femmes*.[33] In Chaucerian fictions, we cannot directly hear women's voices, I have insisted, but we can hear "men's concern," and we can explore the fact that it did not all begin, *sui generis*, with Freud (or with the eighteenth century, as other arguments would have it, or the Renaissance) and that "the historical reality of literature and theory" is indeed "a problematic of sexuality and sexual identity" in more periods than our own.

Finally, as I observed in discussing the Wife of Bath near the beginning of this study, there may be more real and crucial continuity between the humanism of the *Canterbury Tales* and of our day than we want to believe, more actual commonality between the fears that give rise to those "curmudgeonly and old-fashioned" jokes about women like the Wife of Bath or Cleopatra and the fundamental position of modern criticism. In particular, the practice of criticism as many of us learned it may be as threatened by recent feminist and other deconstructive or post-structuralist critiques as Chaucer's representative fourteenth-century man of letters, the Clerk, say, seems to feel that he is menaced by the Wife of Bath "and al hir secte," or as the men of the *Legend of Good Women*, narrator and characters alike, are made nervous by the kind of feminization they experience. According to Chaucerian fiction, such feminization involves both the real presence and the heightened consciousness of limits, external and internal; the paralyzing, even fatal recognition that the position represented by ideals of adult male power, courtly or patriarchal, is unattainable by the most heroic of men; and the further, more frightening and barely visible perception that such power is itself, like clear gender distinctions, unstable, even illusory, at the same time that both the constraints and uncertainties of gender roles are inescapable. The primal fear of feminization in Chaucerian fictions, it seems to me, is the fear that men may be women. Akin to this might be the fear that literary critics occupy a feminine position in modern culture.

33. For a critique of Christine's feminism based particularly on her class bias, see Sheila Delany, " 'Mothers to Think Back Through': Who Are They? The Ambiguous Example of Christine de Pizan," in *Medieval Texts and Contemporary Readers*, ed. Laurie A. Finke and Martin B. Shichtman (Ithaca and London: Cornell University Press, 1987), pp. 177–97.

Literary critics in the late twentieth century may well fear that they practice a "soft" profession.[34] According to recent work by Nancy Armstrong, the basis of our current liberal arts curriculum, with its strong emphasis on certain major British authors, marks the feminization of cultural information, and particularly of literary studies, with meaning grounded in "a private sphere of gendered consciousness." The now standard curriculum began, Armstrong demonstrates, as a female curriculum, intended by eighteenth-century educators to mark and reproduce a new ruling class: "the very program designed specifically to produce daughters who would be desirable to men—if not a station above, then men bent on improving their station—was later extended to provide the standard of literacy for men as well as women."[35] Today, moreover, in the wake of efforts to deprivilege and decenter this curriculum, literary studies may well worry that all criticism will have to become feminist criticism. It is increasingly difficult to deny (as efforts to do so attest) that things like the gender, race, class, ethnicity, and religious affiliation of reader and author do always matter, affect interpretation, and establish what gets read by whom in ways we can no longer ignore or mystify. It is hardly news in many places to announce that textuality and sexuality are related with an unsettling complexity that insists on the continued relevance of questions about the silencing, displacement, and impersonation of women's voices, past and present, in male-authored texts, or that the myth of the great poet's (or the great text's) androgyny or transcendence is the myth on which prevailing traditions of English poetry have been founded.

While the continuity of certain myths of knowledge and interpretation across time and across apparent differences both between and within eras has become one important object of feminist reconsideration, it is rather the breakup of certain assumptions and identities within the critical community that makes that object more visible. It is where the feminist project theorizes and materializes readers who might not always be

34. Margaret Mauer's essay, "Reading Ben Jonson's *Queens*," in Fisher and Halley, *Seeking the Woman*, presents a similar argument: "Jonson's anxiety to assert his poetry's power to an audience of men hardly conceals his fear of appearing impotent in their eyes. No less vulnerable to this fear, though perhaps less literally so, are we professors of literature today, who need to find in poems enough transcendent meaning to make them items of the discourse men speak with men" (p. 235).

35. "The Gender Bind: Women and the Disciplines," *Genders* 3 (November 1988), pp. 1–23.

or want to be in the theoretical and material position of a white Western humanist that it stands to make the most difference to both criticism and history. As Louise Fradenburg points out, modern medieval scholarship of virtually all types seems to be threatened by abandonment and separation from the author; this phenomenon produces in many critics what I have spoken of as adulation and what she calls identification or mirroring.[36] If this is the case, if medievalists (who are surely not alone in this regard) desire to turn history into a mirror, but one that reflects a ground and a unity they cannot otherwise experience or believe in, then this is one difficulty that feminists should not have to face. The feminist medievalist is already separated, in fact excluded, by many still prevalent theories; insofar as she views herself in the position of a female subject in the late twentieth century, she cannot see her reflection in the texts of the Middle Ages, and so her starting point and her ending point are different and her desire is different.[37] Her desire can still be to encounter the masterwork, but from what can be thought of as a partial perspective, in various senses of the word partial.[38]

The knowledge that feminists might have of Chaucer defines itself as partial in one sense, as I have repeatedly argued in this study: redefining the authorial voice and position not just as a place in language, refined out of or transcendent of history, but as a subjectivity only partially knowable, knowable as multiple, contradictory, and strategically in quest of ahistoricity and unity. Chaucer performs this sense of the partiality of the authorial voice. Take the stance of the naive recorder of the *Canterbury Tales*, a stance riddled by the narrator's obvious moral and political judgments and his ultimate literary sophistication; take too the twentieth-

---

36. " 'Voice Memorial': Loss and Reparation in Chaucer's Poetry," *Exemplaria* 2 (1990), pp. 169–202.

37. Leslie Wahl Rabine has made a similar point: "Recognizing in classic works and in their interpretive codes a community of values in which they do not share, feminist critics have engaged in readings which consciously resist and violate the complicity between author and reader upon which rests much of the seduction of classic texts" (*Reading the Romantic Heroine: Text, History, Ideology* [Ann Arbor: University of Michigan Press, 1985], p. 19). Chaucerians, I am suggesting, have not yet resisted the seduction of these classic texts.

38. For a discussion of the partiality of knowledge and subjectivity in both senses that I mean—as "committed and incomplete" (p.7), see *Writing Culture: The Poetics and Politics of Ethnography*, ed. James Clifford and George E. Marcus (Berkeley and Los Angeles: University of California Press, 1986) pp. 1–26. Clifford, author of this introduction to the volume, comments in interesting ways on the omission of feminist work from the essays collected in *Writing Culture*.

century critical division of the author of this masterwork into parts: "Chaucer the pilgrim," "Chaucer the poet," and finally "Chaucer the man." What problems are passed on as if they were solutions by teaching Chaucer this way to generations of students? As a counterweight to all this highly visible instability and self-division, I have argued, women characters and the feminine are deployed as the battleground over which authority, selfhood, and unity can be established. Feminist readings of Chaucer can be part of an effort to open up not only the myth of the great artist as tolerant and sympathetic to women, but also, by extension, the limits of tolerance and sympathy as innocent but knowing positions we can occupy with regard to "others" in our own culture and experience and the difficulties of believing we can see and speak from another's point of view.[39]

The desire of feminists to read Chaucer can be conceived of as partial in another sense too: biased and partisan, but no longer conceived of as therefore lacking some illusory ideal of unsituated objectivity and neutrality. From this perspective, reading Chaucer becomes part of an effort to sustain and redefine an engagement with "oppressive formations."[40] The explicitly partisan nature of the project in this sense protects, as others have argued, against the danger of slipping from a critique of objectivity into apolitical relativism, the mirror image of transcendent totalizing, and against the easy way in which recourse to the partial can become, as we see so clearly in Chaucer, a refusal to be held accountable.[41] Feminist criticism of the canonical male author offers a place in which to examine the risks and benefits of critiquing hegemonic discourses and masterworks from a position of exclusion and to analyze the limits and powers of being constructed, as feminisms are constructed,

---

39. See Armstrong, "The Gender Bind," for fuller development of the tie between a gender-marked body of knowledge and a political empowerment of "the men of a relatively small class of people to speak on behalf of the powerless," together with a critique of Clifford Geertz as a type of the man empowered by a literary education to know others. As Armstrong puts it, "it can also be argued that this benign and politically disinterested discourse produces a common denominator among men, however unwittingly, in order to subordinate those of all other cultures to rational middle-class man" (p. 17).

40. I take this formulation from Elizabeth Ellsworth, "Why Doesn't This Feel Empowering? Working through the Repressive Myths of Critical Pedagogy," *Harvard Educational Review* 59 (1989), pp. 297–324.

41. For one discussion of this possibility, see Mary Poovey, "Feminism and Deconstruction," *Feminist Studies* 14 (1988), pp. 51–65.

in opposition to (rather than outside or beyond) the structures they seek to modify. It may also offer a way in which to make masterworks more available and interesting, open them to interested, partial, situated interpretive acts of those for whom, as interested, partial, situated texts, they were not written, those whom they have hitherto helped to silence and exclude from the game.

Index

Compositor: Impressions, a division of Edwards Brothers
Text: 10/13 Palatino
Display: Palatino
Printer and Binder: Edwards Brothers